INSTRUCTOR'S HANDBOOK
TO ACCOMPANY

Literature for Composition

Essays, Fiction, Poetry, and Drama

FOURTH EDITION

Sylvan Barnet
Tufts University

Morton Berman
Boston University

William Burto
University of Lowell

Marcia Stubbs
Wellesley College

HarperCollins*CollegePublishers*

Instructor's Handbook to accompany LITERATURE FOR COMPOSI-
TION: Essays, Fiction, Poetry, and Drama, Fourth Edition by Sylvan Barnet,
Morton Berman, William Burto, and Marcia Stubbs

ISBN: 0-673-54281-5

95 96 97 98 99 9 8 7 6 5 4 3 2 1

Preface

Our title, *Literature for Composition*, announces the aim of this fourth edition, and our preface to the book clearly, we hope, explains the organization. We want to repeat that the first four chapters offer a good deal of advice about writing, and the next eight chapters are a mini-anthology arranged by genre—four chapters with genres, alternating with four casebooks, a casebook on each genre—again with a good deal of advice about writing. Next are chapters on the nature of literature, on arguing interpretations, on arguing evaluations, and an overview of the writing process. The rest of the book is devoted to a Thematic Anthology.

We have tried to choose works of literature that will interest students in a composition class, and we have suggested topics for essays in the book and in this manual. Some of these topics are the sort that are common in literature courses—"The function of religious imagery in 'Araby,'" for example, or "To what extent is Nora [in *A Doll's House*] a victim, and to what extent is she herself at fault for her way of life?" Such topics need no defense; they help to bring the student into close contact with the work of literature, and they help to develop analytic powers.

But we have also included some topics that invite students to try their hands at imaginative writing: for instance, "Write a dialogue—approximately two double-space typed pages—setting forth a chance encounter between Torvald and Nora five years after the end of Ibsen's play." Such an assignment will, if nothing else, give students some idea of the difficulty of writing dialogue; but of course it will do much more, for again, it will require them to think about the play itself, especially if the instructor cautions them that their dialogue ought to be rooted in Ibsen's play. Similarly, concerning Kincaid's "Girl," we suggest this topic:

Taking "Girl" as a model, write a piece about someone—perhaps a relative, teacher, or friend—who has given you more advice than you wanted.

Still other suggested topics in this manual, however, use the work of literature as a point of departure for expository or persuasive essays. For instance, for an essay that takes off from Grace Paley's "Samuel," we ask:

If you had been on the train, would you have pulled the emergency cord? Why, or why not?

We have just said that such topics use the literary work as a point of departure; we do not mean that the work gets left behind. A good essay will be based on a close reading of the text, but it will also allow the student to develop an argument on an issue larger than the work. Moreover, such topics as those on the Declaration of Independence can easily be made into small-scale research papers if the instructor wishes to teach research methods. In the text, an appendix on "Research Papers" provides information about documentation.

In this manual we discuss, in varying degrees of detail, every literary selection that we reprint, except for a handful that are discussed extensively within the text itself. This means that for a few chapters we include no comments here at all, for example Chapter 13, "What, Then, Is Literature?", which examined in detail Frost's "The Span of Life." We also offer in this manual additional Topics for Critical Thinking and Writing on many of the works. Unfortunately, however, assignments that work well for one instructor may not work well for another, and even an assignment that works well at nine o'clock may not work well at ten. Still, over the years we have had good luck with the selections we include and with the writing assignments given in the text and in this manual. We will be most grateful to any instructors who write to us to suggest additional topics. If there is a fifth edition of the book, we will try to include such suggestions, giving credit to the contributors.

Contents

Part Three Standing Back: Thinking Critically about Literature and Approaches to Literature   89

Part Four A Thematic Anthology 91

20 *Art and Life*   185

PART ONE

*Getting
Started*

CHAPTER 1

The Writer as Reader: Reading and Responding

KATE CHOPIN

Ripe Figs (p. 3)

This story teaches marvelously. Some stories supposedly teach well because the instructor can have the pleasure of showing students all sorts of things that they missed, but of course stories of that kind may, by convincing students that literature has deep meanings that they don't see, turn students away from literature. "Ripe Figs" teaches well because it is a first-rate piece that is easily accessible.

Elaine Gardiner discusses it fully in an essay in *Modern Fiction Studies* 28:3 (1982), reprinted in Harold Bloom's collection of essays *Kate Chopin* (1987), pp. 83-87. Gardiner's essay is admirable, but instructors will be interested to find that their students will make pretty much the same points that Gardiner makes. Gardiner emphasizes three of Chopin's techniques: her use of *contrasts, natural imagery,* and *cyclical plotting.*

The chief contrast is between Maman-Nainaine and Babette, that is, age versus youth, patience versus impatience, experience versus innocence, staidness versus exuberance. Thus, Chopin tells us that "Maman-Nainaine sat down in her stately way," whereas Babette is "restless as a hummingbird," and dances. Other contrasts are spring and summer, summer and fall, figs and chrysanthemums.

Speaking of natural imagery, Gardiner says, "Not only are journeys planned according to when figs ripen and chrysanthemums bloom, but places are defined by what they produce; thus, Bayou-Lafourche, for Maman-Nainaine, is the place 'where the sugar cane grows.'" Gardiner calls attention to the references to the leaves, the rain, and the branches of the fig tree, but of course she emphasizes the ripening of the figs (from "little hard, green marbles" to "purple figs, fringed around with their rich green leaves") and the flowering of the chrysanthemums. The contrasts in natural imagery, Gardiner says, "ultimately convey and emphasize continuity and stability."

Turning to cyclical plotting—common in Chopin—Gardiner says, "With the ripening of the figs in the summertime begins the next period of waiting, the continuance of the cycle, both of nature and of the characters' lives.... The reader finishes the sketch anticipating the movements to follow—movements directed by the seasons, by natural happenings, by the cyclical patterns of these people's lives."

CHAPTER 2

The Reader as Writer: Drafting and Writing

KATE CHOPIN

The Story of an Hour (p. 12)

The first sentence of the story, of course, proves to be essential to the end, though during the middle of the story the initial care to protect Mrs. Mallard from the "sad message" seems almost comic. Students may assume, too easily, that Mrs. Mallard's "storm of grief" is hypocritical. They may not notice that the renewal after the first shock is stimulated by the renewal of life around her ("the tops of trees... were all aquiver with the new spring of life") and that before she achieves a new life, Mrs. Mallard first goes through a sort of death and then tries to resist renewal: Her expression "indicated a suspension of intelligent thought," she felt something "creeping out of the sky," and she tried to "beat it back with her will," but she soon finds herself "drinking the elixir of life through that open window," and her thoughts turn to "spring days, and summer days." Implicit in the story is the idea that her life as a wife—which she had thought was happy—was in fact a life of repression or subjugation, and the awareness comes to her only at this late stage. The story has two surprises: the change from grief to joy proves not to be the whole story, for we get the second surprise, the husband's return and Mrs. Mallard's death. The last line ("the doctors... said she had died... of joy that kills") is doubly ironic: The doctors wrongly assume that she was overjoyed to find that her husband was alive, but they were not wholly wrong in guessing that her last day of life brought her great joy.

In a sense, moreover, the doctors are right (though not in the sense they mean) in saying that she "died of heart disease." That is, if we take the "heart" in a metaphorical sense to refer to love and marriage, we can say that the loss of her new freedom from her marriage is unbearable. This is not to say (though many students do say it) that her marriage was miserable. The text explicitly says "she had loved him—sometimes." The previous paragraph in the story nicely calls attention to a certain aspect of love—a satisfying giving of the self—and yet also to a most unpleasant yielding to force: "There would be no one to live for her during those coming years; she would live for herself. There would be no powerful will bending her in that blind persistence with which men and women believe they have a right to impose a private will upon a fellow-creature."

A biographical observation: Chopin's husband died in 1882, and her mother died in 1885. In 1894 in an entry in her diary she connected the two losses with her growth. "If it were possible for my husband and my mother to come back to earth, I feel that I would unhesitatingly give up every thing that has come into my life since they left it and join my existence again with theirs. To do that, I would have to forget the past ten years of my growth—my real growth."

TOPIC FOR CRITICAL THINKING AND WRITING

> Chopin does not tell us if Mrs. Mallard's death is due to joy at seeing her husband alive, guilt for feeling "free," shock at the awareness that her freedom is lost, or something else. Should the author have made the matter clear? Why, or why not?

KATE CHOPIN

The Storm (p. 32)

Chopin wrote this story in 1898 but never tried to publish it, presumably because she knew it would be unacceptable to the taste of the age. "The Storm" uses the same characters as an earlier story, "The 'Cadian Ball," in which Alcée is about to run away with Calixta when Clarisse captures him as a husband.

Here are some comments on particular issues that are likely to arise while discussing the story

On the characters of Calixta and Bobinôt. In Part I, Bobinôt buys a can of shrimp because Calixta is fond of shrimp. Our own impression is that this detail is provided chiefly to show Bobinôt's interest in pleasing his wife, but Per Seyersted, in *Kate Chopin*, finds a darker meaning. Seyersted suggests (223) that shrimp "may represent a conscious allusion to the potency often denoted by sea foods." (To the best of our knowledge, this potency is attributed only to oysters, but perhaps we lead sheltered lives.) At the beginning of Part II Calixta is "sewing furiously on a sewing machine," and so readers gather that she is a highly industrious woman, presumably a more-than-usually diligent housekeeper. The excuses Bobinôt frames on the way home (Part III) suggest that he is somewhat intimidated by his "overscrupulous housewife." Calixta is genuinely concerned about the welfare of her somewhat simple husband and of her child. The affair with Alcée by no means indicates that she is promiscuous or, for that matter, unhappy with her family. We don't think her expressions of solicitude for the somewhat childlike Bobinôt are insincere. We are even inclined to think that perhaps her encounter with Alcée has heightened her concern for her husband. (At least, to use the language of reader-response criticism, this is the way we "naturalize"—make sense out of—the gap or blank in the narrative.)

Alcée's letter to his wife suggests that he thinks his affair with Calixta may go on for a while, but we take it that the affair is, like the storm (which gives its title to the story), a passing affair. It comes about unexpectedly and "naturally": Alcée at first takes refuge on the gallery, with no thought of entering the house, but because the gallery does not afford shelter, Calixta invites him in, and then a lightning bolt drives her (backward) into his arms. The experience is thoroughly satisfying, and it engenders no regrets, but presumably it will be treasured rather than repeated, despite Alcée's thoughts when he writes his letter.

Clarisse's response. By telling us, in Part V, that Clarisse is delighted at the thought of staying a month longer in Biloxi, Chopin diminishes any blame that a reader might attach to Alcée. That is, although Alcée is unfaithful to his wife, we see that his wife doesn't regret his absence: "Their intimate conjugal life was something which she was more than willing to forego for a while."

Is the story cynical? We don't think so, since cynicism involves a mocking or sneering attitude, whereas in this story Chopin regards her characters affectionately. Blame is diminished not only by Clarisse's letter but by other means. We learn that at an earlier time, when Calixta was a virgin, Alcée's "honor forbade him to prevail." And, again, by associating the affair with the storm, Chopin implies that this moment of passion is in accord with nature. Notice also that the language becomes metaphoric during the scene of passion. For instance, Calixta's "lips were as red and as moist as pomegranate seed," and her "passion... was like a white flame," suggesting that the characters are transported to a strange (though natural) world. There is, of course, the implication that people are less virtuous than they seem to be, but again, Chopin scarcely seems to gloat over this fact. Rather, she suggests that the world is a fairly pleasant place in which there is enough happiness to go all around. "So the storm passed and everyone was happy." There is no need to imagine further episodes in which, for instance, Calixta and Alcée deceive Bobinôt; nor is there any need to imagine further episodes in which Calixta and Alcée regret their moment of passion.

Two additional points can be made. First, there seems to be a suggestion of class distinction between Calixta and Alcée, though both are Creoles. Calixta uses some French terms, and her speech includes such expressions as "An' Bibi? he ain't wet? Ain't hurt?" Similarly Bobinôt's language, though it does not include any French terms, departs from Standard English. On the other hand, Alcée speaks only Standard English. Possibly, however, the distinctions in language are also based, at least partly based, on gender as well as class; Calixta speaks the language of an uneducated woman largely confined to her home, whereas Alcée—a man who presumably deals with men in a larger society— speaks the language of the Anglo world. But if gender is relevant, how can one account for the fact that Bobinôt's language resembles Calixta's, and Clarisse's resembles Alcée's? A tentative answer: Bobinôt, like Calixta, lives in a very limited world, whereas Clarisse is a woman of the world. We see Clarisse only at the end of the story, and there we hear her only through the voice of the narrator, but an expression such as "The society was agreeable" suggests that her language (as might be expected from a woman rich enough to take a long vacation) resembles her husband's, not Calixta's.

CHAPTER 3

Two Forms of Criticism: Explication and Analysis

LANGSTON HUGHES

Harlem (p. 39)

In the eight lines enclosed within the frame (that is, between the first and next-to-last lines) we get four possibilities: The Dream may "dry up," "fester," "crust and sugar over," or "sag." Each of these is set forth with a simile, for example, "dry up / like a raisin in the sun." By the way, the third of these, "crust up and sugar over—like a syrupy sweet," probably describes a dream that has turned into smiling Uncle Tomism. Similes can be effective, and these *are* effective, but in the final line Hughes states the last possibility ("Or does it explode?") directly and briefly, without an amplification. The effect is, more or less, to suggest that the fancy (or pretty) talk stops. The explosion is too serious to be treated in a literary way. But, of course, the word "explode," applied to a dream, is itself figurative. That is, the last line is as "literary" or "poetical" as the earlier lines, but it is a slightly different sort of poetry.

A word about the rhymes: notice that although the poem does use rhyme, it does not use a couplet until the last two lines. The effect of the couplet (load / explode) is that the poem ends with a bang. Of course, when one reads the poem in a book, one sees where the poem ends—though a reader may be surprised to find the forceful rhyme—but an audience hearing the poem recited is surely taken off-guard. The explosion is unexpected (especially in the context of the two previous lines about a sagging, heavy load), and powerful.

A "Voices and Visions" videocassette of Langston Hughes is available from HarperCollins.

TOPIC FOR CRITICAL THINKING AND WRITING

One might keep the first line where it is, and then rearrange the other stanzas—for instance, putting lines 2-8 after 9-11. Which version (Hughes's or the one just mentioned) do you prefer? Why?

The Judgment of Solomon (p. 45)

The story is told chiefly to emphasize Solomon's wisdom, or, more specifically, to indicate that "the wisdom of God was in him, to do judgment" (3.28), but we include the story here because it seems to us to be a moving tale of a mother's love, and (a lesser reason, but a respectable one) because it relates to Raymond Carver's "Popular Mechanics," included later in Chapter 20 ("Love and Hate").

The Biblical story is, in a way, a sort of early detective story: there is a death, a conflict in the testimony of the two witnesses, and a solution by a shrewd outsider. We say "shrewd" because although any of us could have reached the correct judgment after the two women had responded to Solomon's proposal to divide the child, few of us would have been shrewd enough to have devised the situation that led each woman to declare what she really was.

Consider Solomon's predicament. There seems to be nothing that distinguishes the two claimants. There came before him "two women, that were harlots." Until late in the story—that is, up to the time that Solomon suggests dividing the child—they are described only as "the one woman," "the other woman," "the one," "the other." The reader, like Solomon, has nothing to go on, since neither of the witnesses is known to be morally superior, and since there are no other witnesses. Solomon's inspired wisdom, then, is to set up a situation in which each claimant will reveal her true nature—the mother will reveal her love, and the culprit will reveal her hard heart.

Instructors interested in discussing the literary structure of the story may want to call attention to the nice way in which the author takes the cry of the true mother (in which she gives up her suit), "Give her the living child, and in no wise slay it," and then puts these identical words, without change, into Solomon's mouth as his final judgment, though of course the meaning of "her" shifts from (in the first case) the liar to (in Solomon's sentence) the true mother. This exact repetition of a sentence is, of course, especially appropriate in a story about two seemingly indistinguishable women and about a proposal to divide an infant into two.

We have already mentioned that it is important for the two women to be, in effect, indistinguishable, but why did the author make them harlots? We can offer a few guesses: a) the story demands that there be no witnesses, and by making the women harlots the author thus disposed of husbands, parents, and siblings who might otherwise be expected to live with the women; b) the author wishes to show that Solomon's justice extended to all, not only to respectable folk; c) the author wished to dispel or at least to complicate the stereotype of the harlot as thoroughly disreputable by calling to mind another—overriding—stereotype of the mother as motivated by overwhelming maternal love.

One other point: the basic motif of two women fighting over an infant, and the true mother revealing her identity by rejecting a proposal that will kill the infant, is found in many cultures. For instance, in an Indian Jataka story (a story of the lives of the Buddha before he reached his final incarnation as the Buddha child) at a river-bank, where a she-demon claimed it as her own. The two brought the case to a deity, who ordered the child to be divided into two, but the mother yielded her claim rather than destroy the child. See E. B. Cowell and W. H. D. Rouse, *Jataka Stories*, 6 (1912), 63ff.

For a strong feminist reading—a reading very much against the grain of the traditional interpretation that Solomon's deep wisdom solved a difficult problem—see Anne C. Dailey, "The Judgment of Women," in *Out of the Garden*, ed. Christina Buchmann and Celina Spiegel (1994). We quote a few extracts; you may want to try them out with your students.

> Shouldn't we question Solomon's responsibility for raising the sword in the first place? Had he not called for the sword, the other woman might never have expressed her seemingly violent impulse.... (147)

> But does the second woman really *choose* to have the child killed? Maybe she would have picked up the sword and slain the child with her own hands, but we certainly do not know that. All we know is that she says, "Cut him up." Her response may have represented many things besides a heartless desire to see the child killed: futility, hopelessness, anger, or perhaps a disbelief that Solomon would follow through on his murderous threat.... (147)

> The institutional violence that the two women confront in the sword of Solomon mirrors the violence that women face in their everyday lives. Women are expected to back down, negotiate, settle, and accept arbitrary assaults of men at home, on the street, and in the workplace. They are expected to respond with the self-sacrifice of the first prostitute. And when they do not, when they defiantly transgress the laws of men, women must endure, Eve-like, the punishment meted out to them.... (148)

> Blind faith in the correctness of Solomon's judgment can be maintained only because we hear so little from the women. When the sword is raised and the com-

mand given to divide the child, the women know that they have but moments to plead their case. Their speech is uttered in a fearful rush, a female cry in the face of seemingly arbitrary male violence. Had Solomon recognized that the women's initial responses were incomplete, had he desired to *know* these women rather than to judge them immediately according to a preconceived ideal, then, had he been truly wise, he would have listened with a patient ear to all they had to say.... (148)

Solomon succeeds in resolving the dispute over the child in a swift and expedient manner, but he fails to comprehend the cost in human terms of doing so. By judging the women on the basis of a few frantic words, he erases the fullness and complexity of their lives. (148-49)

JAMES THURBER

The Secret Life of Walter Mitty (p. 58)

Class discussion may begin with an examination of the point at which it is apparent that this story is comic. Anyone who knows Thurber's name will of course expect comedy, but not every student has heard of him. The first two sentences do not (on first reading) reveal themselves as comic, though in hindsight one sees that at least the first sentence is from the world of inferior adventure stories. An alert reader may becomes suspicious of the third sentence with its "full-dress uniform" and its "heavily braided white cap pulled down rakishly over one cold gray eye." Suspicions are confirmed with "ta-pocketa-pocketa-pocketa-*pocketa-pocketa*"; the ludicrous "eight-engined Navy hydroplane" and the cliché about the Old Man make the comedy unmistakable.

Instructors may find it useful to introduce the concept of pathos and to lead the class in a discussion of the relation of the pathetic to the tragic and the comic. Here, of course, Mitty's daydreams are comic; we may pity him because of his weakness, but we can only laugh at his daydreams, which (1) are so greatly in contrast with the actual event, and (2) are so indebted to bad movies and pulp magazines.

Brooks and Warren provide an interpretation of the story in *Understanding Fiction*; Charles S. Holmes's *The Clocks of Colombus* is a useful study of Thurber. Carl Sundell examines the structure of the story (e.g., it begins and ends with Mitty dreaming) [*English Journal* 56 (1967): 1284-1287]. James Ellis [*English Journal* 54 (1965): 310-313], points out that Mitty's fantasies are made even more fantastic by various bits of misinformation. For example, Mitty the sea captain calls for "full strength in No. 3 turret," mistakenly thinking that the turrets move the ship; the surgeon nonsensically speaks of obstreosis (primarily a disease of cattle and pigs) of the ductal tract, and thinks coreopsis (a flower) is a disease; the marksman refers to a 50.80 caliber pistol (its diameter would be more than four feet); the pilot speaks of von Richtman but means von Richthofen.

One other study of the story should be mentioned, Ann Ferguson Manx's in *Studies in Short Fiction* [19 (1982): 315-357]. This essay is a vigorous defense of Mrs. Mitty, who is usually thought of as a nag. Manx argues that Mitty's fantasies are not provoked by Mrs. Mitty's naggings. Rather, Mitty is a hopeless fantasist, and it's a good thing for him that he has Mrs. Mitty to see that he wears his galoshes, doesn't drive too fast, and so on. Manx writes: "If we think seriously about what life with a man like Mitty would be like, Mrs. Mitty seems responsible and concerned." Perhaps the best thing is not to "think seriously" about what living with Walter Mitty would be like.

TOPICS FOR CRITICAL THINKING AND WRITING

1. In a paragraph, characterize Mrs. Mitty.
2. In an essay of 500 words, evaluate the view that Mrs. Mitty is exactly the sort of woman Walter Mitty needs.

ALICE WALKER

Everyday Use (p. 72)

The title of this story, like most other titles, is significant, though the significance appears only gradually. Its importance, of course, is not limited to the fact that Dee believes that Maggie will use the quilts for "everyday use"; on reflection we see the love, in daily use, between the narrator and Maggie, and we contrast it with Dee's visit—a special occurrence—as well as with Dee's idea that the quilts should not be put to everyday use. The real black achievement, then, is not the creation of works of art that are kept apart from daily life; rather, it is the everyday craftsmanship and the everyday love shared by people who cherish and sustain each other. That Dee stands apart from this achievement is clear (at least on rereading) from the first paragraph, and her pretensions are suggested as early as the fourth paragraph, where we are told that she thinks "orchids are tacky flowers." (Notice that in the fifth paragraph, when the narrator is imagining herself as Dee would like her to be on a television show, she has glistening hair—presumably because the hair has been straightened—and she appears thinner and lighter-skinned than in fact she is.) Her lack of any real connection with her heritage is made explicit (even before the nonsense about using the churn top as a centerpiece) as early as the paragraph in which she asks if Uncle Buddy whittled the dasher, and Maggie quietly says that Henry whittled it. Still, Dee is confident that she can "think of something artistic to do with the dasher." Soon we learn that she sees the quilts not as useful objects, but only as decorative works; Maggie, however, will use the quilts, and she even knows how to make them. Dee talks about black "heritage" but Maggie and the narrator embody this heritage and they experience a degree of contentment that eludes Dee.

Many white students today are scarcely aware of the Black Muslim movement, which was especially important in the 1960s, and they therefore pass over the Muslim names taken by Dee and her companion, the reference to pork (not to be eaten by Muslims), and so on. That is, they miss the fact that Walker is suggesting that the valuable heritage of American blacks is not to be dropped in favor of an attempt to adopt an essentially remote heritage. It is worth asking students to do a little work in the library and to report on the Black Muslim movement.

Houston A. Baker, Jr. and Charlotte Pierce-Baker discuss the story in *Southern Review* (new series 21[Summer 1985]), in an issue that was later published as a book with the title *Afro-American Writing Today*, ed. James Olney (1989). Their essay is worth reading, but it is rather overheated. Sample:

> Maggie is the arisen goddess of Walker's story; she is the sacred figure who bears the scarifications of experience and knows how to convert patches into robustly patterned and beautifully quilted wholes. As an earth-rooted and quotidian goddess, she stands in dramatic contrast to the stylishly fiery and other-oriented Wangero. (131)

The essay is especially valuable, however, because it reproduces several photographs (in black and white only, unfortunately) of quilts and their makers. Lots of books on American folk art have better reproductions of quilts, but few show the works with the artists who made them. It's worth bringing to class some pictures of quilts, whether from the essay by the Bakers or from another source. Even better, of course, is (if possible) to bring some quilts to class.

TOPICS FOR CRITICAL THINKING AND WRITING

1. "Everyday Use" is by a black woman. Would your response to the story be the same if you knew it were written by a white woman? Or by a man? Explain.

2. How does the narrator's dream about her appearance on the television program foreshadow the later conflict?

3. Compare "Everyday Use" with Bambara's "The Lesson." Consider the following suggestions: Characterize the narrator of each story and compare them. Compare the settings and how they function in each story. What is Miss Moore trying to teach the children in "The Lesson?" Why does Sylvia resist learning it? In "Everyday Use," what does Dee try to teach her mother and sister? Why do they resist her lesson? How are

objects (such as quilts, toys) used in each story? How in each story does the first-person narration enlist and direct our sympathies?

JOSÉ ARMAS

El Tonto del Barrio (p. 79)

If you have any Spanish-speaking students in your class, or even students whose acquaintance with Spanish does not go beyond a few years of high school study, you might ask them how they would translate the title. We thought of glossing "El Tonto" as "The Fool" or "The Idiot," but "Fool" is a bit old-fashioned and "Idiot"—as Armas suggested to us—is too strong. Armas's own suggestion, "Dummy," strikes us as exactly right.

While one is reading the story, say through the first one-third, it may seem to be chiefly a character sketch of Romero and a sketch of the community in which he lives, but then come two sentences that mark a turning point:

> Romero kept the sidewalks clean and the barrio looked after him. It was a contract that worked well for a long time.

"Worked well *for a long time*" implies that something happened that broke the contract, and we are promptly introduced to the disruptive element:

> Then, when Seferino, Barelas' oldest son, graduated from high school he went to work in the barber shop for the summer. Seferino was a conscientious and sensitive young man and it wasn't long before he took notice of Romero and came to feel sorry for him.

In the light of what happens next, some readers may think that the narrator (or the author?) is being ironic, even sarcastic, when he characterizes Seferino as "conscientious and sensitive," but Seferino really is conscientious and sensitive. He just isn't mature, or wise in the ways of the barrio, and (an important point) isn't able to understand that not everyone feels as he does. Thus, when he argues with his father he says, "How would you like to do what he does and be treated in the same way?" That's a reasonable position (we all know that we should do unto others as we would have others do unto us)— but Barelas's answer is wiser than Seferino's question: "I'm not Romero." Further, and this may seem to be a paradox, Barelas is not only wise enough to know that he is not Romero, but he is also wise enough to know (as Seferino does not) *why* Romero sweeps the sidewalks: "He sweeps the sidewalks because he wants something to do, not because he wants money."

Although the conflict between Seferino and Romero is the obvious conflict, the conflict (though that is almost too strong a word) between Seferino and Barelas is worth discussing in class. (The question in the text about Barelas's character is one way of approaching it.) This conflict is amusingly resolved when the well-meaning Seferino disappears into Harvard, thus sparing us a potentially embarrassing or painful scene in which the boy acknowledges his error. Indeed, instead of emphasizing the conflict between Barelas and his son, we get a scene in which Barelas—whose son has caused Romero to misbehave—is pitted against the rest of the community, which now seeks to confine Romero. And although Barelas again is on the right side, in one tiny detail he reveals that he too has been rattled, we might even say corrupted, by his son's well-intentioned plan. When one of the men of the barrio says, "What if [Romero] hurts...?" Barelas interrupts: "He's not going to hurt anyone." Tino replies: "No, Barelas, I was going to say, what if he hurts himself?" It's a lovely touch, showing that Barelas (who is right about so much) can be mistaken, and, more important, showing that even though the community wants to lock Romero up, it is concerned chiefly for Romero's well-being.

These comments are obvious, and perhaps a bit too solemn, since the story has a good deal of delightful humor in it. (One can ask the class what it finds *amusing* in the story.) A favorite passage is the bit recounting how Romero, after breaking with Seferino, at first simply skipped the barber shop in his sweeping, but then refined his action and pushed all of the trash from elsewhere in front of the barber shop.

TOPIC FOR CRITICAL THINKING AND WRITING

The story is about Romero, but almost as interestingly it is about Seferino. We can fairly easily guess what will happen to Romero in the next few years. What would you guess will happen to Seferino? Will his Harvard education lead to his increasing alienation from his community? (Our own response is yes, in the short run, but—since he is a bright and sensitive youth and he has a wise father—we can hope that in the long run he will learn to appreciate and to cherish the ways of the barrio.)

PART TWO

Up Close:

Thinking about Literary Forms

CHAPTER 5

Reading (and Writing about) Essays

BRENT STAPLES

Black Men and Public Space (p. 105)

Although Staples's marvelous first sentence speaks of his "first victim," and his second paragraph speaks of "that first encounter," he doesn't begin his essay with the chronologically earliest event of his narrative. Rather, he begins with an experience that revealed to him the fear he evokes in others and also revealed how that fear alienates and endangers him. He begins, in other words, with an account that dramatizes the focus of his essay. After recounting other incidents which revealed to him that a black male is an object of fear not only to white females but also (at least in some circumstances) to everyone "black, white, male, or female," he goes back in time to explain why at the age of twenty-two he was unaware of the effect he would have on others and then forward again to explain how the "first" experiences altered his behavior. The structure of the essay, beginning in the middle of things and containing a flashback, works so well it may appear artless; it's often useful in a composition class to ask some obvious questions to reveal the writer's options, as well as his decisions and their effects: Where does Staples begin his essay? Why does he begin there? Why not begin with his account of "coming of age" in Chester, Pennsylvania? and so on.

In addition to admiring the effective organization of the essay, we admire the deftness of Staples's language. We've already referred to the electrifying first sentence: "My first victim was a woman—white, well dressed, probably in her early twenties." (The next sentences even heighten the suspense.) We admire too Staples's rigor and his self-assurance as a writer, which enables him to describe himself as others might see him, as a "youngish black man—a broad six feet two inches with a beard and billowing hair, both hands shoved into the pockets of a bulky military jacket." There's a touch of humor in that description, certainly no self-pity. The self-assurance also allows him to acknowledge that there is some basis in fact for pedestrians' fear of black males (paragraph 6) while at the same time characterizing himself as "a softy who is scarcely able to take a knife to a raw chicken" (paragraph 2) and as "timid, but a survivor" (paragraph 9). Other virtues of his prose: the vivid imagery (for example, the memorable "*thunk, thunk, thunk, thunk*" of the car door locks in paragraph 3); the succinct summaries ("being perceived as dangerous is a hazard in itself" in paragraph 2) and the often wry humor ("bear country" in paragraph 12).

Perhaps most of all we admire Staples's restraint. Given the topic and the experiences he recounts (including the loss of a brother to street violence), Staples does not pull out the organ stops of rage to which, we might think, he is entitled. He leaves us instead with the "bright, sunny" warbling of Vivaldi's *Four Seasons*, and a refreshing and important contribution to "New York mugging literature."

TOPICS FOR CRITICAL THINKING AND WRITING

1. Write an essay of approximately 1,000 words explaining how you learned that your behavior and intentions were being misinterpreted, and what you did to alter others' perceptions of you. (An example: a woman or girl whose behavior was being misread as sexually responsive, or even aggressive.)
2. Write a narrative essay (approximately 1,000 words) on "coming of age," focusing on a particular lesson you learned from encounters with others.

JONATHAN SWIFT

A Modest Proposal (P. 114)

Much of the voluminous writing on this short satire is devoted to Swift's use of a persona or mask, and especially to reconciling the persona with those passages in which we hear Swift's voice rather than the projector's. One desperate view, for example, holds that when the persona is apparently speaking out of character, the persona is really using irony and thus—though he is talking sense—he means the opposite of what he says. Our own view is different. We assume that when a satirist uses a persona he wants us at last to see through the mask, and once we have seen through the mask, we enjoy seeing the real face as well as the mask. That is, when we read the title and subtitle of Swift's essay, and even the first few paragraphs, we are at first taken in. But then we begin to suspect that what sounds matter of fact, for example, is cold-blooded or even crazy. And then we get the joke; we realize that we have been taken. We are reading a satire, we see a satirist at work, and there really is no reason why the satirist should consistently keep the mask in front of his face.

One place where we hear Swift's own voice is in the poke at England (paragraph 31): "I could name a country which would be glad to eat up our whole nation." But notice that the satire in this essay is not directed wholly toward England; Swift saves much of his fury for the Irish, especially in the two paragraphs preceding the one from which we have just quoted. In paragraph 29, after saying "Let no man talk to me of other expedients," Swift lists various proposals that he had seriously advocated in earlier writings and that were still available to the Irish, such as the use of locally manufactured clothing and furniture instead of imported goods, and the development of habits of prudence and honesty. The object of the satire is Irish folly quite as much as English rapacity: the Irish have refused to take practical measures and have refused to cure "the expensiveness of pride, vanity, idleness, and gaming in our women," and so Swift now, in fury, tells them there is only one way left. The ironic contrast, then, is not merely between the barbaric solution the projector offers and the compassionate solution that the English should offer, but between one kind of Irish idiocy (the projector's) and another (that of the Irish themselves).

The most admired passages in which the projector speaks are these: the first paragraph, with its slightly crazy reference to "three, four, or six children"; the second paragraph, especially its latter half, in view of what we later learn about how this "preserver of the nation" hopes that children can be made into "useful members of the commonwealth"; the fourth paragraph, with its reference to "a child just dropped from its dam" (the projector thinks of human beings as beasts); the sixth paragraph (beginning "The number of souls"), with its cool mathematical calculations, treating human beings as mere units; the reference (paragraph 14) to the cost of nursing a beggar's child, "two shillings *per annum*, rags included"; the reference (paragraph 19) to dying "as fast as can be reasonably expected"; and the final paragraph.

HENRY DAVID THOREAU

Room for Your Thoughts (p. 120)

One probably does best with most students to start with a simple example of Thoreau's word-play: the ironic play on the word "great" in "It is surprising how many great men and women a small house will contain"; or the derivation from the Greek *oikos* (house) shimmering in the word "economized" in the second sentence.

One might then move to the more difficult sentence near the end: "If we would enjoy the most intimate society with that in each of us which is without, or above, being spoken to, we must not only be silent, but commonly so far apart bodily that we cannot possibly hear each other's voice in any case." Probably most students are aware that different cultures place different values on proximity. The stereotypes (in which there are truths) see the Anglo-Saxons as wanting considerable space between people, and Latinos and Arabs as wanting proximity. For Anglos, Latinos and Arabs are "unrestrained," "pushy," and so forth; for Latinos and Arabs, Anglos are "cold," "distant," "reserved," unwilling to let their bodies give information by means of body-language.

For Thoreau, the self *is* the body but it is also "without" (outside) or "above" the body. The body's needs can send confusing messages; we transcend the body's "case" (container) to attend the higher messages we are all, at our best, attuned to. If we are merely making sociable noises with our talk, "we can afford to stand very near together, cheek by jowl, and feel each other's breath; but if we speak reservedly and thoughtfully, we want to be farther apart, that all animal heat and moisture may have a chance to evaporate." Since spiritual (as opposed to animal) truths are universal, the loftiest conversations can be unvoiced, or silent communion.

But of course it is a mistake to take Thoreau literally; he exaggerates here, as elsewhere, to emphasize a point. And the point is not part of a systematic philosophy but part of a consistent social criticism. We spend too much of our lives on trivia. Thoreau is not so much interested in denying our bodily nature as he is in denying the body the excessive attention we give it, attention that should be reserved for higher things. Hall in "Proxemics" is speaking literally, if generally. He compares a generalized Arab with a generalized Westerner. Thoreau is speaking figuratively in order to contrast our usual selves with our ideal selves.

Thoreau's keen enjoyment of his senses can be inferred even in this passage from his close observation of physical phenomena and his habit of using homely images to explain invisible truths, as in his metaphor (paragraph 2) of thought as a bullet. Or, for students who still think Thoreau is some kind of nut (the wrong kind), one might want to quote his reply on his deathbed to someone who was eager to know Thoreau's thoughts on the next world: "One world at a time."

VIRGINIA WOOLF

The Death of the Moth (p. 121)

The essay begins with a businesslike, or better, scientific tone, its school-teacher-ish opening sentence instructing us that day moths "are not properly to be called moths." But even in this sentence, in the part that follows the semicolon. we hear a personal voice speaking of the writer's sense of pleasure. Moreover, at the end of the sentence she goes so far as to assume, most unscientifically, that we share the pleasure she takes in moths. Notice, too, that the opening paragraph is richly detailed ("narrow hay-colored wings"), and that the detail makes use of the poet's speciality, metaphor, especially in its image of the flock of rooks as "a vast net with thousands of black knots." Paragraph 2 unobtrusively but surely suggests the connection between the life of a moth and of a human being, and indeed, among the whole of creation. Clearly the writer will give us something other than a scientific discourse on moths. We will see moths through a highly perceptive, sympathetic temperament.

About question 4: The season is the harvest, conventional and appropriate enough for an essay about death. But the time, from morning to noon, is a bit less conventional, for we might expect to go from morning to evening, a common enough metaphor for a life-span. The moth's life ends at noon, with the suggestion that the life is cut short. Death comes sooner than we think it should.

LANGSTON HUGHES

Salvation (p. 124)

Most instructors who used the first edition of this book taught several of the stories in "Innocence and Experience." Hughes's essay can serve as an excellent introduction to the themes in "Araby" and "I Want to Know Why," first-person narratives about youngsters.

Hughes, of course, is writing as an adult, but the simplicity of many of his sentences ("But not really saved. It happened like this") and of much of his diction ("there was a big revival") is appropriate to a boy not yet thirteen. This is not really the speech of a youngster ("escorted" in the first paragraph, "dire" in the third, "work-gnarled" in the fourth), but on the whole the style evokes the child's state of mind; we might say that we are chiefly conscious of the youthful subject rather than of the mature writer. But a very artful and adult ironic writing pervades the piece. Notice, for instance, the deflating effect that the last, brief sentence of paragraph 3 has upon the slightly longer previous sentence: "And some of them jumped up and went to Jesus right away. But most of us just sat there." And, of course, the contrast between the hypocritical, grinning Westley (who surely did not cry that night) and the narrator effectively emphasizes Hughes's sense of isolation. If the story is, on the surface, amusing, it is also finally serious and moving.

MAY SARTON

The Rewards of Living a Solitary Life (p. 126)

Sarton's essay is, for the most part, so quiet that it may strike students as flat, but they can learn a good deal about writing by studying it carefully. It begins with a brief bit of narration (often an effective way to begin), and it introduces, still in the first paragraph, the idea of "love"—an idea that, in the final paragraph, will reappear in Sarton's assertion that the person who understands solitude will know that he or she is wedded to an inner self, "till death do us part." Between the first and the last paragraphs we get some rather oracular statements (e.g., "For anyone who can see things for himself with a naked eye becomes, for a moment or two, something of a genius"), but these statements are then given at least a little amplificatio,. and in any case the faintly prophetic mode is appropriate to one who lives in solitude and who wishes to help us to "converse again with [our] hidden powers."

TOPIC FOR WRITING

Write a paragraph discussing whether or not Sarton's essay is sentimental.

GARRISON KEILLOR

Something from the Sixties (p. 128)

Keillor does a good job of sketching the clothing of the 1960s, a period when adolescents and young men and young women—come to think of it, some older ones too—rebelled on campuses, and as part of their rebellion wore pieces of military clothing as a sort of parody of or protest against the war in Vietnam. It was a period when young people with middle class backgrounds rejected the "nice clothes" of their parents, preferred tattered jeans, leather vests, eccentric hats, and so forth. (For an enthusiastic discussion of the phenomenon, written in the midst of it all, see Charles Reich, *The Greening of America*. Reich finds this sort of clothing more honest than the gray flannel suit or the white shirt worn with a necktie: its colors are for the most part those of the earth and sky, the wearer does not constrict the body with a necktie, a patch is nothing to be ashamed of, etc.) In those days the preppie look was unknown on the campus.

The father who writes this essay can hardly conceive of wearing the stuff he digs out for his son, and yet he is pleased, even proud, that his son delights in it. The father is now the "audience," not the bold actor who once wore such clothing, but through his son he again lives those years—even if only briefly—and of course he is delighted by his son's enthusiastic endorsement of the clothing. (What father is not pleased when he gets even a smidgen of respect from his young son? After all, most adolescents—boys, at least—are more or less ashamed of their parents, ashamed of the way they dress and speak and earn their livings.) In Keillor's essay, for the moment a son delights in his father, and a father delights not only in his son but also in his earlier self.

TOPICS FOR WRITING

1. Our fifth question in the text, calling attention to Keillor's remark that he settled down with "what I think of as the Dad look," asks students to describe the clothes, the body stance, and the expression of a man wearing "the Dad look." If you make this assignment, you may want to have students read their descriptions to each other, to find out if there is a consensus or a disagreement. Have students try to explain how they arrived at similar descriptions, or why their descriptions vary.

2. About halfway through the paragraph beginning "We went up to the attic," we read "Military surplus was the basic style then...." Read the rest of the paragraph, and then write a paragraph describing the "basic style" now.

3. Imagine that the writer of this article was a woman and that her daughter had asked her for "something from the sixties." What articles of clothing might the mother have produced? Rewrite the article from the point of view of the mother.

4. If your class has written the article suggested in question 4, have the students exchange papers. Students should then compare the papers they receive with the original article, and should be asked to write about the differences in attitudes toward male and female dress, or assumptions about men and women, that emerged.

FRANCIS BACON

Of Parents and Children (p. 131)

First, a reminder: The topic of Bacon's essay is the topic of one of our chapters. If you teach this essay, you may want to teach it in connection with Chapter 17.

We think there is value in spending classroom time on Bacon's style, hence questions 1 (paraphrase), 2 (on contrasts), and 5 (on imitating) in the text. The point of concerning oneself with Bacon's style is, of course, to help students to see that sentences must have a shape, and that the shape helps to convey—or embody—meaning. Although students can learn very little about the overall organization of an essay from Bacon (if this essay has an organization it has eluded us), they can learn a great deal about the organization of a sentence.

JUANITA MIRANDA

The Pleasures of Tasting Bacon (p. 133)

We'll discuss this essay chiefly as an example of critical writing.

Although the title is a tad coy, the essay strikes us as being perceptive and well-written. The first sentence is rather long but it is easy to follow, and the idea it offers—that one reads for pleasure—is engaging and will probably strike serious college students as a surprising idea.

Miranda tends to use the editorial "we," as in "Let's look... at some of the opening lines," but at least once she uses the first person singular: "I imagine that even a reader who is not committed to the literal truth of the Bible will take delight in this line...." Is this a slip? We don't think so. For the most part Miranda's "we's" imply the reader as well as the writer, but in this case she is clearly speaking only for herself.

Other things one might point out, if one is talking about the essay as a piece of writing: 1) clear transitions (thus, the first paragraph ends with a sentence mentioning "fun," and the second paragraph begins with a sentence mentioning "fun"); 2) engaging examples (the use of Bacon's "Of Truth"—and again notice how this rises out of the end of the preceding paragraph, which raises the question of whether Bacon's assertions are "true"); 3) the focus on a single essay; 4) Miranda's willingness to grant that Bacon's essay has weaknesses (she calls attention to its lack of organization, and to the lack of indisputable truths).

ANNE ROSENBERG

Some Limitations of Bacon's Essays (p. 136)

We talk about Rosenberg's essay chiefly as a piece of writing, but we want to mention at the outset that although her essay and Miranda's are pretty sharply opposed, both make sense. Probably much depends on *why* one reads, i.e. on what one hopes to get from reading. In our view, Bacon's essays do offer the pleasure that Woolf and Miranda speak of. On the other hand, they clearly are of their time, notably in their patriarchal view. The title is not especially inviting, but it is clear and it clearly announces the writer's topic. The opening paragraph begins by conceding something to the subject (the author wisely does not simply dismiss Bacon's essays) and then quickly and clearly states the objections: The essays are dated and boring. In her second sentence ("Let's begin with the second point") she clearly indicates where she is going. It may seem a trifle odd to the reader that she will begin with the second (rather than the first) point, but since she announces what she is doing, the reader is not baffled by what follows, and probably is content to let Rosenberg lead the way.

She makes her first main point effectively by means of a good example, and her discussion of the example is orderly. She cites a sentence from the Bible, and then uses this sentence as a means of getting to her next point, that the essays are dated. By dated she chiefly means that they embody a view of women that is not acceptable today.

The second half of her essay takes another angle: Should we not read Bacon? She judiciously addresses this topic, arguing that Bacon should be read for certain reasons, but maintaining her view that the essays are dated, and she effectively enlists Virginia Woolf to help make the point.

C. S. LEWIS

A Book for Adolescents (p. 138)

One can always count on Lewis to be clear, clear-sighted, and original (even if one disagrees with what he says). Probably most people who teach courses in Renaissance or seventeenth-century literature, or even most teachers of English literature, assume that Bacon is a major figure, who is to be treated reverentially—even if he did not write Shakespeare's plays. Certainly Lewis's idea that Bacon's *Essays* is "a book for adolescents" never struck any of the editors of *Literature for Composition*; in fact, it never occurred to us that Bacon's essays are less than admirable. And even if we had been invited to think very hard about Bacon's line, "There is little friendshipe in the worlde, and least of all betweene equals," it would never have occurred to us to come up with Lewis's view: "A man of 40 either disbelieves it or takes it for granted." Notice that Lewis does not agree or disagree with the idea; he simply says—probably correctly, come to think of it—that only an adolescent would underline the statement.

Our last question in the text seeks to get students to think about Bacon's epigrammatic ("apophthegmatic") sentences. When you come to think of it, it is true that the very *dis*continuity of Bacon's sentences gives each sentence extra weight. If Bacon had gone on to amplify, modify, explain, he might have made a more reasonable and more persuasive case, but not (probably) a more *impressive* case. That is, the sentences, uttered and then abandoned, are like those of an oracle who does not deign to explain.

Perhaps Lewis himself is in Bacon's tradition. The sentence that we just quoted ("A man of 40 either disbelieves it or takes it for granted") has epigrammatic force, partly because of the "either... or" structure, which conveys an authoritative, no-nonsense, all-knowing tone, or, better, a sense that there is nothing more to be said about the topic. Similarly, when Lewis says that "Cunning, even more than virtue, lives in minute particulars," he sounds rather Baconian to us, imitating Bacon's style ("Cunning... virtue") and Bacon's close observation of the ways of the world ("lives in minute particulars").

In a sense, Lewis's essay complements Miranda's, since Miranda puts her emphasis on the pleasure afforded by the style, rather than on the depth of the content.

CHAPTER 7

Reading (and Writing about) Fiction

GRACE PALEY

Samuel (p. 140)

"All those ballsy American stories," Grace Paley has said of much of the American canon, "had nothing to say to me." Is she, then, a feminist writer? She denies it, insisting that she is something rather different, "a feminist and a writer." Some instructors may wish to have a class consider in what ways, if any, "Samuel" is the work of a feminist.

There is a particularly female insight in the last two paragraphs of "Samuel" which (though the second of these mentions Samuel's father) focus on Samuel's mother. The first of these paragraphs emphasizes the mother's agony when she learns of her son's death; the final paragraph, describing a later time, emphasizes a grief that is less visible or audible but that is perhaps even more painful, for this grief is stimulated by the sight of her newborn baby: "Never again will a boy exactly like Samuel be known."

Interestingly, the narrator (can we say the female author?) conveys a good deal of enthusiasm for what some people might regard as offensive *macho* displays of jiggling on the subway, riding the tail of a speeding truck, and hopping on the tops of trucks. Paley makes these actions sympathetic partly by implying that they take real skill, partly by implying that the show-off performing kids usually turn out to be very decent guys (one daredevil has graduated from high school, is married, holds a responsible job, and is going to night school), and partly by mildly discrediting those who oppose them. Thus one lady who disapproves of the jigglers thinks, "Their mothers never know where they are," but the narrator immediately assures us that the mothers of these boys *did* know where they were, and, moreover, the boys had been engaged in the thoroughly respectable activity of visiting a "missile exhibit on Fourteenth street."

Like this woman, the man who pulls the alarm cord is somewhat discredited: he is "one of the men whose boyhood had been more watchful than brave." Although it's no disgrace for a boy to be "watchful," the sentence probably guides most readers to feel some scorn for the man who (so to speak) was never a boy. Many readers will feel that although the man "walked in a citizenly way" to pull the cord, he is motivated less by an impulse of good citizenship than (though probably he doesn't know it) by resentment, by irritation that these children are experiencing a joy that he never experienced in his childhood. On the other hand, Paley does not present him as a villain, and the story is not chiefly concerned with his guilt. By the end of the story, readers are probably so taken up with the mother's grief that they scarcely remember the man.

Although "Samuel" resembles a fable in that it is fairly brief, is narrated in an apparently simple manner, and concludes with a message, it differs significantly from a fable. Most obviously, it does not use the beasts, gods, and inanimate objects that fables commonly use. In fact, these are not essential in fables. More significantly, the characters in "Samuel" are more complicated, since the noisy boys are treated sympathetically and the apparently respectable adults are treated ironically. Finally, where the fable traditionally utters or implies a hard-headed, worldly-wise (and often faintly cynical) message, the message uttered at the end of "Samuel" arouses the reader's deepest sympathy.

TOPICS FOR WRITING

1. If you had been on the train, would you have pulled the emergency cord? Why, or why not?
2. Write a journalist's account (250-300 words) of the accidental death of a boy named Samuel. Use whatever details Paley provides, but feel free to invent what you need for an authentic news story.

EDGAR ALLAN POE

The Cask of Amontillado (p. 153)

Because many students will have read this story in high school, it can be used effectively as the first assignment: they will start with some ideas about it, and at the end of the class discussion they will probably see that they didn't know everything about the story. It may be well to begin a class discussion by asking the students to characterize the narrator. The opening paragraph itself, if read aloud in class, ought to provide enough for them to see that the speaker is probably paranoid and given to a monstrous sort of reasoning, though, of course, at the start of the story we cannot be absolutely certain that Fortunato has not indeed heaped a "thousand injuries" on him. (In this paragraph, notice too the word "impunity," which we later learn is part of the family motto.) When we meet Fortunato, we are convinced that though the narrator's enemy is something of a fool, he is not the monster that the narrator thinks he is. And so the words at the end of the story, fifty years later, must have an ironic tone, for though *in pace requiescat* can apply to Fortunato, they cannot apply to the speaker, who is still talking (on his deathbed, to a priest?) of his vengeance on the unfortunate Fortunato.

The story is full of other little ironies, conscious on the part of Montresor, unconscious on the part of Fortunato:

The narrator is courteous but murderous;

The time is one of festivity but a murder is being planned;

The festival of disguise corresponds to the narrator's disguise of his feelings;

Fortunato thinks he is festively disguised as a fool, but he is a fool;

He says he will not die of a cough, and the narrator assures him that he is right;

Fortunato is a Freemason, and when he asks the narrator for the secret sign of a brother, the narrator boldly, playfully, outrageously shows him the mason's trowel that he will soon use to wall Fortunato up.

But what to make of all this? It has been the fashion, for at least a few decades, to say that Poe's situations and themes speak to our anxieties, our fear of being buried alive, our fear of disintegration of the self, and so on. Maybe. Maybe, too, there is something to Marie Bonaparte's interpretation: she sees the journey through the tunnel to the crypt as an entry into the womb; the narrator is killing his father (Fortunato) and possessing his mother. And maybe, too, there is something to Daniel Hoffman's assertion in *Poe Poe Poe Poe Poe Poe Poe* (223) that Montresor and Fortunato are doubles: "When Montresor leads Fortunato down into the farthest vault of his family's wine-cellar, into a catacomb of human bones, is he not... conducting his double thither? My treasure, my fortune, down into the bowels of the earth, a charnel-house of bones." Maybe.

A video cassette of Edgar Allan Poe's "The Cask of Amontillado" is available from HarperCollins. An audio cassette of Basil Rathbone reading Edgar Allan Poe's "The Cask of Amontillado" and "The Pit and the Pendulum" is also available from HarperCollins.

EUDORA WELTY

A Worn Path (p. 158)

In an essay in the *Georgia Review* (Winter 1979), Eudora Welty (speaking mainly of her first story, "The Death of a Traveling Salesman") says that her characters "rise most often from the present," but her plots are indebted to "the myths and fairy tales I steeped myself in as a young reader.... By the time I was writing stories I drew on them as casually as I drew on the daily newspaper or the remarks of my neighbors."

Clearly "A Worn Path" draws on the myth of the phoenix, the golden bird that periodically consumes itself in flames so that it may be renewed. Phoenix Jackson renews her ancient body on each visit to the doctor's remote office. The chief clues: the woman's name ("Phoenix"), the story's early description of her (her stick makes a sound "like the chirping of a solitary little bird"; "a golden color ran underneath, and the two knobs of her cheeks were illuminated by a yellow burning under the dark"), a reference to cyclic time ("I bound to go to town, mister. The time come around"—and the time is Christmas, i.e., a time of renewal), her "ceremonial stiffness" in the doctor's office, and finally, the words "Phoenix rose carefully."

The myth is wonderfully supported by details, details that are strictly irrelevant (e.g., Phoenix's deception of the hunter, which nets her a nickel, and her cadging of a nickel's worth of pennies from the nurse), but that make the character unsentimental and thoroughly convincing.

A writer in *Studies in Short Fiction* [14 (1977): 288-290] argues: "The journey to Natchez... becomes a psychological necessity for Phoenix, her only way of coping with her loss and her isolation.... Having at first made the journey to save the life of her grandson, she now follows the worn path each Christmas season to save herself" (289). On the other hand, not all of the criticism of the story is on this level. For a good discussion, see Alfred Appel, *A Season of Dreams: The Fiction of Eudora Welty* (1965).

TOPICS FOR CRITICAL THINKING AND WRITING

1. Is the story sentimental? (We'd say no, for several reasons: Phoenix, though old and—at moments—mentally failing, is dignified and never self-pitying; the writer, letting Phoenix tell her own story, never asks us to pity Phoenix; Phoenix exhibits both a sense of humor and a sense of self-reliance, and on those occasions when she needs help she exhibits no embarrassment. Her theft of the nickel and her shrewdness in getting the nurse to give her another nickel instead of "a few pennies" also, as mentioned a moment ago, help to keep her from being the sentimental old lady of Norman Rockwell pictures.)

2.   Write a character sketch (250-300 words) of some old person whom you
      know. If possible, reveal the personality by showing him or her engaged
      in some characteristic activity.

TOBIAS WOLFF

Powder (p. 165)

The first paragraph provides the necessary background: the parents are sepa-
rated, the mother is sensible, and the father is irresponsible—but even at this
stage one may wonder if perhaps there isn't something especially engaging
about a father who sneaks his young son into a nightclub in order to see
Thelonious Monk.

The father's irresponsibility is underlined in the second paragraph. He
promised to get the boy home to the mother for Christmas Eve dinner, but
"he observed some quality [in the snow] that made it necessary for us to get
in one last run. We got in several last runs." The father tries to be reassuring
at the diner, but the boy, a worrier, is distressed. He's a strange kid, as he himself knows, someone who bothers "teachers for homework assignments far
ahead of their due dates" so he can make up schedules. But with a father like
his, and a mother who clearly is not sympathetic to the father's adventurous
(or childish?) enthusiasms, who can blame the boy? And though the boy in
his orderliness is his mother's son, the last paragraph of the story validates the
father. Although the father is "bankrupt of honor," the ride (or the boy's experience of the ride) is something so special that it is "impossible to describe.
Except maybe to say this: if you haven't driven fresh powder, you haven't
driven."

One detail may escape some readers: when the father makes a phone call
from the diner, the boy quite reasonably thinks the father must be calling the
mother, but this man-child in fact is calling the police, with some sort of bull
that causes the officer to drive away and thus gives the father a chance to put
aside the barrier and to drive home. The evidence? After making the call, the
father stares through the window, down the road, and says, "Come on, come
on." (He is impatiently waiting for the result of his call.) As soon as the troop-
er's car passes the window, the father hurries the boy out of the diner. When
the boy asks the father where the policeman may have gone, the father ignores
the question.

"Bankrupt of honor," yes, and one can easily imagine the impossibility of
being married to such a man. But the father desperately wants to keep the family intact, and he wants to get the boy home for dinner with the mother in an
effort to buy "a little more time," though we are not surprised to learn that the
mother decides "to make the split final."

SANDRA CISNEROS

Woman Hollering Creek (p. 167)

One wouldn't exactly call the first paragraph of the story Faulknerian, but it *is* a single sentence of some eighty words, and it *does* have a kind of epic sweep ("The day Don Serafin gave Juan Pedro Martinez Permission" "...already did he divine..."). Other parts of the story give us dialogue, heard by a fly on the wall, in the manner of the traditional "realistic," Hemingway-sort of story ("Felice? It's me, Graciela. / No, I can't talk louder. / I'm at work. / Look, I need kind of a favor"). But surely no reader can feel that this story is a pastiche; rather, Cisneros has displayed wonderful virtuousity in telling a story that has a distinctive style.

One way to get at the story is to think about the concrete details, or, rather, about their relative absence. We are always telling students to notice how the details of, say, the setting help to define the characters. In this story, very little is done in the way of establishing the setting. We are not told if Cleófilas's new home had linoleum on the floor, if the bedspread was gingham, or if the refrigerator was noisy. About all that we know of her house is that the doorways lacked doors, and we know nothing about the hospital to which she goes—how many people were in the waiting room, whether the receptionist was friendly or unfriendly or whether Cleófilas had to wait a long time. Nor are we told much about what any of the characters look like. When we think about it, we may be amazed at how few details are given—one might almost say that the only thing presented in any detail is an episode of a *telenovela*.

What is the effect of this lack of physical detail? The effect, it seems to us, is to isolate Cleófilas, to put her in a world of her own. The narrator's indifference to the appearance of the physical world, and the narrator's emphasis on Cleófilas's states of mind, mark "Woman Hollering Creek" as a story in the "lyrical" rather than the realistic tradition. By using Henry James's method of the central intelligence, Cisneros emphasizes the protagonist's subjectivity and isolation. After all, Cleófilas is isolated from her father, from her husband, from friends in her new town (except for limited contact with her two neighbors), and from television (except occasionally)" Almost any passage will let us hear Cleófilas's distinctive mind, filled with expectations that the real world will not sustain:

> Yes, he has to be back. So they will get married in the spring when he can take off work, and then they will drive off in his new pickup—did you see it?—to their new home in Sequin. Well, not exactly new, but they're going to repaint the house. You know newlyweds. New paint and new furniture. Why not? He can afford it. And later on add maybe a room or two for the children. May they be blessed with many.

About all that Cleófilas has, it seems, is an affectionate connection with the strangely named creek, and this brings us to a discussion of the title. The creek, introduced in the title, is not mentioned again until the third paragraph, where it is ominously associated with the idea that "sometimes love sours." About a third of the way into the story we hear more about the creek, about La Gritona ("the hollering woman" who in folklore haunts the creek), but the title has alerted us to the fact that it may be important. And so it proves to be. On the first leg of the flight back to Mexico, Felice gives a holler when she crosses the creek, "a yell... which startled not only Cleófilas but Juan Pedrito as well." Cleófilas comes to see that this yell is not one of "pain or rage," but, rather, is a "hoot," a "holler like Tarzan," i.e. an assertion of power, of self— not an isolated self like Cleófilas's, but a self-reliant woman who drives a pick-up, not an old woman with a Pontiac. In the last paragraph of the story we learn that Cleófilas adds her own laughter to Felice's, so the story does give the reader a satisfying glimpse of Cleófilas making an important contact, getting out of her isolation at least for a moment. On the other hand, the story does not end with a decisive resolution; we have only the tiniest clue as to what sort of life she will ultimately live when she is back in Mexico.

One way of approaching the story in class is to ask the students to think about the degree to which the story fulfills a reader's expectations. Speaking broadly (and in the company of E. M. Forster, who made this point in *Aspects of the Novel*), we can say that in much good fiction there is, as one moves through the story, a mild sense of surprise, and then the sense of "Oh, that's all right." That is, expectations are set up, and then fulfilled in a way that we had not quite anticipated—hence the surprise—but that, in retrospect, seem right. In this story, the first paragraph tells us that Cleófilas will dream of returning to Mexico. That doesn't necessarily mean that she *will* return, but the possibility has been raised, and it stays in our minds. Then too, because we hear a fair amount about *el otro lado* ("the other side"), perhaps we can guess that the movement to the other side will be followed by a counter-movement, a return. But the emphasis, of course, is not on a plot of adventure. The story could have been a thriller, with a chase (Juan Pedro spots her outside of the Cash N Carry, she jumps into Felice's car, etc.), but Cisneros devotes only a few sentences to this sort of suspense ("All morning that flutter of half-fear, half-doubt"). Cisneros's interest is primarily in Cleófilas's consciousness, and only slightly in an exciting plot of the traditional sort, that is, a plot with an active protagonist who initiates an action that has a beginning, middle, and end. Having said this, however, one should not minimize the boldness of Cleófilas's decision to leave her husband. She had begun with romantic ideas: "You or No One," "One ought to live one's life like that don't you think? You or no one. Because to suffer for love is good. The Pain all sweet somehow, in the end." Then, things happen to her (notably her husband's acts of violence), and in some degree we are in a story in which a relatively passive figure moves from innocence to experience, the sort of story, that is, in which a fairly naive character does not so much act as receive action and finally is forced to per-ceive that life is not what he or she had thought it was. Still, Cleófilas does make an immensely daring decision: she decides to flee. How much has she changed? Probably we can't tell for sure. In the third paragraph from the end, we hear her telling her father and her brothers about the strange Felice ("Can you imagine?"), and it is evident that she herself scarcely comprehends a woman like Felice. Yet the last paragraph tells us that she joined Felice in laughing, and so we feel there is indeed some sort of union, some sort of change in Cleófilas.

CHAPTER 8

Thinking Critically about a Short Story

WILLIAM FAULKNER

A Rose for Emily (p. 177)

The chronology of the story—not very clear on first reading—has been worked out by several writers. Five chronologies are given in M. Thomas Inge, *William Faulkner: "A Rose for Emily"*; a sixth is given in Cleanth Brooks, *William Faulkner: Toward Yoknapatawpha and Beyond* (382-84). Brooks conjectures that Miss Emily is born in 1852, her father dies around 1884, Homer Barron appears in 1884 or 1885, dies in 1885 or 1886, the delegation calls on Miss Emily about the smell in 1885/86. In 1901 or 1904 or 1905, Miss Emily gives up the lessons in china-painting. Colonel Sartoris dies in 1906 or 1907, the delegation calls on her about the taxes in 1916, and Miss Emily dies in 1926.

The plot, of course, is gothic fiction: a decaying mansion, a mysteriously silent servant, a corpse, necrophilia. And one doesn't want to discard the plot in a search for what it symbolizes, but it is also clear that the story is not only "about" Emily Grierson but also about the South's pride in its past (including its Emily-like effort to hold on to what is dead) and the guilt as well as the grandeur of the past. Inevitably much classroom discussion centers on Miss Emily's character, but a proper discussion of her character entails a discussion of the narrator.

(This paragraph summarizes an essay on this topic by John Daremo, originally printed in S. Barnet, *A Short Guide to Writing about Literature.*) The unnamed narrator is never precisely identified. Sometimes he seems to be an innocent eye, a recorder of a story whose implications escape him. Sometimes he seems to be coarse: he mentions "old lady Wyatt, the crazy woman," he talks easily of "niggers," and he confesses that because he and other towns-people felt that Miss Emily's family "held themselves a little too high for what they really were," the townspeople "were not pleased exactly, but vindicated" when at thirty she was still unmarried. But if his feelings are those of com-mon humanity (e. g., racist and smug), he at least knows what these feelings are and thus helps us to know ourselves. We therefore pay him respectful attention, and we notice that on the whole he is compassionate (note espe-cially his sympathetic understanding of Miss Emily's insistence for three days that her father is not dead). True, Miss Emily earns our respect by her aloof-ness and her strength of purpose (e.g., when she publicly appears in the buggy with Homer Barron, and when she cows the druggist and the alderman), but if we speak of her aloofness and her strength of purpose rather than of her arrogance and madness, it is because the narrator's imaginative sympathy guides us. And the narrator is the key to the apparently curious title: pre-sumably the telling of this tale is itself the rose, the community's tribute (for the narrator insistently speaks of himself as "we") to the intelligible humani-ty in a woman whose unhappy life might seem monstrous to less sympathet-ic observers. Another meaning, however, may be offered (very tentatively) for the title. In the story Faulkner emphasizes Miss Emily's attempts to hold on to the past: her insistence, for example, that her father is not dead, and that she has no taxes to pay. Is it possible that Homer Barron's corpse serves as a sort of pressed or preserved will, a reminder of a past experience of love? If so, the title refers to him.

For a feminist reading, see Judith Fetterley, in *The Resisting Reader: A Feminist Approach to American Fiction* (1978), reprinted in *Literary Theories in Praxis*, edited by Shirley F. Staton (1987). Fetterley sees the story as revealing the "sexual conflict" within patriarchy (whether of the South or the North, the old order or the new). Emily's confinement by her father represents the con-finement of women by patriarchy, and the remission of her taxes reveals the dependence of women on men. Emily has been turned into a "Miss," a lady, by a chivalric attitude that is "simply a subtler and more dishonest version of her father's horsewhip." The narrator represents a subtle form of this patri-archy. According to Fetterley, the narrator sees her as "'dear, inescapable, impervious, tranquil, and perverse'; indeed, anything and everything but human."

Fetterley—the "resisting reader" of her title, that is the reader who refus-es to accept that text—argues that the story exposes "the violence done to a woman by making her a lady; it also explains the particular form of power the victim gains from this position and can use on those who enact their violence.... Like Ellison's invisible man, nobody sees *Emily*. And because nobody sees *her*, she can literally get away with murder."

An audio cassette of William Faulkner reading is available from HarperCollins.

TOPICS FOR CRITICAL THINKING AND WRITING

1. How valid is the view that the story is an indictment of the decadent values of the aristocratic Old South? Or a defense of these values (embodied in Emily) against the callousness (embodied in Homer Barron) of the North?
2. Suppose Faulkner had decided to tell the story from Miss Emily's point of view. Write the first 200 or 300 words of such a version.
3. Characterize the narrator.

WILLIAM FAULKNER

Facsimiles of Manuscript and Typescript (p. 185)

In the manuscript page that we reproduce (the first of the five surviving pages) the only significant departure from the printed version is the date of Colonel Sartoris's edict—1904 in the manuscript but 1894 in the printed text.

The typescript of the story is—except for the passages that we reprint— virtually the same as the published version. (To the best of our knowledge, these pages have never been reprinted in a textbook, or, for that matter, in a critical study of Faulkner.) Whatever conjectures we might offer concerning Faulkner's decision to omit from the published version the passage about the dialogue between the servant and Miss Emily, and also Faulkner's slight revision of the ending, are of no more interest than the conjectures that other instructors—and students—may offer. We recommend that you invite your students to examine the typescript and to comment on the changes in the printed text.

WILLIAM FAULKNER

Comments on "A Rose for Emily" (p. 184)

Faulkner's comments on the story provide a chance total about the relevance of the author's intention. (Our own feeling: It's always nice to know what the author has to say, but (1) for most authors before modern times we cannot know what they had to say, and (2) finally we must take the story the way it strikes us. Authors have been known, in their comments on their work, to play with readers, and they have also been known to be poor judges of their own work. After all, if the author says that the story is his or her greatest, we may still prefer some other story. The gist of our view is summed up in D. H. Lawrence's words to the effect that we should trust the tale, not the teller.

Faulkner is probably honest, rather than just modest, when he says that he doesn't know if the story is a criticism of the North or the South, and that he was "simply trying to write about people." The comment (also in his first answer in the text) about symbolism is worth discussing, since students are so eager to find symbols everywhere. (On the other hand, most literature *is* symbolic, at least to some degree.)

CLEANTH BROOKS

On "A Rose for Emily" (p. 196)

In our second question in the text we ask if the student is satisfied with Brooks's formulation, "Heroic isolation pushed too far ends in homicidal murder." Brooks goes on to speak of this as the "moral" (he claims that he is offering this moral for readers who want a moral, but it is Brooks's nevertheless), and he says that "Miss Emily's story constitutes a warning against the sin of pride." Truth to tell, we are surprised that Brooks was willing to offer a moral. Many students, of course, want to know the *theme* of the story, and then they translate this into a moral. In any case, Brooks's moral allows for a good discussion of whether his version is adequate, and whether any version can be adequate.

HAL BLYTHE

Faulkner's "A Rose for Emily" (p. 192)

For what it is worth, we find Blythe's arguments unconvincing. In his second paragraph he says that "Faulkner's major clue to Homer Barron's sexual preference" is his name, but we fail to see how either "Homer" or "Barron" contains the slightest clue. We also fail to see evidence of homosexuality in the fact that Homer likes to drink with the guys, or in the fact that he says he is not the marrying kind. But it will be interesting to hear what students say. The discussion can perhaps be connected with our own comments about the limits of interpretation, in Chapter 14, "Arguing an Interpretation."

JUDITH FETTERLEY

A Rose for "A Rose for Emily" (p. 193)

This selection (from Fetterley's *The Resisting Reader*) seems to us to be one of the few genuinely illuminating comments on the story. Most of the other commentary strikes us as either banal or eccentric, but Fetterley looks at the story from a point of view that lets a reader see things that might otherwise be overlooked. You may want to invite students to notice that Fetterley looks closely at specific passages in the story; she of course has a theory, but she presents the theory in connection with specific passages, and (at least in our eyes) the theory and the passages go together.

CHAPTER 9

Reading (and Writing about) Drama

SUSAN GLASPELL

Trifles (p. 215)

Some students may know Glaspell's other version of this work, a short story entitled "A Jury of Her Peers." Some good class discussion can focus on the interchangeability of the titles. "Trifles" could have been called "A Jury of Her Peers," and vice versa. A peer, of course, is an equal, and the suggestion of the story's title is that Mrs. Wright is judged by a jury of her equals—Mrs. Hale and Mrs. Peters. A male jury would not constitute her equals because—at least in the context of the story and the play—males simply don't have the experiences of women and therefore can't judge them fairly.

Murder is the stuff of TV dramas, and this play concerns a murder, of course, but it's worth asking students how the play differs from a whodunit. Discussion will soon establish that we learn, early in "Trifles," who performed the murder, and we even know, fairly early, *why* Minnie killed her husband. (The women know what is what because they correctly interpret "trifles," but the men are baffled, since they are looking for obvious signs of anger.) Once we know who performed the murder, the interest shifts to the question of whether the women will cover up for Minnie.

The distinction between what the men and the women look for is paralleled in the distinction between the morality of the men and the women. The men stand for law and order, for dominance (they condescend to the women, and the murdered Wright can almost be taken as a symbol of male dominance), whereas the women stand for mutual support or nurturing. Students might be invited to discuss *why* the women protect Minnie. Is it because women are nurturing? Or because they feel guilt for their earlier neglect of Minnie? Or because, being women, they know what her sufferings must have been like, and feel that she acted justly? All of the above?

The symbols will cause very little difficulty. (1) The "gloomy" kitchen suggests Minnie's life with her husband; (2) the bird suggests Minnie (she sang "like a bird," was lively, then became caged and was broken in spirit).

The title is a sort of symbol too, an ironic one, for the men think (in Mr. Hale's words) that "Women are used to worrying over trifles." The men in the play never come to know better, but the reader-viewer comes to understand that the trifles are significant and that the seemingly trivial women have outwitted the self-important men. The irony of the title is established by the ironic action of the play.

Does the play have a *theme?* In our experience, the first theme that students may propose is that "it's a man's world." There is something to this view, but (1) a woman kills her husband, and (2) other women help her to escape from the (male) legal establishment. Do we want to reverse the first suggestion, then, and say that (in this play) it is really a woman's world, that women run things? No, given the abuse that all of the women in the play take. Still, perhaps it is fair to suggest that one of the things the play implies is that overbearing male behavior gets what it deserves—at least sometimes. Of course, when put this way, the theme is ancient; it is at the root of the idea of *hubris*, which is said to govern much Greek tragedy. Glaspell gives it a very special twist by emphasizing the women's role in restoring justice to society.

WENDY WASSERSTEIN

The Man in a Case (p. 226)

In our introductory comments about comedy we mention that comedy often shows the absurdity of ideals. The miser, the puritan, the health-faddist, and so on, are people of ideals, but their ideals are suffocating.

In his famous essay on comedy (1884), Henri Bergson suggested that an organism is comic when it behaves like a mechanism, that is, when instead of responding freely, flexibly, resourcefully—one might almost say intuitively and also intelligently—to the vicissitudes of life, it responds in a predictable, mechanical (and, given life's infinite variety, often inappropriate) way. It is not surprising that the first line in Wasserstein's comedy, spoken by a pedant to his betrothed, is "You are ten minutes late." This is not the way that Demetrius and Lysander speak in *A Midsummer Night's Dream*. True, a Shakespearean lover may fret about time when he is not in the presence of his mistress, but when he sees her, all thoughts of the clock disappear and he is nothing but lover. The Shakespearean lover is, in his way, mechanical too, but the audience feels a degree of sympathy for him that it does not feel for the pedantic clock-watcher.

The very title, *The Man in a Case*, alerts us to a man who is imprisoned— and, it turns out, a man who lives in a prison of his own making. Byelinkov says, "I don't like change very much." His words could be said by many other butts of satire—for example, jealous husbands, or misers. And of course the comic writer takes such figures and puts them in a place where they will be subjected to maximum change. The dramatist puts the jealous husband or the miser, for instance, into a plot in which a stream of men visit the house, and every new visitor is (in the eyes of the comic figure) a potential seducer or a potential thief. In *The Man in a Case*, we meet a man of highly disciplined habits, who is confronted by an uninhibited woman. If you invite students to read the first two speeches—Byelinkov's one line ("You are ten minutes late") and Varinka's rambling account of "the woman who runs the grocery store," they will immediately see the comic juxtaposition.

In this play, then, we have a pedant who unaccountably has fallen in love with a vivacious young woman. (In Chekhov's story, Byelinkov's acquaintances decided that it was time for him to get married, so they conspired to persuade him that he was in love.) The pedant, of course, is a stock comic character going back to the doctor (*il dottore*, not a medical doctor but a pedant) of Renaissance Italian comedy. Such a figure values Latin more than life. True, Byelinkov is in love, but (as his first line, about Varinka being ten minutes late, shows) he remains the precise schoolmaster. Later, when Varinka says "It is time for tea," he replies "It is too early for tea. Tea is at half past the hour." Perhaps tea regularly is served at half past the hour, but, again, a lover does not talk this way; a true lover will take every opportunity to have tea with his mistress. Two other examples of Byelinkov's regimented life: his belief that "heavy cream is too rich for tea-time," and his need to translate two stanzas every day because, he explains, "That is my regular schedule." By the way, speaking of his translation, we are a bit puzzled by the passage in which he says he is translating the *Aeneid* "from classical Greek hexameter into Russian alexandrines." Of course classicists sometimes did translate the *Aeneid* into Greek, as a sort of exercise, but surely a classicist who was going to translate Virgil into Russian alexandrines would translate from Virgil's original Latin, not from Greek. Possibly the joke is precisely that this fool is translating from a translation, not the original; or possibly he is pedantically saying that Virgil used a meter used by the Greeks.

In any case, we are not surprised to hear that Byelinkov describes his career as the teaching of "the discipline and contained beauty of the classics." "Discipline" and containment are exactly what we expect from this sort of comic figure, a man who tells us that he smiles three times every day, and that in 20 years of teaching he has never been late to school. The speech that began "I don't like change very much," went on thus: "If one works out the arithmetic the final fraction of improvement is at best less than an eighth of value over the total damage caused by disruption."

Why, then, is this man talking to Varinka? Because he has fallen in love. Love conquers all, even mathematicians and classicists. For the most part, when such monomaniacs fall in love they are, as we have said, comic objects of satire, but since audiences approve of love, these figures—if young and genuinely in love—also can generate some sympathy from the audience. (Toward the end of this discussion we will talk more about two kinds of comedy, laughing *with* and laughing *at*.) Thus, when Byelinkov says he will put a lilac in Varinka's hair, he almost becomes sympathetic—but when he makes an entry in his notebook, reminding him to do this again next year, he reverts to the pedant whom we find ridiculous.

The end of the play is fairly complex: when Varinka departs, Byelinkov takes out his pad, tears up the note about the lilac, and strews the pieces over the garden. Apparently he has had enough of her; we might almost say that he has come to his senses and has realized that a man of his temperament can not possibly live with a woman of her temperament. But then we are told that he "Carefully picks up each piece of paper and places them all in a small envelope as lights fade to black." What are we to make of this? That he retrieves the paper seems to indicate that he still loves her—or does it just mean that he is fussy enough not to litter the garden and not to leave any evidence of his folly? That is, when he retrieves the paper, is he revealing that he is still the lover, or is he revealing that he is still the pedant, the man who puts everything in its place (tea at a certain hour and at no other hour)? If the former, the audience will respond with a sympathetic chuckle; if the latter, the audience will respond with a mildly scornful laugh. Much will depend on the exact gestures that accompany tearing and strewing the note, retrieving it, and putting the pieces in an envelope. If, for instance, the pieces are fussily retrieved and prissily inserted into the envelope, we will sense the pedant, the figure we laugh *at*. If however, they are tenderly retrieved and lovingly placed into the envelope, we will sense the lover, the figure we laugh *with* as well as at. If there were a blackout while Byelinkov picked up the papers, we are inclined to think that the total effect (because sudden and surprising) would be comic, but Wasserstein's final direction ("lights fade to black") seems to us to allow for sympathy and even pathos.

We suggest that if you assign the play you ask two students to perform it, after rehearsing with a third student who serves as a director at a rehearsal or two. Our own practice—as with scenes from Shakespeare—is to photocopy the work, and to annotate it with some suggestions for stage business. For instance, we would suggest that when Byelinkov delivers his first line ("You are ten minutes late") he says it after carefully consulting a pocket watch. For that matter, you may want to gloss the initial stage direction, "Byelinkov is pacing. Enter Varinka, out of breath." The obvious (farcical?) thing to do is to have Byelinkov pace back and forth, ceremoniously take out and consult his pocket watch, replace the watch, pace back and forth again, and then to have Varinka enter at a moment when Byelinkov is pacing *away* from her. The first two speeches make evident the contrast between the uptight Byelinkov and the effusive Varinka.

Interestingly, soon after this dialogue of opposites, the two are dancing together. Byelinkov has said he is "no dancing bear," and Varinka immediately urges him to dance with her. He complies—probably she grabs him and leaves him no choice. Strangely, when they dance he apparently enjoys the activity; at least we interpret his words "And turn. And turn" to indicate that he is caught up in the dance. A moment later he stops, to place a lilac in her hair, a charming romantic touch that surely makes him sympathetic to the audience—but equally surely he loses this sympathy and becomes merely ridiculous when he takes out his notebook and pedantically writes a memorandum.

A note on Question 1 in the text (about Byelinkov on the motionless bicycle). In Bergsonian thinking, comedy mocks those whose behavior has become fixed and obsessive. What could be more fixed and obsessive than a man furiously pedaling on a bicycle that doesn't go anywhere? Of course the theory has to be modified; the behavior of a tragic hero is also obsessive. The difference, however, is that the tragic hero is obsessed about something that the audience thinks is important (e.g., Desdemona's chastity), whereas the comic hero is obsessed with trivia.

There is, naturally, a good deal more to say about the theory of comedy, but it's probably fair to say that almost all theories of comedy fit into one of two schools: (1) comedy affords the viewer a feeling of superiority (Hobbes's "sudden glory arising from some sudden conception of some eminency in ourselves, by comparison with the infirmity of others"), or (2) comedy helps the viewer to perceive universal absurdity by causing the viewer sympathetically to identify himself or herself with some absurd action. In blunt terms, (1) laughing at (derisive laughter) versus or (2) laughing with (genial, affectionate laughter).

HARVEY FIERSTEIN

On Tidy Endings (p. 232)

The exposition continues well into the play; readers, or viewers, learn the past through explosive bits of dialogue. For instance (Question 1), we are not explicitly told that Collin died of AIDS until we are about one-quarter into the play, though of course the reference to death and to "Uncle Arthur" may incline us to guess that a gay man (Arthur's lover) has died, and that AIDS may have been the cause of his death. On the surface the play is *all* exposition; it seems to be almost entirely about the past. We do not see (again, at least so far as the surface plot goes) characters engaging in actions that then produce consequences that in turn cause further actions. Rather, two characters talk about a dead man.

We say "on the surface" because although nothing much seems to happen—this is not a tragedy in which we see a hero or heroine take a decisive step that will lead to death, or a comedy in which a pair of young lovers will at last be united—the real action in the play is the violent and painful education of Marion and Arthur. Both characters loved Collin, both are deeply hurt by his death and by the behavior of the other, both have some understanding of the other, but both have a great deal to learn. What do they learn (Question 7)?

Marion has already at some point come to realize that she should have included Arthur more openly in the funeral and the obituary, but during the play she learns that she is Arthur's "husband's *ex-wife*," that is, that her relationship to Collin does not equal Arthur's. As Arthur puts it, "After three years you still have no idea of who I am." She learns that although her grief is deep, it cannot equal Arthur's, not only because he is losing his home (not just a profitable piece of real estate) but also because Collin was all that Arthur had, whereas she has a home, a husband, and a son. She learns, too, or perhaps she is violently reminded, that Arthur's love prolonged Collin's life for two years beyond what the doctor thought possible, and she learns some details about Collin's last moments.

Arthur, for his part, learns that Marion knows she could not have equaled Arthur's care for and devotion to Collin. (She admits this when she says she "could never have done what you did. I would never have survived. I really don't know how you did it.") Arthur learns that Collin had not told Marion what his illness was. Further, he learns that although Marion was "jealous" she was "always lovingly" jealous. "I was happy for Collin," she explains, "because there was no way to deny that he was happy." Arthur also learns that she is a carrier, and that (since she and her husband practice safe sex) she may not be able to have the second child that she longs for. He learns, too, that he was wrong when he told Marion that she is not his friend and that he wants her out of his life. (The stage direction tells us that he is "desperate" when he says this. She *is* his friend, and he does not really want her out of his life; at the end of the play he expresses his hope that she will continue to think of him. And, finally, Arthur learns from the lips of the grudging and deeply hurt Jimmy that Collin spoke lovingly about Arthur to Jimmy.

What does Jimmy learn? It's not clear, we think, that he learns anything yet. At the beginning of the play he makes "fey mannerisms," and he quotes a mocking phrase that his friend made about gays. (Later Arthur will say that he has noticed "the snide remarks, the little smirks" that presumably have charac-terized—at least recently—Jimmy's relations to Arthur.) Jimmy delivers Collin's message only when pressured by his mother, but perhaps a reader can feel that Arthur's understanding of the boy is sound. Notice that Arthur does-n't pressure him—for instance, when near the end of the play Jimmy is reluc-tant, as at the start, to enter the apartment, and when Marion forces the boy to give the message. Students might be invited to offer their guesses about whether Jimmy will become reconciled to Arthur.

What do readers or viewers learn? Much depends on one's point of view about whether art teaches, and, if so, how and what? At one extreme are those who hold that works of art can't teach anything because all they do is give details about one imaginary happening. At the other extreme are those who hold that works of art give us insight into reality, give us (in Picasso's famous words) "lies like truth." There is no sign that this quarrel will ever be settled.

A few words about some of the other questions posed at the end of the text. *Question 2:* First, the eagerness with which Marion waits for June shows us that Marion is in fact less composed than her initial appearance might sug-gest. More important, June provides something of a contrast to Marion. She is not hard-hearted, but her businesslike manner helps to make us value Marion. If this assessment is right, viewers are distressed by Arthur's assaults on Marion—though probably most viewers come to understand (and forgive?) these assaults.

Question 6: Should Marion have told Jimmy why Collin left her? Answers doubtless will vary, but probably most readers will agree that the way Marion frames the explanation is grossly wrong. Collin didn't leave her in order to "go sleep with other men." "Love" might be at least part of the explanation.

A good video of the play (same title, 1988, Sandollar Productions) is available. The video is very close to the printed text, except that it begins with shots of traffic, and then of a funeral at which Arthur is in effect snubbed by the other mourners.

CHAPTER 10

Thinking Critically about Drama

WILLIAM SHAKESPEARE

The Tempest (p. 252)

In the late nineteenth century and in the first third of the twentieth, perhaps the chief readings of *The Tempest* were concerned with the degree to which the play was autobiographical. There was much discussion about whether Prospero's return from the island represented Shakespeare's return from London to Stratford, and whether *The Tempest*, as one of the "last plays," represented the work of an artist who had reached some sort of new insight, a vision "beyond tragedy."

In the second third of our century, the emphasis was on New Critical readings, but now, in the last fifteen or so years, the interest has shifted radically, from biographical and formal criticism to two other kinds of criticism, both largely political: in America, New Historicism, and in Britain, Cultural Materialism. Behind these kinds of criticism is a strong concern with British colonialism (which is to say, the exploitation of Caliban) and with contemporary racism.

This criticism has been fruitful, and it is of course inevitable that each age will see Shakespeare in new ways. But new approaches, like the old ones, have their limitations. What is distressing about some recent criticism is first, that it threatens to become a new orthodoxy—quite as narrow as the old—and, second, that it often is written in so unattractive a manner. On the first matter, see Meredith Anne Skura's useful survey of what can be called colonialist readings, in "The Case of Colonialism in *The Tempest*," *Shakespeare Quarterly* 40 (1989): 42-69. As for the second point, the matter of readability, consider as an example this passage by Francis Barker and Peter Hulme, in John Drakakis's collection *Alternative Shakespeares* (1985). (One can understand that a critic of Shakespeare may be chiefly or even entirely concerned with political rather than with aesthetic matters, but one can still hope for writing that does not reveal a tin ear.)

> The ensemble of fictional and lived practices, which for convenience we will sim-ply refer to here as "English colonialism," provides *The Tempest*'s dominant dis-cursive contexts. We have chosen here to concentrate specifically on the figure of usurpation as the nodal point of the play's imbrication into this discourse of colo-nialism." (198)

Or this, from Paul E. Brown, writing in Jonathan Dollimore's and Alan Sinfield's collection *Political Shakespeare* (1985):

> This chapter seeks to demonstrate that *The Tempest* is not simply a reflection of colonialist practices but an intervention in an ambivalent and even contradictory discourse. This intervention takes the form of a powerful and pleasurable narrative which seeks at once to harmonise disjunction, to transcend irreconcilable contra-dictions and to mystify the political conditions which demand colonialist discourse. Yet the narrative ultimately fails to deliver that containment and instead may be seen to foreground precisely those problems which it works to efface or overcome. (48)

One understands the point, but surely one can be pardoned for not wanting to read much of this, and also for feeling that in their lack of concern with aes-thetic matters, these critics neglect something essential to the play.

The view against which New Historicists and the Cultural Materialists are chiefly arguing is usually called the idealist view, which sees an ennobled Prospero as triumphing over his enemies and indeed over his own weaknesses. But of course this is not the only concern of earlier criticism. Probably the most influential work at the middle of this century was Frank Kermode's Arden edition of the play (1954), which, though it discussed the treatises con-cerning the Virginia voyages and of course discussed Caliban at considerable length, did not reduce the play to a colonial enterprise. For Kermode, *The Tempest* was deeply influenced by the ways in which the Old World saw the New World in terms of biblical and classical concepts of unspoiled nature and of providential journeys. Kermode explored the contrasts of Art and Nature, Miranda and Caliban, Ferdinand and Caliban (love versus lust), and so on. Kermode's introductory essay to his edition is some 70 pages long, and it is impossible to summarize it briefly, but the following longish quotation may give some idea of his approach.

> Learning is a major theme in the play; we learn that Miranda is capable of it and

Caliban not, and why this should be so; but we are also given a plan of the place of learning in the dispositions of providence. Prospero, like Adam, fell from his kingdom by an inordinate thirst for knowledge; but learning is a great aid to virtue, the road by which we may love and imitate God, and "repair the ruins of our first parents" [Milton, *Of Education*], and by its means he is enabled to return. The solicitude which accompanied Adam and Eve when "the world was all before them" went also with Prospero and Miranda when they set out in their "rotten carcass of a butt"... They came ashore "by Providence divine"; and Gonzalo leaves us in no doubt that Prospero's fault [*sic*, but perhaps Kermode intended to write *fall*], like Adam's, was a happy one....

He had achieved the great object of Learning, and regained a richer heritage. But he is not learned in only this rather abstract sense; he is the learned prince. Like Boethius, he had been a natural philosopher, and had learnt from Philosophy that "to hate the wicked were against reason." He early shared the view that "no wise man had rather live in banishment, poverty, and ignominy, than prosper in his own country...."

There is nothing remarkable about Prospero's ambition to regain his own kingdom and strengthen his house by a royal marriage. To be studious and contemplative, but also to be able to translate knowledge into power in the active life, was the object of his discipline.... (l-li)

A good deal of recent criticism is Kermode turned inside out, that is, it is an examination of the destructive aspects of "art" (i.e. civilization seen as a bourgeois construction), and a celebration of "nature" (i.e. Caliban). Barker and Hulme, for instance, see in Kermode's discussion—we must quote their very words—"the occulsion of [Caliban's] political claims," and they object that Kermode treats the "nature/art confrontation... totally without the historical contextualization that would locate it among the early universalizing forms of incipient bourgeois hegemony" (195).

A bibliographic note: It would not be difficult to come up with a list of a hundred titles of considerable interest—but such a list would not be useful to a busy instructor. We have therefore decided to offer a much briefer bibliography, though perhaps it is still too long. An instructor who has only an evening or two to devote to reading about the play may want to begin with Kermode's edition, or with Stephen Orgel's more recent edition (1987) in The Oxford Shakespeare.

As for "colonial" criticism, we have already mentioned Barker and Hulme in Drakakis's *Alternative Shakespeare*, and Brown in Dollimore and Sinfield's *Political Shakespeare*. This criticism usually centers on Caliban, who is the subject of a collection of essays, *Caliban*, ed. Harold Bloom (1992), and also the subject of an extremely interesting historical study, Alden T. Vaughan and Virginia Mason Vaughan, *Shakespeare's Caliban: A Cultural History* (1991). For a survey of colonial criticism, see Skura's essay in *Shakespeare Quarterly* 48 (1989), reprinted in Bloom's *Caliban*.

Other recommended reading includes: David L. Hirst, *"The Tempest": Text and Performance* (1984); Richard Levin, *New Readings vs. Old Plays*

(1979); David Young, *The Heart's Forest: A Study of Shakespeare's Pastoral Plays* (1972); Lorie Jerrell Leininger, "The Miranda Trap: Sexism and Racism in Shakespeare's *The Tempest*," in *The Women's Part: Feminist Criticism of Shakespeare*, ed. Carolyn R. S. Lenz et al. (1980), reprinted in the Signet Classic revised edition of *The Tempest* (1987).

What follows is a brief scene-by-scene commentary on the play. No originality is claimed for any of these comments; they are the product of a fair amount of reading and of many hours of discussions with students.

1.1 Shakespeare regularly brings his characters to a strange place (e.g. the wood outside of Athens in *A Midsummer Night's Dream*, the Forest of Arden in *As You Like It*), where they lose their bearings and then come to their senses, or are shaken into sense. What is unusual in *The Tempest* is that the play begins in this disorienting world. This new world, of course, is *not* the New World; it is in the Mediterranean, somewhere between Tunis and Naples—but in writing *The Tempest* Shakespeare drew on materials concerning the expedition to Virginia, and Caliban's name almost surely is derived from *Carib*.

The opening stage direction is authentic, i.e. it is not an addition by a modern editor. The tempestuous noise and the lightning are attempts at realism—the ship is being wrecked—but at the same time they are (we later learn) the product of magic. Further, we may later (if we are so inclined) see symbolism in this realism: the disorder in nature is a sign of the moral disorder in the (ig)noble passengers.

Should Prospero (or perhaps Ariel), presiding over the storm, be visible to an audience? We don't think so; we think the revelation should come later, i.e., at this point the audience should know no more than the characters on the ship—though of course we are at a play, so we know (as the characters on the ship do not know) that there will be some point to all of this bustle. It's our hunch that if Shakespeare had written this play a decade earlier he would indeed have begun with Prospero, but now he is in the period of the Romances, a group of plays (*Cymbeline, The Winter's Tale, The Tempest*) where there is a considerable emphasis on mystery and surprise.

The mariners, trying to do their best, form a contrast to the nobles, who do nothing but offer needless advice (Alonso's first line is "Good boatswain, have care. Where's the master? Play the men"). The boatswain aptly says, "You mar our labor." He is also apt when he says, "What cares these roarers for the name of king?," although in fact the roarers are under the royal control of Prospero, who has raised the storm for a purpose concerned with royalty. In any case, we think the chief point to make in discussing this scene is to call attention to the contrast between the competent and rather witty boatswain and the churlish Sebastian and Antonio. Notice, for instance, Sebastian's "A pox o' your throat, you bawling, blasphemous, incharitable dog!" To which the boatswain replies, "Work you, then." Gonzalo of course is something of an exception among the court party; his last line in the scene ("The will above be done, but I would fain die a dry death") is wryly amusing, and he has our sympathy. Notice, too, that Alonso is far less offensive than Sebastian and Antonio (preparation for what we see later, of course), and Ferdinand—who says nothing—is inoffensive (again, in keeping with his later role). You may want to ask students to characterize the figures on the basis only of what they say in this scene. What do readers *think* Antonio will be like later? Gonzalo? (Antonio and Sebastian are ugly in this scene, as later; Gonzalo's good nature, evident in later scenes, is not very clearly revealed here.)

1.2 The noisiness of the preceding scene ends, and we get this surprise: A young girl is addressing her father, who is wearing a "magic garment" (25) which he speaks of as his "art" (26), i.e. something that empowers him or that is a sign of his power. Miranda (whose name means *to be wondered at*, in effect *admirable*) is full of sympathy for the storm-tossed figures (and so she gains the audience's sympathy): "O, I have suffered / With those that I saw suffer."

With confident words Prospero reassures this emotional, innocent young woman: "Be collected. /... There's no harm done.... / No harm." Notice his incantatory repetitions: "no harm done... No harm... I have done nothing... art ignorant of what thou art." Shakespeare then gives us an almost impossibly long piece of exposition, which some performers seek to make acceptable by hamming it up, for instance by having Miranda fiddle with her garments, or roll her eyes heavenward in mock anguish. It *is* long, and one perhaps can sympathize with Miranda, who falls asleep, but it *can* be successfully performed straight, since in fact as Prospero tells his story he displays a variety of emotions (tenderness, irritability, anger). Further, the lines are so wonderful—so evocative, so (can one put it any other way?) beautiful—that if the speeches are adequately delivered the scene is enthralling. You can't go wrong by reading (or asking two students to read) lines 36-63, which include such wonders as "the dark backward and abysm of time" and

> What foul play had we that we came from thence?
> Or blessèd was't we did?
> *Prospero.*   Both, both my girl!
> By foul play, as thou say'st, were we heaved thence,
> But blessedly holp hither.

(We often tell specific students that they will be asked at the next class meeting to read certain passages, so they can briefly rehearse if they wish.)

But if Prospero in these lines is the loving teacher, a moment later he is the impatient nagging father ("Dost thou attend me?")—the man schooled both by books and by hard knocks (he has experienced even the treachery of a brother), Prospero can scarcely communicate with his utterly innocent daughter, so great is the gap between them.

Prospero tells us a good deal about himself. Among the things you may want to emphasize in class is his confession that he was remiss ("I thus neglecting world ends... "), where he admits that his bookishness and his trust in his brother helped to corrupt his brother ("he needs will be / Absolute Milan," i.e., the brother decided to become Duke of Milan in fact). On the other hand, Prospero's bookishness and his delegation of authority to Antonio are scarcely criminal acts.

We can't resist asking two students to read the passage concerning Prospero and Miranda in the "rotten carcass of a butt" (146), with winds that did them "but loving wrong" (139) to the end of the scene. The emphasis on "providence divine" (159), immediately followed by such words as "food," "fresh water," and "charity" brings us into a world utterly different from the treacherous world that he has been describing.

In 171, "Now I arise" may be literal; perhaps Prospero was seated while he told of his fall, but now he stands, since he is in the ascendant. And having told Miranda all that an innocent can bear to hear, he causes her to fall asleep.

In the course of this long exposition Prospero tells us why he is where he is, but he does not tell us exactly what he plans to do with the visitors. That is, the audience is told a great deal, but a great deal is also withheld, and so suspense is maintained.

Prospero addresses the air—doubtless to our surprise, and Ariel appears. Ariel's entrance (perhaps to the sound of music, and of wind) and his description of how he "flamed amazement" (doubtless accompanied by acrobatic actions miming his narration) give us a moment's relief from what might be called the moral dimension of the play, but only a moment's. He tells us that he has left the king's son "cooling of the air with sighs," i.e., enduring mental pain, and indeed much of the play shows us characters going through various sorts of pain, for instance, Miranda's mental pain for those she thinks are suffering on the ship, and Caliban's physical pain.

Ariel too has experienced pain, and is now threatened with more pain. Truth to tell, Prospero is often not very nice, though perhaps here we can partly excuse him on the ground that his scheme, now at a critical point, demands all of his attention, and he can't tolerate the thought that Ariel's thoughts are elsewhere. Notice, too, that we now learn about Caliban's origin. He is the son of "this damned witch Sycorax" who "for mischiefs manifold, and sorceries terrible" had been banished from Argier (Algiers) and had imprisoned Ariel "into a cloven pine." Prospero now speaks of Sycorax's son, whom we will soon meet. Who is the father? In 1.2.319 Prospero says that Caliban was "got by the devil himself." If this is to be taken literally, Caliban is the son of a witch and an incubus.

Caliban (presumably an anagram of *cannibal*, from *Caniba* and *Carib*, words used of indigenous people of the Western Hemisphere) is described in the *dramatis personae* as "a savage and deformed slave," where "savage" presumably means something like "subhuman." In 4.1 Prospero will say that on Caliban's "nature / Nurture can never stick," i.e. Caliban is (according to Prospero) ineducable. But are we to take this as true, or simply as Prospero's excuse for enslaving Caliban? Even if Caliban is indeed ineducable, was Prospero justified in enslaving him? W. H. Auden suggests, in *The Dyer's Hand*, that when Prospero's educational experiment failed he ought at least to have returned Caliban to the forest. Doubtless this suggestion would have struck Prospero as odd and indeed impossible, since we learn that Caliban is eager "to violate / The honor of" Miranda. A good deal of Prospero's eruptions of anger can probably be attributed to the strain of living with Caliban—a point often made by those who see in Prospero an emblem of the colonizing England, i.e., an emblem of the destruction that colonization does to the colonizer as well as to the colonized.

But to return to Caliban's entrance: his first words are a curse (not surprising) and are in verse (perhaps surprising, and perhaps explicable on the grounds that he is semi-divine, i.e., he is a sort of deity, though a malevolent one).

Caliban's assertion, "This island's mine by Sycorax my mother," has been much quoted, but, as we said at the start of this discussion, Prospero tells us that Sycorax was a witch who was dumped on the island and who imprisoned a resident, Ariel. If this is so, and no one in the play denies it, Caliban's claim to the island is fatally diminished. (Actually, Prospero and Sycorax resemble each other in several ways: both were exiled, and both enslaved Ariel. Further, both are associated with the supernatural, and both are associated with anger [Prospero speaks of Sycorax's rage in 1.22.276]. They even, in a way, share Caliban, since Prospero says, "This thing of darkness I / acknowledge mine [5.1.275-76]. But of course there are also great differences. Prospero renounces vengeance, and he renounces his magic.)

Further, Prospero did not seek out the island in a colonial endeavor; he was forced out of Milan and set adrift. On the other hand, Caliban's speech (telling how Prospero treated him affectionately and in exchange Caliban taught Prospero "all the qualities o' th' isle") undeniably impresses and moves us, as does his report of Prospero's recent treatment of him ("here you sty me / In this hard rock"). Prospero's near-hysterical reply (that Caliban can be moved only by whippings, not by kindness) is understandable, given that Caliban sought to violate Miranda—but Caliban's attempt to violate Miranda is also understandable, and will perhaps seem unexceptional to persons who believe that all men are potential rapists.

Caliban exits (at Prospero's command), bringing the exposition to an end, and Ariel (an obvious foil to the earthy Caliban) enters, charming Ferdinand (also an obvious foil to Caliban) with a song. Notice that the stage direction says Ariel is "invisible." Perhaps he wore some sort of garment that indicated, by convention, that the wearer was invisible. In Shakespeare, music (like everything else, one is tempted to say) is symbolic. Here, though Ferdinand is grieving deeply, its harmonies break through his grief and seize his attention. If we lean heavily on the words "suffer a sea change / Into something rich and strange," we can say that suffering—which of course can be destructive—can also be purifying or redemptive. The play tells us that Prospero has been enriched by his suffering, and it also implies that suffering may benefit other characters. Most obviously, Alonso suffers a sea change during the play.

There is some gentle comedy when Miranda—whose only experience of males is her crabby father and the savage Caliban—at first takes the handsome Ferdinand to be "a spirit," and then, instructed that Ferdinand is a mortal, falls in love with him. This of course is all according to Prospero's plan; one might ask students their opinion of another part of Prospero's plan: "This swift business / I must uneasy make, lest too light winning / Make the prize light."

2.1 The scene begins with the good-natured Gonzalo trying to cheer up Alonso by making the best of a bad situation, while Sebastian and Antonio scoff. Sebastian, in fact, rubs salt into Alonso's wound: "Sir, you may thank yourself for this great loss," and when Alonso pleads "Prithee, peace," Sebastian spitefully renews his attack: "You were kneeled to and importuned otherwise / ... / The fault's your own," to which Alonso can only reply, "So is the dearest o' th' loss." The good Gonzalo quite rightly rebukes Sebastian:

> "The truth you speak doth lack some gentleness,
> And time to speak it in. You rub the sore
> When you should bring the plaster.

Gonzalo, presumably in an effort to divert Alonso's thought from his missing son, goes on to imagine the island as a utopian commonwealth, seeing it as place where, because there is no hierarchy, the potentialities of all individuals can be fulfilled. All of this of course evokes scornful remarks from Sebastian and Antonio.

A question: As we read or witness this scene, do we sometimes find ourselves, almost against our wills, amused by Sebastian and Antonio, and bored by Gonzalo?

Ariel enters, and "all sleep except Alonso, Sebastian, and Antonio," that is, all sleep except those who, because of their corruption, are unable to respond to the harmony of Ariel's "solemn music." Sebastian and Antonio wonder why the others fall asleep, but the very fact that Antonio can say "my spirits are nimble" is (in this context of music) a sign of his discordant or inharmonious state, and indeed in this very speech he goes on to suggest that Sebastian kill his brother in order to gain the crown. In Shakespeare, sleep is frequently a prelude to healing (c.f. Lear's sleep, after his madness.) Students who know *Macbeth* may recall Macbeth's "Methought I heard a voice cry 'Sleep no more! / Macbeth doth murder sleep'" (2.2.35). (By the way, Antonio's suggestion that Sebastian kill the sleeping Alonso may remind us that Macbeth kills the sleeping Duncan.) Antonio's baseness is evident in many speeches, but perhaps is nowhere so evident as in his response to Sebastian's reference to Antonio's conscience: "Ay, sir, where lies that?" (and so on, for some 15 lines).

Ariel, following Prospero's command, wakens Gonzalo, whose first words (so different from the mockery of Sebastian and Antonio) are, "Now good angels / Preserve the King!"

2.2 Caliban's curses while laboring will make a contrast with Ferdinand's willing acceptance (stated in the beginning of the next scene, 3.1) of the chores Prospero assigns to him. With the entry of Stephano and Trinculo we see a comic version of human baseness, and in Stephano's plans for Caliban we hear the voice of the exploiter: "If I can recover him, and keep him tame and get to Naples with him, he's a present for any emperor that ever trod on neat's leather."

The foolish Caliban takes this base creature to be "a brave [i.e. fine] god," and kneels to him. Presumably we are to see that Caliban gives himself into a slavery far more base than his slavery to Prospero. Whereas Prospero—at least at the start—sought to educate Caliban and thus (in a sense) to liberate him, Caliban's new master presumably will use him only for selfish gain. Caliban, having learned nothing, now is eager to show his new master the riches of the isle, as he once showed them to Prospero: "I'll show thee the best springs," etc., whereupon Trinculo aptly comments, "A most ridiculous monster, to make a wonder of a poor drunkard!" The scene ends with Caliban drunkenly singing (c.f. "Ban, 'Ban, Ca—Caliban") a song of liberation ("No more dams I'll make for fish") and shouting about "Freedom," not knowing that he is enslaved to a fool and to liquor. The traditional view is that we see Caliban's base *nature*, but the colonialist interpretation is that Caliban's baseness is due not to nature but to *nurture*, i.e., to the effect on him of colonialism.

3.1 Ferdinand enters, welcoming his task, in contrast to Caliban, who was seen a moment ago exulting in what he thinks is freedom. Ferdinand speaks of loving service:

> The very instant that I saw you, did
> My heart fly to your service; there resides,
> To make me slave to it; and for your sake
> Am I this patient log-man.

Some twenty lines later Miranda, too, offers loving service:

> To be your fellow
> You may deny me; but I'll be your servant,
> Whether you will or no.

3.2 Caliban's degradation is emphasized as we see him offering his services to his new master, Stephano: "How does thy honor? Let me lick thy shoe." Now under the control of Stephano, Caliban's animality becomes particularly vicious as he urges his new master to kill Prospero: "knock a nail into his head," "Batter his skull, or paunch him with a stake, / Or cut his wezand with thy knife." There is also a nice, nasty touch in Caliban's vision of Miranda's future with Stephano: "She will become thy bed, I warrant, / And bring thee forth brave brood." But if here, and in other speeches, he is loathsome, a moment later, in his description of the island, his speech engages us and he gains our sympathy:

> Be not afeard; the isle is full of noises,
> Sounds and sweet airs, that give delight and hurt not.
> Sometimes a thousand twangling instruments
> Will hum about mine ears; and sometimes voices
> That, if I then had waked after long sleep,
> Will make me sleep again; and then, in dreaming,
> The clouds methought would open and show riches
> Ready to drop upon me, that, when I waked,
> I cried to dream again.

Caliban's sensitivity to music does not indicate that he is a noble soul—in 4.1 Ariel reports that wild colts were charmed by his music, and in other plays Shakespeare talks of how Orpheus's music charmed the savage beasts—but the speech surely evokes our sympathy.

3.3 Gonzalo begins the scene with words about a "maze" of "forthrights and meanders." As Northrop Frye points out in his introduction to the Pelican edition of the play, the court party goes on a quest (the pursuit of Ferdinand), undergoes an ordeal (the laborious journey), has a symbolic vision (the illusory banquet), and after confinement and madness (which bring the conviction of sin) achieves self-knowledge and repentance (at least in some cases). In the second speech of this scene Alonso says he will now "put off my hope, and keep it / No longer for my flatterer," i.e. he puts off the deceptions associated with the court party, and thus he unknowingly is preparing himself for regeneration. Notice that a moment later, when the illusory banquet is brought in, Alonso's thoughts immediately turn to guardian angels ("give us kind keepers, heavens!"), whereas Sebastian sees in the illusion only an entertainment ("a living drollery"). Also characteristic is Gonzalo's utopian assumption (25-33) that these strange forms, though of "monstrous shape," are "more gentle, kind, / than of / Our human generation you shall find / Many." And no less characteristic is Sebastian's belly-oriented comment after the forms vanish: "They have left their viands behind... /Will't please you taste of what is here?"

Ariel's appearance in the form of a harpy (52) is an image of the filthiness and the voraciousness of the court party, and the disappearance of the banquet is an image of the deceits of the corrupt courtiers. It is worth reading the whole of Ariel's speech aloud (53-82), calling attention to how the sea—to which Prospero and Miranda were abandoned—has now captured the criminals and brought them to judgment. Ariel's comment in 58 ("I have made you mad") alludes to the loss of mental balance that Shakespeare's characters often undergo before they are regenerated, but we might also say that these corrupt characters were "mad"—i.e. inhumanly cruel, deceitful—even from the start.

Also worth reading entire, and discussing, is Alonso's confession of guilt and his accompanying despair (95-102). Notice the musical imagery: "The winds did *sing* it to me; and the thunder, / That deep and dreadful *organ pipe*, pronounced / The name of Prosper; it did *bass* by trespass...." Alonso's language is now richly metaphoric, and he perceives nature as harmonious (musical) and moral. In short, although in the first scene nature (the storm) seemed to be chaotic and destructive, Alonso has (to quote from Ariel's song in 1.2) "suffered a sea change"; he is now remorseful (he has experienced the "heart's sorrow that Ariel speaks of in line 81) and he sees that there is a moral order in nature. On the other hand, Sebastian and Antonio, unrepentant, madly flail about ("But one fiend at a time, / I'll fight their legions o'er.") Gonzalo rightly perceives that all three are moved by guilt, but he does not see that Alonso's guilt has led him to repentance and regeneration, whereas Sebastian and Antonio's has led them only to madness.

4.1 In line 29 when Ferdinand assures Prospero that his "honor" will never change into "lust," we are reminded yet again of the contrast between Ferdinand and Caliban.

In Prospero's mask-like entertainment—a dramatized Utopia that connects with Gonzalo's vision—we see nature improved by nurture, i.e. not the mere fertility of the island (which Caliban tells us about) but agriculture (harvesting)—nature improved by the working of mankind, nature civilized, one might say. If students read aloud the song in 106-17 they will easily see the emphasis upon and fertility—indeed, upon a golden age without any winter: "Spring come to you at the farthest / In the very end of harvest," though in a moment, when the stupid lustful Caliban and his wicked confederates come into Prospero's mind, this winterless world (the ideal world that Prospero can imagine, as he suggests in line 122) disappears. That is, the mask is an embodiment of Prospero's wishes for an ordered, fertile life for Miranda and Ferdinand, but it is only a vision, not a reality. Prospero can do much, notably he can create the circumstances under which a guilty Alonso will repent, but he cannot compel virtue or wisdom, for instance in Sebastian, Antonio, and Caliban.

The memory of evil, which dispels the imagined harmonious world of the mask, causes Prospero to become so possessed by "anger" (145) that Ferdinand and Miranda are distressed. Prospero sees their discomposure and seeks to cover his own, by suggesting that they are disturbed by the disappearance of the mask, rather than by Prospero's own agitation. The great speech "Our revels now are ended" (which is often taken as an allusion to Shakespeare's retirement) in some modern productions has been transferred to the end of the play, so that the speech is a comment not on the mask but on the play (and Shakespeare's career) as a whole, and, for that matter, on life: The real actors who perform Shakespeare's play will disappear, just as the characters in the mask within the play disappear, and so will the theater (in the reference to "the great globe itself" there is surely a pun on the Globe Theater), and so it is implied, will all of us, and all the order we have tried to establish. This vision, though stated in terms that are meant to reassure Ferdinand and Miranda ("our little life / Is rounded with a sleep"), deeply distresses Prospero, who confesses his agitation in the last six lines: "My old brain is troubled. / ... / A turn or two I'll walk / To still my beating mind."

And why shouldn't he be agitated? As he says a few lines later, "We must prepare to meet with Caliban." The serious enemy is *not* folly (Stephano and Trinculo) but savagery, ineducable animal nature. In a moment Prospero will say that Caliban is "A devil, a born devil, on whose nature / Nurture can never stick" (188-89).

Ariel reports that Caliban and his new friends are in a "filthy pool," up to their necks in mud, presumably an emblem of their filthiness. In a moment they enter, beguiled by the "trumpery" Prospero provides, and it is interesting to notice that Caliban, the primitive, is wiser than Stephano and Trinculo, foolish human beings who are attracted to trivia: "Leave it alone, thou fool! It is but trash." With the "noise of hunters" and the entrance of spirits in the form of dogs, we get a sort of antimask; it is probably not going too far to say that the noise and the dogs are images of the internal chaos in Caliban, Stephano, and Trinculo; that is, their attackers are their own natures. They exit, physically afflicted, a sort of low version of the mental affliction that the more elevated Alonso has undergone.

5.1 You may want to ask two students to read the first lines of this scene (as well as many other passages in this final act). The scene begins with a confident Prospero, in full control, and then moves to Ariel's description of the "distracted" (maddened) Alonso, Antonio, and Sebastian, and the grieving Gonzalo. Ariel says that the sight of them would surely cause Prospero's affections to "become tender" (19)—though in his next speech he makes the point that he himself can feel no pity because he is not human. Prospero (20-32) assures Ariel that, as a human being ("one of their kind") he is indeed "kindlier" moved than Ariel (with a pun on *kind*: 1) more sympathetically; 2) of the same kind, i.e. the same nature). Indeed, he is at some pains to make the point that although he is "struck to th' quick," his "nobler reason" defeats his "fury," since his enemies are "penitent," yet in a moment we will see that his struggle to forgive is not easy. Still, the idea seems to be that Prospero has won a victory not only over his evil foes but also over himself: "The rarer action is / In virtue than in vengeance." It is perhaps appropriate at this point to recall earlier instances of pity or at least of fellow-feeling: (1) Gonzalo pitied Prospero and Miranda when they were set adrift; (2) Prospero pitied Caliban and tried to educate him; (3) Miranda pities those on the storm-tossed ship, and later pities Ferdinand when he is laboring for Prospero; (4) Gonzalo pities the grieving Alonso; (5) Ariel says he would pity the lords if he were human; and now, finally, (6) Prospero is "kindlier" moved.

In Prospero's next speech (32-57), derived from a speech by Medea in Ovid's *Metamorphoses*, Prospero talks about his control over nature. It is customary to say that Prospero is a "white magician," i.e. a practitioner of arts acceptable to God, whereas, for instance, Sycorax—being a witch—was a black magician, a practitioner of forbidden, devilish arts. But, truth to tell, Shakespeare here blurs the line, especially when Prospero reports that he has brought the dead out of their graves (48-49). (We never see him do this in the play—but Shakespeare did bring back from the grave such notables as Julius Caesar and various kings of England.) Of course one of the grand characteristics of Shakespeare is that he blurs the line—Caliban is a murderous brute, and yet he gains out sympathy when he recounts his early association with Prospero and when he talks of the music on the island and of his dreams (3.2); Othello is a hero and yet he is also "ignorant as dirt"; Lear brings his destruction upon himself, despite the good advice of Kent, and yet he is "a man more sinned against than sinning," and so on.

Why does Prospero give up his magic (50-57)? For at least two good reasons: he no longer needs it, now that he has his enemies under control and has brought Miranda and Ferdinand together, and, second, he wishes to rejoin humanity, to be like other human beings.

Again, if you read, or ask students to read, extensive passages, you can hardly skip over 58-87, in which Prospero describes his enemies (their brains "now useless, boiled" in their skulls), says that he weeps along with Gonzalo (6364), and in a marvelous passage compares the recovery of consciousness with the coming of morning "Melting the darkness." But especially noteworthy is the conflict still evident in Prospero, seen in words of forgiveness that are followed by words of rebuke, notably in "I do forgive thee, / Unnatural though thou art." *This* is Prospero, the human being; appropriately, with the words

> I will discase me, and myself present
> As I was sometime Milan,

he takes off the magic garment that he wears (according to the stage direction at the beginning of the scene), and now is seen in his ducal robe. Perhaps he seems *more* splendid as a man than as a magician, that is, perhaps this robe is, say, crimson, in contrast with (perhaps) a magic robe of black with a few arcane symbols in gold.

The repentant Alonso, who had assisted Antonio's overthrow of Prospero in exchange for Antonio subjugating Milan to Naples, begs Prospero's forgiveness (119), but before responding to Alonso Prospero must embrace his old loyal friend Gonzalo. And his thoughts are still on the wickedness of Sebastian and Antonio ("traitors" in 128), especially of Antonio ("whom to call brother / Would even infect my mouth," in 130-31; "wicked sir," in 128). Even here, in this happy ending, we are reminded of evil.

The lovers are discovered playing chess (an aristocratic game, often associated with lovers perhaps because the imagery of warfare was common also in love poetry), and Miranda expresses her wonder ("O brave new world) at the sight of so much of "beauteous mankind," allowing Prospero to remind us of Miranda's innocence: "'Tis new to thee." (Whether or not his line is said with great bitterness depends on one's interpretation of the play.) Gonzalo, seeing the working of divine providence (201-04), sums up (205-13) the gains of the painful experiences (the Duke of Milan was thrust from Milan so that "his issue / Should become kings of Naples"; Claribel found a husband, Ferdinand found a wife, Prospero found a dukedom on an island, "and all of us ourselves / When no man was his own.")

The comic low characters enter—everyone has to be brought together for the grand ending—and, in yet another touch that complicates our view of Prospero, Prospero says of Caliban, "this thing of darkness I / Acknowledge mine" (275-76), suggesting some sort of responsibility for Caliban, and perhaps even suggesting that Caliban—let's say "animal nature"—is a part of Prospero.

An additional touch of darkness here at the end is, again, evident in Sebastian's and Antonio's refusal to confess and repent. Apparently Prospero's magic can go only so far; it can work on Alonso—and it can even cause the bestial Caliban to "seek for grace" (296), but it cannot work on so corrupt a nature as is possessed by Sebastian and Antonio.

The play ends happily—Ariel is freed, and Prospero may even be reconciled with all of the others, if we can take seriously his last words before the epilogue ("Pray you, draw near"), but there are tragic or at least melancholy notes too, especially in "Every third thought shall be my grave" (112). The play of course is a comedy in the sense of a play with a happy ending, but throughout it has been concerned also with tragic themes: treachery, repentance, justice, reconciliation (sometimes suffused with bitterness).

The epilogue is marvelous, and should be read in its entirety. The magic is gone; the speaker is not a magician but is merely the Prospero who has given up magic, and, as the epilogue progresses, this ordinary Prospero turns into a mere actor who, having acted generously toward his enemies, now asks his audience to act generously toward him, i.e. to applaud and to speak well of the play:

> But release me from my bands
> With the help of your good hands.
> Gentle breath of yours my sails
> Must fill, or else my project fails....

When the play ends with Prospero asking to be set "free," perhaps we remember that he freed Ariel, and that, in a way, he freed Alonso from villainy. Most important, however, Prospero suggests in his final two lines that our generosity toward him is, in a sense, a sign of our awareness that we too—no less than the actors—hope for forgiveness.

MICHEL EYQUEM DE MONTAIGNE

Of the Cannibals (p. 316)

Students who wish to pursue the ideas of *nature* versus *nurture* and of European attitudes toward the inhabitants of the New World—perhaps for a research paper—will find much valuable information in Hugh Honour, *The New Golden Land*. Also useful is the handsome, massive catalog of an exhibition at the National Gallery, Washington, *Circa 1492: Art in the Age of Exploration*.

JANE LEE

The Tempest *in Its Age and in Our Time* (p. 317)

This essay is rather old fashioned in its approach, that is, in its assumption that the play has an enduring—can we say "universal"?—meaning, but we think it is perceptive. Some students of criticism would say that it belongs to the "idealist" school, with its assumptions that (1) the meaning is contained within the play itself; (2) this meaning is evident if we read closely, and (3) the play has a moral effect ("Like all other great drama, it gives us a memorable image of life *to live up to*"). All three of these points can be discussed in the classroom.

STEPHEN GREENBLATT

The Best Way To Kill Our Literary Inheritance (p. 320)

This short essay can be effectively juxtaposed with the preceding essay, since both touch on early colonialism. Although Greenblatt grants that the play "is, of course, about many other things as well..." he puts the emphasis on colonialism. It's our guess that Lee would agree with much of what Greenblatt says—she seems open minded—but that Greenblatt would find Lee's essay too inclined to overlook what he takes to be the darker aspects of the play.

RALPH BERRY AND JONATHAN MILLER

A Production of The Tempest *(p. 322)*

In his production, Miller (as the interview indicates) cast both Caliban and Ariel as blacks. He did this, he explains, in order to force the audience to think about the effects of colonialism. You may want to invite students offer opinions about whether early plays should be produced in ways that force the audiences to see them in the light of contemporary society. (The next essay in the text, by Errol G. Hill, also talks about casting Caliban and Ariel.)

ERROL G. HILL

Caliban and Ariel (p. 325)

Hill's idea that, if one wants to introduce matters of race, Ariel should be played by a black actor and Caliban by a white, is engaging and is worth discussing in class, especially in connection with the preceding piece by Ralph Berry and Jonathan Miller.

LINDA BAMBER

The Tempest *and the Traffic in Women (p. 326)*

This is the only essay in the casebook that may cause the average student a little difficulty, but if your students are fairly strong you will probably find that it is the essay that interests them the most.

CHAPTER 11

*Reading
(and Writing
about)
Poetry*

EMILY DICKINSON

Wild Nights—Wild Nights! (p. 333)

A reader tends to think of Emily Dickinson as the speaker of "Wild Nights" and therefore is perhaps shocked by the last stanza, in which a woman apparently takes on the phallic role of a ship mooring in a harbor. But perhaps the poem is spoken by a man. (In one of her poems the speaker says, "I am a rural man," in another the speaker refers to "my brown cigar," and in "A narrow fellow in the Grass"—included in our text—the speaker identifies himself as male in lines 11-12.)

Possibly we are superficial readers, but we don't attach to "Might I but moor—Tonight—/ In Thee!" the strong sexual associations that several critics have commented on. Some but not all assume that the image suggests male penetration. Albert Gelpi, in *The Tenth Muse* (1975), 242-43 says that "the sexual roles are blurred." He adds, "Something more subtle than an inversion of sexual roles is at work here, and the point is not that Emily Dickinson was homosexual, as Rebecca Patterson and John Cody have argued," but he doesn't clarify the point. (Patterson's discussion is in *The Riddle of Emily Dickinson* [1951]; Cody's is in *After Great Pain* [1971].) Paula Bennett, in *My Life a Loaded Gun* (1986), drawing on a discussion by L. Faderman, seems to reject the idea of a male speaker. She says that "the imagery of the poem, with its emphasis on entering rather than being entered, is… far more appropriate for one woman's experience of another than for a woman's experience with a man" (61). Christine Miller too insists that the speaker is a woman. In *Feminist Critics Read Emily Dickinson,* ed. Suzanne Juhasz (1983), Miller says that the speaker is a woman but she adds that "The woman is the ship that seeks to 'moor—Tonight—/ In Thee!'—an activity more representative of male than of female social behavior" (137). Our own simple view: a reader need not find an image of penetration in "moor;" rather, we think that in this poem the word suggests a longed-for security.

Is the poem sentimental? We don't think so, chiefly because it is brief, controlled, and (in "Tonight") it does not claim too much.

In *Explicator* 25 (January 1967), Item 44, James T. Connelly pointed out that in letter No. 332 (T.H. Johnson's edition, *Letters,* II, 463), Dickinson writes, "Dying is a wild Night and a new road." Looking at the poem in the light of this letter, Connelly concludes that "to die is to experience a wild night on a turbulent, surging sea. Only by plunging into this uncharted sea of Death can one at last reach the port of rest and calm. The poem, thus considered, is an apparent death wish: a personification and apostrophe to Death whose presence and company are paradoxically exhilarating luxury." We are unconvinced, partly because the poem speaks not of "a wild night" but of "Wild Nights," and we cannot see how the plural form lends itself to this reading.

ROBERT FROST

The Telephone (p. 335)

A student of ours, Jane Takayanagi, wrote an entry in a journal that we think is worth reprinting. In our opinion she is right in seeing that a quarrel has precipitated the speaker's walk ("When I was just as far as I could walk / From here today"), but it is hard to convince someone who doesn't sense it. In any case, here is the entry from her journal:

> As the poem goes on, we learn that the man wants to be with the woman, but it starts by telling us that he walked as far away from her as he could. He doesn't say why, but I think from the way the woman speaks later in the poem, they had a fight and he walked out. Then, when he stopped to rest, he thought he heard her voice. He really means that he was thinking of her and he was hoping she was thinking of him. So he returns, and he tells her he heard her calling him, but he pretends he heard her call him through a flower on their window sill. He can't admit that *he* was thinking about her.
>
> This seems very realistic to me; when someone feels a bit ashamed, it's sometimes hard to admit that you were wrong, and you want the other person to tell you that things are OK anyhow. And judging from line 7, when he says "Don't

say I didn't," it seems that she is going to interrupt him by denying it. She is still angry, or maybe she doesn't want to make up too quickly. But he wants to pretend that *she* called him back. So when he says, "Do you remember what it was you said?" she won't admit that she *was* thinking of him, and she says, "First tell me what it was you thought you heard." She's testing him a little. So he goes on, with the business about flowers as telephones, and he says "someone" called him. He understands that she doesn't want to be pushed into forgiving him, so he backs off. Then she is willing to admit that she did think about him, but still she doesn't quite admit it. She is too proud to say openly that she wants him back but does say, "I *may* have thought as much." And then, since they both have preserved their dignity and also have admitted that they care about the other, he can say, "Well, so I came."

Two other (small) points: (1) Why in line 11 does Frost speak of having "driven a bee away"? We think that maybe in a tiny way it shows the speaker's willingness to exert himself and to face danger. It's a miniature ordeal, a test of his mettle. (2) In line 17 the speaker says, "I heard it as I bowed." Of course "bowed" rhymes with "aloud," but putting aside the need for a rhyme, surely the phrase is better than, say, "I heard it as I stood," since it conveys a gesture of humility.

WILLIAM BLAKE

The Sick Rose (p. 340)

"The Sick Rose" has been much interpreted, usually along the lines given in the text. (See Reuben Brower, *The Fields of Light,* and Rosenthal and Smith, *Exploring Poetry.*) But E. D. Hirsch, Jr., in *Innocence and Experience*, argues that "The rose is being satirized by Blake as well as being infected by the worm. Part of the rose's sickness is her ignorance of her disease. Her ignorance is her spiritual disease because in accepting 'dark secret love' she has unknowingly repressed and perverted her instinctive life, her 'bed of crimson joy. '" Hirsch argues his point for a couple of pages.

We especially like Helen Vendler's comment on this poem in her introduction to *The Harvard Book of Contemporary American Poetry:*

> The world of the poem is analogous to the existential world, but not identical with it. In a famous created world of Blake's, for instance, there is a rose doomed to mortal illness by the love of a flying worm who is invisible. We do not experience such a poem by moving it piecemeal into our world, deciding what the rose "symbolizes" and what the worm "stands for." On the contrary, we must move ourselves in to its ambience, into a world in which a dismayed man can converse with his beloved rose and thrust upon her, in his anguished jealousy, diagnosis and

fatal prognosis in one sentence.... After living in Blake's world for the space of eight lines, we return to our own world, haunted and accused.

Allen Ginsberg has "tuned" the poem (MGM Records FTS-3083).

ROBERT HERRICK

Upon Julia's Clothes (p. 342)

A good deal has been published on this tiny poem. Much of what has been published seems odd to us, for instance, an argument that in the first stanza Julia is clothed but in the second is imagined as nude ("free" is alleged to describe her body, not her clothes), or that the first stanza describes her from the front, the second from the rear.

One of our students Stan Wylie, seems to us to have written a far better discussion of the poem. We print it in the book.

Other things, of course, might be said about this poem. For instance, Wylie says nothing about the changes in the meter and their contributions to the poem. Nor does he say anything about the sounds of any of the words (he might have commented on the long vowels in "sweetly flows" and shown how the effect would have been different if instead of "sweetly flows" Herrick had written "sweetly flits," and he might have commented on the spondees in "Then, then" and "O, how" and the almost-spondees in "Next, when," "each way free," and "that glittering"), but such topics might be material for another essay.

CHRISTINA ROSSETTI

In an Artist's Studio (p. 346)

The octave seems devoted to the "nameless girl," who appears again and again as "A queen" and as "A saint, an angel." Although her "loveliness" is mentioned, a reader may sense that the woman herself is stifled, for she is "hidden," seen in a "mirror," and characterized as "nameless." Furthermore, "every canvas means / The same one meaning, neither more nor less," a passage suggesting not only her limitations but also those of the painter. That is, the painter apparently keeps repeating himself, a trait that in the nineteenth century, as well as in our times, suggests some sort of dehumanization.

In the sestet further attention is paid to the artist, who (vampire-like?) "feeds upon her face." Still, the emphasis probably is on the woman, who is further dehumanized by being deprived of her own identity. Once she was "joyful" and full of "hope," but now, transformed by his imagination into works of art, she is not a creature of flesh and blood with her own identity, but is an image that "fills his dream."

Having said all this, we want to mention that we have heard students and colleagues argue a very different reading: The artist relentlessly pursues his idea, nourished by the "loveliness" and the "kind eyes" of the woman. Still, we stubbornly think that this reading overestimates the nobility of the artist, and underestimates the woman's loss of identity.

ROBERT BROWNING

My Last Duchess (p. 358)

Robert Langbaum has a good analysis of "My Last Duchess" in *The Poetry of Experience*. On this poem, see also Laurence Perrine, *PMLA* 74 (March 1959): 157-59. W.J.T. Mitchell, in "Representation," in *Critical Terms for Literary Study*, ed. Frank Lentricchia and Thomas McLaughlin, discusses the poem at some length. One of his points is: "Just as the duke seems to hypnotize the envoy, Browning seems to paralyze the reader's normal judgment by his virtuosic representation of villainy. His poem holds us in its grip, condemning in advance all our attempts to control it by interpretation...."

It may be mentioned here that although every poem has a "voice," not every poem needs to be a Browningesque dramatic monologue giving the reader a strong sense of place and audience. No one would criticize Marvell's "To His Coy Mistress" on the grounds that the "lady" addressed in line 2 gives place (in at least some degree) to a larger audience—let us say, a general audience—when we get to "But at my back I always hear / Time's winged chariot hurrying near."

EDWIN ARLINGTON ROBINSON

Richard Cory (p. 360)

The point is not that money doesn't bring happiness; even a thoroughly civilized spirit (grace, taste, courtesy) does not bring happiness. The protagonist's name is significant. "Richard" suggests "Rich," and probably his entire name faintly suggests Richard Cœur de Lion (and *cœur* = heart and core, and also suggests *cour* = court). These suggestions, along with "crown," "favored," "imperially," "arrayed," "glittered," "king," emphasize his superiority. Other words emphasize his dignity, courtesy, and humanity: "gentleman," "clean favored," "quietly," "human," "schooled," "grace." Everything combines to depict him as a man of self-sufficiency, dignity, and restraint—yet he kills himself. Still, even his final act has some dignity: it is stated briefly, and it takes place on "one calm summer night." Students might be asked if anything is lost by substituting (what might on first thought seem more appropriate) "one dark winter night." If this rewriting is not bad enough, listen to Paul Simon's version of the poem. He sings it, with Art Garfunkel, on *Sounds of Silence*, Columbia CS 9269.

E. E. CUMMINGS

anyone lived in a pretty how town (p. 361)

It can be useful to ask students to put into the usual order (so far as one can) the words of the first two stanzas, and then to ask students why cummings's version is more effective. Here are a few rough glosses: l.4: "danced his did" = lived intensely (versus the "someones" who in l.18 "did their dance," that is, unenthusiastically went through motions that might have been ecstatic); l.7: "they sowed their isn't they reaped their same" gives us the little-minded or small-minded who, unlike "anyone," are unloving and therefore receiving nothing; l.8: "sun moon stars rain" = day after day; l.10: "down they forgot as up they grew" implies a mental diminution that accompanies growing up; l.17: "someones," that is, adults, people who think they are somebody; l.25: "anyone died," that is, the child matured, stopped loving (and became dead as the other adults). The last two stanzas imply that although children grow into "Women and men" (l.33) as the seasons continue. (This reading is heavily indebted to R. C. Walsh, *Explicator* 22 no. 9 [May 1964], Item 72. For a more complicated reading, see D. L. Clark, *Lyric Resonance*, 187-94.)

An audiocassette of e. e. cummings reading is available from Harper-Collins.

LOUISE ERDRICH

Indian Boarding School: The Runaways (p. 362)

The speaker is one of the "runaways." From the title and the first two lines ("Home's the place we head for in our sleep/ Boxcars stumbling north in dreams") we know that the speaker dreams of running away from school, and probably *has* run away, more than once. Calling the railway lines "old lacerations that we love" announces at once what the rest of the poem recalls: the runaways, having been captured by the sheriff (line 12) and taken back to school, are physically punished. The image of punishment is repeated in "Riding scars" (line 7), "it hurts/ to be here" (lines 10-11), and the concluding lines of the first stanza:

> The highway doesn't rock, it only hums
> like a wing of long insults. The worn-down welts
> of ancient punishment lead back and forth.

The "ancient punishment" refers to the punishment of the runaways but it may also recall the punishment meted out by whites who laid down the railroad tracks as they gradually subdued the Native Americans. "Home" is not described in the poem, but making "Home's" the first syllable, rather than Home is," accentuates it.

TOPIC FOR WRITING

In a paragraph, describe a place you "head for in [your] sleep." Or, describe "shameful work" that you were given, which you did not deserve, or did. (If you are lucky, you can use a color as Erdrich uses green as "the color you would think shame was" in lines 17-18.)

RITA DOVE

Daystar (p. 363)

The poem comes from Dove's Pulitzer-prize book *Thomas and Beulah* (1986), which contains sequences of poems about African-Americans who migrated from the South to the North.

In thinking about a poem, one can hardly go wrong in paying attention to the title. Here, why "Daystar"? "Daystar" can refer either to a planet—especially Venus—visible in the eastern sky before sunrise, or to the sun. Both meanings are probably relevant here. The speaker's brief period of escape from (at one extreme) the children's diapers and dolls and (at the other) Thomas's sexual demands are perhaps like the brief (and marvelous) appearance of a planet at a time that one scarcely expects to see a heavenly body; and this moment of escape—a moment of wonderful independence—is perhaps also like the sun, which stands in splendid isolation, self-illuminating. Sometimes, as she sits "behind the garage," she is closely connected to the visible world around her (the cricket, the maple leaf), but sometimes, with her eyes closed, she perceives only her self. (The mention, in the last line of the poem, of "the middle of the day" perhaps indicates that the chief meaning of "daystar" here is the sun, but we see no reason to rule out the suggestion of the other meaning.)

BASHO

An Old Pond (p. 364)

Basho's poem has engendered an enormous body of commentary in Japanese, and more than enough in English. It is not unusual to find someone arguing that the "ancient pond" is the enduring spiritual world, and the frog that jumps in is the material, transient world; or the ancient pond is the body of traditional literature (today we would say the canon), and the frog is the new writer. And so on.

Here is the poem (originally published in 1686) in transliterated Japanese, with a literal English translation next to it:

Furu ike ya	old pond place
Kawazu tobikomu	frog jumps
Mizu no oto	water's sound

The *ya* in the first line, a suffix often added to a noun, is used to denote a place. Thus, the word for *fish* is *sakana*, but a fish store is *sakanaya*. In the third line, *no* is a possessive, something like our *'s*, which turns (for instance) water into *water's* (here, *the water's sound*, or *the sound of water*).

Next, six versions we have collected. One difficulty, it will immediately be recognized, is that the original has more syllables than a close translation will have. *Frog* is one syllable, but the Japanese *kawazu* is three; similarly, *jumps* is one syllable, but *tobikomu* is four. Translators have tended to pad their poems by adding an *ah* here or there.

You may want to write two or more of these on the board, and invite students to discuss the differences.

1. The old pond, ah!
    A frog jumps in:
    The water's sound.

2. There, in the old pond—
    A frog has just jumped in
    With a splash of water.

3. The ancient pond—
    A frog jumps in,
    The sound of water.

4. A frog
    Jumping into the ancient pond.
    Splash.

5. Ah, the ancient pond.
    A frog makes the plunge.
    The sound of water.

6. An old pond.
    A frog jumps in—
    Plop!

The translator of this last version justifies *plop*—which might seem too crude or whimsical—on the grounds that it is onomatopoeic, and that the Japanese *oto* (= sound) is closer to *plop* than are such words as *splash* or *sound*.

The wittiest translation that we have come across is by D. J. Enright, in *Old Men and Comets* (1994). It preserves the 5-7-5 count:

> An ancient bayou
> A batrachian flops in—
> Sound of H$_2$O.

And, for good measure, here are two responses to Basho, by the Zen priest Sengai (1750-1837):

1. An old pond;
   Basho jumps in,
   The sound of water!

2. If there were a pond around here
   I would jump in
   And let him hear the splash.

The haiku in our text, along with the editorial comment, is enough to give students an idea of the form, and to allow them to write their own haiku. We have found that most students enjoy—because they can achieve at least a decent degree of success— writing haiku.

For collections of haiku, with substantial commentaries, see Harold G. Henderson, *An Introduction to Haiku,* and Kenneth Yasuda, *The Japanese Haiku.* For a shorter but still moderately detailed history of the form, see the article on haiku in *The Kodansha Encyclopedia of Japan.* We summarize the last part of the Kodansha article, "On Writing Haiku in English." As you will see in a moment, the author takes us through several versions of a haiku. You may want to write the first version on the board, discuss it, and then move on to the second, and so on.

The author begins by saying what a haiku does: "When a haiku is successful, it endows our lives with freshness and new wonder and reveals the charm and profundity of all truly simple things." Almost any subject is possible, from the stars on a stormy night to a heron in the evening breeze. He gives as an example (in the traditional 5-7-5 syllable pattern) a roadside encounter:

> Meeting on the road,
> we chat leisurely awhile
> and go on our ways.

"The problem with this verse," he says, "is that it tells us something but evokes nothing. It is flat and one-dimensional. What is needed, among other things, is a sharper 'cutting' (usually indicated by a colon or dash) after either the first or the second line," thus:

A roadside meeting:
we chat leisurely awhile
and go on our ways.

But there still is not enough of a cutting here; there is no imaginative distance between the two elements. Another try:

A baby's crying:
we chat leisurely awhile
and go on our ways.

Here, however, the distance between the two parts is too great. One
would have to be deaf or cruel to chat while a baby cries. The two images don't
somehow connect. The next version:

A peaceful country:
we chat leisurely awhile
and go on our ways.

Not bad; the peaceful country provides a grand background for this pleasant encounter between two friendly people; or, to put it the other way around,
the encounter between the two people "crystallizes the abstract notion of a
peaceful country."

The two parts of the poem, then, must be remote to a degree and yet
must somehow connect, and each must enhance the other. Further, in the traditional Japanese haiku there must be a seasonal theme. When does a leisurely chat occur? Probably not in winter (too cold to stand chatting); nor does
spring (the author says) seem right for this sort of talk, since spring is the time
for "the fresh encounters of the young." Autumn? No, "Autumn is too suggestive of reflective maturity and eventual partings." Only summer is right:

Another hot day:
we chat leisurely awhile
and go on our ways.

But the author of the article says, the word "leisurely" is wrong here; one
wouldn't chat in a leisurely fashion on a hot day. A summer chat is characterized not by leisureliness but by "involuntary lethargy." The final version:

Another hot day:
yawning "good-bye" and "take care"
we go on our ways.

The author's final judgment of this work: "Not a haiku masterpiece, but not discreditable for a first try."

WILLIAM BLAKE

London (p. 366)

"London," from *Songs of Experience*, is a denunciation of the mind-forged manacles, that is, of manmade repressive situations, not a denunciation of cities with a glorification of rural life. The church assists in exploitation by promises of an eternal reward, the monarchy slaughters men for private gain, and marriage drives the unmarried (or the unsatisfactorily married) to harlots. "Chartered" (2), that is, not merely mapped but licensed, is perhaps almost acceptable for streets, but that the river, an image of freedom, should also be chartered is unnatural and intolerable. As the poem develops, it is evident that children are licensed (as chimney sweeps), soldiers are licensed (to kill and to be killed), and harlots are licensed (bought and sold). E. D. Hirsch, Jr., *Innocence and Experience,* suggests that there is a further meaning: The English were proud of their "chartered liberties," rights guaranteed by Magna Carta, but "these chartered liberties are chartered slaveries." For "ban" in line 7 Hirsch offers four references: a summons to arms (king), a formal denunciation or curse (church), a proclamation of marriage, and a prohibition (king, church, marriage).

A few additional points: The church is "blackening" because (1) it is covered with the soot of an industrial (mechanistic) society; (2) it is spiritually corrupt; and (3) it corrupts people. The chimney-sweeper's cry appalls the church because the cry is a reproach, and "appalls" hints at "pall" (suggestive of the dead church) and at its literal meaning, "to make pale," that is, the hypocritical church is a whited sepulcher. In line 14, "the youthful Harlot's curse" may be a cry (thus linked with the infant's cry, the chimney sweeper's cry, and the soldier's sigh), or it may be the disease that afflicts her and is communicated to others. In *Poetry and Repression*, Harold Bloom offers the astounding suggestion that "the harlot's curse is not, as various interpreters have said, venereal disease, but is indeed what 'curse' came to mean in the vernacular after Blake and still means now: menstruation, the natural cycle in the human female.... [Blake knows that one] curse or ban or natural fact (menstruation) blasts or scatters another natural fact, the tearlessness of the newborn infant."

In an earlier version, "dirty" stood in lines 1 and 2 instead of "chartered," and "smites" instead of "blights" in line 16.

For an analysis of several reading of "London," see Susan R. Suleiman and Inge Crosman, *The Reader in the Text*. Also important is an essay by E. P. Thompson in *Interpreting Blake*, ed. Michael Phillips.

ALLEN GINSBERG

A Supermarket in California (p. 367)

The poem evokes Walt Whitman by name and evokes his poetry in the long, unrhymed lines and in the catalogs of commonplace objects of American life. But Ginsberg's America is not Whitman's, for Ginsberg makes the point that Whitman too was lonely while he lived and finally encountered the loneliness of death. The allusion to the Spanish poet Garcia Lorca is to his poem on Walt Whitman, and also calls to mind yet another homosexual poet whose love was unreciprocated. As we see it, the "self-conscious" poet, his head aching (1), draws inspiration from Whitman, who lived in an earlier and more innocent age, an age when a man could unselfconsciously celebrate male beauty and comradeliness. But that age is "the lost America of love" (11), and in any case the Whitman who celebrates it and who is the poet's "courage-teacher" (13) was himself "lonely" (again 13) and, like all mortals, at last lost all. By the way, in the first sentence, Ginsberg seems to confuse the Lethe (the river of forgetfulness) with the Styx (the river across which Charon poled his ferry).

ELIZABETH BISHOP

Filling Station (p. 368)

We hope that we are not being sexist pigs (doubtless something that sexist pigs often say) when we say that we hear a woman's voice in "Oh, but it is dirty!" (It's a good idea to ask students to read this line aloud—and, indeed to read the entire poem aloud.) We even hear a woman's voice, though less obviously, in "Be careful with that match!" (One can ask students if they hear a woman's voice. If they do, it can be interesting to ask them to alter the line to something a man might say—perhaps, "Watch out with that match," or some such thing.) Other words that seem to us to indicate a female speaker: "saucy" (describing the sons, in line 10), "all quite thoroughly dirty" (13), "comfy" (20), though here perhaps the speaker is consciously using the diction of the woman who may live at the gas station), "Why, oh why, the doily?" (30), and the knowledgeable remarks about embroidery in lines 30-33.

The somewhat snobbish tone of the first stanza is moderated in the third, when the speaker begins to take an interest in the *life* of this station, and if snobbery continues in the fourth and fifth stanzas (21-30), it is also moderated by the speaker's interest in the technique of the doily. In the last stanza there is a bit of snide humor in "Somebody waters the plant,/ or oils it, maybe," but clearly by now the speaker is won over. However coarse the taste of the owners, they have tried to add a bit of order and a bit of beauty to life—not only to their own lives, but to the lives of passersby. The cans that spell out ESSO of course advertise a product, but they speak "softly" (38), their "so-so-so" serving to soothe the drivers of "high-strung automobiles," as a groom might soothe a horse or a mother her fretful baby. "Somebody loves us," the poet ends, referring most obviously to the owners of the filling station, but surely the reference is also larger, perhaps even unobtrusively hinting at the existence of a loving God. The close attention to detail, for which Bishop is widely known, is in fact loaded with moral value. Students might be invited to think of the poem partly in terms of Frost's comment about a poem as "a clarification of life… [and] a momentary stay against confusion."

The movement in this poem from the rather prim and disapproving opening line, through the sympathetic union with what she observes—achieved especially when the speaker, taken out of herself by her rapt attention to the embroidery—and finally to the larger or more generous view reminds us of a comment about her poetry in one of Bishop's letters. The arts, Bishop says, begin in observation. "Dreams, works of art,… unexpected moments of empathy…, catch a peripheral vision of whatever it is one can never really see full-face but that seems enormously important…. What one seems to want in art, in experiencing it, is the same thing that is necessary for its creation, a self-forgetful, perfectly useless concentration" (quoted by Helen McNeil in *Voices and Visions,* ed. Helen Vendler, 395).

A "Voices and Visions" video cassette of Elizabeth Bishop is available from HarperCollins.

X. J. KENNEDY

Nothing in Heaven Functions as It Ought (p. 370)

The poem is a Petrarchan sonnet, with the traditional contrast between the octave and the sestet. Kennedy's contrast of heaven and hell is not surprising, then, but in the contrasting rhymes and versification he plays an unexpected game. The off-rhymes and the hypermetric lines of the octave of course imitate the statement of the octave (things are askew), and the mechanical perfection of the sestet imitates the sestet's statement ("Hell hath no freewheeling part").

Kennedy has let us see an earlier version of the poem. You may want to invite students to compare the following version with the one in their text.

Nothing in Heaven Functions as It Ought (an early version)

Nothing in Heaven functions as it ought:
Peter snaps off a key stuck in the lock,
And his creaky gates keep crowing like a cock
(No hush of oily gold as Milton thought).
Gangs of the martyred innocents keep whoofing
The nimbus off the Venerable Bede
Like that of an old dandelion in seed.
The beatific choir take fits of coughing.

But Hell, sweet Hell, holds no unsteady part,
Nothing to rust nor rip nor lose its place.
Ask anyone: How did you come to be here?—
And he will slot a quarter into his face
And there will be a click and wheels will whir
And out will pop a neat brief of his case.

EMILY DICKINSON

I like to see it lap the Miles (p. 371)

This poem provides an excellent introduction to the uses of figurative language, and especially to the idea that much of the interest in poetry comes from the poet's perception of resemblances. (Aristotle said that metaphor is the mark of the poet.)

Resemblances—described obliquely—are at the heart of riddles, and Dickinson often has a riddling manner, as in this poem. She never specifically says the poem is about a train, and she never specifically says that the train is being compared to a horse, though the words *neigh* (14) and *stable* (17) introduce the horse pretty clearly. Because Dickinson's poem is so close to a riddle, we think it is worth spending some time in class talking about the nature of riddles, and the pleasures that they afford. It is also worth pointing out that the word *riddle* is the same as the word *read*, and that both words mean *interpret, understand.*

A riddle, like a highly metaphoric poem, is based on perceiving an analogy. Thus, to take the most famous riddle in Western culture, if we see a day as analogous to a lifespan, we can ask the riddle of the Sphinx:

What walks on four legs in the morning, two in the afternoon, and three in the evening?

There is even a further analogy here, in seeing a staff (used by the elderly) as a leg. You may want to invite students to offer riddles—disguised descriptions—and then discuss the metaphors involved. (Some students may at first not get the exact point, and may propose riddles that involve puns, such as "When is a door not a door? When it's ajar," or the venerable "What's black and white and red all over." Fine, this provides an opportunity to discuss the difference between a riddle and a conundrum.

In the text we ask, in our second question, how the reader responds to the idea that the poem is about poets and poetry. This idea is put forth by William Freedman in *Explicator* 40:3 (Spring 1982): 31-32. Freedman accepts the idea that the poem compares a train to a horse, but he suggests that it also is about poets and poetry, and especially about the poem as both a thing of power and also a thing controlled by the writer: "For the resistance of rebellious matter to conventional form, emerging as subject, shapes and ultimately determines the form this poem about poetry assumes." Why not? Although we are getting a bit tired of hearing that all poems are really about poetry (they are all "self-reflexive," it is said), and we certainly are not going to stop saying that the poem is chiefly about a train, we are willing to see something in Freedman's argument. We are reminded of a comment about interpretation that Robert Frost once made. Asked if had intended something or other in a poem, he said that the writer is entitled to credit for anything good that the reader sees in a poem.

And now for a few comments on the poetics of this riddling description of a train. (1) It is a single sentence, and the first three stanzas each end with a run-on line, presumably suggesting the forward motion of the train (though we are told that the train does "stop to feed itself at Tanks"). (2) The lines vary in length, and the pauses vary, presumably suggesting the changing speed of the train. Notice especially the pause after "Tanks—" which is followed by only two words ("And then") before we get another heavy pause, in which the train gathers strength for its "prodigious step / Around a Pile of Mountains." (3) When the train does make its final stop, the word "Stop"—the first word in the line—gets an unexpected stress (perhaps very faintly anticipated by a lesser stress in the first word of the preceding line, "Then"). Further, *Stop* itself ends in an explosive sound. The poem of course goes on for a few words, so perhaps we can say that *Stop*, with its unexpected stress, represents the first (and unexpected) braking of the train, before the train actually comes to a full stop. Come to think of it, *Stop* is followed by a dash and then by a trochee, *docile*, so we get two consecutive stresses with a pause between them ("Stop—do"), again perhaps suggesting the jerkiness of the stopping train? And then, as the train recovers and comes to an orderly halt, we get a few more words in a predominantly iambic rhythm. Is this going too far? Well, remember, Robert Frost said....

One final note: The poem says nothing about the train as a symbol of progress, nothing about the train as a symbol of America's manifest destiny, nothing about the train as sullying the environment. There are lots of things some readers find in the poem that we are unwilling to accept.

TOPICS FOR WRITING

1. Compare a train to something other than a horse—perhaps to a stream, or an ox, or a runner. Jot down two columns, indicting the parallels. What qualities in a train have you been able to capture that Dickinson necessarily missed by choosing to compare a train to a horse?

2. Again jot down two columns, making a comparison of two things, but this time beginning with something other than a train—perhaps an airplane, a college, a sporting event, or a concert. Then, imitating Dickinson, turn it into a poem.

JOHN KEATS

Ode to a Nightingale (p. 372)

Many students are quick to find symbolism in whatever poems and stories they read, but surely we can all agree that Keats's nightingale *is* a symbol, and we can probably agree more or less on what it symbolizes. The nightingale is a nightingale, of course, but as the poem progresses it also becomes a symbol of what has been called visionary art—that is, an art produced by the imagination or fantasy, presumably in favored moments, rather than an art produced by keen observation of external reality. Speaking of "Ode to a Nightingale," David Perkins says in *The Quest for Permanence* (1959), "By means of the symbol the ode explores the consequences of a commitment to vision, and as it does so, comes close to implying that the destruction of the protagonist is one of the results" (245).

The poem begins with the poet experiencing "a drowsy numbness," as though he had drunk hemlock or consumed an opiate. This dulling of consciousness is a prelude to the release of the imagination, which sees the nightingale as a "Dryad" (7) from the world of classical mythology. We soon learn that the cause of this sensation is the poet's perception of the bird's happy song. Further, the experience "pains" because the poet is "too happy" in his experience of the nightingale's "happiness." In other words, the initial stimulus to the imagination, which begins the movement toward vision, is a sweetly painful experience that includes the deadening of ordinary consciousness. In fact, even in this early stage there is a movement toward death (c.f. "Lethe" [4]).

How to join the bird, and with it "fade away into the forest dim"? The second stanza, with its description of the "draught of vintage," imaginatively evokes a world of wine, of southern France, and of medieval love poetry. The third stanza shows us the world he seeks to escape from, a world

> where men sit and hear each other groan;
> Where palsy shakes a few, sad, last grey hairs,
> Where youth grows pale, and spectre-thin, and dies....

The bird, then, clearly represents an ideal state, a condition beyond mortal suffering and transience. In the fourth stanza we learn that the poet has rejected wine (Bacchus) as a means of joining the bird, and instead will use the "viewless wings of poesy," that is, imaginative (visionary) poetry, or the imagination. By the middle of this stanza he has joined the bird ("Already with thee!"), and he seems almost amazed at his success. We have left the world of suffering, described in the third stanza, and are in a realm beyond the rational world, beyond the place where "the dull brain perplexes and retards." It is the world of the moon and of "Fays," where there is "no light," and a world of "embalmed darkness." In this visionary world the usual methods of knowing (e.g. by means of the eye) are of no avail, and we notice that (paradoxically) the poet can now describe the flowers with special richness (stanza 5). That is, this fifth stanza is not a world of fantasy, but is the real world freshly experienced and keenly described by the imagination. The famous example, of course, is the poet's statement that he "cannot see... what soft incense hangs upon the bough," where the synesthesia (incense imagined as a weighty substance, hanging) gives us a new awareness. At the same time, despite the fresh and loving description in the stanza, there is also a sense of longing for the transient world that he now cannot see.

As the passages just quoted imply, this rich world, with its "embalmed darkness" and its "fast fading violets," is in fact a world close to death. It is not surprising, therefore, that in the sixth stanza the poet says, "Now more than ever seems it rich to die, / To cease upon the midnight with no pain."

Death, then, offers a more complete escape from life than does wine or Poesy—but of course death would also separate the speaker from the song of the nightingale. By the end of the sixth stanza he realizes that his drift toward the nightingale is a drift toward extinction, and thus death is no longer attractive. (Everyone points out, by way of objecting to the poet's assertion that the bird is immortal—"not born for death"—whereas the poet will die, that in fact this particular bird also will die. David Perkins offers a possible reply to the objection: "In its distance from the poet the nightingale has now been openly transformed into symbol.... By referring only to the voice of the nightingale, he can identify it with all nightingales and so find a natural basis" for claiming that it endures [254].)

In the seventh stanza Keats pushes the nightingale back and back in time, first to a world of "emperor and clown," then to the world of the biblical *Ruth*, and finally he sets it in an utterly remote sphere, "faery lands forlorn," a realm where human beings cannot live. In line 35 the poet had said, "Already with thee," but now, when the word "forlorn" reminds him that sorrow has existed in all realms—real and imagined—the vision disappears and the poet is alone.

The nightingale, no longer a symbol, is a bird that flies away in a real land-scape with a "still stream" and "valley-glades." The departure of the bird is accompanied by the departure of the vision. The imagination can let us escape reality for a while, but only for a while. The analytic mind returns, pointing out that one is not with the bird but is a "sole self." And the song of the nightingale will fade and finally die away, "buried deep" in a remote valley, whereas the poet of course is still alive.

The poem ends with a question: Did the speaker experience a "vision" (a revelation of a supernatural reality) or did he experience a "waking dream" (a fantasy, an illusion)? The nightingale's song is gone, and the speaker is unsure of the nature of the moment of vision. Still, it seems to us that the speaker, back in the real world, has learned that "fancy" (i.e. the imagination) may "cheat" (deceive), and that the imagined world is ultimately "forlorn."

You may want to teach this poem in conjunction with Keats's "Ode on a Grecian Urn," which we include later in our text.

Bibliographic Note: For a detailed analysis of the poem, see Helen Vendler, *The Odes of John Keats* (1983); for briefer discussions, see the books on Keats by Walter Jackson Bate, Douglas Bush, and Aileen Ward. Also useful is a collection edited by Jack Stillinger, *Twentieth Century Interpretations of Keats's Odes* (1968), which includes a good introductory essay by Stillinger, as well as essays by Cleanth Brooks, Richard Harter Fogle, and Anthony Hecht. Stillinger's introductory essay is reprinted in his *The Hoodwinking of Madeline* (1971).

WALLACE STEVENS

Anecdote of the Jar (p. 374)

Stevens's poem has evoked controversy, chiefly on whether the jar is a symbol of man's superiority to nature or a symbol of man's corruption of natural beauty. For a survey of various interpretations, see *College English* 26 (April 1965): 527-32. William York Tindall, in *Wallace Stevens,* 24, argues that "the theme is interaction: The effect of the round jar on its surroundings and of them on it. This artifact composes nature, but not entirely; for the slovenly place still sprawls. Wilderness of bird and bush makes jar stand out, gray and bare" (24). Frank Kermode, in *The Romantic Image,* dismisses the controversy over whether "the poet is *for* Nature or *for* Art." Kermode says:

This is irrelevant, because the point of the jar's *difference,* and the manner of its difference, are what matters. It belongs to a different order of reality already completely significant and orderly, fixed and immortal. In one sense it is more vital, in another sense less so, than the "slovenly wilderness" around it; the poem itself reconciles opposites by using a jar as a symbol… of what moves in stillness, is dead in life, whose meaning and being are the same.

See also Joseph N. Riddell, *The Clairvoyant Eye* 43-44, and Harold Bloom, *Kabbalah and Criticism.*

A "Voices and Visions" videocassette of Wallace Stevens is available from HarperCollins. An audiocassette of Wallace Stevens reading is also available from HarperCollins.

ELIZABETH BISHOP

The Fish (p. 375)

Bishop's poem gives a highly detailed picture of a "venerable" heroic fish that, with its "medals" and its "beard of wisdom," becomes a symbol of courageous endurance. From the colors of the fish, seen and imagined ("brown skin," "darker brown," "rosettes of lime," "tiny white sea-lice," "white flesh," "dramatic reds and blacks," "pink swim-bladder," "tinfoil"), and from the colors of the old fish-lines, the poem moves to the rainbow in the oil in the bilge (the lowest part of the hull). The rainbow—the sign of hope and of God's promise to Noah to spare humanity—grows in the imagination until it fills "the little rented boat," illuminating (we might say) the speaker, who, perceiving the heroic history of the captive, forbears to conquer and returns the fish to the water.

For a discussion of the poem, see Bonnie Costello, *Elizabeth Bishop.*

TOPICS FOR CRITICAL THINKING AND WRITING

1.   Underline the similes and metaphors, and think about their implications. Of course they help to describe the fish, but do they also help to convey the speaker's attitude toward the fish?

MARGE PIERCY

Barbie Doll (p. 377)

The title alerts us to the world of childhood, so we are not surprised in the first line by "This girlchild" (like "This little pig") or by "peepee" in the second line. The stanza ends with the voice of a jeering child. The second stanza drops the kid-talk, adopting in its place the language of social science. (The stanza has much of the sound of Auden's "The Unknown Citizen.") We have not, then, made much progress; the "girlchild" who in the first stanza is treated like a Barbie doll is in the second treated like a healthy specimen, a statistic. The third stanza sounds more intimate, but she is still an object, not a person, and by the end of this stanza, there is a painful explosion. The two preceding stanzas each ended with a voice different from the voice that spoke the earlier lines of the stanza (in 6, "You have a great big nose and fat legs," we hear a jeering child, and in 11, "Everyone saw a fat nose on thick legs," we hear an adolescent imagining how others see her), but the third stanza ends with something of the flatly stated violence of a fairy tale: "So she cut off her nose and her legs / and offered them up." In the fourth and final stanza she is again (or better, still) a doll, lifeless and pretty.

In recent years, in addition to white Barbies there have been African-American, Hispanic and Asian Barbies, but until the fall of 1990 the TV and print ads showed only the fair-skinned blue-eyed version. For additional information about Barbie, see Sydney Ladensohn Stern and Ted Schoenhaus, *Toyland: the High-Stakes Game of the Toy Industry*. Barbie's wardrobe has changed from flight attendant to astronaut, and from garden-party outfits to workout attire. She has a dress-for-success and a briefcase—but they are pink.

CHAPTER 13

Thinking Critically about Poetry

A Casebook on Emily Dickinson, I heard a Fly buzz—when I died—

GERHARD FRIEDRICH

I heard a Fly buzz—when I died— (p. 380)

Our first question in the text is perhaps a clue that we found the focus of the article a bit obscure. Although Friedrich's opening paragraph is clear, and announces that he will address "two major problems" (the significance of the buzzing fly, and the meaning of "see" in the final line), it seems to us that the ensuing argument slips around. In the second paragraph we learn that the fly is sufficient "to blur the vision, to short-circuit mental concentration, so that spiritual awareness is lost," but in the next paragraph we learn that the buzzing is an "untimely reminder of man's final, cadaverous condition and putrefaction." Well, isn't awareness of "man's final, cadaverous condition" part of "spiritual awareness"?

Friedrich's final paragraph suggests that the reader compare this poem with another poem, and contrast it with two others—but since we don't fully accept his comment on the poem in question, it is hard for us to see how the other poems that he cites help to clarify his reading of this poem.

JOHN CIARDI

Dickinson's "I heard a Fly buzz—when I died—" (p. 384)

Ciardi takes issue with Friedrich's argument that the fly impedes the speaker's spiritual insight. In its place he suggests that the fly is "the last kiss of the world, the last buzz from life." He supports this reading by speaking (briefly, of course, since his whole essay is less than one page long) of "Emily's tremendous attachment to the physical world." This statement rings true for us, and we think it is evident to anyone who reads a number of her poems—though of course each poem is unique, and readers should be cautious about generalizing.

CAROLINE HOGUE

Dickinson's "I heard a Fly buzz—when I died—" (p. 385)

Hogue takes Friedrich's view, and dismisses Ciardi's, but it is not clear to us that she offers anything in the way of evidence beyond the assertion that Dickinson "could not possibly have entertained any such view [as Ciardi's] of a blowfly. She was a practical housewife, and every housewife abhors a blowfly." Well, as a "housewife" Dickinson probably did not want flies around, but as a poet…. We come back to Ciardi's comment about Dickinson's "tremendous attachment to the physical world."

Hogue's use of a remark in one of Dickinson's letters to Higginson especially puzzles us, since the remark (in our opinion) takes a somewhat light-hearted attitude toward "hallowed things." If anything, Dickinson's unconventional comment lends some support to support Ciardi's view. In our comment on the next interpretation we will offer a few more words about using Dickinson's letters as keys to the poems.

EUGENE HOLLAHAN

Dickinson's "I heard a Fly buzz—when I died—" (p. 386)

As we indicate in our question, in the text, it is usually a good idea for the reader of a lyric poem to think about the speaker and the setting, but we cannot imagine why one should imagine that the speaker of this poem is "possibly or certainly damned to Hell." Hollahan begins by asserting that he will study the poem "in the light of the theological tradition the author was nurtured in," but if anything is apparent in Dickinson's letters and in her poems it is that her writing does *not* echo "the theological tradition" that she was nurtured in. One has only to recall the famous comment (25 April 1862) to Higginson about her family: "They are religious—except me—and address an Eclipse, every morning—whom they call their 'Father.'" Or recall that she speaks of God as "Burglar! Banker—Father," and she says that "The Bible is an antique Volume—Written by faded Men." The more one knows of "the theological tradition the author was nurtured in," the less she seems to be part of that tradition.

But how might one disprove the idea that the poem is spoken by a damned soul. We don't know how to *dis*prove *any* interpretation that any reader offers of any poem, except to ask for the evidence that the reader believes supports the interpretation, and then to try to test the alleged evidence against the text of the poem. In this case, we would find ourselves talking about Dickinson's religious views, in so far as they can be garnered from her specific statements in letters; we would find her own comments a lot more valuable than a vague reference to "the theological tradition the author was nurtured in").

KARL KELLER

A Playful Poem (p. 388)

Keller, rather like Hollahan, puts a strong emphasis on the speaker's context. He sees the speaker as "a woman sitting somewhere hereafter telling other dead how *she* died. There was, she remembers with her flip tale, really nothing to it." In our view, this reading (like Hollahan's) sees the poem as a Browningesque dramatic monologue. It is all very well to urge students to think of the speaker's situation, and of a possible audience (e.g. the count's emissary, in "My Last Duchess"), but in a good many lyrics the speaker's status and locus are not highly particularized. (The words of almost any poem indicate a very particular state of mind, but the speaker's social station and physical placement may not be indicated at all.) We find Keller's strongly imagined scene an invention that gets in the way.

PAULA BENNETT

Dickinson's "I heard a Fly buzz—when I died—" (p. 389)

Bennett has affinities with Friedrich and with Hollahan, in that she finds the poem "horrifying," though in her final paragraph she also takes it be "at the very least a grim joke." We agree that there is a descent from the expected "experience of awe" (second paragraph), but we do not find that the poem turns into a "grim joke"; we continue to think that Ciardi's reading is the closest to our own.

PART THREE

Standing Back

Thinking Critically about Literature and Approaches to Literature

CHAPTER 15

Arguing an Evaluation

GWENDOLYN BROOKS

We Real Cool (p. 428)

The unusual arrangement of the lines, putting what ordinarily would be the first syllable of the second line at the end of the first line, and so on, of course emphasizes the "we"—and therefore emphasizes the absence of "we" in the final line, which consists only of "Die soon," the "we" having been extinguished. The disappearance of the "we" is especially striking in a poem in which the "we" is so pleased with itself.

By emphasis we don't necessarily mean a heavy stress on the word. An emphasis can be gained by the slightest of pauses (even though the word is not followed by a comma or a shift in tone). In *Report from Part One,* Brooks comments on this poem:

> The ending WEs in "We Real Cool" are tiny, wispy, weakly argumentative "Kilroy-is-here" announcements. The boys have no accented sense of themselves, yet they are aware of a semidefined personal importance. Say the "we" softly. (185)

"We" presumably refers to a gang of seven confident pool players, but if seven is traditionally a lucky number, it brings these people no luck. The subtitle allows one to infer that at the Golden Shovel they are digging their own graves.

An audio cassette of Gwendolyn Brooks reading is available from HarperCollins.

PART FOUR

A Thematic Anthology

CHAPTER 17

Parents and Children

JOAN DIDION

On Going Home (p. 455)

In a first-year writing course with traditional age students (17-19 years old), some students reading Didion will find her style heady and her topic compelling for their own writing. Others will be irritated, some without knowing why. Still others will be indifferent. Typically, whatever their intellectual range, students at this age vary markedly in emotional maturity. Some, we find, are not ready for the confrontation with their own ambivalence toward their families that a serious engagement with Didion's essay demands. So, although we would assign the essay and discuss it in class, we wouldn't *require* essays written about it. For students who can and will use them, the questions following the piece provide some sample essay topics.

DAVID MASELLO

In My Father's House (p. 457)

When we first saw the essay, in *The New York Times Magazine*, the title immediately brought to mind a famous line from the Gospel according to John: "In my father's house are many mansions." When we had finished reading the essay, we were not quite clear about the relevance of the line. Maybe it is a sort of private joke; or maybe a reader is supposed to feel, "Yes, just as there are many mansions in the house of the Lord, so there are many kinds of sexuality." If something like this *is* implied, then perhaps one can go further and say that Masello is also implying in his allusion that his sort of sexuality is (or ought to be) sanctified by religion. But maybe we are making too much of the title—though if we are, what *is* implied in this title?

You may want to discuss the narrative strategies that Masello employs. After all, he could have told us at the start that he has a boyfriend. Instead, he keeps this information from the reader, and even as late as the seventh paragraph he is speaking of "the person" who sent the flowers. It's our impression that at this point, precisely because the expression is so strained—surely a reader expects "the woman," or possibly "the man," but certainly *not* "the person"—a reader probably understands that "the person" is a man, and so this is not an essay about a son and a father who share an interest in the Civil War, etc. etc., but is about a gay son's relation to his father. (If readers don't get the idea from "a person," they get it at the end of the next paragraph, when Masello comes out of the closet.) Students might be asked to discuss whether the surprise works, or whether the essay might have been as good or better if it had begun by announcing the topic.

By the way, when we tried this essay out on a friend, she said that her chief response was that the father must be a simpleton. You might ask students to characterize the father—and, for that matter, to characterize the son.

LUKE

The Parable of the Prodigal Son (p. 460)

A bibliographic note about parables may be useful. In the *Encyclopedia Britannica,* in a relatively long article entitled "Fable, Parable, Allegory," fable and parable are defined as "short, simple forms of naive allegory," and yet a few paragraphs later the article says that "The rhetorical appeal of a parable is directed primarily toward an elite, in that a final core of its truth is known only to an inner circle, however simple its narrative may appear on the surface...." Perhaps, then, a parable is not a "naive allegory." Two other passages from the article are especially interesting: "The Aesopian fables emphasize the social interaction of human beings," whereas "parables do not analyze social systems so much as they remind the listener of his beliefs." That may not always be true, but it is worth thinking about.

The traditional title of this story is unfortunate, since it makes the second half of the story (the father's dealings with the older brother) superfluous. Joachim Jeremias, in *The Parables of Jesus,* suggests that the work should be called "The Parable of the Father's Love."

Here is a way to provoke thoughtful discussion of the parable. Roger Seamon, in "The Story of the Moral: The Function of Thematizing in Literary Criticism," *Journal of Aesthetics and Art Criticism* 47 (1989): 229-36, offers an unusual way of thinking about this parable. He summarizes his approach as follows:

> I want to reverse the traditional and common sense view that stories convey, illustrate, prove or emotionally support themes. Morals and themes, I argue, convey to audiences what story is to be made out of sentences. The story flows, so to speak, from theme, rather than the theme following from the story. (230)

He goes on to suggest an experiment. "Imagine," he says, that instead of reading a story that traditionally is called "The Prodigal Son,"

> we were to find the same set of sentences in another book under the title "The Prodigal Father," and at the end we found the following moral: "waste not your heart on the unworthy, lest you lose the love of the righteous." We now go back and re-read the sentences, and we find that *we are now reading a different story*. In the new story the father's giving the son money is wrong.

Seamon goes on to say that in *this* story the son's confession is "a way of evading responsibility for his error," and that the father is as prodigal with his love as he was with his property. In this version (remember: the sentences are identical, but the title is different), Seamon claims "The story concludes with the father happily returning to his error. The absence of poetic justice at the end is meant to arouse our indignation" (232).

It's interesting to hear students respond to this view. Of course Seamon's title, "The Prodigal Father," is merely his own invention, but the conventional title ("The Prodigal Son") has no compelling authority. The question is this: Once we apply Seamon's title, do we read the story the way he suggests—that is, do we see the father as blameworthy and the stay-at-home son as justified? If not, why not? Again, Seamon's point is that although the common-sense view holds that the story yields a moral, in fact the reverse is true: the moral (i.e. the theme we have in mind) yields the story. For Seamon, "A thematic statement conveys information about how the critic constructs the *nature and motivations of the characters, [and] the value of their actions...*" (233). True, but can't we add that the skilled critic, i.e., reader, is in large measure guided by the author who knows (again, at least in large measure) how to control the reader's response? Seamon apparently takes a different view, for he holds that "the sentences used to project the events are not, in themselves, sufficient to tell us how we are to characterize or evaluate what is going on." Our response to Seamon is of no importance; what is important is to get students to think about why they do or do not accept the view that the story might be entitled "The Prodigal Father."

We spend some time in class teaching this parable because we find the artistry admirable—and also because the story is profound. One small but telling artistic detail may be noted here, a detail mentioned by Joachim Jeremias, who points out that the elder son, speaking to his father, "omits the address"; we had never noticed this, but now it seems obvious, and surely it is revealing that when the younger son addresses his father he says, "Father," and that when the father addresses the older son he says, "Son." The older son's lack of address, then, speaks volumes: he refuses to see himself as bound by family ties of love—a position evident also when, talking to his father, he identifies the prodigal not as "my brother" but as "this thy son." The story is (among many other things) an admirable example of work in which a story-teller guides an audience into having certain responses.

It's also worthwhile in class to spend some time cautioning against a too-vigorous attempt to find meaning in every detail. (Professionals as well as students sometimes don't know when to leave well enough alone. For instance, a writer in *Studies in Short Fiction* 23 (1986), talking about Updike's "A & P," says that Queenie's pink bathing suit "suggests the emerging desires competing with chastity." But come to think of it, this statement isn't surprising, considering what has been said about the pink ribbon in "Young Goodman Brown." One writer, for instance, says it symbolizes feminine passion, and another says it symbolizes a state between the scarlet of total depravity and the white of innocence.)

To illustrate the danger of pressing too hard, you might mention medieval allegorizations of the story. The gist of these is this: the older brother represents the Pharisees and teachers who resented the conversion of the Gentiles. Thus the fact that the older brother was in the fields when the prodigal returned was taken as standing for the remoteness of the Pharisees and the teachers from the grace of God. The younger brother, according to medieval interpretations, represents the Gentiles, who wandered in illusions and who served the devil (the owner of the swine) by tending the devil's demons (the swine). The pods that the prodigal ate represent either the vices (which cannot satisfy) or pagan literature (again, unsatisfying). The father represents God the Father; his going forth to meet the prodigal stands for the Incarnation; his falling on the neck of the prodigal stands for the mild yoke that Christ places on the neck of his followers (Matthew 11:29-30). The music which the older brother hears represents the praise of God, and the feast of the fatted calf represents the Eucharist. A great deal more of this sort of thing can be found in Stephen L. Wailes, *Medieval Allegories of Jesus' Parables* (236-45). The point should already be clear. On the other hand, it's also worth mentioning that the medieval interpreters of the parable at least paid it the compliment of taking it seriously. Odd as the interpretations now seem, they were the result of an admirable love of the word, and surely such an excess is preferable to indifference.

Is the parable an allegory? No, and yes. Certainly it does not have the detailed system of correspondences that one associates with allegory. Moreover, since the prodigal says, "Father, I have sinned against heaven and... thee," the father cannot be said to represent heaven, i.e., God. And yet, as Jeremias says (131):

> The parable describes with touching simplicity what God is like, his goodness, his grace, his boundless mercy, his abounding love.

Need a reader believe in God or in the divinity of Jesus in order to value this story? The point is surely worth discussing in class. Most students will agree that such belief is not necessary, and from here one can go on to discuss stories as ways of imaginatively entering alien worlds.

KATE CHOPIN

Regret (p. 461)

It is plain that Mamzelle Aurelie regrets that she does not have a family of children... to feed, to sort out their games, to put to bed, to cherish. She understands it in two weeks when she baby-sits for Odile's children, while Odile visits her ailing mother in another parish. At the end of the two weeks, Odile returns home, and "her beaming face indicated that her homecoming was a happy one." Odile picks up the children, and Aurelie looks around her in the evening shadows, and cries.

It is not plain to most of our students that Mamzelle Aurelie is masculine, though we ask them what Mamzelle Aurelie looked like, why she isn't married, why she cries "like a man." We offer the opinion that perhaps she is a lesbian, though probably unconscious of it (she is "quite alone in the world"). But most of our students (we have taught this story twice, early in the semester) are confident in their own opinions—that M. Aurelie is strong, self-reliant, wears what is comfortable, and is *not* a lesbian—and without giving in ourselves, we let the story rest there.

We want them to see, of course, the use Chopin makes of setting. Mamzelle Aurelie is alone on a farm, she receives the children on a bright morning, and she watches them leave "as the evening shadows were creeping and deepening around her solitary figure." One has the gratifying sense of a beginning, a middle, and an end. And then there is Chopin's humor, present here and in everything we've read by her. We read paragraph 4:

> One morning Mamzelle Aurelie stood upon her gallery, contemplating, with arms akimbo, a small band of very small children who, to all intents and purposes, might have fallen from the clouds, so unexpected and bewildering was their coming, and so unwelcome. They were the children of her nearest neighbor, Odile, who was not such a near neighbor, after all.

It is Chopin who is telling the story, of course, but the intonation is decidedly Mamzelle Aurelie's—solid, respectable, and with her own brand of wit. And we might contrast that with:

> But this coming, unannounced and unexpected, threw Mamzelle Aurelie into a flutter that was almost agitation. The children had to be gathered. Where was Ti Nomme? Yonder in the shed, putting an edge on his knife at the grindstone. And Marceline and Marcelette? Cutting and fashioning doll-rags in the corner of the gallery.

And so on. The military discipline M. Aurelie had wanted to impose is, of course, dissipated; she has indeed learned how to take care of the children, but from them. And when they leave she cries. "She cried like a man, with sobs that seemed to tear her very soul."

FRANK O'CONNOR

My Oedipus Complex (p. 464)

The story has three parts: (1) Larry's satisfactory relation to his mother during his father's absence; (2) Larry's defeat when his father returns home and displaces him; and (3) Larry's new satisfactory relation—this time with his father—when Sonny displaces the father in the mother's affections. Still, though there really is a plot or action here (the resolution of the boy's conflict with his father), much of our interest in "My Oedipus Complex" centers on the boy's character, especially on the delightful mixture of egotism and naiveté revealed by using a first-person narrator. The egotism itself is engaging (he feels "rather like the sun, ready to illumine," and he is confident that his prayers have saved Father, "a total stranger who had cajoled his way back from the war into our big bed"), and it arises in large part out of a touching need for affection.

It should be mentioned that according to Freud, the Oedipus complex is universal. A boy wishes to possess his mother, and he therefore sees his father as a rival. (Freud held that a girl, too, has these desires, but he accounted for them in different ways during his career, and he never seems to have solidified his views of the female Oedipus complex.) The boy has further rivals—his siblings—in his desire for the mother. Sibling rivalry and the Oedipus complex, then, are aspects of the same thing, but the murderous feelings toward the sibling can be shown more openly because the sibling (usually a younger child) is a less threatening rival. One other point: Freud says that the boy's castration complex (fear that the father will punish him by castration) ends the Oedipus complex, for the boy then suppresses his sexual interest in the mother, identifies himself with his father's sexuality, and seeks a woman of his own.

Although we put *Hamlet* in the chapter "Innocence and Experience" and *Oedipus* in "Men, Women, God, and Gods," an instructor may want to teach these two plays along with O'Connor's story. For some further comments on the Oedipus complex, see page 307 of this manual, where Sophocles' *Oedipus* is discussed.

Although Freud's discovery was rooted in a tragic play, the Oedipus complex seems to be at the heart of much comedy, especially those plays that show a young male lover outwitting an older male (a father surrogate) and winning an attractive young woman.

TOPIC FOR WRITING

Is the story serious or humorous or both?

TONI CADE BAMBARA

My Man Bovanne (p. 472)

It is a truth universally unacknowledged that children are ashamed of their parents—perhaps of their speech, their way of dressing, their occupation, almost anything and everything. In Bambara's story the children are ashamed of their mother's clothing, of her hair (a wig), and especially of her apparent sexuality. According to Task, Mama's "dress is too short... and too low-cut for a woman of [her] age"; according to Elo, Mama dances with Bovanne as though she is "a bitch in heat." Mama denies the charges, explicitly saying that her dancing is a sort of "chest to chest like talkin. Not jammin my breasts into the man. Wasn't bout tits. Was bout vibrations." She also wittily picks up the young people's interest in African drums and insists she "was just talkin on the drums... just drummin that's all." On the other hand, there is no need—at least there is no need for the reader—to deny an element of sexuality, especially since Mama tells us that she has "men friends" who sometimes "get messy." Students might be invited to talk about why (for the most part) young people are so prudish when it comes to the thought of older people having sexual feelings.

Much of the irony in the story is that the young people, proud of their liberation from the old conventions, e.g. from playing the role of Uncle Tom, do not see (as we see from their reaction to their mother) that they are tightly bound by new conventions. (One is reminded of a story Picasso tells about the conventions that constrict those who think they are unconventional. Some anarchists were conscripted into the army; when the sergeant ordered "right face," they all faced left.) Mama in fact is less conventional than her children; further, and more important, she is also a good deal more humane. The young people at the meeting supposedly are concerned about the needs of others, but Mama, who values people more than politics, notices that they are short on action:

"They ain't said boo to the man yet. Cause he blind and old and don't nobody there need him since they grown up and don't need they skates fixed no more."

Bambara has written an engaging essay on her work—though it makes no reference to this story—in *The Writer on Her Work,* edited by Janet Sternberg (1980). In this essay she characterizes herself (with some mock-solemnity) as "a Pan-Africanist-socialist-female." One of the points she goes on to make is that she is not interested in expressing "rage, bitterness, revenge," and that she does not "conjure up characters for the express purpose of despising them" (156). Nor is she keen, she says, on "Sylvia Plath and the other obligatory writers on women's studies lists—the writers who hawk despair, insanity, alienation, suicide, all in the name of protesting woman's oppression, are not my mentors. I was raised on stories of Harriet Tubman, Ida B. Wells, Paul Robeson, and my grandmother, Annie, whom folks in Atlanta still remember as an early Rosa Parks" (163).

For an interview with Bambara (though, again, it does not mention this story), see *Sturdy Black Bridges: Visions of Black Women in Literature,* edited by Roseann P. Bell and others (1979). For a useful survey of Bambara's writing (again with no specific reference to this story), see Susan Willis, *Specifying: Black Women Writing the American Experience* (1987).

TOPICS FOR CRITICAL THINKING AND WRITING

1. Compare Mama with the mother in Alice Walker's "Everyday Use."
2. Rewrite a paragraph or two in Standard English and evaluate the effectiveness of each version.
3. Rewrite part of the story (the opening paragraph, for instance) from the point of view of an omniscient narrator, or from the point of view of one of Mama's children.

MAX APPLE

Bridging (p. 477)

The biographical headnote in the text quotes Apple's belief that "the most powerful question in narrative" is "What happens next?" It also quotes his belief that the writer of fiction must "create a character whom... your reader can care about."

Students might be invited to examine their responses to "Bridging" in the light of these two points. (They might also be reminded of Henry James's comment about the intertwining of character and plot, quoted in Chapter 6: "What is character but the determination of incident, What is incident but the illustration of character?")

Most students care about Jessica and find her of interest—but they also care about the narrator and find him of interest. The reader's interest in the characters generates an interest in what the characters will say and do and in what will happen to them. After all, a man who is an assistant Girl Scout leader is not the sort of person one meets every day. He is not afraid to defy the usual views of sex roles, but as a loving father he can't easily tolerate his daughter's defiance—her rejection of young companions, and her absorption in the world of male sports, where she is never a participant but always a spectator. Gradually we learn about his thoroughly understandable desire to bring Jessica into a world of friends (refreshingly, he also entertains the thought that "She'll grow up like everyone else does"), and about his own need to trust a world that has taken his wife from him. We perceive his interest in Kay Randall, and perhaps (thinking of "What happens next?") we anticipate some sort of union, but then we perceive his sad awareness that she and he are not characters in a Robert Redford / Barbra Streisand film. Unlike his daughter, however, he seems to be well on the road toward recovery. Picking flowers with the girls, he realized that he was "not watching and keeping score and admiring from the distance but a participant, a player."

Will he be able to bring Jessica back into the world where she participates? One has every reason to believe so, partly because Jessica (despite her withdrawal from others) trusts her father in some things, and partly because the father seems to know what he is doing. The last paragraph of the story is full of good sense: "I promise to take you everywhere, my lovely child, and then to leave you. I'm learning to be a leader." The narrator is learning to "bridge"— to make contact—and although Jessica "won't bridge,… won't budge," presumably he, if anyone, will be able to help Jessica to construct and cross her bridges.

This discussion, however, has been too solemn. The story is, after all, amusing as well as touching, and it is amusing not only because (for example) we see Kay Randall pin a promptness badge on him, but also because Jessica has a keen sense of humor: "She tells me to wear it to work." Even Jessica's bitter comment about her mother's death ("I just tell them she fell off the Empire State Building") is funny. Her sense of humor, even if it is now dark, as well as her father's determination and affection, somehow encourages us to feel that the two of them will get through their difficulties.

AMY HEMPEL

Today Will Be a Quiet Day (p. 484)

The first question following the story in the text, asking the reader to consider the ominous talk in the first page, seems to me to get at the heart of traditional storytelling. What is the connection between the beginning and the end of a story? What does it mean to speak of unity, or to say that a story has a beginning, a middle, and an end? Why, one may ask, do experienced readers simply *know* that this story will turn out well? Why don't we take the talk of disaster as foreshadowing? For that matter, why don't we take the title as a hint of imminent death? (Later the reader learns that the father has jokingly suggested that he wants his tombstone to say, "Today will be a quiet day.")

Probably the simple answer is that (putting aside the title) the story begins playfully—the boy is teasing—and then continues with a cozy domestic image comparing the children to dogs carrying their own leashes. Only the bit about the suicide, and the father's comment that "You think you're safe... but it's thinking you're invisible because you closed your eyes" disturb the reader's sense of comfort. But the next thing we hear about is "Petaluma—the chicken, egg, and arm-wrestling capital of the nation." This *can't* be a story that will end unhappily (although, if Flannery O'Connor were writing it, it could). Robert Louis Stevenson, speaking of the inappropriateness of an unhappy ending in a work by Barrie, offers a relevant observation: "If you are going to make a book end badly [i.e. unhappily], it must end badly from the beginning." Somehow "Today Will be a Quiet Day" lets us know, from the brother's teasing remark about the bridge collapsing, that nothing will collapse in this story. The tone is simply too genial, too good-natured, for it to turn out badly. Again, in Stevenson's words, if a story is going to end badly, it should end badly from the beginning.

We see, almost from the start, that despite the absence of the mother this family is OK.. The teasing reveals affection, not aggression. Only once does the boy inflict pain on his sister—when he reveals that the dog was killed rather than sent to a ranch—but his remark is inadvertent rather than malicious.

Where is the mother, or, better, why is the mother never mentioned? Is she dead, divorced, away on vacation, hospitalized, or locked up? The narrator gives us no dues, though surely we can infer that she is not away temporarily; if she were, the others would mention her. Similarly, we can infer that her absence is not of recent origin. But we need not worry about her absence. Judging from the absence of comment about her, we probably can say that she plays no role in their lives—and plays no role in our view of their lives.

JAMAICA KINCAID

Girl (p. 489)

Jamaica Kincaid, like her fictional heroine Annie John, lived in Antigua, a much doted-on only child, until she was seventeen, when she came to the

United States to continue her education. In an interview in the *New York Times Book Review* (April 7, 1985, p. 6), she said, "I did sort of go to college but it was such a dismal failure. I just educated myself, if that's possible." She has published three collections of short stories based on her life in the West Indies.

In this story we meet a girl in her early adolescence, under the constant tutelage of her mother for her coming role as a woman. In today's terminology, we see the social construction of gender. The mother is a powerful presence, shrewd and spirited as well as overprotective and anxious about her daughter's burgeoning sexuality. The girl is attentive to her mother, and mostly submissive; we sense that it is through her reverie that we hear her mother's monologue, which the daughter twice interrupts briefly. But the repetition of instruction and correction in the monologue, especially of the incessant "this is how to," suggests the tension between the two that we know, from our own experience, will lead to a confrontation that will permanently alter the relationship. Despite the references to the Island culture, which provide the story's rich, exotic texture, the central drama of coming of age could be happening anywhere.

A good way to teach the story is to have two students read it aloud in class. It's short, humorous, and in passages pleasantly rhythmical. The students will hear the shift in voices, and will want to discuss the characters and the conflict.

A video cassette of Jamaica Kincaid reading "Girl" is available from HarperCollins.

TOPICS FOR CRITICAL THINKING AND WRITING

1. What is the conflict in this story?
2. Is the girl naive? Explain.
3. Taking "Girl" as a model, write a piece about someone—perhaps a relative, teacher, or friend—who has given you more advice than you wanted.

AMY TAN

Two Kinds (p. 491)

It's not a bad idea to ask a student to read the first two paragraphs aloud, and then to invite the class to comment. What, you might ask them, do they hear besides some information about the mother's beliefs? Probably they will hear at least two other things: (1) the voice of a narrator who does not quite share her mother's opinion, and (2) a comic tone. You may, then, want to spend some time in class examining *what the writer has done* that lets a reader draw these inferences. On the first point, it may be enough to begin by noticing that when someone says, "My mother believed," we are almost sure to feel some difference between the speaker and the reported belief. Here the belief is further distanced by the fivefold repetition of "You could." The comedy—perhaps better characterized as mild humor—is evident in the naiveté or simplicity of ambitions: open a restaurant, work for the government, retire, buy a house with almost no money down, become famous. Many readers may feel superior (as the daughter herself does) to this mother, who apparently thinks that in America money and fame and even genius are readily available to all who apply themselves— but many readers may also wish that their mother was as enthusiastic.

The second paragraph adds a sort of comic topper. After all, when the mother says, in the first paragraph, "you could be anything you wanted to be in America," the ambitions that she specifies are not impossible, but when in the second paragraph she says, "you can be prodigy too," and "you can be best anything," we realize that we are listening to an obsessed parent, a woman ferociously possessive of her daughter. (In another story in Tan's *Joy Luck Club* a mother says of her daughter, "How can she be her own person? When did I give her up?") Obsessions, of course, can be the stuff of tragedy—some students will be quick to talk about Macbeth's ambition, Brutus's self-confidence, and so forth—but obsessions are also the stuff of comedy; witness the lover who writes sonnets to his mistress's eyebrow, Harpo Marx in pursuit of a blonde, the pedant, and all sorts of other monomaniacs whose monomania (at least as it is represented in the work of art) is not dangerous to others.

The third paragraph, with its references to the terrible losses in China, darkens the tone, but the fourth restores the comedy, with its vision of "a Chinese Shirley Temple." The fifth paragraph is perhaps the most obviously funny so far: when Shirley Temple cries, the narrator's mother says to her daughter: "You already know how. Don't need talent for crying."

There's no need here to belabor the obvious, but students—accustomed to thinking that everything in a textbook is deadly serious—easily miss the humor. They will definitely grasp the absurdity of the thought that "Nairobi" might be one way of pronouncing Helsinki, but they may miss the delightful comedy of Auntie Lindo pretending that Waverly's abundant chess trophies are a nuisance ("all day I have no time to do nothing but dust off her winnings"), and even a deaf piano teacher may not strike them as comic. (Of course, in "real life" we probably would find pathos rather than comedy in a deaf piano teacher—and that's a point worth discussing in class.) So the point to make, probably, is that the story is comic (for example, in the mother's single-mindedness, and in the daughter's absurd hope that the recital may be going all right, even though she is hitting all the wrong notes) but is also serious (the conflict between the mother and the daughter, the mother's passionate love, the daughter's rebelliousness, and the daughter's later recognition that her mother loved her deeply). It is serious, too, in the way it shows us (especially in the passage about the "old Chinese silk dresses") the narrator's deepening perception of her Chinese heritage.

As a child, she at first shares her mother's desire that she be a "prodigy," but she soon becomes determined to be herself. In the mirror she sees herself as "ordinary" but also as "angry, powerful"; she is an independent creature, not an imitation of Shirley Temple. The question is, Can a young person achieve independence without shattering a fiercely possessive parent? Or, for that matter, without shattering herself? We can understand the narrator's need to defy her mother ("I now felt stronger, as if my true self had finally emerged"), but the devastating effect when she speaks of her mother's dead babies seems almost too great a price to pay. Surely the reader will be pleased to learn that the narrator and her mother became more or less reconciled, even though the mother continued to feel that the narrator just didn't try hard enough to be a genius. It's worth reading aloud the passage about the mother's offer of the piano:

> And after that, every time I saw it in my parents' living room, standing in front of the bay window, it made me feel proud, as if it were a shiny trophy that I had won back.

As a mature woman, the narrator comes to see that "Pleading Child" (which might almost be the title of her early history) is complemented by "Perfectly Contented." Of course, just as we have to interpret "Pleading Child" a bit freely—let's say as "Agitated Child"—so "Perfectly Contented" must be interpreted freely as, say, "Maturity Achieved." We get (to quote the title of the story) "two kinds" of experience and "two kinds" of daughter, in one.

ROBERT HAYDEN

Those Winter Sundays (p. 499)

The poem begins in the midst of a reflection, "Sundays too my father got up early," a meditation on how the speaker neglected his father on these Sundays, and doubtless on other occasions. The boy was (perhaps) six to eight, aware that there were "chronic angers" in the house, though unaware what they were about. He spoke "indifferently" to his father, a word that nicely reflects the boy's attitude, knowing that much was wrong, yet not knowing what it was. But the scene has lasted, until, one feels, this moment, when the grown son, looking back, understands the father's "austere and lonely offices." Like the father in the poem, who drives out the cold and brings warmth (by means of love, of course, as well as coal) to an unknowing child, an "austere and lonely" writer performs an office, shaping experience for another person's use.

Students can read the poem without difficulty (except for the word "offices") but we like to pause at such lines as

made
banked fires blaze. No one ever thanked him.

to get them to say what is special about them. We hope that some student, if we've done it right, will see that the four syllables at the end of a sentence of four lines are all stressed. And the brevity of the next sentence reinforces its content; no one thanked him. The last two lines of the poem are again brief and cogent, especially with the repetition of "What did I know? What did I know? Our last question assumes that all of us have such memories. We ask students to create a scene in which gratitude was the appropriate response, which we failed to give.

THEODORE ROETHKE

My Papa's Waltz (p. 500)

Writing of Roethke's "My Papa's Waltz" in *How Does a Poem Mean,* John Ciardi says that the poem seems to lack a "fulcrum" (Ciardi's word for a "point of balance" or point at which there is a twist in the thought), but that the fulcrum "occurs after the last line." In his terminology, "The fulcrum exists outside the poem, between the enacted experience and the silence that follows it."

An audiocassette of Theodore Roethke reading is available from HarperCollins.

GWENDOLYN BROOKS

The Mother (p. 501)

It's our guess that discussion in class will concentrate on the last three lines. For what it's worth, we find those lines convincing, partly because of their simplicity (no metaphors, no inversions, no unusual diction) and partly because of the repetition. Of course the repetition *might* suggest insincerity, the speaker's awareness that she does not sound convincing and so she piles it on (some readers may feel that the lady doth protest too much), but we do not hear any such suggestion.

SYLVIA PLATH

Daddy (p. 502)

C. B. Cox and A. R. Jones point out, in *Critical Quarterly* 6 (Summer 1964): 107-122, that literature has always been interested in perverse states of mind

(Greek and Roman interest in the irrational; Elizabethan interest in melancholy, jealousy, madness, etc.; and Browning's dramatic monologues). The "fine frenzy" of the poet himself (in the words of Shakespeare's Theseus), once associated with inspiration and even divinity, in the twentieth century links the poet with the psychotic personality. And apparently a sensitive (poetic) mind can make only a deranged response in a deranged world. Plath's "Daddy" begins with simple repetitions that evoke the world of the nursery rhyme (and yet also of the witches in *Macbeth*, who say, "I'll do, I'll do, and I'll do"). The opening line also connects with the suggestion of the marriage service ("And I said I do") in line 67. The speaker sees herself as tormented yet also as desiring the pain inflicted by her father/love ("Every woman adores a Fascist"). She recognizes that by accepting the need for love she exposes herself to violence. The speaker's identification of herself with Jews and the evocation of "Dachau, Auschwitz, Belsen" suggest some identity between the heroine's tortured mind and the age's. Death, Cox and Jones go on to say, is the only release from a world that denies love and life. The "Daddy" of the poem is father, Germany, fatherland, and—life itself, which surrounds the speaker and which the speaker rejects.

In *Commentary* (July 1974 and October 1974), there is an exchange of letters on the appropriateness of Plath's use of Nazi imagery in a poem about her father. Roger Hoffman, in the July issue, argues that the imagery is valid because in a child's mind an authoritarian father is fearsome. Irving Howe, in October (9-12), replies that this argument is inadequate ground "for invoking the father as a Nazi." The speaker of the poem is not a child, Howe says, but "the grown-up writer, Sylvia Plath." He goes on: the "unwarranted fusion of child's response and grown-ups' references makes for either melodrama or self-pity." Howe also rejects Carole Stone's argument (July) that the images are acceptable because "one individual's psyche [can] approximate the suffering of a people." Howe replies that the victims of the concentration camps didn't merely "suffer"; they were methodically destroyed. He questions the appropriateness of using images of the camps to evoke personal traumas. There is, he says, a lack of "congruence" between the object and the image, "a failure in judgement." Some useful criticism can also be found in *The Art of Sylvia Plath*, ed. Charles Newman.

A "Voices and Visions" videocassette of Sylvia Plath is available from HarperCollins. An audiocassette of Sylvia Plath reading is also available from HarperCollins.

TOPIC FOR WRITING

The speaker expresses her hatred for her father by identifying him with the Nazis, herself with the Jews. Is it irresponsible for a poet to compare her sense of torment with that of Jews who were gassed in Dachau, Auschwitz, and Belsen?

LUCILLE CLIFTON

Wishes for Sons (p. 505)

We take it that the speaker feels a love-hate relationship, wishing that her sons—presumably as arrogant as most other males—may feel the pains (physical and mental) of being a woman in a man's world. The implication, we think, is not only that the sons should suffer as women suffer, but that such suffering would improve them by knocking the arrogance out of them. They may think they know what arrogance is, but not until they encounter a (male) gynecologist will they really know what women put up with.

RUTH WHITMAN

Listening to grownups quarreling (p. 506)

The poem will cause readers no difficulty, and the suggested writing assignment ("In a paragraph [or a journal entry] compare yourself to some non-human figure, as you overheard grownups quarreling") will produce interesting material that can be discussed in class.

SHARON OLDS

I Go Back to May 1937 (p. 506)

One way of getting a lively discussion going is to mention that although poets often adopt a persona, Olds's "I Go Back" strikes most readers as autobiographical. What do the students think about Olds disclosing such intimate (and potentially embarrassing) family history?

ADDITIONAL TOPICS FOR CRITICAL THINKING AND WRITING

1. Summarize the poem in a sentence or two. (In summarizing, try to convey a sense of the speaker's changes of attitude, a sense of development. You may want to use a structure something like this: "The speaker begins by envisioning her parents at college and thinks... but... because... and then...." That is, if you find in the poem *a sequence* of thought, rather than a collection of unconnected thoughts, try to give your reader a sense of that sequence.)

2. What do you take to be the speaker's attitude toward her parents? Does the poem give us enough information to let us comment on the speaker's attitude toward herself? If so, what is this attitude?

3.   Discuss the poem with a friend or two, then read it aloud, and compare your oral interpretations. How do they differ (for example, in the tone in which you read a certain line), and why?
4.   A collaborative exercise: Divide the class into groups of five, and ask each group to discuss the poem and to come up with one paragraph interpreting the poem. Then have a member of each group read the paragraphs aloud in class, and have the class discuss the differences.
5.   "I Go Back to May 1937" doesn't rhyme, and its lines vary in length. Do you agree that it is a poem, or is it really prose printed in a strange way? Explain.

JUDITH ORTIZ COFER

My Father in the Navy: A Childhood Memory (p. 508)

Most students will quickly see the imagery of death ("stiff and immaculate / in the white cloth, / an apparition") and the Christian imagery ("halo," "When he rose," "kept vigil," "like an angel / heralding a new day"). The sailor-father comes back to the living world from "below," and thus would seem to resemble the risen Jesus. If one assumes that the father is dead, one notices an irony: in Christian thinking it is Jesus who animates human beings—that is, who gives them the possibility of eternal life, but in the poem it is the living (the speaker and her siblings) who, so to speak, bring life to the "apparition."

However, we take a different view. It is our sense that the father is alive, and the speaker is remembering how her sailor-father—presumably often away for long periods—would reappear, almost miraculously, as though from the dead.

DAVID MURA

An Argument: On 1942 (p. 509)

Mura is a *sansei*, a third-generation Japanese-American. Born in 1952, he of course did not experience internment in the relocation camps of 1942. The poem is rooted in the fairly widespread difference today between the attitude of, on the one hand, most of those who experienced the camps (chiefly *issei* [first-generation] and their American-born children, *nisei* [second-generation]), and on the other hand, many *sansei*, who were born after World War II, and who cannot understand how their parents and grandparents allowed themselves to be so subjugated.

Mura's poem—in effect an argument between the poet and his mother—begins in the son's voice. Between the fourth and the fifth lines, however, the mother interrupts (or at least she does so in the son's imagination), and the poet reports her words: "—No, no, she tells me. Why bring it back? The camps are over." The mother wishes to forget the experience, or at least not to dwell on it, but her son, she says, is "like a terrier... gnawing a bone." For her, the experience was chiefly boring (line 9). (Of course one can say that she has repressed her memories of humiliation—but one can also entertain the possibility that for a child the experience was indeed chiefly boring.) For the son, who did not experience it but who now looks at it through the eyes of a mature Japanese-American writing in the late 1980s, the thought of the indignity is galling.

What does a reader make of the conflict? Presumably the reader can hold both views, sharing the youth's sense of outrage but also understanding the mother's view—which, incidentally, is given the climactic final position: "David, it was so long ago... how useless it seems..." In fact, it seems entirely possible that the poet himself holds both views. At least to our ear he voices them with equal effectiveness.

After we had written the preceding remarks we received the following comment from David Mura:

> The poem starts with an imaginary poem in my voice, a lament for the world that was destroyed by the internment order. I'm both attracted to and wary of the romantic cast to such a voice, and in the poem, my mother gives another version of the past, one which downplays the effect of the camps and argues against over-romanticizing both the past and past sufferings. In the end, I think there's a great deal of denial in my mother's version of the past, and yet, her version is a reality with which I must contend; after all, she was there, and I wasn't (of course, her presence at these events doesn't necessarily mean her interpretation of them can't be wrong). Both her version and my version exist in the poem as realities which the reader must confront. As with much of my work, I think of this poem as a political poem.

For another poem about the internment of Japanese-Americans in 1942, see Mitsuye Yamada, "To the Lady" (1026).

TENNESSEE WILLIAMS

The Glass Menagerie (p. 511)

The books on Williams that have appeared so far are disappointing. The best general survey is Henry Popkin's article in *Tulane Drama Review* 4 (Spring

1960): 45-64; also useful is Gordon Rogoff, in *Tulane Drama Review* 10 (Summer 1966): 78-92. For a comparison between the play and earlier versions, see Lester A. Beaurline, *Modern Drama* 8 (1965): 14249. For a discussion of Christian references and motifs (e.g., Amanda's candelabrum, which was damaged when lightning struck the church), see Roger B. Stein, in *Western Humanities Review* 18 (Spring 1964): 141-53, reprinted in *Tennessee Williams,* ed. Stephen S. Stanton. Stein suggests that the play shows us a world in which Christianity has been replaced by materialism.

Perhaps the two points that students find most difficult to understand are that Amanda is both tragic *and* comic (see the comments below, on the first suggested topic for writing), and that Tom's quest for reality has about it something of adolescent romanticism. Tom comes under the influence of his father (who ran away from his responsibilities), and he depends heavily on Hollywood movies. This brings up another point: It is obvious that Amanda, Laura, and Tom cherish illusions, but students sometimes do not see that Williams suggests that all members of society depended in some measure on the illusions afforded by movies, magazine fiction, liquor, dance halls, sex, and other things that "flooded the world with brief, deceptive rainbows," while the real world of Berchtesgaden, moving toward World War II, was for a while scarcely seen. If Amanda, Laura, and Tom are outsiders living partly on illusions, so is everyone else, including Jim, whose identification with the myth of science may strike most views as hopelessly out of touch with reality.

The Glass Menagerie has twice been filmed, most recently in 1987, directed by Paul Newman. Newman followed Williams's sequence of scenes, and he kept almost all the dialogue, yet the film strikes us as unsuccessful. Why? Probably this "memory play" needs to be somewhat distanced, framed by a proscenium. Further, the film's abundant close-ups seem wrong; they make the play too energetic, too aggressive. Such are our impressions; instructors who rent the film (Cineplex Odeon) can ask students to set forth their own impressions—in writing.

An audiocassette of Tennessee Williams reading is available from HarperCollins.

ADDITIONAL TOPICS FOR CRITICAL THINKING AND WRITING

1.   Comedy in The *Glass Menagerie.* (Students should be cautioned that comedy need not be "relief." It can help to modify the tragic aspects, or rather, to define a special kind of tragedy. A few moments spent on the Porter scene in *Macbeth*—with which almost all students are familiar— will probably help to make clear the fact that comedy may be integral.)

2.   Compare the function of Tom with the function of the Chorus in *Antigone.* (Williams calls his play a "memory play." What we see is supposed to be the narrator's memory—not the dramatist's representation—

of what happened. Strictly speaking, the narrator is necessarily unreliable in the scene between Laura and Jim, for he was not present, but as Williams explains in the "Production Notes," what counts is not what happened but what the narrator remembers as having happened or, more exactly, the narrator's response to happenings.)

3.   Cinematic techniques in *The Glass Menagerie*. (Among these are fade-ins and fade-outs; projected titles, reminiscent of titles in silent films; the final "interior pantomime" of Laura and Amanda, enacted while Tom addresses the audience, resembles by its silence a scene from silent films, or a scene in a talking film in which the sound track gives a narrator's voice instead of dramatic dialogue. By the way, it should be noted that Williams, when young, like Tom, often attended movies, and that this play was adapted from Williams's rejected screen play, *The Gentleman Caller*, itself derived from one of Williams's short stories.) Topic 3 and 4 are ways of getting at the importance of *un*realistic settings and techniques in this "memory play."

4.   Compare the play with the earlier Williams short story, "Portrait of a Girl in Class," in *One Arm and Other Stories*.

EDWARD ALBEE

The Sandbox (p. 557)

We begin by offering a few generalizations about the "theater of the absurd" (it got its name from Martin Esslin's useful critical study, *The Theatre of the Absurd*), and then turn to Albee's play.

Some students may already have read a play by Beckett or Ionesco, or perhaps another play by Albee, and they can be encouraged to try to define the type by seeing what *The Sandbox* shares with what they have read earlier. We think it is fairly accurate to say that an "absurd" play usually has most of the following characteristics:

1.   The plays are "theatrical" rather than realistic, often setting forth obviously impossible situations with obviously unreal characters.

2.   The works are serious but often (or at least intermittently) comic, especially satiric.

3.   The basic themes are
      (a)   human loneliness in a world without God;
      (b)   the inability to communicate;
      (c)   the dehumanization and impotence of individuals in a bourgeois society;
      (d)   the meaninglessness of death.

4.   Characters behave illogically, speak in clichés, rarely if ever communicate
      with each other, and seem to have no clearly defined coherent character.
5.   The plays are relatively plotless (nothing much seems to happen).

So far as *The Sandbox* goes, the last two points need considerable modifica-
tion. Mommy and Daddy certainly speak in clichés, but they are fairly
coherent (Mommy is stupid and cruel, or at least cold; Daddy is vapid), and
so far as plot goes, death comes to Grandma. The play thus ends in a rather
conventional way, especially when compared (for example) to *Waiting for
Godot,* whose ending is open, ambiguous, unresolved: The characters
announce that they will leave but remain on the stage. The other characteristics in our list are evident in *The Sandbox.*

We have suggested approaching the play by drawing on students' famil-
iarity with some other play of the type. If, however, most students are unfamiliar with any plots of the "theater of the absurd"—or even if they are familiar with some—you may prefer from the start to deal with the play itself, or
perhaps with the play in the light of the quotations from Albee and Esslin
given in the questions appended to the text.

We prefer, if the class will let us, to postpone discussion of the symbolism
of the sandbox, and to begin with easier material, Mommy and Daddy.
Mommy's callousness and moral imperceptiveness, like Daddy's vacuity, are
easily seen. One can begin with the description in the *dramatis personae.*
Mommy is "well-dressed" and "imposing." Now, there is nothing wrong with
being well-dressed, or even with being imposing, but students can easily see
that in the context of the play, "well-dressed" suggests materialism, a concern
for the self, and superficiality; "imposing," being self-centered and stupidly
cruel, Daddy is "small," "gray, thin," and in the play this comes to mean that
he is negligible, emasculated, and colorless,

Grandma is described as "tiny, wizened," but also as possessing "bright
eyes." That is, though physically weak, she is animated, spirited. We learn, too,
that she married a farmer (suggesting closeness to the soil, fertility, hard work)
when she was seventeen, was widowed when she was thirty, and was left to
raise her daughter "all by my lonesome. You can imagine what *that* was like."
This is not a loving maternal comment, but since we see the dreadful Mommy,
we can easily sympathize with Grandma. (In our experience, students often
start blaming Grandma for behavior that presumably made Mommy what she
is. We try to counter this by asking them if they really believe that *they* are what
their parents made them. Most students, we have found, are quite willing to
see the bad influence of parents on others, but not on themselves.)

Although Grandma at first utters the meaningless sounds that in much of
the "theater of the absurd" stand for the gibberish that passes for human conversation, she soon becomes articulate, engaging, and very human. Where
Mommy says nothing but an empty "Hello" and "Hello there" to the Young

Man, Grandma does "a mild double-take" at his inane "Hi," addresses coherent words to him, gives him "the once-over," and sizes him up ironically with "Bright, too." Of course Grandma is not precisely the sort of person one would like to have as one's own grandmother, but she has worked hard, and she has a sense of moral and intellectual values.

The Young Man—a simpleton who, appropriately, wants to be an actor, that is, wants not to have an identity of his own—begins merely as a hunk, a male beauty engaged in mindless repetitive physical activity, but he develops—in response to Grandma's vitality—into a more sympathetic, loving figure (he kisses Grandma), and his kiss brings her comfort and evokes from her a highly civilized response.

What of the sandbox? It seems clear to us that it is an image of the sterile world (contrasted with the farm of Grandma's earlier years): it stands for the barrenness of today's society, and it anticipates the grave.

Finally, brief though the play is, it can be put into the context of traditional tragedy; that is, it can be discussed as a play that (to use the Aristotelian terms introduced in text, 205) evokes both pity and terror.

CHAPTER 18

Innocence
and
Experience

PLATO

The Myth of the Cave (p. 563)

The form of the dialogue, of course, has a dramatic effectiveness (we see and hear the give-and-take), but it is also a philosophic device. We arrive at a truth by asking questions and answering them, or by having other people try to answer them. In a dialogue, the problem is studied from more than one point of view, not simply to add opinion on top of opinion but to refute irrational points of view, thereby coming to a rational resolution. Moreover, this method (for the dialogues are imitations of Socrates' dialectic method) assumes that teaching is not so much a matter of pouring ideas into an empty head as it is a matter of drawing out ideas that are dormant in the soul. Perhaps one of the grandest things that Socrates taught through his dialectic method was that we can find answers ourselves if we are skeptical of authority and if we ask ourselves questions.

We have spoken of a rational resolution, and of course when one thinks of Plato (or of Socrates) one thinks of reason. But one also thinks of Plato's occasional myths, such as "The Myth of the Cave." These myths work, we might say, poetically; they supplement rational discourse by providing us with images that make us see and feel. Take, as a simple example, the passage in which Socrates asks Glaucon to imagine chained prisoners in a cave, looking at shadows, and Glaucon is moved—as we are—to say, "You have shown me a strange image, and they are strange prisoners." Socrates' cool but startling response is, "Like ourselves." Here we are not convinced rationally; surely we feel as well as see.

Question 3 following the text, on the painfulness involved in learning, can be related effectively to Toni Cade Bambara's story "The Lesson" (pages 993-999), where Sylvia experiences pain and shows irritation.

About question 4, concerning metaphoric uses of light as intellectual comprehension—in addition to "enlighten" and "illuminate" and "see," expressions such as, "to throw light on a subject," "to clarify," "to clear up," "it dawned on me," and "I had a bright idea" are relevant.

TOPIC FOR CRITICAL THINKING AND WRITING

According to "The Myth of the Cave," what emotions do the unenlight-ened prisoners feel? What emotions do the freed people feel? (We want students to notice that the prisoners compete for "honors and glories" and "fight with one another about shadows only." These prisoners—such is the complacency of ignorance—ridicule the enlightened person. Note too, that the enlightened person pities the prisoners but has no wish to go back into the cave to enlighten them. Our point: these characters are not flat abstractions but are indeed "like ourselves.")

MAYA ANGELOU

Graduation (p. 570)

Many students do not perceive that the elevated or heroic diction of the first part (e.g., "glorious release," "nobility" "like travelers with exotic destinations" all in paragraph 1) is an essential prelude to the descent in the middle ("It was awful to be Negro"). Neither do these students see the comedy, mixed of course with pathos, in such a passage as "My academic work was among the best of the year. I could say the preamble to the Constitution even faster than Bailey." Nor, often, do they see the comedy in the paragraph beginning with "The school band": "We stood," "we sat," "we rose again," "we remained standing for a brief minute before the choir director and the principal signaled to us, rather desperately I thought, to take our seats." Nor do they always real-ize, even after finishing the essay, that this confusion about sitting and stand-ing resulted from the deletion of the Negro national anthem, presumably out of deference to the white speaker. The difficult thing about teaching this essay, then, is showing some students that they missed a good part of an essay that they read with ease and believed they fully understood. Probably they miss some of the comedy because they can scarcely believe that an essay on graduation can be even partly amusing—unless it is an out-and-out spoof.

We try, then, in teaching this chapter from *I Know Why the Caged Bird Sings*, to help students see the difference between the youthful (and, from an adult's point of view, touching yet amusing) excitement and confidence of the beginning, and the mature, partly understated knowledge of the final three paragraphs. In this narration of the movement from innocence to experience, the last paragraph is especially tightlipped and tough-minded, with its "If we were a people much given to revealing secrets," "slavery cured us of that weakness," and "it may be enough, however..."

TOPICS FOR CRITICAL THINKING AND WRITING

1.   Question 3 following the essay can be used as an assignment for writing one paragraph; question 2 for a brief essay of two to four paragraphs.
2.   In 500 to 750 words describe your own graduation from grade school or high school. (Before setting out on your first draft, think about your experience and jot down some words that summarize your chief impression—"exciting," "boring," "hot," "nervous," "disappointing," "fun," or whatever. Think about these, and pick out one or two that on reflection seem truest to the experience. You may even choose two that are contradictory. Then, with this as a thesis, jot down supporting details, and finally begin to draft your essay.)
3.   Narrate an experience that disclosed a lesson of some value to you. (Students should be cautioned not to look exclusively at momentous events in their lives or to expect to make startling discoveries. Most of us can, on reflection, recall experiences from which we learned—however dimly we perceived the lesson at the time—something that was and continues to be of value to us.)
4.   "From Innocence to Experience—A Comparison of 'Graduation' and 'The Lesson'" (Toni Cade Bambara's "The Lesson," text p. 579).

NATHANIEL HAWTHORNE

Dr. Heidegger's Experiment (p. 579)

Wryness rather than cynicism, and sympathy rather than bitter mockery characterize this story about the inability of some fallen people to recognize that perfection is not of this world. The narrator's tone (a good subject for class discussion) is of course largely responsible for the way in which a reader interprets the plot of any story, and here most readers find a rather genial narrator rather than a currish fellow. Students can be invited to consider the first seven words,

"That very singular man, old Dr. Heidegger." To help them, you might invent a new opening sentence, such as "A certain old man, Dr. Heidegger...," and ask them to consider the difference. To our ear Hawthorne's opening, with "That," implies that we already have some knowledge of Dr. Heidegger; presumably we have heard of him; at least the narrator, caught up in his thoughts about Heidegger, seems to assume that we know of the doctor. And surely "singular," at least in this context along with "old Dr. Heidegger," suggests that the speaker has in mind some sort of engaging (i.e., sympathetic) eccentric. In short, Hawthorne's opening words establish a degree of intimacy between narrator and subject, and between subject and reader. The story is largely an exposure of folly—the folly of others, not of Dr. Heidegger—but the narrator's tone is benign, whereas a cynic's tone is unsympathetic and scoffing.

The story is largely the exposure of "folly" rather than of "evil," because the antics of the rejuvenated oldsters seem comic, but of course the story does not overlook evil. Heidegger's warning to his guests includes the words "sin" and "shame," and so their subsequent behavior is to be regarded (or at least *may* be regarded) as wicked. Nor is immoral behavior first introduced at this point; the opening paragraph hints at avarice (Mr. Nedbourne's "frantic speculation") and at assorted other vices. Still, the first paragraph presents the four visitors with some sympathy; looking at the old wrecks, Hawthorne seems more inclined to smile at than to denounce the errors of their youth. The comment, for instance, that the three men were once at each other's throats is not so much a cynical comment as it is a reminder that the angry passions of our youth fortunately do not always endure. It quickly becomes clear, of course, that Hawthorne is being ironic in his first sentence when he calls the four visitors "venerable," but they are now so decayed, and their behavior is so absurd, that they seem foolish rather than wicked. In one passage, however, their folly turns ugly: when heightened with the potion, the "merry youngsters" felt

> an impulse to mock the infirmity and decrepitude of which they had so lately been victims. They laughed loudly at their old-fashioned attire.... One limped across the floor, like a gouty grandfather; one set a pair of spectacles astride of his nose, and pretended to pore over the black-letter pages of the book of magic; a third seated himself in an armchair, and strove to imitate the venerable dignity of Dr. Heidegger.

It is convenient at this point to comment on the doctor. Like his visitors, he is old; the word "venerable" here, of course, is not ironic. And like his visitors, he once had aspirations, for what is a doctor but a person who aspires to restore the sick to health? But early in the story, in the second paragraph, we hear of a terrible reversal: Dr. Heidegger administered medicine to his beloved, and she died of the treatment. The narrator does not explicitly tell us that this experience purged the doctor of high hopes, or reconciled him to death, but as we read the story we are forced to believe that Heidegger understands that unchanging perfection embodied in the portrait of Sylvia Ward—is not the way of life. This knowledge separates old Heidegger from his four old guests, who, after drinking the potion, repeat the errors of their youth, revealing an inclination toward violence motivated by greed, jealousy, and sensuality.

The second question in the text asks about Dr. Heidegger's study. A list of its properties (cobwebs, a skeleton, and other usual paraphernalia of Gothic stories and films) suggests that it is the study of a mad scientist, the sort of place intended to thrill readers. But consider the way in which Hawthorne describes it. To take a single example, Hawthorne says the study is "festooned with cobwebs," thereby making the cobwebs decorative rather than menacing. Hawthorne is not, in fact, presenting the doctor as a mad scientist or as a diabolical figure. If anything, the "venerable" doctor, seated in his armchair and beholding the follies of the people he has (in a sense) newly created, seems almost godlike. But (as many students will say) this is going pretty far; it's better to say that Heidegger presents us with a bittersweet pageant showing human folly and—in his own behavior—a pattern of virtue.

Only one extended discussion thus far has been of some interest, Lawrence E. Scanlon's "That Very Singular Man, Dr. Heidegger," Nineteenth-Century Fiction, 17 (1962-63), 253-63. To support his assertion that the story contains "lighter elements," Scanlon finds it necessary to argue at length that the names of Hawthorne's five characters all evoke names of people who were associated with the theater: George Gascoigne (1525?-77), Thomas Killigrew (1612-83), William Wycherley (1640?-1716), Matthew Medbourne (d. 1679), and John James Heidegger (1659-1749). The last two of these are very minor figures, but Hawthorne could indeed have come across their names. In any case, Scanlon suggests that the theatrical evocation should help us to see the doings in Heidegger's study "as a kind of experiment or masquerade."

Scanlon's main point, however, is that a bumbling physician such as Dr. Heidegger (who accidentally killed his beloved, and who now engages in such trivial scientific experiments as "the murder of a mouse in an air pump") could not really possess an elixir of life; the effervescent fluid must, therefore, be "champagne or some equally potent liquor." Hawthorne of course never says that the four drinkers actually are transformed by a magic drink; indeed, he says that the seeming change is "not unlike what might have been produced by a glass of generous wine." He reports, too, that "the tall mirror is said to have reflected the figures of the three old, gray, withered grandsires, ridiculously contending for the skinny ugliness of a shriveled grandam." Notice also such expressions as the assertion that the four "*fancied* that some magic power had readily begun to smooth away the deep and sad inscriptions which Father Time had been so long engraving on their brows." Scanlon's point is that Dr. Heidegger, presiding over a revel, deceives his friends into thinking they are young. Scanlon argues that if (as he believes) Heidegger uses liquor rather than an elixir, the story is "a good deal less solemn than it is usually thought to be." The broad moral point in any case remains: the four visitors reveal that they have learned nothing from their long experience, and Heidegger asserts that a second chance is not worth the effort.

Scanlon's view that the story is not especially solemn is evident throughout the story and it does not depend on associating the five names with persons of the theater. One of Scanlon's other points must be mentioned. He suggests that in Dr. Heidegger Hawthorne presents a sort of comic view of himself as one who tries to bring back the past: Heidegger with his elixir, Hawthorne with his tales (such as "The Maypole of Merry Mount") set in olden times. The magic powers of Heidegger and Hawthorne last only a few moments; Heidegger's butterfly and the rose wither, Hawthorne's evocations of the past last only until a reader closes the book.

For a good survey of the rather weak commentary that the story has evoked, see Lea B. V. Newman, *A Reader's Guide to the Short Stories of Nathaniel Hawthorne* (1979).

JAMES JOYCE

Araby (p. 586)

Probably the best discussion of "Araby" remains one of the earliest, that of Cleanth Brooks and Robert Penn Warren in *Understanding Fiction*. Among more recent discussions, L. J. Morrissey, "Joyce's Narrative Strategies in 'Araby'" *Modern Fiction Studies* 28 (1982): 45-52, is especially good.

Students have difficulty with the story largely because they do not read it carefully enough. They scan it for what happens (who goes where) and do not pay enough attention to passages in which (they think) "nothing is happening." But when students read passages aloud in class, for instance the first three paragraphs, they *do* see what is going on (that is, they come to understand the boy's mind) and enjoy the story very much. To help them hear the romantic boy who lives in what is (from an adult point of view) an unromantic society it is especially useful to have students read aloud passages written in different styles. Compare, for instance, "At night in my bedroom and by day in the classroom her image came between me and the page I strove to read" with "I asked for leave to go to the bazaar on Saturday night. My aunt was surprised and hoped it was not some Freemason affair."

That the narrator is no longer a boy is indicated by such passages as the following:

her name was like a summons to all my foolish blood.

Her name sprang to my lips at moments in strange prayers and praise which I myself did not understand. My eyes were often full of tears (I voted not tell why).

What innumerable follies laid waste my waking and sleeping thoughts....

Morrissey points out that in addition to distancing himself from his past actions by such words as "foolish" and "follies" (and, at the end of the story, "vanity"), the narrator distances himself from the boy he was by the words "imagined" and "seemed," words indicating that his present view differs from his earlier view.

The narrator recounts a story of disillusionment. The first two paragraphs clearly establish the complacent middle-class world into which he is born—the houses "conscious of decent lives within them" gaze with "imperturbable faces." This idea of decency is made concrete by the comment in the second paragraph that the priest's charity is evident in his will: He left all of his money to institutions and his furniture to his sister. (Probably even the sister was so decent that she too thought this was the right thing to do.) Morrissey, interpreting the passage about the priest's will differently, takes the line to be the boy's innocent report of "what must have been an ironic comment by adults."

As a boy he lived in a sterile atmosphere, a sort of fallen world:

The house is in a "blind" or dead-end street.
The rooms are musty.
The priest had died (religion is no longer vital?).
A bicycle pump, once a useful device, now lies rusty and unused under a bush in the garden.
An apple tree in the center of the garden in this fallen world.
Nearby are the odors of stable and garbage dumps.

Nevertheless the boy is quickened by various things, for instance by the yellow pages of an old book, but especially by Mangan's sister (who remains unnamed, perhaps to suggest that the boy's love is spiritual). He promises to visit " Araby" (a bazaar) and to return with a gift for her.

The boy for a while moves through a romantic, religious world:

He sees her "image".
He imagines that he carries a "chalice."
He hears the "litanies" and "chanting" of vendors. He utters "strange prayers."

Delayed by his uncle, whose inebriation is indicated by the uncle's "talking to himself" and by "the hall-stand rocking" (his parents seem not to be living; notice the emphasis on the boy's isolation throughout the story, e.g. his ride alone in the car of the train), he hears the clerks counting the days' receipts—moneychangers in the temple.

"The light was out. The upper part of the hall was now completely dark." The darkness and the preceding trivial conversations of a girl and two young women reveal—Joyce might have said epiphanize—the emptiness of the world. The boy has journeyed to a rich, exotic (religious?) world created by his imagination and has found it cold and trivial, as dead as the neighborhood he lives in.

The boy's entry through the shilling entrance rather than through the sixpenny (children's) entrance presumably signals his coming of age.

This brief discussion of "Araby" of course seems reasonable to its writer, even the remarks that the rusty bicycle pump suggests a diminished world, and that the entry through the shilling entrance rather than the sixpenny entrance suggests, implies, or even—through one hesitates to use word—symbolizes (along with many other details) his initiation into an adult view. But how far can (or should) one press the details? An article in *James Joyce Quarterly* 4 (1967): 85-86 suggests that the pump under the bushes stands for the serpent in the garden. Is there a difference between saying that the rusty pump—in the context of the story—puts a reader in mind of a diminished (deflated) world, and saying that it stands for the serpent? Is one interpretation relevant, and the other not? Students might be invited to offer their own views on how far to look for "meaning" or "symbols" in this story, or in any other story. They might also be advised to read—but not necessarily to swallow—the brief discussions of symbolism in the text and in the glossary.

An audio cassette of James Joyce reading is available from HarperCollins.

TOPICS FOR CRITICAL THINKING AND WRITING

1. What do the first two paragraphs tell us about the boy's environment? What does the second paragraph tell us about his nature?
2. Of course none of us can speak authoritatively about what life was *really* like in Dublin around 1900, but would you say that Joyce gives—insofar as space allows—a realistic picture of Dublin? If so, was his chief aim to give the reader a slice of Dublin life? What do you think Joyce wants us to believe that life in Dublin was like?
3. The boy says that when his uncle returned he heard his uncle talking to himself, and he heard the hallstand (coattree) rocking. Then he says, "I could interpret these signs." What do "these signs" mean? How is the uncle's behavior here consistent with other details of life in Dublin?
4. Reread the story, underlining or highlighting religious images. What is the point of these images?

FRANK O'CONNOR

Guests of the Nation (p. 590)

We once began teaching this story by asking, "What is this story about?" The first answer, "War," brought the reply, "Yes, but what about war? Is it, for example, about the heroism that war sometimes stimulates?" Another student replied, "No, it's about the cruelty of war." The point: though it is obvious to all instructors that the story is Bonaparte's, specifically about his growing up or initiation or movement from innocence to experience, this movement is not so evident to inexperienced readers.

This is not to say, of course, that it is not also about the conflict between the ideas of society and the ideals of the individuals. Jeremiah Donovan, though he thinks of himself as experienced, seems never to have grown up, never to have come to any sorrowful awareness of human loneliness. The bickering between Noble and Hawkins is, however, not a sign of enmity but a sort of bond. They may quarrel, but at least they share a relationship. Hawkins's offer to join the Irish cause indicates not so much his cowardice as his intuitive awareness that life and fellowship are more important than blind nationalism that excuses murder by an appeal to "duty."

Question 4, below, lends itself well to a theme. The old woman is a "simple... countrywoman," but she knows (as the narrator finds out) that "nothing but sorrow and want can follow the people that disturb the hidden powers." An interview with O'Connor in *Writers at Work,* edited by Malcolm Cowley, reveals some of O'Connor's ideas about fiction. Asked why he chose the short story as his medium, O'Connor said, "Because it's the nearest thing I know of to lyric poetry.... A novel actually requires far more logic and far more knowledge of circumstances, whereas a short story can have the sort of detachment from circumstances that lyric poetry has." O'Connor's ideas about the short story are expressed at some length in his book on the topic, *The Lonely Voice.*

HISAYE YAMAMOTO

Yoneko's Earthquake (p. 599)

Despite the title, the story can be thought of primarily as the mother's story, rather than as Yoneko's; that is why the questions below concentrate on the mother.

On the other hand, it is entirely right that classroom discussion consider Yoneko in some detail. Strictly speaking, the story is not told from her point of view, but we nevertheless learn of the events as she sees them. Students might be invited to discuss her character in an effort to help them see that part of a reader's interest in the story depends on perceiving the gap between what Yoneko sees (she is a sort of innocent eye) and what the reader understands to have happened—first between Mrs. Hosoume and Marpo (they have had an affair, and Mrs. Hosoume has become pregnant), then to Mrs. Hosoume (she has an abortion, and when Seigo dies she takes his death as a punishment visited upon her by God for having taken the life of the fetus), and finally to Mr. Hosoume (he seeks to comfort his wife). One might say, perhaps a bit too simply, that Yoneko's loss of Christian faith is ironically contrasted with Mrs. Hosoume's acquisition of Christian faith, and with Mr. Hosoume's ultimate Christian (charitable) behavior. But this way of putting things makes the story sound too solemn: it is largely Yoneko's engaging character that gives the reader immediate pleasure. The story is in many ways warm and even humorous.

If the title refers to Yoneko's loss of faith in God—a powerful experience—it also puts us in mind of the "earthquake"—the disastrous event—that the girl does *not* perceive. Is Yoneko to be regarded as conspicuously imperceptive? Surely not. She is an engaging child, genial, affectionate (despite her teasing of her brother), and in some ways thoughtful, as when she wonders if Jesus was exempted "from stinging eyes when he shampooed that long, naturally wavy hair of his." But, not unnaturally, she is more concerned with the pretty ring than with wondering about where it came from, and when (in the last two paragraphs) she perceives that her mother is examining "with peculiarly intent eyes," her distress at having lost the ring preoccupies her.

The domestic tragedy—how Mr. Hosoume's incapacitation leads to Mrs. Hosoume's increasing dependence on Marpo, and then to Mr. Hosoume's perception that his role has been (in one way or another) usurped—is perceived only dimly by Yoneko, who is "thunderstruck" when her father slaps her mother, but who does not understand the implications. None of this should lead a reader to think that Yoneko is in any way slow, though perhaps today, when the issue of abortion is aired daily on television, the unstated happenings of the story might seem evident even to a youngster.

JOHN UPDIKE

A & P (p. 608)

It may be useful for students to characterize the narrator and see if occasionally Updike slips. Is "crescent," in the third sentence too apt a word for a speaker who a moment later says, "She gives me a little snort," and "If she'd been born at the right time they would have burned her over in Salem"? If this is a slip, it is more than compensated for by the numerous expressions that are just right.

Like Frank O'Connor's "Guests of the Nation," "A & P" is a first-person story, and in its way is also about growing up. Invite students to characterize the narrator as precisely as possible. Many will notice his hope that the girls will observe his heroic pose, and some will notice, too, his admission that he doesn't want to hurt his parents. His belief (echoing Lengel's) that he will "feel this for the rest of his life" is also adolescent. But his assertion of the girls' innocence is attractive and brave.

Some readers have wondered why Sammy quits. Nothing in the story suggests that he is a political rebel, or that he is a troubled adolescent who uses the episode in the A & P as a cover for some sort of adolescent emotional problem An extremely odd article in *Studies in Short Fiction*, 23 (1986): 321-23, which seeks to connect Updike's story with Hawthorne's "Young Goodman Brown," says that "Sammy's sodden quitting is not only a way of attracting the girls' attention but also a way of punishing himself for lustful thoughts." Surely this is nonsense, even further off the mark than the same author's assertion that Queenie's pink bathing suit "suggests the emerging desires competing with chastity" (322). Sammy quits because he wants to make a gesture on behalf of these pretty girls, who in appearance and in spirit (when challenged, they assert themselves) are superior to the "sheep" and to the tedious Lengel. Of course Sammy hopes his gesture will be noticed, but in any case the gesture is sincere.

What sort of fellow is Sammy? Is he a male chauvinist pig? An idealist? A self-satisfied deluded adolescent? Someone who thinks he is knowledgeable but who is too quick to judge some people as sheep? Maybe all of the above, in varying degrees. Certainly his remark that the mind of a girl is "a little buzz, like a bee in a glass jar," is outrageous—but later he empathizes with the girls, seeing them not as mindless and not as mere sex objects but as human beings who are being bullied. If we smile a bit at his self-dramatization ("I felt how hard this world was going to be to me hereafter"), we nevertheless find him endowed with a sensitivity that is noticeably absent in Lengel.

TOPIC FOR CRITICAL THINKING AND WRITING

Sammy: comic yet heroic?

LILIANA HEKER

The Stolen Party (p. 613)

This short, easy story can be effectively taught early in the semester; in conjunction with chapter 7 it can even be used as a sort of textbook model to illustrate principles of irony, foreshadowing, character, plot, conflict, and symbolism.

The story begins with a conflict between the mother and the daughter; the mother proves to be right (not about the monkey but about a more important matter, the way in which rich people perceive their servants), but the point of the story is neither to vindicate the mother nor to emphasize the opposition between mother and daughter. Midway in the story we are sure that the mother in fact is fond and proud of her daughter, and by the end we find ourselves responding very sympathetically to the mother.

Señora Ines bothers some of the students, who say that she snobbishly puts Rosaura in her place. But one may doubt that there is any malice, and one may even argue that Señora Ines is courteous, charming, and sincere. She just can't help thinking of Rosaura as part of "the help." It is not surprising that Señora Ines offers Rosaura money; probably she is right in assuming that the family can use a little extra cash. True, a more imaginative woman might at the outset have understood that the child would like a gift comparable to (or better than!) the gifts given to the other children, whereas Señora Ines comes to that understanding only when Rosaura's arms stiffen. Still, Señora Ines *does* come to this understanding; a less intelligent or less sympathetic person would not have understood or even noticed the child's response. Señora Ines is guilty, then, of a lack of insight, a lack of sympathetic imagination that would take her beyond social distinctions, but nothing in the story suggests that she is not well-intentioned .

What of Señora Ines's evaluations of Rosaura, such as "What a marvelous daughter you have, Herminia," and "You really and truly earned this"? Of course, having seen Rosaura carry a jug of juice, and serve cake, Señora Ines is impressed with Rosaura as a domestic servant, but Rosaura had won Señora Ines's praise even before performing these tasks: "How lovely you look today, Rosaura." And if Señora Ines allows Rosaura to enter the kitchen, where the monkey is, we can conjecture that permission is granted not just for one reason but for two reasons: Rosaura, as "the daughter of the employee," is familiar with the kitchen, but second, Rosaura *is* (as Señora Ines says) better behaved than the "boisterous" children. Rosaura's superior nature soon is confirmed when she is contrasted with the fat boy who drops the monkey. Presumably her virtues are evident to all—except to the snobbish girl with the bow.

The point of these remarks is this: although Señora Ines destroys the day by offering Rosaura money—i.e., by revealing that Rosaura doesn't quite belong among the guests—she need not be thought of as cruel or even as stupid. She seems to us to be a person of intelligence and good will, but she cannot quite go beyond the way persons of her class think.

What is a reader to make out of the comment that Rosaura "had always loved… having power of life or death?" This remark, which might surprise some readers, might well characterize a wicked queen in a fairy tale. Still, readers do not judge her severely; despite the unexpected revelation, Rosaura remains attractive. Or, possibly, there is nothing at all sinister in the remark. It might characterize a precocious child, already better educated than her mother, who smarts at her mother's position, language, and distrust of the people whom the child loves and seeks to emulate (the people "who live in the big house"). That is, in this view it is both psychologically and politically sound for her to wish for power—and indeed she is a forceful figure, the winner of the sack race and a person whom the boys want on their side.

PATRICIA GRACE

Butterflies (p. 617)

Because this story is very short and very engaging, it can be used as a way of introducing students to fiction. One can, for instance, discuss the effectiveness of the objective point of view. It seems to us that much of the charm of the story is that we do *not* get inside any of the characters' minds. We don't need to hear what the grandparents think. We know all we need to know from the few things that they say: they are respectful of knowledge and authority (the teacher); they are proud of their granddaughter, and they want her to succeed. In fact, the delightful suspense evoked by the last paragraph, in which the grandparents "were quiet for a long time," would be destroyed if we were brought inside their minds. In its present form, the reader waits, wondering what the oldsters will say, and then we get exactly the right statement.

Stories about innocence and experience usually concern the innocence of a child. Here we do get an innocent child, but, more important, we get an innocent adult, the well-meaning but naive teacher. And we realize that the grandparents, despite their uneducated speech, are wiser than the teacher.

TOPIC FOR WRITING

Students can write a paragraph concerning the first question in the text *before* they come to class. Or, you can close discussion of the story by having students write a paragraph *in* class.

WILLIAM BLAKE

Infant Joy (p. 619)

In addition to the infant there is a second speaker, an adult—presumably the mother, but nothing in the text rules out the possibility that the adult speaker is the father.

The infant speaks the first two lines, the adult (asking what to call the infant) speaks the third. The infant replies, "I happy am, / Joy is my name," and the adult is then moved to say, "Sweet joy befall thee." Is it too subtle to detect a difference between the infant, who knows only that it is happy, and the adult, who, in saying "Sweet joy befall thee" is introducing (to the edges of our mind, or, rather, to the depths of our mind) the possibility that—life being what it is—joy may *not* befall the infant? That is, even here, in the *Songs of Innocence*, we may detect an awareness of a fallen world, a world where in fact people do not always encounter "Sweet joy."

The second stanza apparently is spoken entirely by the adult, but the language of the first two lines ("Pretty joy! / Sweet joy but two days old") is close to the language of the infant—not to the language of a real infant, of course, but to the language of Blake's infant, who began the poem by saying "I have no name, I am but two years old." Still, there is a difference between the speakers. The mother sings (a lullaby?), partly out of her own joy, and partly, perhaps, to reassure the infant (at least that is more or less the function of lullabies in real life). Speaking of lullabies, elsewhere in the text we include Willa Cather's poem of a mother singing to a child.

What of Blake's illustration for the poem? The best discussion of the picture is Andrew Lincoln's, in his edition of Blake's *Songs of Innocence and Experience* (1991), which is volume 2 in the series called *Blake's Illuminated Books*, gen. ed. David Bindman. We quote Lincoln's chief points:

> The figures within the opened petals enact an Adoration scene. A mother in a blue dress nurses a baby in her lap, while a winged girl-angel stands with arms reaching out towards the infant.

> The petals of the flower seem protective, although those that curl over from the left may suggest containment, hinting perhaps at the potential constraints that face the newborn child.

> There are other images of constraint here. In the design, the drooping bud at the right may recall the temporal process in which flowers unfold and decay, while in the song joy is at once a present state of being and a hope for an uncertain future.

WILLIAM BLAKE

Infant Sorrow (p. 620)

In "Infant Joy" we saw not only the child's view but also the parent's. Here we see only the child's view, which regards the adult embrace not as an act of love but as a threatening constraint. It's not a question of which view—"Infant Joy" or "Infant Sorrow"—is truer. Both are true. In "Infant Sorrow" Blake lets us see life from the point of view of the infant, a creature who is helpless, distrustful of the parents, presciently aware that it has entered a "dangerous world" and aware that its cries sound like those of a "fiend" to all who cannot understand its distress.

The first stanza emphasizes physical actions—of the mother in labor, of the sympathetic father, and of the babe itself ("piping loud"). There is action in the second stanza too, but there is also something more; there is thought, really strategy. Confined by the father at the beginning of the second stanza, the infant decides it is best to turn to the mother ("I thought best / To sulk upon my mother's breast"), but in any case the infant is still trapped.

Andrew Lincoln points out that the illustration seems to represent a rather "comfortable and secure interior." He goes on to say that "In the light of the poem, the protection that surrounds the child here must itself seem threatening, potentially stifling."

WILLIAM BLAKE

The Echoing Green (p. 621)

E. M. W. Tillyard discusses this poem in *Poetry Direct and Oblique*. Among his points are these:

> Blake "finds in the traditional village sports and pieties a type of his world of innocence";

> The poem moves from dawn in the first stanza, to midday in the second (presumably Old John sits under an oak to protect himself from the noonday sun), to evening in the third stanza, and thus "the form is a stylized day-cycle";

> beginning and end are balanced (echoing green, darkening green; waking birds, birds in their nest);

> "the old unfreeze and join their mirth to make up a full chorus with children."

According to Tillyard, all of this is an indirect way of expressing "desire satisfied" and "fruition." He goes on: "At the end of the 'echoing green' is 'the darkening green' because its function is fulfilled." All of this seems reasonable to us, if fulfillment is recognized as including weariness and the coming of darkness.

Some other points: Who is the speaker? Apparently a young person, if one leans on lines 9 ("our sports"), 15 ("our play"), and 24 ("our sports"), but not a child; the vision is that of a mature person, at least someone mature enough to know that "our sports have an end."

In the first stanza, one action almost automatically generates the next: the sun rises, making the skies happy; the merry bells ring, stimulating the birds, who "Sing louder around / To the bells' chearful sound."

Why "echoing green"? Because it resounds with the noise of children playing, of course, but also because the children are a renewed version of the old people, or, to put it the other way around, the old people are the distant echoes of the children. There are other echoes, too, in the repeated words: the title is repeated in the last lines of the first and second stanzas, and it is varied ("the darkening green") at the end of the third stanza. Other repeated words are "sun" (1, 23), "bells" (3, 6), "birds" (6, 27), "seen" (9, 19, 29), "sports" (9, 24, 29), "laugh" (12, 15), "such" (in 17 we get "Such, such").

Allen Ginsberg sings "The Echoing Green" on *Songs of Innocence and Experience by William Blake, Tuned by Allen Ginsberg.*

GERARD MANLEY HOPKINS

Spring and Fall: To a Young Child (p. 622)

In our experience, students will have considerable difficulty if they simply read the poem silently to themselves, but if they read (and reread) it aloud, it becomes clear—and more important, it becomes something they value.

We begin, then, as we usually do with poems, by having a student read the poem aloud, and then we invite comments about the title and its connection with the two people in the poem. Students usually see that the poem presents youth and age, that Margaret is associated with spring and the speaker with the fall, and this leads to discussion of the Fall in Christian thought. Many students, however, do not know that in Christian thought the disobedience of Adam and Eve brought consequences that extended to nature, and that the perennial spring of Eden therefore yielded to autumn and winter; that is, "Goldengrove" inherited death. ("Goldengrove," incidentally, might seem to suggest preciousness and eternity, but here the golden leaves are a sign of transience and death.)

In the original version of "Spring and Fall" (1880), line 8 ran, "Though forests low and leafmeal lie." When he revised the poem in 1884, Hopkins changed "Though forests low and" to "Though worlds of wanwood," thus introducing the pallor of "wanwood" and also wonderfully extending the vista from "forests" to "worlds." Margaret's sorrow for the trees stripped of their golden foliage is finally sorrow for the Fall, whose consequences are everywhere. Her mouth cannot formulate any of this, but her spirit has intuited it ("ghost guessed").

On "Spring and Fall," see Paul L. Mariani, *A Commentary on the Complete Poems of Gerard Manley Hopkins*; Marylou Motto, *The Poetry of Gerard Manley Hopkins*; and Peter Milward's essay in Milward and R. V. Schoder, *Landscape and Inscape*. George Starbuck has a modern version ("Translations from the English") in his book of poems, *White Paper*.

A. E. HOUSMAN

When I Was One-and-Twenty (p. 623)

The "wise man" seems to offer two pieces of wisdom, but they are closely related. One is, in effect, "Don't give your heart away," that is, don't fall in love; the second is, "If you do give your heart away, you will suffer." The speaker ignored the advice, and now, at twenty-two, has learned its truth. The last line of the poem, with its repetition, suggests that the speaker takes his youthful sorrow very seriously ("And oh 'tis true, 'tis true"), but surely the line strikes readers (and is intended to strike them) as a trifle maudlin. And since the poem jingles nicely and almost suggests a nursery rhyme, we can hardly take the grief too seriously. We listen with sympathetic amusement to this tale of disillusionment.

E. E. CUMMINGS

in just (p. 624)

Of course a reader's response to any sort of print on a page is partly conditioned by the appearance of the page. Nice margins and creamy paper can make a so-so story seem pretty good, and double columns and thin paper that allows for show-through can make reading even an absorbing work difficult. And probably any poet would be distressed to find the first twelve lines of his or her sonnet printed on a right-hand page, and the final couplet—invisible to the reader of the three quatrains—on the next page.

Our point, again, is that the physical appearance of any work counts, but of course with cummings's work it counts a great deal more, in a variety of ways. For instance, "eddieandbill" catches the child's way of speaking, and also conveys a sense of an inseparable pair, just as "bettyandisbel" does. (When the youngsters grow up, they will be Eddie and Betty, and Bill and Isabel, but cummings is giving us children in the stage when boys play with boys and girls with girls.) As for the variations in which the words "far and wee" appear, we can say only that the spaces (in line 5, "far and wee"; in line 13, "far   and   wee"; in lines 22-24, "far / and / wee") convey the variations in the balloonman's whistle, and the last of these perhaps suggests that he is moving away.

The allusion to Pan (via the goatfoot and the whistle) seems clear to us. Pan is the woodland god of Arcadia, a land usually depicted as a world of perpetual spring. Of course Pan is especially associated with the pursuit of nymphs, but cummings here gives us a rather sexless world, though we can hardly repress the thought that this world of childhood (with its inseparable boys and its inseparable girls) and of springtime play (marbles, dancing) will in time become something else.

One other point: Most students, in the course of class discussion, will see that the repeated "wee" (5, 13, 14) works several ways. The balloon man is "little" (3); his whistle makes the sound of "wee"; "wee" is a child's exclamation of delight; and "we" children go running to buy balloons.

e. e. cummings reads on two audiocassettes that are available from HarperCollins.

LOUISE GLÜCK

The School Children (p. 625)

On the surface, the poem seems loaded with pictures of cute children on their way to school, bringing the traditional apples for the teachers: "with their little satchels," "apples, red and gold," "their overcoats of blue or yellow wool." Even "how orderly they are" (said of the nails on which the children hang their coats) can be taken as a benign comment on this happy scene.

But of course by the time we finish the second stanza we realize that this is not a Norman Rockwell scene. The children must cross to "the other shore" where they are confronted by people "who wait behind great desks." Further, these people are not presented warmly. Rather, they are presented (we never *see* them) as godlike figures who wait "to receive these offerings."

The third stanza is perhaps even more menacing, with that orderly row of nails, waiting to accept the pretty coats. The text speaks—horribly—of "the nails / on which the children hang…." As we continue to read the sentence the meaning changes radically, of course, and we see that it is not the children but "their overcoats" that hang on the nails, but the thought lingers; the mind retains a vision of the children hanging from nails.

The last stanza reintroduces us to the teachers, who "shall instruct them in silence," a menacing expression that we take to mean (1) shall teach them silently (a terrifying way of teaching), and (2) shall teach them to be silent (a terrifying condition). The stanza does not end, however, with the teachers or with the children. Rather, it ends with the mothers, who "scour the orchards for a way out," i.e. who seek to equip their children with the "offerings" (line 7) that the gods require. That is, the mothers seek (by propitiating the gods) to protect their children from the severe socialization that awaits them, but it is already too late, because "the gray limbs of the fruit trees" (it is now autumn) bear "so little ammunition."

In the last stanza, why "The teachers *shall* instruct them," and "the mothers *shall* scour the orchards," rather than "will instruct" and "will scour"? Although older handbooks say that *shall* expresses simple futurity in the first person (and *will* expresses determination in the first person), it is our impression that *shall* has almost disappeared. Indeed, part of what made Douglas MacArthur's "I shall return" so memorable was that he used an unusual construction. To our ear, the use of *shall* in the last stanza of Glück's poem has a voice-of-doom quality; the teachers must act as they will, and the mothers must act as they will—and the children will be the victims.

LOUISE GLÜCK

Gretel in Darkness (p. 626)

In *New Voices in American Poetry*, ed. David Allan Evans (1973) 106, Ms. Glück comments on her poem:

To Hansel the escape from the forest was a means to an end: a future. To Gretel the escape is an end in itself. No moment in the ordinary existence she made possible by killing the witch and rescuing her brother can touch for her the moment of the escape. That moment was her triumph: it provided Gretel with an opportunity to experience herself as powerful. The whole episode, the drama in the forest, remains for her charged and present. It is in that episode that she wishes to imbed herself. Unfortunately, she is alone in this desire. Their adventure grows increasingly remote to Hansel, presumably because the new life answers his needs. The Gretel of the poem perceives, and passionately wishes to alter, the discrepancy between her investment in the forest and Hansel's.

WILLIAM SHAKESPEARE

The Tragedy of Hamlet, Prince of Denmark (p. 628)

Probably the best short study of *Hamlet* is Maynard Mack's "The World of Hamlet" *Yale Review* 41 (1952), 502-23, reprinted in the Signet paperback edition of *Hamlet*, in *Tragic Themes*, ed. Cleanth Brooks, and elsewhere. Maurice Charney's *Style in Hamlet* is excellent, and so too is Harley Granville-Barker's book-length essay in *Prefaces to Shakespeare*. For an essay that draws on the tenets of reader-response criticism, see Stephen Booth, "On the Value of *Hamlet*" in *Reinterpretations of Elizabethan Drama* (1969), 137-76.

The nature of the Ghost has produced a good deal of commentary, most of it summarized in Eleanor Prosser's *Hamlet and Revenge*. She says that for the Elizabethans a ghost can be only one of three things: the soul of a pagan (impossible in this play, for the context is Christian); a soul from Roman Catholic purgatory (impossible in this play, because it seeks revenge); or a devil (which is what Prosser says this Ghost is). Prosser argues that the Ghost is evil because it counsels revenge, it disappears at the invocation of heaven, and it disappears when the cock crows. But perhaps it can be replied that although the Ghost indeed acts suspiciously, its role is to build suspense and to contribute to the play's meaning, which involves uncertainty and the difficulty of sure action. Prosser sees Hamlet as a rebellious youth who deliberately mistreats Ophelia and descends deep into evil (e.g., he spares Claudius at his prayers only in order to damn him), but when he returns from England he is no longer the "barbaric young revenger... but a mature man of poise and serenity" (217). He is generous to the gravediggers and Laertes, "delightful" with Osric. In short, the young rebel has been chastened by experience and by the vision of death, and so he is saved. He "has fought his way out of Hell" (237). Prosser offers a useful corrective to the romantic idea of the delicate prince, as well as a great deal of information about the attitude toward ghosts, but one need not accept her conclusion that the Ghost is a devil; her evidence about ghosts is incontrovertible on its own grounds, but one may feel that, finally, the play simply doesn't square with Elizabethan popular thought about ghosts.

Note: As we mention on page 98 of this manual, the instructor may wish to teach *Hamlet* in connection with Frank O'Connor's "My Oedipus Complex" (in the section on "Love and Hate") and *Oedipus Rex* (in "Men, Women, God. and Gods"). We comment on the Oedipus complex in our discussion of the two works. The view that *Hamlet* can be explained by reference to the Oedipus complex is most fully set forth in Ernest Jones, *Hamlet and Oedipus*. Briefly, Jones's points are that Hamlet delays because of "some unconscious source of repugnance to his task"; this repugnance is rooted in the fact that Claudius had done what Hamlet unconsciously desired to do (kill Hamlet Senior and sleep with Gertrude). Thus far Jones follows Freud. But Jones adds another reason: The desire to kill the father is *repressed* in infancy, and this repression continues to operate in maturity, which means that Hamlet can scarcely act on his desire to kill Claudius, for Claudius is now in effect his father.

TOPICS FOR WRITING

Many of the questions printed in the text lend themselves to themes, but here are two more possibilities,

1. Cut 1,000 lines from the play so that it can be performed in a reasonable time, and justify your omissions.
2. The uses of prose in *Hamlet*.

CHAPTER 19

Love
and Hate

SEI SHONAGON

A Lover's Departure (p. 738)

Our first question in the text, concerning a reader's initial response and a subsequent response, derives from our experience in teaching this selection. On first reading it, most students don't see much here—they are too intent on looking for an important message. When they reread it, however, they usually enjoy the visual picture of the lover's departure, and, more important, they enjoy the strong irritation that Sei Shonagon displays at the end.

We are reminded of two remarks by John Keats: "The excellence of every Art is its intensity, capable of making all disagreeables evaporate," and

> the poetical character [i.e. the artist]... enjoys light and shade; it lives in gusto, be it foul or fair, high or low, rich or poor, mean or elevated—It has as much delight in conceiving an Iago as an Imogen.

So, too, readers delight in villains as well as heroes, or, in this case, we delight both in the lover's conceit and also in Sei Shonagon's detestation of him. (She was, of course, no Keats, no practitioner of "negative capability." Rather, she was what Keats called "the egotistical sublime," but this quality is part of what delights the reader.)

The second question in the text asks students to speculate about Sei Shonagon's personality. Almost nothing is known about her other than what she reveals in her book, but the book amply testifies to the one significant external comment about her, a remark in a diary by the other great prose writer of the period, Lady Murasaki (author of *The Tale of Genji*): "Sei Shonagon: The very picture of conceit and arrogance." Murasaki goes on to say that Shonagon is "pretentious," "inane," and "notorious for her triviality. Anyone who reads Shonagon's *Pillow-Book* (in Arthur Waley's translation, or, even better, in Ivan Morris's) will agree—but will probably also add, "yes, and isn't she marvelous!"

Our third question suggests that students emulate Sei Shonagon and write some observations about hateful things. Among Shonagon's entries are comments on an unwelcome visitor who chatters, elderly people who have the gall to warm themselves near a brazier in a most unceremonious way ("I have seen some dreary old creatures actually resting their feet on the brazier and rubbing them against the edge while they speak"), crying babies, and people who tell a story that she was about to tell. Her writings reveal her keen perceptions and her self-centeredness—and one doesn't know which to enjoy more. She apparently was the Erica Kane of her day.

JUDITH ORTIZ COFER

I Fell in Love, Or My Hormones Awakened (p. 739)

Our first question in the text asks about the humor in the essay. Almost every paragraph provides examples. For instance, in the first paragraph there is (in the first sentence) the comic drop from "I fell in love" to "my hormones awakened"; later in the paragraph we hear that she fell in love with "an older man"—a senior, when she was a first-year student. But the humor does not consist entirely in defeating the reader's expectations; much of it is in the author's genial presentation of her silly, romantic—and very human—self, for instance in the second paragraph the revelation that she drank milk, which she hated, so that she would have an excuse to go to the store to see the boy who worked there.

Nothing in the essay will cause readers any difficulty, we think, and it lends itself very well to writing assignments, some of which we suggest in the text.

GARY SOTO

Like Mexicans (p. 744)

There is of course a serious issue in the essay—the suggestion that poor people are pretty much all alike, i.e. that class is as least as significant as race—and we try to get at this issue in the first question in the text. We think, however, instructors in writing courses will also want to discuss Soto's strategies as a writer.

Chiefly he adopts a deadpan manner, as when he reports, without comment, his grandmother's view that Italians, Jews, and Asians are all okies, or that he should become a barber because barbers have good lives because "they made good money and listened to the radio all day" (although he does indeed comment on this point, calling it "bad advice"). The deadpan manner is most evident in the last two sentence of the first paragraph, where he communicates a slightly bawdy joke by *not* telling it but leaving it to the reader's imagination.

Repetition too plays a role. In traditional ballads we speak of incremental repetition, where slight variations advance the story ("Edward" is the classic example), but here we get, as in much comedy, something that might be called non-incremental repetition. Thus, when we first meet his mother, she is slapping a steak with a knife, and she agrees with him about becoming a barber and about marrying a Mexican girl; when we next meet her, she is slapping hamburger, and she agrees with him about marrying the Japanese girl.

OSCAR WILDE

The Happy Prince (p. 747)

We include this story for several reasons, partly in order to allow for discussion about very different kinds of love (*eros* and *agape*) and partly to allow for a possible gay reading of a story by a known gay writer.

When Wilde wrote the story, he had not yet become involved in the disastrous trial that led to his fall and, in effect, his banishment from England, but he had already moved (though he was still married) to a homosexual life. Even after the trial, it should be noted, although Wilde's name became anathema his work continued to be published and read in the most respectable places. Little or no connection was made between the man and his writing, except, perhaps, by persons who assumed that almost any male writer probably was effete, and by persons who especially associated the Aesthetic Movement, with its emphasis on beauty, with homosexuals. That is, Wilde's fairy tales, of which "The Happy Prince" is universally regarded as the best, continued to be read, and were not in any particular way related to Wilde's sexual orientation.

Robert K. Martin, however, in *Studies in Short Fiction* 16 (1979): 74-77, interestingly connects the story to the author. The most important point, available to all readers of the story, is that the swallow is male, just like the Prince. When you think about this, it becomes evident that Wilde is saying something special when the Prince says,

> I am glad that you are going to Egypt at last, little Swallow, you have stayed too long here; but you must kiss me on the lips, for I love you.

As Martin says, commenting on this passage,

> The dynamics of the fairy tale allow Wilde to present two men kissing on the lips, a taboo relationship which would be "inconceivable" in serious fiction; ironically, such forbidden love can only be portrayed in the world of children's literature, where nothing is "real." (76)

Martin's other chief point is that the general public's linking of homosexuality with concern for beauty is wrong-headed. Wilde's story emphasizes social awareness. The prince *was* a hedonist when he lived in Sans-Souci ("I never cared to ask what lay beyond" the surrounding walls), but now, when he sees (as a statue) the suffering around him, he is moved to tears. and he intervenes in the world. Martin puts it this way:

> "The Happy Prince" remains an important inner journal, an account of the way in which for Wilde the recognition and acceptance of his homosexuality coincided with the rejection of his previously held Aestheticism. Far from being the cause of frivolity and his Aesthetic Camp, Wilde's homosexuality led to a deepening of the human capacity for love and the willingness to sacrifice all for a beloved. The only literary form in which he could record this change of heart was the fairy tale. (77)

Martin does not comment on a few other passages that seem strongly homosexual, and that perhaps could pass for the same reason that the same-sex kiss could pass—i.e. because, as Martin says, in children's literature nothing is taken as real. Consider, for instance, the following lines:

> Under the archway of a bridge, two little boy were lying in one another's arms to try and keep themselves warm. "How hungry we are!" they said. "You must not lie here," shouted the watchman, and they wandered out into the rain.

The passage, about two boys, is perfectly appropriate in the story, but it is difficult to believe that Wilde wrote it without any thought of the law's attitude toward two men "lying in one another's arms."

Now for a brief comment on a matter that we raised at the start of this discussion, *agape* and *eros*. *Agape* is the chief Greek word used in the New Testament for *love*, and although the meaning in Greek varies somewhat, depending on the context, the word has now come to mean spiritual (as opposed to erotic) love. (*Agape* is also distinguished from *philos*, yet another Greek word translated as love, for instance in *Philadelphia* [brotherly love], *philosophy* [love of wisdom], and *philanthropy* [love of man]. *Agape* is the love God shows to humankind, or, when used of human beings, it is selfless love, not at all to be confused with erotic or fleshly love.)

In Wilde's fairy tale, the surface story is one of *agape:* The prince, when at last he perceives human suffering, bestows *agape*. The swallow, at first a rather inconsequential creature who loves a reed—he is especially "attracted by her slender waist"—is moved by the Prince's desire to alleviate suffering. He remains even into the dangerous winter season, assisting the Prince, though it finally costs the bird its life. In the dying kiss we seem to get a union of *agape* with *eros*.

If one's concern is largely with the *form* of the fiction, one may want to relate it to traditional fairy tales. The most obvious resemblance perhaps is the supernatural element (animals can talk, a statue can have feelings), and especially the intervention of the supernatural into the natural world (with the Prince's wonderful gifts to the poor, compare, for instance, the gifts of the fairy godmother to Cinderella). But other connections between Wilde's story and traditional fairy tales are evident. For instance, (1) the characters are flat (in fairy tales, the characters are usually no more complicated than The Wicked Witch or The Handsome Prince); (2) the swallow is given three tasks to perform (the usual number in fairy tales); (3) the action takes place in a virtually unspecified place. (We do get a few details about place, such as the comment that the bird "passed over the Ghetto," but the story can take place anywhere, just as fairy tales take place "once upon a time, in a land far away," and that's about all we learn.)

On the other hand, readers familiar with fairy tales, for instance the collections made by Jacob and Wilhelm Grimm or Hans Christian Andersen, know that Wilde's story is very different. For one thing, Wilde the Wit can't resist satirizing the mathematics teacher and the professor of ornithology. And the exoticism—Egypt with its lotuses and with its "crocodiles [who] lie in the mud and look lazily about them" is uncharacteristic of traditional fairy tales. Fairy tales of course include the strange—especially in the form of magical creatures, but they don't dwell on the remote. What is strange in a fairy tale is, say, that fairies can turn hay into gold, or that horses can talk, but these things are presented matter of factly, and are not lingered over.

The difficulty in discussing in class this issue—the connection between Wilde's story and traditional fairy stories—is that many students know "traditional" fairy tales only through their Walt Disney or Golden Book transformations, where much of the acerbity and the conciseness of the nineteenth-century versions has been replaced by doses of sentimentality.

For a somewhat overwhelming formal study of the story against the paradigms established by Axel Olric (thirteen elements) and Vladimir Propp (thirty one elements) see David M. Monaghan, "The Literary Fairy-Tale," *Canadian Journal of Comparative Literature* 1 (1974) 156-166.

VIRGINIA WOOLF

Lappin and Lapinova (p. 754)

Although the narrator enters only Rosalind's mind in any detail in this story, the point of view is omniscient. One hesitates to generalize about point of view (the editorial material in chapter 4 expresses some doubt about commonplaces such as a first-person point of view lending a sense of reality), but it does seem true that an omniscient point of view is especially suited to conveying a sense of human smallness or, to put the matter more charitably, it is especially suited to an ironic or faintly cynical view of life. Consider the first paragraph of the story:

> They were married. The wedding march pealed out. The pigeons fluttered. Small boys in Eton jackets threw rice; a fox terrier sauntered across the path; and Ernest Thorburn led his bride to the car through that small inquisitive crowd of complete strangers which always collects in London to enjoy other people's happiness or unhappiness. Certainly he looked handsome and she looked shy. More rice was thrown, and the car moved off.

The first three sentences, and the beginning of the fourth (until the description of the crowd), objectively present an attractive scene. The last two sentences of the paragraph are also objective. Although readers may suspect (especially if they know some of Virginia Woolf's other fiction) that this marriage will not be happy, the picture is a pretty one—a pleasant snapshot of a wedding. But now look again at the middle of the paragraph. The wry Olympian and mildly cynical comment on the mind of the crowd complicates the whole, diminishing the mental and moral stature of the London crowd and also—a sort of guilt by association—diminishing the marriage.

The second paragraph, taking a closer view, so to speak, enters Rosalind's mind. The whole paragraph is important, but the observation that "Perhaps she never would get used to the fact that she was Mrs. Ernest Anybody" is especially crucial. There are two important points here: one is the name "Ernest" (with all of its Victorian associations, emphasized in the last sentence of the paragraph, which evokes the Albert Memorial); the other calls attention to the transformation of a woman with an identity of her own into a woman whose identity depends on her husband. By the end of the story the reader sees that once Rosalind becomes Mrs. Ernest Thorburn she has no identity in the "real" world—the world of the Thorburns—other than that of Ernest's wife.

An unsympathetic reader might say that Rosalind neurotically and self-destructively takes refuge in a fantasy world, but a more sympathetic reader might say that in order to sustain her sanity she must enter a fantasy world:

> Without that [fantasy] world, how, Rosalind wondered, that winter could she have lived at all?

The narrator then shows us the world that has been thrust upon Rosalind. By showing us the golden-wedding celebration of Ernest's parents, Woolf gives us a strong sense of the oppressive world that is Rosalind's fate now that she has married Ernest. John, "Ernest's sporting brother," is dreadful enough when he talks about the "price rabbits were fetching that autumn in Wiltshire, skins and all," but he becomes positively monstrous when he talks about keeping down the rabbit population: "Shoot'em! Jump on'em with big boots! That the only way to deal with 'em… rabbits." Rosalind's imagination, scarcely neurotic and escapist, sees truly: Ernest's father is a poacher, his mother a bullying squire, and his sister Celia a wretched ferret.

But of course Rosalind has two fantasy worlds, the imagined world that is an accurate if heightened version of the real world (again, the world of the poacher et al.), and, second, the imagined forest world that offers some shelter from this world, though it turns out that she cannot sustain this second world. At first Ernest offers a little help, twitching his nose and mildly indulging her, but Ernest soon tires of the game; since he is at ease in the crass Thorburn world, he has no need to invent an escape and, further, is not sufficiently imaginative to do so. At first Ernest is pleased to be King Lappin, but later he doesn't play the game, and it therefore takes Rosalind longer (i.e. requires a stronger imaginative effort) to turn this brute of a man into a fit partner. During the interval required for this effort, she feels "a load on the back of her neck, as if somebody were about to wring it." Later she has a vision of her own golden-wedding day, herself as an elderly Thorburn; "She could not bear it." When she wakes her sleeping husband and whimpers that she thought her rabbit was dead, his reply is, "Don't talk such rubbish, Rosalind"; he immediately falls asleep and starts to snore. In short, Ernest crudely and with unthinking cruelty dismisses her, with results that are scarcely surprising.

The second question (below) asks if a description in the story (of Ernest and Rosalind as Lappin and Lapinova) is accurate: "They were the opposite of each other; he was bold and determined; she wary and undependable." (Presumably this is the way Rosalind sees her husband and herself, since the invention is hers, not his.) Responses will, of course, vary, but most students see that a good deal of amplification is needed. First of all, it is significant that even in her fantasy she accepts the traditional stereotypes; the male is "bold," the female is "undependable." Second, to characterize Ernest as "bold and determined" is to put matters in the most favorable light; "insensitive and unthinking" would be another and more accurate way of describing him. And how fair is it to say that Rosalind is "wary and undependable"? Certainly Ernest and his clan would think of her as undependable—she would probably at the last minute decide she couldn't go with them to hunt rabbits, or if she did accompany them she would faint when someone pulled the trigger—but if the favorable description of Ernest was highly inaccurate, this unfavorable description of Rosalind is equally inaccurate.

How can we account for the inaccuracy, which is Rosalind's own perception? We can't be positive about why Rosalind denigrates herself, but there is ample evidence in the story that a woman of a sensitive nature would perceive that she has no place in the world of the Thorburns. She is married to a Thorburn, but (even though she has been taught to see him as "bold and determined") she cannot become his sort of clod; she cannot possibly live (in any but a purely physical sense) the life of Mrs. Ernest Thorburn. And, on the other hand, there apparently is no other sort of life available to her, except the fantasy life that sustains her for a time. (Most—but not all—students will know that a woman of Rosalind's time and place could not engage in a career; she could read books, and even write them, but most of her life would still be lived not as a person in her own right but as Mrs. Ernest Thorburn.) In sum, the overly favorable characterization of Ernest and the overly negative characterization of Rosalind show us the crippling, self-deprecating way in which Rosalind has been taught to think by a patriarchal society. She sees her inability to function in the brutal male world as a sign of her undependability. But readers surely judge Rosalind less harshly than she judges herself.

An interesting discussion of this story, as well as some others by Woolf, can be found in an essay by Selma Meyerowitz in *New Feminist Essays on Virginia Woolf* edited by Jane Maracus (1981). Meyerowitz concludes her discussion thus:

> Although Rosalind in "Lappin and Lapinova" rejects the social conventions of the class into which she marries, she cannot establish viable conventions outside that class's life-style. She accepts the typical role of a submissive wife, remaining sheltered from contact with the outside world and exalting her husband's status. Her position in her marriage and in society does not allow her to develop a sense of identity or the resources necessary for a continuing emotional relationship. As a result, her fantasy world proves ineffectual and destructive. Sadly, Rosalind's awakening to the truth is painful, yet Woolf implies that her fantasy retreat ensured her immaturity and fruitlessness, as well as her inability to communicate and achieve emotional fulfilment in her marriage. (244)

TOPICS FOR CRITICAL THINKING AND WRITING

1. What is the point of view and the tone of the first paragraph? Of the second?
2. We are told that Rosalind and Ernest—King Lappin and Queen Lapinova—"were the opposite of each other; he was bold and determined; she wary and undependable." Are these brief characterizations adequate or are the characters more complex? What, by the way, do you make of the fact that Rosalind fantasizes that she is a hare, not a rabbit?
3. Why, at the golden-wedding party, does Rosalind feel that she is being "dissolved into nothingness"?
4. The story ends with this sentence: "So that was the end of that marriage." Why did the marriage end? What, if anything, does this rather flat sentence add to the story?

ZORA NEALE HURSTON

Sweat (p. 760)

Zora Neale Hurston was not simply a black writer, or a woman writer; she was a black woman writer, and much of her fiction comes from this perspective. (bell hooks, in *Ain't I a Woman*, interestingly discusses black women and feminism.)

The contrast between the two chief characters is boldly drawn—clearly Delia is good and Sykes is bad—but it is not without complexity. After all, Delia does allow Sykes to die, and Sykes, though a brute, obviously suffers (despite his boasting and his bullying) from a sense of inferiority which apparently is heightened by the sight of his wife engaged in a menial task for white people: "Ah done tole you time and again to keep them white folks' clothes outa dis house." Though Hurston does not explicitly make the point that black men had a harder time than black women in finding employment, a reader presumably is aware of the fact that an oppressive white society made black men feel unmanly, and that they sometimes compensated by brutal expressions of what they took to be manliness. When Sykes deliberately steps on the white clothes, we understand that he is expressing not only a cruel contempt for his wife but also hostility toward white society.

Still, that Sykes is a brute cannot be doubted; the other black men in the story testify to this effect. This is the intent of question 2, below. Notice especially the longish speech to the effect that some men abuse women simply because the men are bad:

Taint no law on earth dat kin make a man be decent if it aint in 'im.... Dey knows whut dey is doin' while dey is at it, an' hates theirselvs fuh it but they keeps on hangin' after huh tell she's empty. Den dey hates huh fuh bein' a cane-chew an' in de way.

Further, even before Sykes came to hate his wife, he never loved her but only lusted after her.

She had brought love to the union and he had brought a longing for the flesh.

In this respect, however, he apparently is not much different from the other men in the story, who seem to regard an attractive woman only as a commodity, not as a person with ideas and feelings. Thus one of them, commenting on Delia's good looks in her earlier days, says, "Ah'd uh mah'ied huh mahself if he hadn'ter beat me to it." It does not occur to him that she might have had a say in the choice of her husband.

Classroom discussion will probably focus on Delia, especially on the question of whether a woman as devout as Delia would stand by and allow even the worst of husbands to die. (Question 3 approaches this point.) But "stand by" is misleading, since Hurston takes pains to emphasize not only the suffering that Delia has undergone at Sykes's hands but also the helplessness she experiences when the snake bites him. She becomes "ill," and we are told that "Delia could not move—her legs were gone flabby." Seeing him in agony, she experiences "a surge of pity," but "Orlando with its doctors was too far." All of these statements extenuate—indeed, eliminate—any blame that otherwise a reader might conceivably attach to Delia.

Further, Sykes is responsible for his own death since he malevolently introduces the snake into the house, and it is presumably Sykes who has transferred the snake from the box to the laundry basket, in an effort to murder Delia. He is thus justly punished, undone by his own hand. Interestingly, a passage in Ecclesiastes (10: 8-9) uses the image of a snake:

> He that diggeth a pit shall fall into it; and whoso breaketh an hedge, a serpent shall bite him.
> Whoso removeth stones shall be hurt therewith; and he that cleaveth wood shall be endangered thereby.

We are thus in a world of tragedy, where a person aiming at good (doubtless in his brutal mind Sykes thinks that it will be good—for him—to eliminate Delia) destroys himself. With the passage from Ecclesiastes in mind, one can almost speak of the physics of the world: for every action, there is an equal and opposite reaction. Delia, one notices, tells Sykes that she now hates him as much as she used to love him, and he counters that his hatred for her equals her hatred for him. At the start of the story he torments Delia by terrifying her with what seems to be a snake, and at the end of the story he is terrified by a snake. He puts the snake in her laundry basket, but the snake crawls into his bed—where Sykes is bitten. A final comment on the reciprocal structure or geometry of the story: "Sweat" begins late at night, and ends with "the red dawn," which gradually changes into full light, as "the sun crept on up." The image of daylight implies a new day, a new life for Delia, though of course nothing can bring back her youth or her love.

For an extensive discussion of the economics of the sexist and racist society depicted in "Sweat," see Kathryn Lee Seidel, "The Artist in the Kitchen: The Economics of Creativity in Hurston's "Sweat," in *Zora in Florida*, ed. Steve Glassman and Kathryn Lee Seidel.

TOPICS FOR CRITICAL THINKING AND WRITING

1. Summarize the relationship of Delia and Sykes before the time of the story.
2. What function, if any, do the men on Joe Clark's porch serve?
3. Do you think Delia's action at the end of the story is immoral? Why, or why not?

ALICE MUNRO

How I Met My Husband (p. 769)

One way of teaching this story is to approach it as a delightful semi-comic version of the usually portentous (and usually male) story of initiation, or of the movement from innocence to experience. The narrator, Edie, is now mature, but she is reporting (like, say, the narrator of Joyce's "Araby") an early experience.

"I was fifteen and away from home for the first time"—such words suggest considerable naiveté, and indeed in the course of the story we learn that Edie was inexperienced in all sorts of ways, especially in the ways of young men. We learn too that she was not much of a student (she left high school after one year), that she is childish enough to put on Mrs. Peebles's makeup and one of her dresses, etc. If you ask a student to read the opening paragraph aloud in class, students will probably hear a fairly naive voice in "We heard... and we were sure... so we all ran out... the first close-up plane I ever saw." (On the other hand, it is Mrs. Peebles, not the narrator, who screams.) The title of the story itself has a naive (or at least matter-of-fact) tone to it, and one can argue that the story reveals the narrator's naiveté, since it tells the reader what caused her to smile while she waited for the mailman, and how her smile charmed the man who did become her husband.

If Edie is in some ways naive, she is also endowed with lots of native smarts. Of course, strictly speaking, one can't be sure that what she now reports is what she felt when she was 15 years old, but the reader gets the feeling that much of the report, though delivered by a mature woman, accurately conveys Edie's original perception. Since some passages are explicitly said to be later interpretations (e.g., "I wasn't even old enough then to realize how out of the common it [was]… for a man to say a word like *beautiful*"), we naturally take the rest of the story to be a fairly accurate report of her original responses. For instance:

> Dessert was never anything to write home about, at their place. A dish of Jell-O or sliced bananas or fruit out of a tin. "Have a house without a pie, be ashamed until you die," my mother used to say, but Mrs. Peebles operated differently.

Although the expression "Mrs. Peebles operated differently" has the wryness of maturity, the earlier words expressing scorn for desserts that are not home-made presumably represent the view she held at the time.

Readers who are familiar both with Jell-O and with home-made pies will not be quick to call Edie naive. As one reads the story one keeps encountering an inexperienced girl who nevertheless is extremely perceptive, for instance about human ways (Dr. Peebles "had a calming way of talking, like any doctor"), and especially about class distinctions ("Dr. Peebles was only an animal doctor"). The comments on the behavior of the others reveal a quick mind. Example: "Asking people to stay, just like that, is certainly a country thing, and maybe seemed natural to [Dr. Peebles] now, but not to Mrs. Peebles, from the way she said, oh yes, we have plenty of room." Edie also is an adept housekeeper, and she shows an awareness of professional responsibility: "I was scared, but I never admitted that, especially in front of the children I was taking care of." Her naiveté is chiefly confined to sex and to the belief that Chris Watters will send her a letter.

Most important, Edie is a very *good* person. For instance, she excuses Mrs. Peebles's unthinking remark about gawking farmers: "She didn't say that to hurt my feelings. It never occurred to her." Somewhat similarly, she tells Chris that his sign is attractive, and, more important, she continued to smile at the mailman because he was "counting on it, and he didn't have an easy life, with the winter driving ahead." In the last line of the story she explicitly says that she likes people to be happy, but the line gains its force from what we have seen earlier.

Her desire that people be happy does not extend to the dreadful Alice Kelling. Students might be invited to discuss their attitude toward Edie's lie. Almost all will probably excuse Edie, on various grounds: (1) Edie admits that lying is wrong; (2) Edie lies in part to protect someone else; (3) Alice is awful. By the way, it's interesting to notice that although Edie lies to Alice *before* Alice reveals her full loathsomeness, even the few readers who are uneasy about Edie lying tend to excuse Edie retroactively, so to speak, after Alice unleashes a torrent of abuse. Another point about Alice, or about Alice and Edie: Edie does not do much in the way of offering negative comments about Alice. Munro lets us form an opinion on our own, and thus preserves Edie from speaking harshly.

One way of teaching this story is to compare it with stories of male initiation (e.g. Joyce's "Araby").

TOPICS FOR CRITICAL THINKING AND WRITING

1. Since Edie tells the story, we know about the other characters only as much as she tells us. Do you think her view of Mrs. Peebles and of Loretta Bird is accurate? On what do you base your answer?
2. Edie offers explicit comments about Mrs. Peebles and Loretta Bird, but not about Alice Kelling, or at least not to the same degree. Why?
3. Characterize Edie.
4. What do you think of the title? Why?

RAYMOND CARVER

Popular Mechanics (p. 782)

The usual characteristics of Minimalism are alleged to be:

*   lower-middle-class characters, who are relatively inarticulate and out of touch with others and with themselves
*   little if any setting
*   little action of any apparent importance
*   little if any authorial comment, i.e., little interpretation of motive
*   a drab style—fairly simple sentences, with little or no use of figurative language or allusions

Almost no story perfectly exemplifies this textbook paradigm. In fact, "Popular Mechanics" is an excellent way of seeing the inadequacy of such a view of minimalism.

Let's look at this very short story—certainly minimal in terms of length—from beginning to end, though for the moment we'll skip the title. Here is the first paragraph:

> Early that day the weather turned and the snow was melting into dirty water. Streaks of it ran down from the little shoulder-high window that faced the back-yard. Cars slushed by on the street outside, where it was getting dark. But it was getting dark on the inside too.

If the paragraph is read aloud in class, students will easily see that Carver very briefly establishes an unpleasant setting ("dirty water," "streaks," "cars slushed by"), giving us not only a sense of what we see but also the time of day ("dark"). But of course Carver is *not* giving us mere landscape and chronology. When we read "But it was getting dark on the inside too," we anticipate dark passions. A reader can't be sure that such passions will materialize, or how the story will turn out; the darkness may dissipate, but at this stage a reader is prepared for a story that fits the rotten weather. (Another way of putting it is to say that Carver is preparing the reader, i.e., is seeking to control our responses.) Perhaps, then, it is incorrect to say that minimalists do not use figurative language; surely the dark weather is figurative. And on rereading the story a reader may feel that the metamorphosis of snow into dirty water is an emblem of the history of this marriage.

The second question printed at the end of this discussion asks students to compare the opening paragraph with an earlier version. Perhaps the chief differences are the elimination of the sun from the revised version—there is no sunshine in this world—and the emphasis, in the last sentence of the revised paragraph, on the internal darkness. In the earlier version, "It was getting dark, outside and inside;" in the later version, the inside darkness gets a sentence to itself: "But it was getting dark on the inside too." The real point of asking students to look at the revisions "to account for the changes" is to help them to look closely at what Carver has written, so that they will give his words a chance to shape their responses.

As we read the story, we never get inside the heads of the characters. The author tells us nothing about them, other than what they say and what they do. We don't know *why* they behave as they do. We know very little about them, not even their names, since Carver calls them only "he" and "she." The first line of dialogue is angry, and all of the remaining dialogue reveals the terrific hostility that exists between the two speakers. As the author presents them to us, the alienation of these characters does seem to fit the textbook description of minimalist writing.

The quarrel about the picture of the baby leads (because Carver is an artist, not a mere recorder) to the quarrel about the baby. (These people may hate each other, but apparently they both love the baby, although of course it is possible that each wants to possess the picture and the baby simply in order to hurt the other. Again, the author gives no clues.) The adults' angry passions contaminate the baby, so to speak, for the baby begins to cry and soon is "red-faced and screaming."

Even a little detail like the flowerpot is relevant. In the fight, the adults could have knocked over some other object, for example a kitchen chair. But it is a flowerpot—a little touch of life and presumably a small attempt at beautifying the house—that is upset. Norman German and Jack Bedell, *Critique* 29 (1988): 257-60 make the interesting point that no plant is mentioned, only a pot. "The empty pot," they suggest, "is like the house, a lifeless hull." Carver isn't just recording; he is choosing what he wishes to record, because he wants to evoke certain responses.

We can't tell what ultimately happened to the baby, but there is every reason to believe that he is physically harmed, possibly even killed, and this point gets back to the title, a topic raised below, in question 4. Why did Carver change the title from "Mine" to "Popular Mechanics"? The new title of course summons to mind the magazine of that name, but the magazine is never mentioned. What then, is the relevance of the title? First, it probably calls to mind the male blue-collar world, the chief readership of *Popular Mechanics*. Second, by the time one finishes the story and thinks about the title, one sees a sort of pun in "popular," one of whose meanings is "Of or carried on by the common people" (*Webster's New World Dictionary*). And in "mechanics" we see the forces at work—the physical forces operating on the baby as the two adults each pull him.

The last sentence surely is worth discussing in class: "In this manner, the issue was decided." The language seems flat, unadorned, merely informative. But "decided" is monstrously inappropriate. The word suggests thought rather than sheer violence; even if, say, we decide an issue by tossing a coin, the decision to toss a coin is arrived at by thinking and by common consent. Perhaps the word "issue," too, is significant; German and Bedell find in it a pun (*offspring* as well as *argument*). To find a parallel for Carver's last sentence we probably have to turn to the world of Swiftian irony.

Question 3, below, invites students to compare the last line with Carver's earlier version, "In this manner they decided the issue." In the revision, by means of the passive, Carver makes the sentence even flatter; the narrator seems even more effaced. But he is therefore, to the responsive reader, even more present. As Tobias Wolff puts it, in the introduction to *Matters of Life and Death*, "Irony offers us a way of talking about the unspeakable. In the voices of Swift and Nabokov and Jane Austen we sometimes hear what would have been a scream if irony had not subdued it to eloquence."

The circumstances and the word "decided" may remind the reader of another decision concerning a disputed child, the decision Solomon made (1 Kings 3:16-27) when confronted with two prostitutes who disputed over which was the true mother of the child. One woman, you'll recall, was even willing to murder the child in order to settle the dispute. (see p. 46)

In short, Carver's language is not so drab as it sometimes appears to be, which disputes the contention that his stories—especially the early ones—are "thin." As the three stories in this book indicate, he changed as a writer, but in some ways the body of his work is consistent. Late in his life, in the preface to *The Best American Short Stories 1986*, he described his taste:

> I'm drawn toward the traditional (some would call it old-fashioned) methods of storytelling: one layer of reality unfolding and giving way to another, perhaps richer layer; the gradual accretion of meaningful detail; dialogue that not only reveals something about character but advances the story.

In interviews shortly before his death he freely admitted that his view of life had changed; he was in love, and things didn't seem as bleak as they had seemed earlier. But this does not mean that his early stories are less skillfully constructed than are his later, more tender stories.

TOPICS FOR CRITICAL THINKING AND WRITING

1.   Some readers object to "minimalist" writings on the grounds that the stories (1) lack ideas, (2) do not describe characters in depth, and (3) are written in a drab style. Does Carver's story seem to you to suffer from these alleged weaknesses?

2.   When Carver first published the story, the opening paragraph was slightly different. Here is the earlier version:

> During the day the sun had come out and the snow melted into dirty water. Streaks of water ran down from the little, shoulder-high window that faced the back yard. Cars slushed by on the street outside. It was getting dark, outside and inside.

Which version do you prefer? Why?

3.   The last line—"In this manner, the issue was decided"—in the original version ran thus: "In this manner they decided the issue." Do you consider the small change an improvement? Why, or why not?

4.   The original title was "Mine." Again, what do you think of the change, and why?

RAYMOND CARVER

What We Talk about when We Talk about Love (p. 783)

This story is Carver's dark version of Plato's *Symposium*, even though there are no direct echoes beyond the situation (people talking and drinking) and the subject (love). Carver's story begins in daylight and moves into darkness, with the talk seeming (at least on the surface) to clarify nothing, whereas Plato's dialogue moves from late afternoon or evening through the night and into the daylight. True, at the end of *The Symposium* we are told that some of the participants have fallen asleep and others are drowsy and unable to follow the argument that Socrates is presenting, but presumably the reader has been persuaded by Socrates's words (Socrates modestly attributes them to the priestess Diotima) concerning the nature of love.

In ordinary talk, love means many things, ranging from (say) a passion for the movies or for shopping to more serious things, such as love of one's country, love of God, love of humanity, love of parents for children, and erotic love of human beings. Even if we confine our attention to erotic love—the only kind of love discussed in Carver's story—we probably can hardly come up with a narrow definition; rather, when we think about what love is, we think of three things. First, we think of our own experiences; second, we think of the lovers around us, whose secrets we don't know but whose relationships we can guess to be widely (and wildly) varied, and, third—or perhaps really first—we think of famous stories of love, for it probably is these (e.g. Romeo and Juliet, Othello and Desdemona, Beatrice and Benedict, Petruchio and Kate, Tristan and Isolde, perhaps even Edward VIII and Wallie Simpson) that give us our clearest and most memorable ideas about what love is. These fictions help to create life. (Someone—maybe La Rochefoucauld—said that people would not fall in love if they had not read about it in a book.) In *The Symposium*, too, there is a range of kinds of love, though it is clear that for Plato the highest is love of wisdom.

Carver's story resembles Plato's *Symposium* not only in the setting and in the topic of discussion, but in form. We say that "What We Talk About" is a short story, but perhaps we ought to call it (following Northrop Frye) an anatomy, a prose fiction characterized by debates or dialogues. Frye used the word to distinguish such long prose fictions as *Gulliver's Travels* and *Point Counterpoint* from the novel; he pointed out that it was not very useful to discuss all long prose fictions as though they are novels, with realistic characters and plots that moved to resolutions. Similarly, we can say that not all short works of fiction need be short stories, if by "short story" we mean, again, a work with realistic characters participating in a plot that is resolved. Frye himself saw some short prose fictions as *tales* (narratives with the emphasis on the improbable), and perhaps we can see others—those that explore ideas and that do not come to a resolution—as anatomies.

In any case, it is evident that we can distinguish between literature of *resolution* and literature of *revelation*, that is, between (1) literature that stimulates us to ask, "And what happened next?" and that finally leaves us with a settled state of affairs, and (2) literature that causes us to say, "Ah, I understand what they mean." But we should add that in Carver, and, for that matter, in *The Symposium* too, the more the characters talk, the more mysterious the topic becomes. Doubtless one reason Socrates attributed to the priestess Diotima his vision of the love of the ideal was to make it unearthly, mysterious, overpowering—in short, to make it emotionally appealing.

In the case of "What We Talk about when We Talk about Love," we can—by "consistency-building," to use a term from reader-response criticism—try to make some sense of the characters. There is, for instance, Mel, the cardiologist who had been a seminarian and who "would like to come back again in a different life, a different time and all,... as a knight." Yet this knight—if we have stock ideas we think of chivalry—fantasizes killing his wife by releasing a swarm of bees in her home. We can put together all that we see and hear of each character, and can try to make sense of the bundle, but the characters remain elusive. Terri, for instance, insists that the man who beat her up and who tried to kill her *did* love her, and though Mel can say, "I just wouldn't call Ed's behavior love," *we* are hardly in a position to pass judgment. The reader can only say what the narrator says: "I'm the wrong person to ask…. I didn't even know the man…. I wouldn't know. You'd have to know the particulars." Terri *did* know the particulars, and she says that Ed—a suicide—died for love (paragraph 37), to which Mel replies, "If that's love, you can have it."

That is, the characters are insulated from each other just as we are insulated from the characters. The extreme example is the old couple in the hospital, swathed in bandages with only "little eye-holes and mouth-holes…. The man's heart was breaking because he couldn't turn his goddam head and *see* his goddam wife." These two characters are probably pretty clear to the reader, and they are clear to Mel, too, but (given his experience with his former wife) he can hardly believe what he knows is true. In any case, the image of the elderly swathed lovers, unable to communicate, is connected with the image of knights in heavy armor—protective but also suffocating—and with the image of the beekeeper wearing "a helmet with the plate that comes down over your face, the big gloves, and the padded coat." A moment after he gives us this description, Mel decides not to telephone his children (by his first marriage), again emphasizing the gaps between people. Immediately after Mel makes this decision, the narrator speaks of heading "out into the sunset," to which the narrator's wife asks, "What does that mean, honey?" "It just means what I said," the narrator curtly replies, "That's all it means." This communication that does not communicate is immediately paralleled by words that do not lead to actions or, more precisely, by words that are not accompanied by the appropriate action: Terri offers to get some cheese and crackers but in fact she makes no move to do so, and the characters remain sitting in the dark room, their heartbeats audible.

We can, of course, chart some patterns. There is the bandaged couple (old, devoted lovers); Mel and Terri (lovers for a considerable time, but not old); the narrator and Laura ("going on a year and a half"); but these characters are not set within a traditional plot, and nothing in the way of obvious action happens. Nothing is resolved, but (paradoxically) something is revealed in the darkness; readers may feel that Carver has drawn them more deeply into the mystery of love—perhaps even given them one more picture of lovers, to add to the literary gallery that helps to give us an idea of what love is.

TOBIAS WOLFF

Say Yes (p. 792)

In line with Question 1 in the text, students might be invited to give their responses to the man, based only on the first paragraph. (You may want to make this assignment before the students read the story, and ask them to jot down their responses immediately after reading—or reading twice—the first paragraph.) Is he a decent guy? Is his "I try" nicely modest, or is it a bit too self-congratulatory? In the last sentence of the first paragraph ("Helping out with the dishes was a way he had of showing how considerate he was") do we hear the voice of an objective narrator—or do we get inside of the husband's mind, and hear him congratulating himself on how considerate he is? (Of course this issue gets into matters of point of view—a topic discussed in the next chapter—but there is no harm in anticipating the discussion.)

How do students respond to the husband and wife during the quarrel? (It will be interesting to see if the class divides along the lines of sex.) Perhaps the husband is at his nastiest when, saying "These are dirty," he dumps the silver back into the sink. His aggressive (and defensive?) action is understandable—we probably have all done something like this—but it is also revealing. And, even more important, this perfectly normal (if nasty) action leads to something significant; his wife, reaching into the sink, cuts her hand. We didn't expect that, but now it has happened and it seems perfectly natural. Her action, in turn, leads to further actions: his solicitude (genuine, no doubt, but, since "he hoped that she appreciated how quickly he had come to her aid," a very self-conscious and therefore somewhat tainted display of his goodness), her continuation of the argument (though by now the issue has somewhat turned from the general topic of interracial marriage to whether he would marry *her* if she were black), his rejection ("No"), his pretense of indifference (in order to equal her pretended indifference), the glimpse of the outside world (a few stars, light traffic, two dogs that scrap but then amicably trot off).

The effect of the husband's (and our) brief contact with the outdoors, and especially with the scrapping dogs who apparently really get along well together, is to bring him to his senses. One might almost say that nature helps to heal him. He apologizes to Anne. Because a reader feels the sincerity of the apology ("Anne, I'm really sorry.... I'll make it up to you, I promise"), when Anne (apparently rather coldly) says, "How?" and "We'll see," a reader may at first be taken aback but then will see the appropriateness of her response.

In short, everything naturally follows from what has come before, and yet perhaps nothing could easily have been predicted. It's pretty much in accord with E. M. Forster's statement (quoted in Chapter 2),

> Shock, followed by the feeling, "O, that's all right," is a sign that all is well with plot: characters, to be real, ought to run smoothly, but a plot ought to cause surprise.

The final paragraph is complex, maybe even ambiguous. On one level, their wedding night is repeated. He has said that he will marry her, and now the bride, insisting that he turn out the lights (she is modest?) approaches, and his heart pounds "the way it had on their first night together." At the same time, the paragraph introduces the menacing idea of a stranger in the house, an intruder who awakens one and who causes anxiety. Have the husband and wife, by means of the quarrel, become strangers to each other? Adam and Eve after the Fall? *Is* the final effect that of a menacing estrangement between the husband and wife? Or is it rather of the excitement of newlyweds, going to bed for the first time—strangers (sexually) to each other, but united by love? Perhaps the ultimate effect of the final paragraph is to convey the trepidation and excitement of a first sexual experience, an experience during which the stranger becomes the beloved spouse. Some such experience is now relived by this couple, who had been briefly estranged, and now are in the process of becoming reunited.

GLORIA NAYLOR

The Two (p. 795)

Although instructors will be interested in matters of technique—especially the metaphors of the quilt and of the smell, and the shift in point of view from (at the start) the outside view of the two women to (midway) the inside view of Lorraine and Theresa—discussion in class is likely to center on the characterization of "the two" (we don't learn even their names until we have read about one-third of the story), their relationship to each others, and society's relationship to them.

The differences between the two women are clear enough—Lorraine is shy, soft, and in need of the approval of the community; Theresa is tougher (but "the strain of fighting alone was beginning to show")—but both are at first lumped together as "nice girls," and this point is worth discussing in class. Why, at first, does the community find them acceptable? Because they don't play loud music, they don't have drunken friends, and—the next most important point—they do not encourage other women's husbands to hang around, that is, they are not a threat to the married women. But it is precisely this "friendly indifference to the men on the street" that (when its source is detected) becomes "an insult to the [neighborhood] women."

By the way, we have fairly often encountered in the popular press articles with such titles as "Why Are Gay Men Feared?" (the usual answer is that men insecure about their own heterosexuality feel threatened by gay men, who, the theory goes, in effect tell the supposed straight men that maybe they aren't really so straight), but we don't recall ever encountering an article on the response of heterosexual women to lesbians. Perhaps some students will want to confirm or dispute Naylor's view of why the straight community resents "the two." As we understand the story, Naylor is suggesting that heterosexual women welcome other women who are not threats to their relationships with men, but then reject lesbians (who fit this category) because lesbians, by virtue of their indifference to or independence from males, seem to be a criticism of heterosexuality. (Can we go so far as to say that lesbians, in this view, upset straight women because lesbians make other women aware of their need for men?)

There are two stories in this story, the story of the relationship between the community and "the two," and the story of the relationship between Lorraine and Theresa. This second story, we take it, is about two women who (like the members of most straight couples) differ considerably in personality and who have their problems, but who are tied to each other by deep affection. The last we hear in the story is a bit of good-natured bickering that reveals Lorraine is doing her best to please Theresa. Lorraine, who had tried to talk Theresa into avoiding fattening foods, is preparing a (fattening) gravy for the chicken, and Theresa is pretending to disapprove.

RITA DOVE

Second-Hand Man (p. 802)

In "real slow," in the first paragraph, we hear a voice that is speaking something other than Standard English, and discussion in class may well spend some time on the narrator. Technically the narrative point of view is editorial omniscience, but that seems like an awfully highfalutin' term for this folksy narrator who, admittedly, knows what is going on in everyone's mind ("All the girls loved James") but who surely seems to be a voice of common sense, speaking the idiom of the characters in the story. Thus, if the narrator knows what is going on in Virginia's mind (for instance, that she hated to be called *Ginny*), well, any sensible person in this part of the woods would know that. And if we want to say that Dove uses the technique known as editorial omniscience, one might add that only a very self-satisfied system of critical theory would apply so heavy-handed a term to a narrator who says, "It was time to let the dog in out of the rain, even if he shook his wet all over the floor." In any case, the narrator's voice surely is close to Virginia's, and the narrator's wisdom probably is close to hers too.

The story is very much in the oral tradition, not only in its occasional moralizing ("But people are too curious for their own good") but also in the narrator's concern that the hearer understand the way the characters feel:

"Virginia," he said. He was real scared. "How can you shoot me down like this?"

That gratuitous but thoroughly welcome "He was real scared" wonderfully catches the voice of the oral reporter.

And like much oral narrative, this story deals with archetypal material (though it is set in the 1920s)—a courting (briefly imperiled by a snake in the garden) that produces a happy marriage (the happiness is in this world proved by the production of a beautiful baby). The oral flavor is emphasized, of course, by the five passages of song. The story is told with great sobriety: ("No, he courted her proper"), and yet with humor too, as in the story about Virginia dumping hot water on an unwelcome suitor ("She only got a little piece of his pant leg"), or in pictures of the unsuccessful wooer Sterling Williams, who "kept buying root beers [for Virginia] and having to drink them himself." And the narrator can value both ritual and common sense, as when he speaks approvingly of the formal courtship ("He courted her just inside a year, came by nearly every day"), and yet can say, of James Evans's proposing while kneeling on one knee, "There's a point when all this dignity and stuff get in the way of destiny." (James is so taken by his role as suitor that he can't believe the woman of his dreams has actually said *yes*.)

If the courting is both realistic and ritualistic, so is Virginia's threat to shoot James. She proceeds according to ritual (and the narrator emphasizes the ritual by using the same syntax in successive sentences):

> She took off her coat and hung it in the front closet. She unpinned her hat and set it in its box on the shelf. She reached in the back of the closet and brought out his hunting rifle and the box of bullets. She didn't see no way out but to shoot him.

She means it, or thinks she does, but, "No, she couldn't shoot him when he stood there looking at her with those sweet brown eyes, telling her how much he loved her." What to do? She'll wait until he sleeps. But "He didn't sleep for three nights." We are in the world of battling heroes—he won't sleep or run, and she won't put aside her standards—but fortunately she finds a way out. "Sitting there, Virginia had plenty of time to think." He had lied—but only to win her, so the lie is forgivable. She lays down the rifle, and lays down certain conditions that domesticate her man ("You will join the choir and settle down instead of plucking on that guitar at the drop of a hat"). She plans to bring James's child to Ohio, but we learn that the child had died some time before this episode. Why? Perhaps because we have to see that even the wonderful Virginia can't have everything her way, and perhaps because since James *did* lie—even though only for the perfectly good reason of gaining Virginia— in the world of folk tale he has to be punished. We think the point is worth discussing.

ANONYMOUS

Western Wind (p. 806)

"Western Wind" has been much discussed. Probably most readers will find acceptable R. P. Warren's suggestion (*Kenyon Review,* 1943, 5) that the grieving lover seeks relief for the absence of his beloved in "the sympathetic manifestation of nature." But how do you feel about Patric M. Sweeney's view (*Explicator,* October 1955) that the speaker asserts that "he will come to life only when the dead woman returns, and her love, like rain, renews him"? In short, in this view the speaker "cries out to the one person who conquered death, who knows that the dead, returning to life, give life to those who loved them." We find this reading of the poem hard to take, but (like many readings) it is virtually impossible to *dis*prove.

One other point: Some readers have asked why other readers assume that the speaker is a male. A hard question to answer.

ANONYMOUS

Edward (p. 807)

Bertrand Bronson, in *The Ballad as Song,* suggests that "Edward" may not be a pure folk ballad. Perhaps the strongest evidence of a "literary" touch is the fact that the surprise ending in the last line—which forces us to reconstruct our understanding of the mother—is unusual for a ballad. In traditional ballads, Bronson points out, people ask questions in order to learn what they do not know (or, in the case of riddling ballads, in order to test someone), but in "Edward" the questions and answers serve a sophisticated technique of character revelation and of plot-telling. By the way, the motifs of questions and answers and last will and testament, found in "Edward," are also in "Lord Randal," which is fairly well known among undergraduates.

TOPICS FOR CRITICAL THINKING AND WRITING

1. The poem consists of two parts. How does the structure of the first part parallel that of the second?
2. What might have been the mothers motives? Do you think that the story would be improved if we knew the motives behind her "counseils"? Explain.
3. How can you explain Edward's statements about his wife and children?
4. Line 21 offers a surprise, but it is topped by the surprise in the final four lines. Can you reread the poem with pleasure once you know the surprises? Explain.

CHRISTOPHER MARLOWE

Come Live with Me and Be My Love (p. 809)

SIR WALTER RALEIGH

The Nymph's Reply to the Shepherd (p. 810)

JOHN DONNE

The Bait (p. 811)

Marlowe's poem will probably cause no problems. We hope, however, that students do not reject it because it depicts an idealized, idyllic, pastoral world. It gives us, of course, not the real world but a world that we might sometimes dream of.

Raleigh's bitter (but engaging) response does not quite say that Marlowe's world is utterly fanciful. Raleigh seems to grant the truth of Marlowe's spring-time world, but he points out that there is a further truth—the truth of change. Spring becomes fall and winter. (Topic 2 in the text asks about line 12. We hear puns in *spring* [the season, and also the watery source] and *fall* [the season, and a downfall].)

We find the last stanza of Raleigh's poem especially interesting. The poem does not cynically glory in debunking Marlowe's poem; rather, the final stanza expresses a poignant wish that Marlowe's vision were true.

Donne's "The Bait" begin with Marlowe's words, and the shift to "golden sands, and crystal brooks" hardly seems to change the landscape, though of course it does in fact get us into the world of fisherfolk. The idealized motif is continued in the second stanza, though "betray" in line 8 introduces a dark note. Still, the next stanza (9-12) seems chiefly to continue the motif of a golden world, but in lines 13-16 we get two additional words that cause unease, *loath* and *darknest.* The next two stanzas vigorously introduce the real world of hardships; fishing is no longer a delightful sport, but something that requires people to *freeze,* and it will *cut* their legs. Further, we now hear of *poor fish,* and the fisherfolk behave *treacherously.* This is a bit odd, since at the start the speaker invited the beloved to fish in a world of *golden sands* and *crystal brooks,* with *silken lines* and *silver hooks.* That is, as the poem continues, the act of fishing is seen as less pleasant (to those who fish and to the fish themselves). In fact, where the speaker was a fisherman in the first stanza, in the last stanza he is a victimized fish, taken by the bait (attractiveness?) of the beloved. The beloved, therefore, is (at the start) a fellow-fisher or a companion at the start and (at the end) is also a deceiver who snares the speaker. On the other hand, although the speaker seems to lament his lot, he also evidently enjoys it. The idea that lovers enjoys suffering, enjoy thralldom, is of course commonplace.

MICHAEL DRAYTON

Since There's No Help (p. 812)

The first quatrain (though joined to the next quatrain by a semicolon) is in effect a complete sentence. The speaker seems resolute, though perhaps in retrospect we feel that the repetition of "glad" in line 3 ("I am glad, yea, glad with all my heart") is a clue that insincerity causes him to protest too much. The second quatrain, which also can stand as a sentence, continues the matter-of-fact tone. But then, after the eighth line, comes the turn, or *volta*, so often found in sonnets. In the third quatrain and couplet—this quatrain cannot stand as a sentence, but passionately overflows into the couplet, and so the quatrain and couplet together can be taken as a sort of sestet—we hear a new breathlessness or sense of urgency that dispels the earlier apparent confidence. The personified abstractions, too, are new (Passion, Faith, etc.); they do *not* indicate insincerity or lack of feeling, but, on the contrary, take us into a world of bruised feelings, evident earlier in such an expression as "you get no more of me." Even the shift from "you" in line 2 to the more intimate "thou" in line 13 is significant in establishing the change. The poem ends with a feminine rhyme, probably to keep it from ending too emphatically or, to put the matter a bit differently, to indicate that the speaker is not the master of the situation.

WILLIAM SHAKESPEARE

Sonnet 29, Sonnet 116 (pp. 813-814)

Shakespeare's 154 sonnets were published in 1609, although it is thought that most of them were composed in the middle 1590s, around the time *Romeo and Juliet* and *A Midsummer Night's Dream* were written. Francis Meres spoke of Shakespeare's "sugared sonnets" in 1598, and two were published in an anthology in 1599. The order of the sonnets is probably not Shakespeare's, but there are two large divisions (with some inconsistent interruptions). Sonnets 1-126 seem to be addressed to, or concerned with, a handsome, aristocratic young man who is urged to marry and thus to propagate his beauty and become immortal. Sonnets 127-152 are chiefly concerned with a promiscuous dark woman who seduces a friend, at least for a while.

Wordsworth thought the poems were autobiographical ("With this key Shakespeare unlocked his heart"), to which Browning replied, "If so, the less Shakespeare he." Scholars have not convincingly identified the friend or the lady, and of course the whole thing may be as fictional as *Hamlet.* Certainly it *sounds* like autobiography, but this is only to say that Shakespeare is a writer who sounds convincing. The chief argument that the poems really may be autobiographical is that the insistence that the friend marry is so odd a theme. As C. S. Lewis says in *English Literature in the Sixteenth Century,* what man (except a potential father-in-law) cares if another man gets married? One other point: Do the poems addressed to the beautiful friend suggest a homosexual interest? Certainly they suggest a *passionate* interest, but it doesn't seem to be erotic. "Sonnet 20," a bawdy and witty poem, expressly denies any interest in the friend's body. It seems reasonable to say that what the speaker of the sonnets wants from the friend is not sex but love.

Sonnet 29 (When in disgrace with Fortune and men's eyes) (p. 813)

The rhyme scheme of "Sonnet 29" is that of the usual Shakespearean sonnet, but the thought is organized more or less into an octave and a sextet, the transition being emphasized by the trochee at the beginning of line 9. The sense of energy is also communicated by the trochee that begins line 10 and yet another introducing line 11, this last being especially important because by consonance and alliteration it communicates its own energy to the new image of joy ("Like to the lark"). As in most of Shakespeare's sonnets, the couplet is more or less a summary of what has preceded, but not in the same order: line 13 summarizes the third quatrain: line 14 looks back to (but now rejects) the earlier quatrains.

The first line surely glances at Shakespeare's unimpressive social position, and line 8 presumably refers to his work. Possibly the idea is that he most enjoyed his work before it became the source of his present discomfort. Edward Hubler, in *The Sense of Shakespeare's Sonnets,* notes that "the release from depression is expressed through the image of the lark, a remembrance of earlier days when the cares of his London career were unknown."

To this it can be added that although the poem employs numerous figures of speech from the start (e.g., personification with "Fortune," synecdoche with "eyes" in line 1, metonymy with "heaven" in line 3), line 11, with the image of the lark, introduces the poem's first readily evident figure of speech, and it is also the most emphatic run-on line in the poem. Moreover, though heaven was "deaf" in line 3, in line 12 it presumably hears the lark singing "hymns at heaven's gate." "Sullen" in line 12 perhaps deserves some special comment too: (1) The earth is still somber in color, though the sky is bright, and (2) applied to human beings, it suggests the moody people who inhabit earth.

TOPIC FOR CRITICAL THINKING AND WRITING

Disregarding for the moment the last two lines (or *couplet*), where does the sharpest turn or shift occur? In a sentence, summarize the speaker's state of mind before this turn and, in another sentence, the state of mind after it.

Sonnet 116 (Let me not to the marriage of true minds) (p. 814)

Although the poem is almost certainly addressed to a man, because it is a celebration of the permanence of love it can apply equally well to a woman or, in fact, to a parent or child.

The first words, "Let me not," are almost a vow, and "admit impediments" in the second line faintly hints at the marriage service in the Book of Common Prayer, which says, "If any of you know just cause or impediment...." In line 2 "admit" can mean both "acknowledge, grant the existence of" and "allow to enter."

The first quatrain is a negative definition of love ("love is not..."), but the second quatrain is an affirmative definition ("O no, it is..."). The third begins as another negative definition, recognizing that "rosy lips and cheeks" will indeed decay, but denying that they are the essence of love; this quatrain then ends affirmatively, making a contrast to transience: "bears it out even to the edge of doom." Then, having clinched his case, the speaker adopts a genial and personal tone in the couplet, where for the first time he introduces the word "I."

Speaking of couplets, we can't resist quoting Robert Frost on the topic. Once, in conversation with Frost, the boxer Gene Tunney said something about the price of a poem. Frost replied: "One thousand dollars a line. Four thousand for a quatrain, but for a sonnet, $12,000. The last two lines of a sonnet don't mean anything anyway." Students might be invited to test the sonnets against this playful remark.

TOPICS FOR CRITICAL THINKING AND WRITING

1.   Paraphrase (that is, put into your own words) "Let me not to the marriage of true minds / Admit impediments." Is there more than one appropriate meaning of "Admit"?

2.   Notice that the poem celebrates "the marriage of true minds," not bodies. In a sentence or two, using only your own words, summarize Shakespeare's idea of the nature of such love, both what it is and what it is not.

3.   Paraphrase lines 13-14. What is the speaker's tone here? Would you say that the tone is different from the tone in the rest of the poem?

4.   Write a paragraph or a poem defining either love or hate. Or see if you
     can find such a definition in a popular song. Bring the lyrics to class.

JOHN DONNE

A Valediction: Forbidding Mourning (p. 815)

Instructors may be so familiar with this poem that they may not recognize the
difficulties it presents to students. The title itself leads many students to think
(quite plausibly) that it is about death, an idea reinforced by the first simile.
But this simile is introduced to make the point that *just as* virtuous men can
die quietly because they are confident of a happy future, *so* the two lovers can
part quietly—that is, the speaker can go on a journey—because they are confident of each other.

The hysterics that accompany the separation of less confident lovers are
ridiculed ("sigh-tempests," "tear-floods"); such agitation would be a "profa-
nation" of the relationship of the speaker and his beloved and would betray
them to the "laity."

Thus the speaker and the beloved are implicitly priests of spiritual love.

The poem goes on to contrast the harmful movement of the earth (an
earthquake) with the harmless ("innocent") movement of heavenly bodies,
thereby again associating the speaker and the beloved with heavenly matters.
(The cosmology, of course, is the geocentric Ptolemaic system.) The fourth
stanza continues the contrast: other lovers are "sublunary," changeable, and
subject to the changing moon. Such earthbound lovers depend on the physical things that "elemented" their love ("eyes, lips, and hands"), but the love of
the speaker and his partner is "refined" and does not depend on such stuff.
Moreover, if their love is like something physical, it is "like gold to airy thin-
ness beat."

The three last stanzas introduce the image of a draftsman's (not an explorer's) compass, and they also introduce the circle as a symbol of perfection.

See Theodore Redpath's edition of *The Songs and Sonnets of John Donne,*
and see especially Clay Hunt, *Donne's Poetry,* and Patricia Spacks, *College
English* 29 (1968): 594-95. Louis Martz, *The Wit of Love,* 48, says of line 20:
"'Care less,' but is it so? The very rigor and intricacy of the famous image of
the compass at the end may be taken to suggest rather desperate dialectical
effort to control by logic and reason a situation almost beyond control."

TOPICS FOR CRITICAL THINKING AND WRITING

1.   The first stanza describes the death of "virtuous men." To what is their
     death compared in the second stanza?

2. Who is the speaker of this poem? To whom does he speak and what is the occasion? Explain the title.
3. What is the meaning of "laity" in line 8? What does it imply about the speaker and his beloved?
4. In the fourth stanza the speaker contrasts the love of "dull sublunary lovers" (i.e., ordinary mortals) with the love he and his beloved share. What is the difference?
5. In the figure of the carpenter's or draftsperson's compass (lines 25-36) the speaker offers reasons—some stated clearly, some not so clearly—why he will end where he began. In 250 words explain these reasons.
6. In line 35 Donne speaks of his voyage as a "circle." Explain in a paragraph why the circle is traditionally a symbol of perfection.
7. Write a farewell note—or poem—to someone you love (or hate).

JOHN DONNE

The Canonization (p. 816)

Cleanth Brooks's discussion of this poem, in his essay entitled "The Language of Paradox" in *The Well Wrought Urn* (1947), became almost the classic new-critical reading of the poem, and it can still be recommended. Another good reading—almost as old but also enduring—is by Clay Hunt, in *Donne's Poetry* (1954).

The opening line, with its explosive "For God's sake hold your tongue, and let me love," perhaps suggests to the reader that we will get an amusing, cynical male's view of love, i.e. of sexual satisfaction. Readers who notice that the first and last lines of the stanza each end with the word "love"—in fact the first and last line of every stanza ends with "love"—will admire the cleverness, but in fact the poem is more than cynical and clever; it goes on to become a serious statement about the spiritual aspects of sexual love.

In the second stanza Donne invokes the traditional Petrarchan lover, whose sighs are stormy winds at sea, whose tears are heavy rains, and so forth—but he invokes this lover with a difference. Although the speaker claims to be such a lover, sighing and weeping abundantly, he points out that in fact his emotional expressions do no damage whatsoever to the surrounding world. The stanza is amusing, but it also devalues the "real" world, i.e. shows it as a place of transience (the seasons, shipwrecks) and of unattractive activities (war, lawsuits, dying).

Even by the end of the second stanza, then, the poem seems to be chiefly a somewhat satirical love poem. In the third stanza, however, another voice begins to take over. The speaker's listener is still present ("Call us what you will"), but the speaker now is less concerned with joking, and (having diminished the outside world) he begins to argue his own case more seriously. As Clay

Hunt says, "the poem loses the lively conversational immediacy of an answer to an actual opponent and takes on instead the character of an analytic private meditation" (75). Hunt rightly adds, however, that up to the very end the poem "maintains the logical structure, if not the dramatic character of a debate" (75).

A few details about the third stanza. Why does the poet say that the onlooker may call the lovers flies? Several answers can be given—and we need not choose among them. First, perhaps the idea is that the lovers circle around each other—aimlessly, in the view of the onlooker. Second, in the Renaissance the fly was a standard emblem of the brevity of life (as was the "taper," in line 21), and, third, the fly was also an emblem of lust. The lovers "die," i.e. reach a sexual climax (a standard Renaissance meaning for "die") and also shorten their lives by their sexual activity.

The fly also, in an almost grotesque way, anticipates the eagle and the dove, and these in turn lead to the phoenix. In the eagle and the dove we get images of strength and docility, or activity and passiveness, and in the phoenix we get a similar reconciliation of opposites, since the phoenix engenders itself, i.e. seems to contain the male and the female ("to one neutral thing both sexes fit"). And this gets us to Renaissance Platonic ideas of spiritual love (either between two men, or between a man and a woman but unadulterated by physical passion).

The phoenix also contains a religious allusion, since in the Middle Ages and Renaissance it was an emblem of the resurrection of Christ. Thus the "riddle" of 22 becomes associated with the mysteries of religion (cf. "religious" in 27). All of this of course is a development of the title, "The Canonization." The lovers are not the self-indulgent sensuous persons envisioned by the onlooker at the start of the poem. Rather (Donne argues) they are saints of love. Their story ("legend") may not appear on tombs and hearses, and their names may not be in a "chronicle" (i.e. a history book), but they will survive in "verse" (29), in "sonnets" (31, i.e. love poems), and these poems are "hymns" (35—again the religious imagery).

In the final stanza the poet imagines later lovers invoking the deceased speaker and his beloved. This later age is a degenerate world ("love... now is rage"), in accordance with the tradition that nature is decaying and that this decay is accompanied by a loss of spirituality. Lovers of the future, then, will call on the earlier saints of love for intercession with God ("Beg from above / A pattern of your love").

ROBERT HERRICK

Corrina's Going A-Maying (p. 818)

The poem is discussed at length in Cleanth Brooks's *The Well-Wrought Urn*.

The motif is *carpe diem*, "seize the day," a motif found also in Marvell's

"To His Coy Mistress." If you want to teach yet another *carpe diem* poem, consider photocopying Herrick's "To the Virgins, to Make Much of Time":

To the Virgins, to Make Much of Time

Gather ye rosebuds while ye may,
    Old Time is still a-flying;
And this same flower that smiles today,
    Tomorrow will be dying.

The glorious lamp of heaven, the sun,
    The higher he's a-getting,
The sooner will his race be run,
    And nearer he's to setting.

That age is best which is the first,
    When youth and blood are warmer;
But being spent, the worse, and worst
    Times still succeed the former.

Then be not coy, but use your time;
    And while ye may, go marry:
For having lost but once your prime,
    You may for ever tarry.

[1648]

ANDREW MARVELL

To His Coy Mistress (p. 812)

Marvell's "To His Coy Mistress" is well discussed by J. V. Cunningham, *Modern Philosophy* 51 (August 1953): 33-41; by Francis Berry, *Poets' Grammar;* by Joan Hartwig, *College English* 25 (May 1964): 572-75; by Bruce King, *Southern Review* 5 (1969): 689-703; and by Richard Crider, *College Literature* 12 (Spring 1985):113-21. Incidentally, "dew" in line 35 is an editor's emendation for "glew" in the first edition (1681). Grierson suggests "glew" means a shining gum found on some trees. Another editor, Margoulieth, conjectures "lew"—that is, warmth.

Marvell's poem can be the subject of a paper involving a comparison with Herrick's "To the Virgins." Although both poems take as their theme the *carpe diem* motif, their tone and imagery differ greatly. For example, the sun in Herrick's poem ("the higher he's a-getting") does not race through the sky, but in Marvell's poem the lovers will force the sun to hurry. Or, again, in Herrick's poem the speaker is concerned not with satisfying his own desires but with the young women, whereas in Marvell's poem one strongly feels that the speaker is at least as concerned with himself as with the woman.

We have usually found it best to teach Herrick's poem before Marvell's partly because Herrick's is shorter, but chiefly because most students find it simpler.

Naturally none of the early discussions of the poem consider whether it is outrageously sexist—and, if it is, whether it should be taught. Such a discussion is probably inevitable in the classroom today, and no reader of this manual can be in need of our opinion on this topic. We will therefore comment only on some formal matters.

The poem consists of three parts, developing an argument along these lines: "If... But... Therefore." The first of these three parts is playful, the second wry or even scornful or bitter, and the third passionate. Or, to put it in slightly different terms, the poem is an argument, spoken (as the title indicates) by a male suitor to a reluctant woman. It begins with a hypothetical situation ("Had we but world enough and time") in which the speaker playfully caricatures Petrarchan conventions (fantastic promises, incredible patience). Then (21-32), with "But at my back," he offers a very different version of life, a wry, almost scornful speech describing a world in which beauty is fleeting. Finally (33-46) he offers a passionate conclusion ("Now therefore").

The conclusion, and especially the final couplet, perhaps require further comment. The "amorous birds of prey" of line 38 replace the doves of Venus found in more traditional love poetry. The destructiveness suggested by the birds is continued in the image of a "ball," which is chiefly a cannonball hurtling "thorough the iron gates of life" but is also the united lovers—that is, the ball is made up of their "strength" (chiefly his?) and "sweetness" (chiefly hers?). Some commentators find in "Tear" a suggestion of a hymen destroyed by "rough strife." The violence and the suggestions of warfare are somewhat diminished in the final couplet, but they are not absent, for the sun, though advancing, is partly imagined as an enemy that is being routed ("yet we will make him run").

We have some small uncertainties about the metrics of lines 21-22, "But at my back I always hear / Time's winged chariot hurrying near." Are "chariot" and "hurrying" disyllabic or trisyllabic? If they are trisyllabic the line contains two extra syllables, forcing the reader to hurry through the line. But of course different readers will read almost any line differently. For instance, in the first of these lines some readers will put relatively heavy stresses on the first four syllables ("But at my back"); others may rush through the first three words and put an especially heavy stress on "back," compensating for the lack of an earlier stress. In any case, these two lines surely are spoken differently from the earlier lines. Similarly, the third section, beginning with line 33, starts by sounding different. In this case almost everyone would agree that "Now therefore" gets two consecutive stresses.

WILLIAM BLAKE

The Clod and the Pebble (p. 822)

TOPICS FOR CRITICAL THINKING AND WRITING

1. What does it mean to say (lines 1-4) that self-sacrificing love "builds a Heaven in Hell's despite"? And (lines 9-12) that selfish love "builds a Hell in Heaven's despite"?
2. What would be the effect of beginning with lines 9-12, and ending with 1-4—and, of course, revising the middle stanza?

WILLIAM BLAKE

The Garden of Love (p. 822)

Instead of the freedom and innocence of the echoing green we now have the restraint of the priest-ridden garden, where desires are constrained by repressive authority.

The chapel is closed (a sign of repressiveness), priests are dressed in black, the garden has become a cemetery, and "Thou shalt not" is the prevailing spirit. To our ear, the tone is jingly, which might suggest merriment but (given the context) perhaps is meant to indicate a mechanical, lifeless place. All of the lines except the last two have three stresses each; in each of the last two lines there are four stresses, and there are also internal rhymes, which, in the context, serve to "bind" the poem, i.e. to emphasize the oppressiveness of the place.

In the illustration, children stare into a grave, and the window in the church is dark.

WILLIAM BLAKE

A Poison Tree (p. 824)

The first three lines of the last stanza are primarily trochaic, each beginning with a heavily stressed hammer-stroke emphasizing the speaker's deliberation. The last line, however, is iambic, and the shift probably contributes to our sense of the speaker's relief in contemplating the result of his perverse activity.

Fruitful images ("I watered," "I sunned," "it grew," "it bore") are used here to describe a death-giving repressive activity, the speaker delighting in his sick productivity. E. D. Hirsch, Jr., in *Innocence and Experience*, calls attention to the fact that the poem is not simply an attack on hypocrisy but is also a description of "the causes and characteristics of human fallenness."

What is the reader's attitude toward the speaker? Do we listen with horror—or are we engaged, and even delighted? After all, a reader's response to a work of literature is not at all the same as a viewer's response to a real-life happening. (The problem has been discussed at least since the days of Aristotle, who in the course of his remarks on tragedy sought to explain why we take delight in literary versions of actions that in real life would distress us.) But even in real life some morally repulsive actions may give us pleasure. One thinks of Keats's famous remark, in a letter of March 19, 1819: "Though a quarrel in the streets is a thing to be hated, the energies displayed in it are fine." Is the energy displayed in this poem "fine"?

One can, of course, disagree with Keats's general comment—or even if one agrees with Keats one can say that Keats does not speak for Blake. Does Blake give us any guidance? If we turn to *The Marriage of Heaven and Hell*, we find many statements suggesting that Blake, like Keats, delighted in energy, and (we are going a bit further) that Blake might approve of the speaker of "A Poison Tree." Here, from *The Marriage*, are some of the "Proverbs of Hell":

> Drive your cart and your plow over the bones of the dead.
> The road of excess leads to the palace of wisdom.
> If the fool would persist in his folly, he would become wise.

On the other hand, also among the "Proverbs of Hell" is this:

> He who desires but acts not, breeds pestilence.

And from elsewhere in *The Marriage of Heaven and Hell*:

> Expect poison from standing water.
> The weak in courage is strong in cunning.
> Sooner murder an infant in its cradle than nurse unacted desires.

If we were to choose a single line that seems best to represent Blake—that is, our understanding of Blake—it would be (also from *The Marriage of Heaven and Hell*) this:

> Energy is Eternal Delight

The question, then, is whether the speaker of the poem is indeed showing admirable energy, and whether we (in line with Keats's view) inevitably delight in his delight however wicked its sources, or, on the other hand, whether the speaker is one of those who are "weak in courage," a person equivalent to "standing water," someone who "desires but acts not," i.e. who acts only in piddling ways (watering, sunning, smiling) and therefore is someone who "breeds pestilence."

Perhaps, too, the whole issue is complicated by the fact that the speaker's foe is disreputable, since he steals into the garden at night. (Surely we *can* believe the speaker on this matter.)

If in class you raise the issue of to what degree, if any, we can approve of the speaker, you might wish to compare the poem with Browning's "Soliloquy of a Spanish Cloister."

EDGAR ALLAN POE

To Helen (p. 826)

The best discussion that we have come across is an old one, by M. L. Rosenthal and A. J. Smith, in *Exploring Poetry* (1955), 603-604, in a chapter on symbolism. Rosenthal and Smith begin by pointing out that the speaker is telling a sort of story: "Helen's beauty, the speaker says, has borne him 'homeward' gently and pleasurably—'o'er a perfumed sea.'" If the poem had ended with the second stanza, they add, it might seem to argue that the beauty of the woman who is addressed (if he is not addressing the original Helen) "has led him to appreciate the kindred beauty of classical art." But in the third stanza "the emphasis on classical beauty is minimized." Helen has brought the speaker, who has sailed on "desperate seas," to security, but she is nevertheless still remote, strange, and statuelike in a window-niche. By calling her Psyche he endows her "with a spiritual, unreachable quality." Further, Rosenthal and Smith suggest, because the name Psyche reminds us of the legend of Cupid and Psyche, in which the beautiful Psyche inadvertently burned Cupid with a drop of oil from her lamp and thus lost him as a husband, she is a "symbol both of beauty and of frustration." The poem therefore is not chiefly about the values of classical art. Rather, it may be about "the speaker's feelings for a particular woman," or it may even be "a confession of failure in love or in poetic achievement."

Thomas O. Mabbott, in his valuable edition, *Collected Works of Edgar Allan Poe* (1969) I,164, confidently offers a simpler, no-nonsense summary of the theme:

> It is spiritual love that leads us to beauty, a resting place from sorrow and the homeland of all that is sacred in our being. Beauty is the lasting legacy of Greece and Rome, and its supreme symbol is the most beautiful of women, Helen of Troy, daughter of Zeus, who brings the wanderer home and inspires the poet.

Who is the wanderer? Candidates include Odysseus, Dionysus, Menelaus, and Catullus. For instance, lines 2-5 may faintly recall Book XIII of the *Odyssey*, in which a Phaeacian bark carries the sleeping Odysseus to his native Ithaca. The various claims—none wholly convincing—are summarized in Mabbott's edition. Incidentally, the "desperate seas" of line 6 offer a nice example of a transferred epithet; the traveler is desperate, not the seas.

Poe revised the poem steadily, from 1831 to 1843. The most notable revisions are these:

Line 9: *from* beauty of fair *to* glory that was
Line 10: *from* And the grandeur of old *to* And the grandeur that was
Line 11: *from* that little *to* yon brilliant
Line 13: *from* folded scroll *to* agate book *to* agate lamp

ROBERT BROWNING

Porphyria's Lover (p. 827)

Compared with "My Last Duchess," this poem has more story and less of the diction of a particular speaker, but students can fairly soon see that the interest in "Porphyria's Lover" is not only in what happened but also in the speaker's mind. His insane egotism led him to attempt to preserve forever Porphyria's love for him. He believes that although she struggles to offer her love, her weakness (21-25) made her require his assistance. (Interestingly, in 6-15 she seemed energetic and efficient; perhaps there is even something a bit too efficient in making the fire before speaking to her lover.) But his egotism is tempered with solicitude (41-42,50-54), making him less monstrous but certainly mad. Inevitably, discussion in class centers on the lover's motives (do we believe them?), but it is useful to spend some time on the question of why readers enjoy the story of a mad strangler.

As for question 2 below, which asks the students to serve as the murderer's lawyer: probably the best defense is a plea of insanity, which in some twenty-five states in the United States means that a defendant who did not know what he or she was doing or that the acts were morally wrong is not criminally liable. Evidence that the speaker is insane: (1) he sees nature as hostile (the wind is "sullen," vexing the lake and tearing down the trees "for spite"); (2) he thinks Porphyria "worships" him—though perhaps she does, we can't tell; (3) he thinks that Porphyria, now dead, has her "utmost will"; and (4) he has sat "all night long" with her head on his shoulder.

By the way, a plea of insanity is usually accepted to mean that the defendant not only was mentally ill but was so ill that he did not have the capacity to control his actions or (and this is rather different) to appreciate the wrongfulness of the action. Thus a killing may be carefully planned and executed exactly according to plan, but the defendant may be judged not guilty by virtue of insanity. John Hinckley, Jr., who shot President Reagan, was so judged, although the prosecution argued that Hinckley planned carefully and was aware that he would get attention by attacking the president. In reaction to the Hinckley decision, some states have recently changed the laws governing the use of the insanity plea. That is, some states that used to allow juries to acquit a defendant if the prosecutor failed to prove beyond a reasonable doubt that the defendant was sane at the time the crime was committed now shift the burden to the defense: the defense must prove that the defendant was insane. The change is a big one, for the traditional constitutional concept of a criminal trial was that the defendant need do nothing to prove his or her innocence; the burden of proof was on the prosecutor. Students wishing to do some research on the insanity plea might look at two books: William J. Winslade and Judith Wilson Ross, *The Insanity Plea,* and Norval Morris, *Madness and the Criminal Law.*

TOPICS FOR CRITICAL THINKING AND WRITING

1.   Exactly why did the speaker murder Porphyria?
2.   You are a lawyer assigned to defend the speaker against the charge of murder. In 500 to 750 words, write your defense.

ROBERT BROWNING

Soliloquy of the Spanish Cloister (p. 828)

Because the speaker of "Soliloquy" is soliloquizing rather than addressing someone, technically the poem is not a dramatic monologue. Still, the poem is Browningesque; as in Browning's dramatic monologues, the speaker reveals himself; here, although the monk is soliloquizing about Brother Lawrence, we learn more about the speaker (he begins and ends with a growl) than we do about his ostensible subject. For example, note that his condemnation of Brother Lawrence's interest in "brown Dolores" (stanza 5) really tells us only that the speaker lusts for her, The malicious speaker, of course, though filled with hatred, is proud of his pious adherence to mealtime rituals (stanza 5), and he can, at the end, mechanically pray to the Virgin although his mind is obsessed by his hatred of Brother Lawrence.

   Whether any of us could have observed Brother Lawrence's sweetness without lapsing into hatred is a nice question, akin to what *our* response would be to the duke's ever-obliging last duchess.

If you are insatiably interested in the possible sources of line 70 ("Hy, Zy, Hine"), you will want to consult *Victorian Poetry* 17 (Winter 1979), 377-83.

TOPIC FOR WRITING

Write a soliloquy, in verse or prose, spoken by Brother Lawrence.

WALT WHITMAN

When I Heard at the Close of the Day (p. 831)

First, a few words about Whitman's sexual orientation. As the biographical note indicates, Whitman's heterosexual poems (partly remarkable because of their passages about female eroticism) aroused more indignation than what we take to be his homosexual ones, which were passed off as celebrating some sort of pure "manly love." For instance, in the first biography of Whitman, *Walt Whitman* (1883), written by Dr. Richard Maurice Bucke in collaboration with the poet, one reads that "Calamus" presents "an exalted friendship, a love into which sex does not enter as an element" (166). Some admirers saw the poems differently, but in a letter (written in response to an inquiry by John Addington Symonds, famous for his interest in "Greek love") Whitman wrote, "Though unmarried, I have had six children." Symonds apparently accepted this at face value, and in his *Walt Whitman* (1893) he said that what Whitman calls "the 'adhesiveness' of comradeship is meant to have no interblending with the 'amativeness' of sensual love" (93). But Symonds also wrote:

> Those unenviable mortals who are the inheritors of sexual anomalies, will recognize their own emotions in Whitman's "superb friendship... latent in all men."
> (93)

In the text, in our discussion of gay criticism, we mention some recent work on Whitman.

Now for a few words about "When I Heard." David Cavitch, in *My Soul and I: The Inner Life of Walt Whitman* (1985), places the poem in the context of Whitman's development:

> "When I Heard at the Close of the Day" reveals Whitman's dissatisfaction with his long-standing discipline of ambition and solitary creativity. His achievements, his acclaim, and his cronies no longer delight him, he says; he is happy only when he withdraws from it all to be with his lover at a rendezvous. But Whitman is not just on vacation: He dismisses the rewards of national fame and high accomplishments, and he emphasizes his perfect gratification in actual, private intimacy.
> (132)

We may add two points to this comment: 1) the "plaudits in the capital" were in fact muted; Whitman seems to be alluding to a single cautious newspaper review; 2) nature—the sound of the water and the sand—seems to "congratulate" him, offering an approval beyond what the public can offer.

Some commentators speak of this poem as a sort of free verse sonnet. We discuss this idea in our comment on the next poem.

WALT WHITMAN

I Saw in Louisiana a Live-Oak Crowing (p. 832)

Whitman spent two months in New Orleans, in the spring of 1848.

As Whitman sees it, the tree is like him in that it is "rude, unbending, lusty" (this is the Whitman who from the first version of *Leaves of Grass* onward celebrated himself as "one of the roughs, a kosmos, / Disorderly, fleshly and sensual… eating drinking and breeding"), but the tree is *un*like him in that it grows in solitude.

In line 3 "uttering" ("uttering joyous leaves") strikes us as especially interesting, since it attributes to the tree a voice, or, rather, sees its organic growth as akin to human speech. Whitman conceived himself as one who by nature writes poetry, as a tree by nature produces leaves.

On at least one occasion Whitman suggested that the poems in "Calamus" could be thought of as something like a group of sonnets, and some readers have felt that this poem has the feel of a sonnet with an octave and a sestet, even though it is not rhymed, is not in iambic pentameter, and has thirteen rather than fourteen lines.

The first four lines can be thought of as a quatrain (or, in terms of the structure of the whole, as roughly equivalent to the octave in an Italian sonnet) in which the poet presents the image—the tree—and relates it to himself. Then, at the beginning of line 5, comes a turn (the *volta* in an Italian sonnet), strongly marked by "But," and we get a sort of comment on the first unit, rather as a sestet in an Italian sonnet may comment on the octave. (Here the second unit runs to nine lines rather than to six.) The gist is this: the poet dwells on his difference from the tree—even as he talks about the souvenir twig that he has brought back with him. One can of course divide this second unit variously, for instance one can distinguish between the first five lines (5-9)—a group about the twig—and the remaining four lines (10-13)—a group in which the poet's thought returns to the original tree that is not only like him ("joyous") but is also unlike him ("without a friend a lover near").

WALT WHITMAN

We Two Boys Together Clinging (p. 836)

Students can learn a great deal by comparing the draft (printed in the text) with the final version. As a small example, notice the important shift in the last line from "my foray" to "our foray." One wonders, in fact, how—in a poem celebrating partnership—Whitman could have originally written "my."

The use of the present participles (cling*ing*, leav*ing*, etc.) to convey an ongoing action is not unusual, but what is unusual here is the great degree to which Whitman uses them. Similarly, the rather jingling meter of the first two lines seem uncharacteristic.

The poem has greatly interested the British painter David Hockney (now a resident of California), who has painted a picture called *We Two Boys Together Clinging*, showing two boys kissing. It is reproduced in almost all books on Hockney. In the picture the first line of the poem is written across the shoulders of the boys, and down the side of the boy at the right. The word "never" appears near the mouth of one boy (cf. the second line of the poem, "One the other never leaving"), and the word "yes" near the mouth of the other. ("Yes" is not a word found in the poem, but presumably here it is an affirmation).

MATTHEW ARNOLD

Dover Beach (p. 836)

"Dover Beach" begins with the literal—the scene that hits the eye and ear—and then moves in the second stanza to Sophocles' figurative tragic interpretation, in the third to Arnold's figurative religious interpretation, and finally—the image of the sea now being abandoned—to the simile of the world as a "darkling plain" whose only reality is the speaker and the person addressed. The end thus completes the idea of illusion versus reality that began in the first stanza, where the scene that was "calm" (1), "fair" (2), and "tranquil" (3) actually contained the discords implicit in "grating roar," "fling," and so on. In fact, even the "tonight" of the first line implies some conflict, for the word suggests that on other nights the sea is *not* calm.

For a thought-provoking reading of "Dover Beach," consult A. Dwight Culler, *Imaginative Reason: The Poetry of Matthew Arnold*. Culler argues (perhaps too ingeniously) that although some critics complain about a lack of unity in the imagery (no sea in the last section, and no darkling plain in the first), "the naked shingles *are* the darkling plain, and that we have no sea in the last section is the very point of the poem. The sea has retreated from the world...." To this point of Culler's we add that the "pebbles" flung about by the waves (10) are an anticipation of "ignorant armies" that are "swept with confused alarms of struggle and flight" (36).

Gerald Graff includes a chapter called "How to Save 'Dover Beach'" in his *Beyond the Culture Wars: How Teaching the Conflicts Can Revitalize American Education* (1992). As the title of the essay and the subtitle of the book indicate, Graff believes that works such as "Dover Beach" can best be taught by recognizing that many of today's readers find some of their assumptions unconvincing and even incomprehensible. Graff imagines an older male professor (OMP) who throws up his hands at his students' indifference to the poem, and a young female professor (YFP) who says she understands how the students feel. In fact Graff's YFP goes on not to express indifference but rather to offer a challenging reading of the poem, or at least of the last lines ("Ah, love...."). She says that this passage adds up to this:

> In other words, protect and console me, my dear—as it's the function of your naturally more spiritual sex to do—from the "struggle and flight" of politics and history that we men have been assigned the regrettable duty of dealing with. It's a good example of how women have been defined by our culture as naturally private and domestic and therefore justly disqualified from sharing male power. (38)

She goes on to say that it is precisely for this reason that we *should* teach the poem—"as the example of phallocentric discourse that it is." OMP objects that such a label "misses the whole point of poetry," and that YFP and her colleagues treat poems "as if they were statements about gender politics" rather than expressions of "universal concerns." YFP replies that literature *is*—among other things—about "gender politics." She goes on:

> What you take to be the universal human experience in Arnold and Shakespeare, Professor OMP, is male experience presented as if it were universal. You don't notice the presence of politics in literature—or in sexual relations, for that matter—because for you patriarchy is simply the normal state of affairs and therefore as invisible as the air you breathe. My reading of "Dover Beach" seems to you to reflect a "special-interest" agenda, but to me yours does, too. You can afford to "transmute" the sexual politics of literature onto a universal plane, but that's a luxury I don't enjoy. (39)

Again, Graff's chief point is that we should face the controversies—should let them enter into our teaching—and not ignore them. "For disagreements about 'Dover Beach' are not peripheral to humanistic culture; they are central to what we mean by humanistic culture" (56). And: "Controversies from which we have been trying to protect 'Dover Beach' can do a lot to save it" (63).

TOPICS FOR CRITICAL THINKING AND WRITING

1. What are the stated and implied reasons behind Arnold's implication that only love offers comfort?
2. The sea, described in the first stanza, puts the speaker in mind of two metaphors, one in the second stanza and one in the third. Explain each of these metaphors in your own words. In commenting on the first, be sure to include a remark about "turbid" in line 17.
3. Is there a connection between the imagery of the sea in the first three stanzas and the imagery of darkness in the last stanza?

WILLIAM BUTLER YEATS

For Anne Gregory (p. 838)

One can imagine Yeats, at 65, writing about a woman of 19, in response to her somewhat petulant and innocent assertion that she wants to be loved "for herself alone." Presumably she means by this her intellectual and psychological characteristics, her mind and her personality. Yeats, more or less in the role of The Wise Old Man, asserts in the first stanza that it is simply a fact that youthful lovers will be taken by her physical beauty—a beauty, by the way, that seems formidable (note "ramparts")—and thrown into despair. The old Yeats presumably remembers his own youthful feelings, but note his reference to "an old religious man" who "found a text" to prove that only God could overlook her hair and love her for herself alone. If the old man "found" the text, presumably he was looking for it. The implication seems to be that beauty captivates not only "a young man, / Thrown into despair" (1 and 2), but also "an old religious man"—to say nothing of an old irreligious man, or of Yeats—and that such a man, feeling ashamed, might well search for a text that would explain or justify his apparently indecorous feelings.

Of course Yeats is speaking somewhat playfully, even teasingly, but the overall intention is to help this young female friend ("my dear," 16) accept her exceptional beauty. She may think of her hair as yellow, and she may imagine dying it "Brown, or black, or carrot," but for Yeats, and for "young men in despair," it is "great honey-colored / Ramparts," sweet, yet magnificent and beyond reach.

If one wants to move away from the poem a bit and turn to a larger issue, one might ask whether the poem is sexist. Can we imagine a poem consisting of a dialogue between an older woman and a young man, in which the woman assures the man that young women can never love him for himself alone, but only for his blond (or raven-black) hair (or profile, or body)? If one can't imagine such a poem, *why* can't one? Is it because a sexist view prevents us from imagining an old woman giving good advice to a young man? Or is it perhaps because Yeats's poem touches on a truth, that is, young men are captivated by youthful female beauty, whereas the hypothetical poem is false; that is, young women are not taken chiefly by youthful male beauty? Or is it sexist to assume that, confronted with the opposite sex, the primary interests of young men and young women differ?

TOPICS FOR CRITICAL THINKING AND WRITING

1. What can you imagine Anne saying that provoked the poem?
2. In the first stanza Anne's hair is described both as "great honey-colored ramparts" and as "yellow." Why does the speaker use these two rather different characterizations? Judging from the second stanza, how would Anne describe her hair?
3. If you did not know that Yeats was 65 when he wrote the poem, would you be able to deduce from the poem itself that the speaker of the first and third stanzas is considerably older than Anne?
4. Anne says that she wants to be loved "for myself alone." Exactly what do you think this expression means?
5. Why would "an old religious man" search until he found a text that would prove that only God could love her for herself alone? Do you think Yeats shares this view?
6. In a sentence or two characterize Yeats as he reveals himself in this poem, and then characterize Anne.

An audiocassette of W. B. Yeats reading is available from HarperCollins.

EZRA POUND

The River-Merchant's Wife: A Letter (p. 839)

One of Pound's comments to William Carlos Williams may be useful (from *Letters of Ezra Pound, 1907-41*, edited by D. D. Paige, 3-4):

> To me the short so-called dramatic lyric—at any rate the sort of thing I do—is the poetic part of a drama the rest of which (to me the prose part) is left to the reader's imagination or implied or set in a short note. I catch the character I happen to be interested in at the moment he interests me, usually a moment of song, self-analysis, or sudden understanding or revelation. And the rest of the play would bore me and presumably the reader.

Pound, of course, learned much from Browning's dramatic monologues, and this comment could, in a general way, apply to Browning's poems. But it is worth exploring with students the way in which "The River-Merchant's Wife" differs from "My Last Duchess." For one thing, Pound's speaker (like so many of the speakers in his early poems) is relatively naive, and so the poem gives us an impression of a "pure" and universal sort, whereas Browning's gives us an impression of a particular case history. Moreover, Browning customarily gives us considerably more sense of a particular period than Pound does or, to put it a little differently, Browning—even in "My Last Duchess"—gives us a greater sense of a particular character interacting with particular circumstances of the age. Pound based his poem on a prose translation by Ernest Fenollosa of a poem by the Chinese poet Li Po (in Japanese, called Rihaku). A transcription of the Fenollosa manuscript is printed in Michael Reck, *Ezra Pound: A Close-up*, 168-71.

EDNA ST. VINCENT MILLAY

The Spring and the Fall (p. 840)

We begin with the rhyme scheme of the poem.

year	*a* (with internal *a*)
dear	*a*
wet	*b*
year	*a* (with internal *b*)
peach	*c*
reach	*c*
year	*a* (with internal *a*)
dear	*a*
trill	*d*
year	*a* (with internal *d*)
praise	*e*
ways	*e*
falling	*f* (with an internal *f*, but as an off-rhyme)
calling	*f*
hear	*a*
year	*a* (with internal *d*)
days	*e*
ways	*e*

Obviously there's lots of rhyme here; this is a highly lyrical lyric, close to song. In addition to the repetition of sound gained through rhyme, there are other repetitions—not only in the form of alliteration (e.g., "bough... blossoming," "rooks… raucous") and consonance (e.g., "trees… see") but also in the form of entire words: the first half of the first line is repeated verbatim in the second half of the line; "In the spring of the year" (1) becomes "In the fall of the year" (7), words repeated verbatim in the second half of the line, and in the third stanza the two phrases about the seasons are joined in 1.16, but with a significant change: "the" year becomes "a" year.

Many highly lyrical poems employ what can be called a repetitive or perhaps an intensifying structure, each stanza going over the same ground, deepening the feeling but not advancing a narrative, even a narrative of the progress of a feeling. "The Spring and the Fall," however, is a lyric that includes a narrative, a progression, as a reader probably suspects immediately from the title. The first stanza deals with spring, the second with fall. Further, in the first stanza the lovers are physically and emotionally united (they walk together, and he obligingly—lovingly—presents her with "a bough of the blossoming peach"); in the second stanza the lovers are together only physically, not emotionally: "He laughed at all I dared to praise." Instead of giving her a gift, he laughs at (not with) her, and we hear of rooks making a "raucous" sound. The last line of the second stanza explicitly announces the break: "And broke my heart, in little ways." (The word "way," incidentally, was introduced in the first stanza—the peach-bough he gave her a sign of his love, "was out of the way and hard to reach." And in the last stanza "ways" appears again, in the last line, where we are told that when love went it "went in little ways.")

Another notable difference between the first two stanzas: ordinarily the stanzas in a lyric poem repeat a metrical pattern, but in this poem the last two lines of the second stanza are shorter than the last two lines of the first two stanza, thus conveying a sense of something cut short. The difference is made especially evident by the fact that the change is unanticipated; the first two lines of the second stanza closely resemble (as one expects) the first two lines of the first stanza.

The narrative, then, in effect is completed at the end of the second stanza. Or nearly so: although at the end of the second stanza we learn that the speaker's heart was broken "in little ways," we don't learn until the last two lines of the third stanza that what especially hurts is that love went "in little ways." The third stanza, as has already been mentioned, brings the two seasons together; its first four lines seem joyous and loving, but its last two lines comment on the end of this love affair. The third stanza differs from the first two in several technical details. For example, as we have already mentioned, the first line of the first stanza, like the first line of the second stanza, repeats a phrase ("In the spring of the year, in the spring of the year," "In the fall of the year, in the fall of the year"). The third stanza, however, reflecting a different state of mind, begins with a different form of repetition: "Year be springing or year be falling." Another difference, admittedly small, is that the third stanza is the only stanza to use a feminine rhyme ("falling… calling").

EDNA ST. VINCENT MILLAY

Love Is Not All: It Is not Meat nor Drink (p. 841)

Late in the poem a phrase in line 12 (" the memory of this night") identifies the speaker (a lover), the audience (the beloved), and the time (a night of love), but the poem begins drily, even rather pedantically. A somewhat professorial voice delivers a lecture on love, beginning authoritatively with four almost equally stressed monosyllables ("Love is not all"). Then, warming to the subject, the speaker becomes more expansive, with "It is not... nor... Nor... nor... And... and... and... and... can not... Nor... nor," all in the octave. Of course, in saying that love cannot do this and that we sense, paradoxically, a praise of love, if we have read a fair amount of love poetry, perhaps we expect the octave to yield to a sestet that will say what love *can* do. But this sestet too begins with apparent objectivity, as if making a concession ("It well may be"). Then, like the octave, the sestet introduces a romantic note while nominally proclaiming realism, although its images are somewhat less exotic (there is nothing like the "floating spar" of line 3, for instance) than the images of the octave. On the other hand, insofar as it introduces a more personal or a more intense note ("the memory of this night"), and reveals that the poem is addressed to the beloved, it is *more* romantic. In any case the sestet comes down to earth, and at the same times reaches a romantic height, in its last line, which consists of two sentences: "It may well be. I do not think I would." The brevity of these two sentences, and the lack of imagery, presumably convey a dry humor that the octave lacks, and at the same time they make an extremely romantic claim. (Surely "I do not think I would" is an understatement; in effect, it is a passionate declaration.) Put it this way: although the octave asserts, for example, that love is not meat and drink and cannot heal the sick, and the first part of the sestet asserts that the speaker "might" give up the beloved's love in certain extreme circumstances, the understated passion of the conclusion serves to dismiss these assertions as unlikely—indeed, a reader feels, as untrue. Although to the rational mind "love is not all," to the lover it is "all," and a lover here is doing the talking.

ROBERT FROST

The Silken Tent (p. 842)

The idea of comparing a woman to a silken tent in the summer breeze seems fresh enough to us (probably swaying silken tents have been compared to young women, but did anyone before Frost see it the other way around?), and given this idea, one would expect passages about gentle swaying. If one knew the piece were going to be an allegory worked out in some detail, one might expect the tent pole to be the soul. But who could have expected the brilliant connection between the cords and " ties of love and thought," and the brilliant suggestion that only rarely are we made aware—by "capriciousness"—of our "bondage"? The paradoxical idea that we are (so to speak) kept upright—are what we are—by things that would seem to pull us down is new to most students, who think that one "must be oneself." With a little discussion they come to see that what a person is depends largely on relationships. We are parents, or students, or teachers, or— something; our complex relationships give us our identity. Sometimes, in trying to make clear this idea that our relationships contribute to (rather than diminish) our identities, we mention the scene in Ibsen's *Peer Gynt* where, in an effort to get at his essential self, Peer peels an onion, each removed layer being a relationship that he has stripped himself of. He ends with nothing, of course.

In short, we think this poem embodies a profound idea, and we spend a fair amount of our class time talking about that idea. But we also try to look at the poem closely. Students might be invited to discuss what sort of woman "she" is. What, for instance, do "midday" and "summer" in line 2 contribute? Frost could, after all, have written "In morning when a sunny April breeze" but he probably wanted to suggest—we don't say a mature woman—someone who is no longer girlish, someone who is of sufficient age to have established responsibilities, and to have experienced, on occasion, a sense of slight bondage. Among the traits that we think can be reasonably inferred from the comparison are these: beauty, poise, delicacy (in lines 1-4), and sweetness and firmness of soul (5-7).

TOPICS FOR CRITICAL THINKING AND WRITING

1. The second line places the scene at "midday" in "summer." In addition to giving us the concreteness of a setting, do these words help to characterize the woman whom the speaker describes? If so, how?
2. The tent is supported by "guys" (not men, but the cords or "ties" of line 10) and by its "central cedar pole." What does Frost tell us about these ties? What does he tell us about the pole?
3. What do you make of lines 12-14?
4. In a sentence, a paragraph, or a poem, construct a simile that explains a relationship.

ADRIENNE RICH

Diving into the Wreck (p. 844)

Most responses identify the wreck as either (1) the speaker's life (persons familiar with Rich's biography may identify it specifically as her unhappy marriage to a man who committed suicide in 1970, about three years before the poem was published) or (2) more broadly, our male-dominated society. Another way of putting it is to say that the poem is about sexual politics. The poem is discussed by Wendy Martin and by Erica Jong in *Adrienne Rich's Poetry*, ed. Barbara C. Gelpi and Albert Gelpi. Part of the following comment is indebted to their discussions.

Armed with a book of myths (an understanding of the lies society has created?) and a camera and a knife (an instrument of vision and an instrument of power?) she goes, alone, in contrast to Cousteau assisted by a team, to explore the wreck. (This sort of exploration can be done only by the individual. One might add, by the way, that it is a new sort of exploration, an exploration for which Rich had no maps. Before the second half of the twentieth century, there was virtually no poetry about what it was like to be a wife or a woman living in a male-dominated society. The earlier poetry written by women was chiefly about children, love, and God.) More exactly, she is there, exploring the wreck ("I came to explore the wreck" implies that she is speaking from the site itself). She has immersed herself in the primal, life-giving element and has now arrived in order "to see the damage that was done / and the treasures that prevail," that is, to see not only what is ruined but also what is salvageable. Her object is to find truth, not myth (62-63).

Lines 72-73, in which she is both mermaid and merman, and line 77, in which "I am she; I am he," suggest that she has achieved an androgynous nature and thus has become the sort of new woman who will tell the truth. According to lines 92-94, the names of such true persons, or androgynes, persons who may rescue civilization, do not appear in the book of myths.

ADRIENNE RICH

Novella (p. 846)

The third-person point of view (for what the reader almost surely takes as an episode from the author's life), the flat tone, and the title serve to distance the work, serve, we might say, to make it prosaic, since poems usually express passion. But of course these devices, like other devices such as understatement, mask deep feeling.

Despite the man's return to the house, and the somewhat absurd situation where he finds that because he has forgotten his key he must ring the bell of his own house in order to enter, we take it that the quarrel is not resolved. That is, he *does* return, and "The lights go on in the house"—this might seem to be a sign of reunion, the dispelling of the darkness of anger, etc.—but the last two lines ("Outside, separate as minds, / the stars too come alight") seem to us to indicate that the man and the woman remain "separate." Some of our students have disagreed with us.

ADRIENNE RICH

XI (from Twenty-One Love Poems) (p. 847)

Nothing in this poem specifies the sex of the speaker, but since the author is a woman perhaps most readers assume that the speaker is a woman. Such an assumption is usually fairly safe but certainly not always. In this case, however, it is true; the surrounding poems make it clear that the speaker is a woman.

TOPIC FOR CRITICAL THINKING AND WRITING

We know from the context—the poem is one of a group of twenty-one poems—that it is about two women in love. But can the poem—at least out of context—be read equally well as a poem about heterosexual lovers?

ROBERT PACK

The Frog Prince (p. 848)

The tale recorded by the Grimm Brothers is not quite as we remembered it. In our memory—and we think that perhaps most people share this view—a handsome young prince has been turned into a frog by a witch, and he cannot regain his human shape until a beautiful woman kisses him, i.e. loves him, or at least pities him. It all works out all right, and the implicit moral is (as in the story of "Beauty and the Beast") that love is so powerful that it can transform the beloved, or that those who pity the unfortunate will themselves be rewarded, or something along those lines.

In fact, the Grimm story is rather different. The trouble is, even the earliest English translation of Grimm, *German Popular Tales* (1823), changed the story considerably. (The version given in this first English translation is reprinted in Iona and Peter Opie, *The Classic Fairy Tales* [1974].) The Grimm version is, however, readily available in *The Juniper Tree*, trans. Lore Segal. In the original story (i.e. the German version printed by the Grimm Brothers), the girl does not love the frog; she promises him that she will let him live with her if he retrieves a golden ball. She makes the promise lightly, assuming that the frog cannot get out of the well. Her father, however, insists that she keep the promise. In a fit of anger, she throws the frog against a wall, and it becomes the human being that it earlier was. Folklorists believe that the Grimm Brothers probably added the bit about the father insisting that the girl keep her promise, in order to make the story suitably instructive for children, but even with this added bit of moralizing the story as a whole remains morally chaotic. As Maria Tatar says, in *Off with Their Heads! Fairy Tales and the Culture of Childhood* (1992),

> Although the princess of "The Frog King" is selfish, greedy, ungrateful, and cruel, in the end she does as well for herself as all the modest, obedient, magnanimous, and compassionate Beauties of "The Search for the Lost Husband." Much as the Grimms tried to rewrite the tale with paternal prompts about the importance of keeping promises and showing gratitude, they could not succeed in camouflaging the way in which the tale rewards indignant rage. (154)

This is not really surprising. Nineteenth-century versions of fairy tales *don't* usually have nice morals; on the contrary, they are often nightmarish things, especially nightmarish because their arbitrariness seems meaningless. We should mention, however, that in Freudian thought the meaning is evident: The slimy frog who seeks to get into the princess's bed is a scarcely veiled phallic symbol; the penis attains completeness only when accepted by a partner.

It may be useful to ask students if they have encountered the story of the prince who, transformed into a frog, can regain his human shape only when accepted by a beautiful woman. Probably some will report a saying popular among young women, "You have to kiss a lot of frogs before you find a prince."

We don't know what version of the story Robert Pack started from, but since he does not mention the startling episode of the princess hurling the frog against the wall, we suspect that he may have drawn on a moralized version of the sort we mentioned at the outset, where the princess out of love or tenderness or sympathy accepts the frog. Pack's first quatrain deals chiefly with the princess's surprise at the change in the frog; in the second quatrain and in the first part of the third quatrain her thoughts turn from the frog to herself—first, to the thought that *she* has transformed him, and then to the thought that in turn *she has been transformed* by the sexual act. The second half of the third quatrain, and the final two lines of the poem (we can't quite call them a couplet since they don't rhyme with each other, and in fact the fourteenth line rhymes with the twelfth) bring us down to earth when the mother sees the girl with the prince: "What was it that her mother said?" Obviously Pack is making a little joke; he takes a myth (a puzzling one, if he is working from the original version, or a pretty one, if he is working from the moralized version) and he subjects it to a common-sense mentality. But the joke is also serious; the poem forces the reader to think of the gap between the mother and the transformed girl. In line 6 the word "wonder"—in the sense of "marvelous thing"—explicitly refers to the transformation of the frog, but we can apply it also to the transformation of the girl. Of course the mother once was similarly transformed, but in the poem the contrast is between the girl, who has suddenly entered into a marvelous new world, made by love, and the mother, whose remarks, though not given, can easily be imagined.

ELLEN BRYANT VOIGHT

Quarrel (p. 848)

We know that the people quarreling are a married couple, with some children. They have been quarreling since morning, and through lunch, and all afternoon, and through dinner, and "the sun long gone," even in bed, back to back. They will continue to quarrel the next day, or the next. We don't know what they quarrel about, but that doesn't matter. They might not even use words to quarrel. The last lines tells us that they need to wound each other as they have been and are being wounded by others. (Many students will be unwilling to agree that "love" is the right word in our third question.)

We ask students to try to characterize the landscape, beginning with

> the sun pouring its implacable white bath
> over the birches, each one undressing
> slyly, from the top down....

The rich tide of human energy here in the sun and in the birches—hardly neutral, with the sun's "implacable white tide" and the birches "undressing/slyly from the top down"—suggests to us someone already in the quarrel, the speaker, who can also speak the last lines. It is interesting, too, that after, in lines 7-8,

> the plush clouds lowering a gray matte
> for the barn

(again, odd human energy for the approach of noon) the language for the quarrel and the landscape are fused:

> they see the top of this
> particular mountain, its glacial headwall

The "particular mountain" is, we believe, what stands between the quarrelers, not outside. "The pitch is terrific all through dinner" deliberately confuses the images, as the pitch can be of the mountain's slope or of the sound of the quarrel. (We believe, however, that the ambiguity of "they" in line 12 intends to refer to the adults.) And

> the two of them back to back in the
> blank constricting bed, like marbles on aluminum—

turns the quarrelers into inanimate beings, moved by their circumstances, in a "constricting" bed and "on aluminum."

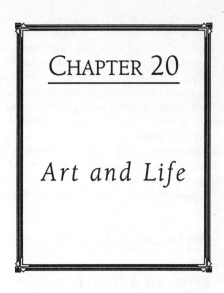

CHAPTER 20

Art and Life

PABLO PICASSO

Talking about Art (p. 853)

We think that all of these comments are extremely engaging, and all (or almost all) of them can provoke lively responses from students.

The comment about roosters ("roosters have always been seen but seldom so well as in American weather vanes") can be related to the first comment (about art as a lie that makes us realize truth), which is the subject of the first question in the text. At bottom it gets to the idea that art gives us the essential. The idea more or less is in accordance with Aristotle's distinction between history and poetry: History tells us what happened, poetry tells us what happens.

CAMILLE PAGLIA

Madonna: Animality and Artifice (p. 856)

Perhaps the heart of the essay is the beginning of the fifth paragraph: "The video is pornographic. It's decadent. And it's fabulous." For Paglia, the most interesting art is strongly sexual, bringing the reader or spectator into close contact with animality. But (as the rest of her title indicates) there must be "artifice" too. In these few pages Paglia doesn't argue this point—she barely asserts it beyond her title—but it is implicit in such a sentence as this, in paragraph 10: "She shows girls how to be attractive, sensual, energetic, ambitious, aggressive, and funny—all at the same time." Obviously it takes "artifice"— skill, cunning, artistry—to do all this at once.

A point that many students (and others) find objectionable or at least difficult to grasp is that art can be strongly sexual—indecent, in the view of many—and yet educational, life-enhancing, or whatever words one wants to use. Notice, that is, Paglia's assertion (again in paragraph 10) that "Madonna has taught young women to be fully female and sexual while still exercising control over their lives." Plenty here for classroom discussion.

WILLA CATHER

Light on Adobe Walls (p. 858)

We don't know why Cather gave this essay the title that she did. Perhaps the essay—which was unpublished at her death—is incomplete, and she never got around to talking about the adobe walls.

The first few sentences, about freedom, will probably come as something of a surprise to most students, many of whom associate art with freedom. But Cather is really not saying anything very surprising. After all, as soon as a writer writes the first line, or the painter applies the first brushstroke, the beginning of a pattern is established. This is obviously true when a poet uses a strict form: as soon as Shakespeare wrote, "That time of year thou may'st in me behold," he knew he had to find, in the third line, a rhyme for "behold." Of course there were many possibilities—"fold," "bold," "sold," and so on— but that first line limited his freedom. In fact, even before he got to the end of the line he was limited, since from the first word onward his form required a line that was primarily iambic pentameter.

Robert Frost may have thought he was relatively free when he started to write "Stopping by Woods," since his first stanza rhymes *aaba,* but then he had to do something with that *b,* and it became the rhyming word at the end of the first line of the next stanza, which rhymes *bbcb.* The next stanza therefore *had* to rhyme *ccdc.* The only problem was, How to end this? What to do with the unrhymed line? His solution, of course, is famous: *dddd.* It seems obvious, inevitable; but it was a stroke of genius for Frost to see exactly how his fetters might best be fastened.

If you do assign this essay, and dwell on this point, you may find it effective to call attention to Picasso's anecdote (in the text) about the anarchists in the army. The command was "Right face," and (Picasso says) "since they are anarchists, they all face left.... There you are again, in chains."

The gist of our second question, about Cather's response to Shakespeare's *The Tempest*, probably will already have come up in class if you have assigned the play. Cather is echoing the dominant early twentieth-century view, that the play smacks of a declaration to cease writing. (This idea is especially associated with Lytton Strachey, whose essay we give in the text.) The idea arose in an age when biographical criticism was highly popular, and it seemed to make sense, since it was known that *The Tempest* was Shakespeare's last play, or at least the last play for which he was entirely responsible. (People persist in thinking that after *The Tempest* he may have given John Fletcher a hand in later plays.) Although most of today's criticism of the play eschews biographical motifs, and concentrates on politics and gender, it is hard to dismiss the old idea that the play includes Shakespeare's farewell to the stage—you know, that business of Prospero saying

> I'll break my staff,
> Bury it certain fathoms in the earth,
> And deeper than did ever plummet sound
> I'll drown my book. (5.1. 54-57)

And if that isn't convincing enough, how about this:

> And thence retire me to my Milan, where
> Every third thought shall be of my grave. (5.1.310-311)

Still, if we didn't know that this is Shakespeare's last play, would we see in these lines the dramatist's retreat to Stratford? (And of course we don't know if Shakespeare himself knew, when he wrote this play, that it would be his last.) In any case, Cather's view was pretty much the view of the age, and a view that is entirely understandable and that (although now out of fashion) may be right.

NATHANIEL HAWTHORNE

The Artist of the Beautiful (p. 859)

Commentary on Hawthorne's story has not changed greatly since 1979, when Lea Bertani Votar Newman, in *A Reader's Guide to the Short Stories of Nathaniel Hawthorne* said that

> The spectrum ranges from an affirmation of the value of art and the triumph of the Romantic idealist over a materialistic society to a condemnation of the artist

and his ignominious defeat by the forces of life. A great many middle positions between these two extremes have been taken, some of the defined by the degree of irony that each reader perceives. (23)

In short, is Owen an idealistic artist who takes risks in an insensitive material-istic society, or is he a hybristic fool, who detaches himself from society—or is he something in between? Or did Hawthorne bungle the story? Millicent Bell (*Hawthorne's View of the Artist* [1962]) thinks that Hawthorne began by pre-senting Owen's story (and Transcendentalism) sympathetically, but then began to undercut what he himself had just written, and, in the end, "felt, like Annie, 'a secret scorn' for the artist" (105).

What of Owen? On the one hand, the text calls him a "genius" and a "being of thought, imagination, and keenest sensibility"; on the other hand, he is said to be "full of little petulances" and of a "morbid sensibility." Or take his foil, Robert Danforth. Danforth is a philistine when he says, "There is more real use in one downright blow of my sledge hammer than in the whole five years' labor that our friend Owen has wasted on this butterfly" (par. 96), but Hawthorne in several passages makes Danforth sympathetic, saying (for instance) that Danforth's "massage substance [was] thoroughly warmed and attempered by domestic influences."

And what of Annie's baby, who destroys Owen's butterfly? The baby is "a little personage who had come mysteriously out of the infinite, but with some-thing so sturdy and real in his composition that he seemed moulded out of the densest substance which earth could supply."

In her survey of the commentary Newman ably lays out the bases (philo-sophical, sociological, and psychological) for the differences in interpretation. The conflicting philosophical or ideological forces are Puritanism distrustful of art) and Romanticism (glorifying art as a spiritual value). And for some read-ers, the story shows Hawthorne's wavering; he could not accept the Puritan dismissal of art, but he also could not accept the elevated romantic view of art, or the romantic view that the artist's imagination is greater than any work of art that this imagination may produce.

This last idea, that what counts is the imagination, and not the finished things that the imagination produces, is perhaps best known in several lines by Robert Browning, for instance "What's come to perfection perishes," or "faultless to a fault," or "Less is more." In this last quotation, from "Andrea del Sarto," the idea is that it is better to aim high, and to fail to achieve what one can imagine, than to aim low and to fulfill one's aspirations. Tennyson, too, has passages along these lines, such as "Faultily faultless, icily regular, splendidly null, / Dead perfection, no more." In Hawthorne's story, the destruction of the butterfly has sometimes been taken as of no great importance; what *is* important, in this view, is the artist's aspiration. The narrator tells us that Owen contemplates the child's destructive act with equanimity, for he had caught a far other butterfly than this. When the artist rose high enough to achieve the beautiful, the symbol by which he made it perceptible to mortal senses became of little value in his eyes, while his spirit possessed itself in the enjoyment of the reality.

These are the last words of the story, and their place gives them special force. True, in earlier pages in the story Owen has been subjected to criticism, and we may remember those passages, but the final words seem pretty positive. The story can be read as the narrative of Owen's growth; he had had his lapses, and he has behaved foolishly, but by the end he understands (as he had not understood earlier, for instance when he was distressed that Annie tinkered with his "little whirligig") that art, like life, is subject to destruction. There are, however, readers who find the ending solipsistic, i.e. who insist that Owen is deluding himself. Nina Baym, for instance, in *The Shape of Hawthorne's Career* (1976), says that Owen's greatest creation is only "an ideal which is lifeless and depthless; he creates a fragile cold bauble which literally represents the belittling of Imagination" (126).

This brings Lea Newman to the issue of the artist and society. She points out that some critics blame the materialistic society for Owen's alienation (and here they see Hawthorne complaining about his own lot in an unsympathetic environment). But many readers notice that Hawthorne does not simply present an unattractive material world and a sensitive artist; rather, he makes the material world fairly attractive (Danforth may be a bit crude, but he seems to be a decent fellow) and he makes Owen rather unattractive. The question really is this: Does the story show Owen's spiritual progress, or does it show his progressive folly—or something of both?

In her survey of psychological responses, Newman finds that most commentators are hostile to Owen; he is said to be paranoid, narcissistic, attempting to sublimate homosexual tendencies, impotent, and so on. Frederick Crews, for instance, in *The Sins of the Fathers* (1966) says that Owen (like Hawthorne's other artists) is a "sexual escapist" (166) who sublimates his sexual desires, and turns to "the ideal only as a refuge from his weakness of temperament and physique" (167). Owen "has turned to the ideal only as a refuge from his weakness of temperament and physique, and it is notable that he is "conspicuously wanting in masculinity" (167). In this view, the victory of art is the failure of manhood. Crews says,

> The baby's destruction of the butterfly is superficially presented as one last act of ungrateful disbelief on the part of the world, before Owen's Platonism has the final say; but Hawthorne has taken pains to remind us that the source of that Platonism is impotence. (169)

On the other hand, Richard Yoder convincingly suggests, in an essay originally published in *Studies in Romanticism* 7 (1968), and reprinted in *Critical Essays on Hawthorne's Short Stories* (1991), ed. Albert J. von Frank, that

The moral of the tale... is that art's highest achievement is to make a man of the artist. Hawthorne is saying that the artistic life is worthwhile even if the artist is unproductive or his work is lost; the artist is still a finer person for it. Given this view, one cannot agree with... Crews' idea that the victory of art coincides with the failure of manhood. (179)

WILLA CATHER

A Wagner Matinee (p. 876)

The headnote in the text mentions that Cather revised the story when she republished it. Most of the revisions were in the direction of cutting unfavorable descriptions of the aunt. To take a single example: In the first (1904) version, the second paragraph began thus:

> The name of my Aunt Georgiana called up not alone her own figure, at once pathetic and grotesque, but opened before my feet a gulf of recollections....

In the 1920 version the corresponding passage reads thus:

> The name of my Aunt Georgiana opened before me a gulf of recollection....

But the revisions consist of additions, too, the most interesting of which we call attention to in our questions at the end of the story. There is, of course, throughout the story an opposition between the musical (i.e. high cultural) life of Boston and the farm life in Nebraska, but it seems to us that the added passage, describing the moment after the performance, when the performers leave "the stage to the chairs and music stands, empty as a winter cornfield," presents a devastating comparison. The deserted stage, with its sticks of furnishings, Cather suggests, is an image of the life in the West to which the aunt must return.

Biographers point out that Cather indeed had an aunt, by marriage, who had musical interests, who had been educated at Mount Holyoke Female Seminary, and who married and went off to Nebraska with her husband, and who did make a brief return to the East. Biographers further point out that Cather wrote the story while she was living in Pittsburgh, and some of them suggest that the story expresses her fear that she too may some day be forced to return to the bleak frontier life that awaits the aunt. Certainly the picture of life in Nebraska is unattractive, and Cather rubs it in, for instance by juxtaposing *within a single paragraph* the frontier, "where, as in a treadmill, one might walk from daybreak to dusk without perceiving a shadow," against the clean profiles of the musicians, the gloss of their linen, the dull black of their coats, the beloved shapes of the instruments, the patches of yellow light on the smooth, varnished bellies of the 'cellos and the bass viols in the rear, the restless, wind-tossed forest of fiddle necks and bows....

But the story is not really, at bottom, about two parts of the country, or even about two ways of life. And even less is it about the extinction of sensibility that overtakes those who live on the frontier. Quite the opposite. The story is about the aunt's ability to respond to the music, or, we might generalize, about the ability of music to raise us above ourselves. Not that even without music we are such bad creatures. The aunt displays a thoroughly commendable concern for "a certain weakling calf," and for "the freshly-opened kit of mackerel in the cellar," but somehow the music makes even such humane considerations evaporate.

Some readers emphasize the change in the narrator. Thus, Susan J. Rosowski, in *The Perilous Voyage: Willa Cather's Romanticism* (1986) suggests that Clark moves "from cold objectivity to empathy" (27). Certainly the story is about emotions, rather than about geography, but to say that the narrator undergoes a great change is (we think) to overlook such early explicit statements of feeling as Clark's assertion, in the fourth paragraph, that he regarded his aunt with "awe and respect," and (the first sentence of the next paragraph) that he "owed to this woman most of the good that ever came [his] way in [his] boyhood," and that he "had a reverential affection for her." True, he says he judged her "superficially" in thinking she might be embarrassed by her clothing, but this is only to say he made an intellectual error, not that he regarded her coldly. Similarly, Clark sounds a trifle condescending when in the middle of the story he begins to think perhaps he ought to get his aunt "back to Red Willow County without waking her," but this thought strikes us as not only well-intentioned but also as perfectly natural. In fact, by the end of the story, although presumably readers are glad that the aunt has been deeply moved, they probably also are distressed on her behalf. That is, we would not want to deprive her of the ecstasy, but we realize that the experience immensely heightens the pain of her return to Nebraska, and surely we don't condemn Clark for entertaining the idea of sparing her this distress. In brief, our view is that during the progress of the story a reader of course gets deeper into Clark's mind as well as into the aunt's, but we think it is a mistake to turn the story into one about a callow youth who comes to respect his aunt.

We are also unconvinced by the suggestion in Loretta Wasserman, *Willa Cather: A Study of the Short Fiction* (1991), that (in the paragraph we quote above, where Cather juxtaposes the shadowless plains of Nebraska with the contours and colors of the orchestra) Cather "hints, just hints, that there is a link between the austere beauty of the plains and the designs of musical form" (30). But the point is worth raising in class.

KURT VONNEGUT, JR.

Who Am I This Time? (p. 881)

The story is easy, and can be taught effectively as an introduction to fiction if you don't want to begin with our chapter on fiction.

The gist of the story, of course, concerns characterless people who achieve characters through literature. Harry is a mousy clerk of uncertain parentage, and Helene is a rootless girl without hope or curiosity, but this very lack of personality—this negative capability, to use Keats's term—proves to be an asset to the actors, and finally proves to be the means by which they achieve emotion and character. Helene, if not Harry, rises not only to the play but also to a lasting emotion; when the play is over Harry fades back into his normal life as clerk, but Helene, continuing to love him, is transformed from a hopeless nothing into a girl with a purpose. Note too that it was through art (i.e., movies) that she was at first enabled to perform satisfactorily the role of Stella. One doesn't want to press the story too hard, but it is fair to say that it deals with the role of art in life, and that it implies that life imitates art, in contrast to the old idea that art imitates life.

HISAYE YAMAMOTO

Seventeen Syllables (p. 890)

Of course the story is largely concerned with the conflict between the parents, and with the naive daughter's responses—we might have included this story in the section called "Parents and Children"—but it is also concerned with the role of art (here, *haiku* poetry) in the mother's life.

We are not told exactly why the mother turned to writing *haiku*, and it is easy to assume that she did so in an effort to escape from her brusque hard-working husband. But this view is needlessly reductive. And in any case she apparently is skilled in writing poetry. It seems reasonable, then, to assume that her interest, whatever its origins, is thoroughly genuine. The unfortunate result, however, is that it increasingly isolates her from her husband. His isolation is emphasized in the scene at the Hayano's, where the children form one group, and her mother and Mr. Hayano form another. Rosie's father, alone, leafs through the magazine, and occasionally shows a photo to Mrs. Hayano, speaking to her in an unnecessarily loud voice.

Presumably the mother's interest in literature exasperates the father not so much because it takes her away from work—though this is his excuse for his actions—but because it is a world that he cannot enter. Appropriately, the prize that he destroys is a work of art, a print by Hiroshige.

Students interested in thinking about psychological explanations for the appeal of the arts may want to look at Freud's "Writers and Day-Dreaming" (1908), in volume 10 of *The Standard Edition of the Complete Psychological Works of Sigmund Freud*, ed. James Strachey. Freud here argues that a work of art embodies (in an acceptable form) the writer's fantasies, and we readers take pleasure in a work of art because it offers fantasies in a harmonious form. For a quick introduction to Freud and the appeal of the arts, see Lionel Trilling's "Freud and Literature," in Trilling's *The Liberal Imagination* (1950).

JANE FLANDERS

Van Gogh's Bed (p. 902)

Ms. Flanders has kindly furnished us with some remarks about her poem. She writes:

> The desire for simplicity [expressed in van Gogh's letters] would seem to be at the heart of the painting. Likewise the poem is "simple," even crude, especially the stubby first line of each stanza with its list of rudimentary adjectives. But what we are given, in both instances, is, of course, the illusion of simplicity. In the painting the room ought to seem restful, Actually it excites the eye with its bright colors, bold strokes, and odd angles. Even the bed itself looks as if it might levitate or drive off like some magical conveyance. A childlike playfulness invites the poet's reverie.
>
> By what wonderful process was it made? What did he dream about when he slept in it? The artist's absence (the empty bed) which may at first seem innocuous or self-evident (he's busy painting the picture, isn't he?) also reminds us that he would have his first mental crisis a few months later and his suicide at the age of thirty-seven was little more than a year away. Likewise, in the poem's final stanza, concrete details give way to something more elusive—light, fragrance, and not happiness itself, but the memory of happiness, with its hint of loss and melancholy.

We hope we are not being presumptuous if we add a few remarks of our own.

1) Using the title as the beginning—the reader more or less has to go back and repeat the title at the start of each stanza—is unusual, interesting, and witty.

2) The bed is orange, "like Cinderella's coach." The coach, of course, was a transformed pumpkin (hence orange), and transforming things is what artists do.

3) The coach-pumpkin-sun image continues into the second stanza, where van Gogh is conceived as being carried "bumpily to the ball." Possibly the idea is that the pumpkin-coach carries him also toward the sun, i.e., he is brought violently toward one of his chief subjects.

4) Although we get some violence in the second stanza ("slept alone, tossing," "bumpily"), in the third stanza we get a glimpse of the "friendly... peasant" world that he moved in. If there is violence here ("beat") it is for good domestic purposes ("beat his mattress till it rose like meringue").

5) The last stanza begins a bit desolately ("empty") but immediately is filled with nature ("Morning light pours in"), nature transformed by human beings ("wine"), nature and humanity ("fragrance"), and humanity ("the memory of happiness").

WILLIAM CARLOS WILLIAMS

The Great Figure (p. 905)

The biographical headnote in the text gives Williams's account of the origin of the poem.

When one first encounters the poem, perhaps one takes the title—"The Great Figure"—to be a notable person. Certainly the first two lines, taken in conjunction with the title, allow us to assume that the speaker met someone on a rainy night ("Among the rain / and lights"), but beginning with the third line we adjust this impression, and learn that the encounter is not with a notable person but with a notable, even heroic, thing, the number 5, in gold, on a red fire engine. The third line, the line which introduces the fire engine's number, is the longest in the poem (six syllables), suggesting its importance. On the other hand, the very short lines, especially "in gold" and "on a red" are emphatic because of their brevity as well as because of the strong colors.

"Fire truck" appears in the sixth line, just above the middle of the 13-line poem. The central line consists of only one word, "moving," and from here on the truck apparently has moved out of sight, because the remaining lines about the truck are about its sound ("clangs," "howls"), not its appearance, though the sentence (and the poem) ends with a visual image, but not of the truck; the speaker now sees not the truck but "the dark city."

The poem has been much praised. Dare one say that two lines, each consisting of a single word, are perhaps weak spots? We have in mind "tense / unheeded," words that strike us as weak. The "gong clangs" and the "siren howls" make "tense" unneeded, and we can't quite imagine how anyone, even the most jaded New Yorker, can let a screaming fire engine go by "unheeded." And if New Yorkers *do* let fire engines go by unheeded, well, perhaps it is not for Dr. Williams to announce his superiority to them by saying in effect that *he* is heeding the engine, witness this poem. In fact, "unheeded" seems to shift attention away from the engine, which we take to be the real subject, and to an irrelevant audience.

Now for a brief comment on Demuth's painting. In our headnote we mention that Demuth is sometimes called a Cubist-Realist, a term that more or less fits this atypical painting; more typically Demuth's work is (like the work of Charles Sheeler) characterized as "Precisionist," with reference to the almost sterile way in which he delineated architecture. In *I Saw the Figure 5 in Gold* the realism is evident chiefly in the lack of distortion of the number 5; the cubism—of a very tame sort—is a bit more evident, in the diagonals and the planes, and especially in what we take to be the simultaneous treatment of the front (the headlights) and the side (the number 5) of the fire engine.

The three concentric 5s presumably give a violent in-and-out sensation, imitating (with the assistance of the converging diagonals) the onrushing engine. Incidentally, although one often reads, in students' discussions of pictures, that "the eye first sees..., and then moves to...." Experiments have shown that all such discussions are misguided. The eye does not travel along a path, but rather jumps back and forth all over the place.

A few more words about the figure 5. John Malcolm Brinnin, in *William Carlos Williams* (1963), said that "the possibility that the figure 5, or any other figure, on a fire engine might be 'tense' is absurd" (28). This remark distressed Bram Dijkstra, who, in *The Hieroglyphics of a New Speech: Cubism, Steiglitz, and the Early Poetry of William Carlos Williams* (1969), replied:

> One look at Charles Demuth's visual interpretation of the poem, executed in close association with Williams, should suffice to indicate the appropriateness and accuracy of Williams' use of the word "tense." Demuth's figure 5 strains and pulls, receding and projecting itself again onto the canvas, its original movement in time transformed into visual tensions, caught within the warring pressure lines of darkness and lamplight, a golden object held suspended on the red fires of sound. (78)

You may want to ask students if this is a useful way to talk about the picture—and if it indeed shows that (to go back to Brinnin's point) a digit on a fire engine can be "tense."

The fact that the picture was a sort of portrait of a friend accounts for the inscription of Williams's first name at the top (the letters are partly cut off) and middle name (without the final *s*) in barely discernable letters just below the top of the figure 5. (Conceivably the trimmed names may correspond to the fragmentary glimpses of the moving engine.) The friendly personal connection between Demuth and Williams also accounts for the whimsical "Art Co" at the right, written on what probably is a representation of a storefront. At the bottom left, in small letters, Demuth has written his own initials, and in the bottom center, again in small letters, Williams's initials.

ADRIENNE RICH

Mourning Picture (p. 906)

Edwin Romanzo Elmer's painting has something of the stiffness that one associates with Sunday painters, who until the 1970s were called primitive
painters. These painters lacked formal training in art, and as a consequence
they were likely to be unskilled in linear perspective and in other ways of suggesting gradual recession in space. They were, however, usually deeply concerned with their own sort of realism, with (for instance) depicting all four legs
of a cow because, after all, most cows *do* have four legs—even though in fact
in certain positions a leg or two might be invisible. Another characteristic of
the work of Sunday painters is that the figures seem posed, as though a pho-
tographer using a slow film had arranged his subjects and then told them to be
sure not to move.

In fact, Elmer, a native of rural Massachusetts, did receive some formal
training in New York at the Academy of Design, but this undated painting
probably antedates his stay in New York.

Rich's poem seems to us to have something of the painting's almost unnatural specificity. For instance, the first line is careful to tell us—in a rather flat,
unemotional and yet rather solemn tone—that the chair is mahogany and that
the rocker is cane: "They have carried the mahogany chair and the cane rocker / out under the lilac bush...." But if the speaker's voice is akin to the world
of the painting, matter-of-fact and yet hyper keen (unblinking one might say)
and otherworldly, these qualities are especially appropriate, since the speaker is
the dead girl. That is, the speaker sees things as, in a way, they are but in a way
that is not quite natural. For instance, she speaks of "the map of every lilac
leaf." When you think of it, leaves do resemble maps because of their veins,
but the perception seems unnatural, a sort of perception through a magnifying glass. (By the way, another of Elmer's paintings shows a landscape as seen
not simply through a window but through a magnifying glass perched on a
vase on a table.)

We don't want to overemphasize the strangeness of the voice, however;
the perception of the maplike leaf leads to a more usual perception, "the net
of veins on my father's / grief-tranced hand." This chain continues in lines
25-26 with the image of silk thread, which in 27 becomes "a web in the dew."
But what exactly do we make of 25, "the silk-spool will run bare"? These
words constitute the end of a sentence about the grieving mother; we might
have thought that the silk spool would remain unconsumed, that is, the
mother might have put away her domestic work when the child died. But
Rich tells us, on the contrary, that the "silk-spool will run bare," possibly suggesting the three fates, who spin, measure, and cut a thread, thereby ending a
person's life.

After writing the preceding paragraph, with its conjecture about the silk-spool, we came across an article about Elmer, written by his niece, Maud Valona Elmer (*Massachusetts Review* 6 [1964-65]:121-44). She mentions that as a boy Elmer worked in a spool-silk factory (presumably a factory that wound silk thread on spools, or perhaps a factory that prepared silk to be wound on spools). She also mentions that after the death of the daughter, Elmer and his wife left the house shown in the picture and went to live with the wife's mother, in Baptist Corner (cf. line 24). Since other information about Edwin Romanzo Elmer is virtually nonexistent, one can safely say that the article in *Massachusetts Review*—and, in all probability, the painting, which the niece sold to the Smith College Museum of Art—inspired Rich to write the poem.

The veins of the leaf become, in line 30, the "skeleton" of the leaf, thereby continuing the death imagery and continuing, too, the somewhat strange quality of the imagery. This strangeness is evident, too, in the "shadowless" house (32), shadowless because the time is noonday (31), when the sun is directly above us, but also "shadowless" because death and sadness have not yet come to the house. At the end of the poem the speaker (we think, but we are far from certain) says that if she recreated the world she—having experienced death—could not leave out death from what had seemed an idyllic world, a world of loving parents, placid sheep, and a doll to be cared for.

One other point: We learn from Maud Valona Elmer's article that the lamb in the picture indicates that the child is dead. In old New England cemeteries the tombstones of children are sometimes adorned with a lamb, suggesting that the deceased was "a Lamb of God."

Having said all this, we still remain unsure about the poem, but here are the main lines of our thought:

1) In "Mourning Picture," Effie describes Elmer's picture. In the first stanza she sees that "they" (probably the parents, possibly servants, but it doesn't matter) have carried our the chair and the rocker, that the parents "darkly sit there," the house "stands fast," the doll lies in her pram. She sees the mourning, but interestingly she does not see herself, with the lamb, the largest figures in the picture. Effie believes that she could remake (like the artist) every particle of that world ("I could remake... [I could] draw out"), but does not.

2) The second stanza describes Effie's present self, which we are inclined to think means in the hours after death, while she (the shade of the dead) still inhabits the house. What she experiences is that "the dream condenses." (Life here, as at the poem's end, *is* a dream.) It doesn't vanish yet. During this period, while the family mourns, she is "visible and invisible / remembering and remembered."

3) In the last stanza she foresees her parents' future. She imagines making the world "again" (line 29) but will not. Her death ("*this*") is part of her life. She remains "Effie"; "you" (meaning her parents, the painter, the reader?) are *her* dream.

CATHY SONG

Beauty and Sadness (p. 908)

The poem concerns the unhappy artist who creates enduring beauty. In some versions, the artist creates beauty *because* he or she is unhappy, as the oyster creates a pearl out of its discomfort, and this apparently is what Song is suggesting when she says that the "inconsolable" Utamaro—inconsolable presumably because the women were "indifferent" (42)—"graced these women with immortality" (50). We can go a little further and say that when she speaks of "the dwarfed and bespectacled painter" (53) Song implies the Freudian idea of the artist who, suffering from unsatisfied longings, engages in fantasy wish-fulfillment—in this case, making pictures of the beauties he cannot in reality win. Speaking more generally, we can say that Song's poem touches on the venerable theme of *ars longa, vita brevis.*

A few notes: The term *ukiyo* originally was a Buddhist term for "the world of suffering," i.e., the transient world of incarnation, but in Japan in the late seventeenth century, by means of a pun, it became "the floating world," i.e., the world of transient pleasure. (The pronunciation is the same, but the initial character is different.) Pictures of the floating world—e.g., of women and of actors—are called *ukiyo-e.* In Song's poem notice "floating world" in line 26, and "fleeting loveliness" in line 13. In line 12, "transfer" probably alludes on the literal level to the thin paper on which the artist drew his design. This paper, placed on the block, provided the carver with a guide for cutting.

MARY JO SALTER

The Rebirth of Venus (p. 910)

Botticelli's *The Birth of Venus* (which we will discuss in a moment) is one of the most frequently reproduced paintings in the world. And it does indeed seem to be a favorite of sidewalk artists; we have on several occasions seen the face of Venus done in chalk on the street.

In line 3 Salter mentions chalk, an almost comically inappropriate medium for this goddess who was born in the sea, who is depicted as standing on a floating shell, and who is associated with life-giving fluids. Salter wittily compounds the irony by saying, in her first line, that the artist has "knelt to *fish* her face up from the sidewalk."

In the text we ask students what Salter may mean (lines 6-8) when she refers to "that woman men divined / ages before a painter let them look / into the eyes their eyes had had in mind" (6-8). We take it that Salter is saying that in this picture of Venus the painter gives form ("an earthly habitation, and a name," to quote Hippolyta, from *A Midsummer Night's Dream*) to what we vaguely intuit or "divine." Perhaps the idea is close to a point that the painter Paul Klee made, when he said, "Art does not reproduce the visible; rather, it renders visible."

A query: in lines 5-6, which immediately precede the passage we have just discussed, is Salter getting at the Platonic notion that a work of art is a copy of a copy, i.e. a copy of something on earth, and the something-on-earth is itself only a copy of a heavenly (Platonic) ideal? That is, is Salter saying that the sidewalk artist is copying a reproduction in a book, which itself is a copy of Botticelli's work, and Botticelli's work is the copy of an ideal? (As we will mention in a moment, scholars agree that Botticelli was influenced by Neo-Platonism, and it is likely that Salter knew this.)

In "let there be light" (line 21), we take Salter to be expressing the hope that the afternoon will last long enough for this earnest artist to complete his chalk drawing on the sidewalk, although it is clear that rain is impending and that Venus therefore will soon be returned to her watery element. The tone is genial, even wry ("it's clear enough the rain / will swamp her like a tide") but the poet clearly respects this painstaking artist ("he won't rush") who is constantly "envisioning faces."

A few words about *The Birth of Venus* (c. 1482), by Sandro Botticelli (1445-151) may be relevant. It is a Renaissance painting, of course, but the nude Venus has little of the obvious voluptuousness—the sense of a ripe, weighty, physical body, we might almost say—that one finds in other Renaissance paintings, especially the Venetian paintings. (Botticelli was a Florentine.) Similarly, there is surprisingly little sense of depth in this picture; aside from the shell, almost everything seems to be at the front. That is, Botticelli has treated his material in a highly decorative manner (the waves are indicated by little V-shaped squiggles on a flat surface), and has produced a painting of a Venus who has a somewhat etherealized or spiritual quality.

According to a simple, brutal, ancient legend, Saturn (Greek: Cronus) castrated his father Uranus, and threw the severed genitals into the sea. From the organs, as they gathered foam (*aphros*) was born Venus (Greek: Aphrodite), goddess of love. Botticelli's contemporaries, the Neo-Platonists, in particular Marsilio Ficino, interpreted this myth in an elaborate allegory concerning the birth of beauty in the human soul or mind; when we create or generate some work of beauty, we experience pleasure because we have been fertilized by divinity.

Putting aside allegorical interpretations of the picture—and all scholars agree that Botticelli painted in a Neo-Platonic climate—we can say that the picture shows, at the left, two embracing wind gods (flying Zephyrs) who are blowing Venus (standing on a cockle shell) to her sacred island of Cyprus. At the right a female figure, variously interpreted as representing the Hours or as the nymph Pomona (descended from the ancient goddess of fruit trees) extends to the naked goddess a flower-embroidered cloak.

In the middle of the painting, between these energetic figures and under a shower of roses, stands Venus herself, modestly posed (the posture is called *Venus pudica,* i.e., modest Venus). Although the pose is classic, the rhythmic curve of her body is not, since her weight does not really rest on her feet. As Kenneth Clark puts it, in *The Nude* (1956), "She is not standing, but floating" (102). The figure is also unclassical—that is, it is Gothic (medieval) in the steeply sloping shoulders and the elongated body. On the other hand, the nudity of course is a sign of classical influence; in the Middle Ages the only nude figures were Adam and Eve, or damned souls.) The nudity here, as we have already suggested, is perhaps more ethereal than voluptuous; she looks virginal, and indeed Kenneth Clark has pointed out that Botticelli used the same head for his Madonnas. Clark characterizes her expression as "wistful" (102).

W. H. AUDEN

Musée des Beaux Arts (p. 913)

Useful pieces on "Musée" are in *College English* 24 (April 1963): 529-31; *Modern Language Notes* 76 (April 1961): 331-36; *Textual Analysis,* ed. Mary Ann Caws (a relatively difficult essay by Michael Riffaterre); and *Art Journal* 32 (Winter 1972-1973): 157-62—the last useful primarily because it includes reproductions of Brueghel's work and reprints other poems relating to his pictures. We reproduce Brueghel's picture of Icarus (in the Brussels Museum of Fine Arts, hence Auden's title); for a color reproduction see Timothy Foote, *The World of Brueghel.* Auden glances at some of Brueghel's other paintings (the children skating in *The Numbering of Bethlehem* are indifferent to Joseph and Mary, who are almost lost in a crowd; the dogs and the horses in *The Massacre of the Innocents),* and his poem accurately catches Brueghel's sense of nature undisturbed by what rarely happens to the individual.

As Otto Benesch points out (*The Art of the Renaissance in Northern Europe,* 99), in *Icarus* Brueghel gives us a sense of cosmic landscape. Plowman, shepherd, and fisherman go about their business, unaware of Icarus, who is represented in the lower right-hand corner simply by his lower legs and feet, the rest of him being submerged in the sea. Daedalus is nowhere represented; the yellow sun sets in the west, and the sea, coasts, and islands are transfigured with a silvery light. It should be noted that in Ovid's account in *Metamorphoses* 8: lines 183-235, the plowman, shepherd, and fisherman beheld Icarus and Daedalus with amazement, taking the two for gods. Given Brueghel's diminution of Icarus—legs and feet, unnoticed by the other figures in the picture— it is fair to say that Brueghel is offering a comment on the pride of scientists. James Snyder, who makes this point in *Northern Renaissance Art,* 510, also calls attention to the shiny pate of a recumbent man, a dead man, at the left margin, halfway up and all but invisible even in the original painting. This image,

Snyder says, "assuredly is meant to express the old Netherlandish saying, 'No plow stops over the death of any man,' or over Brueghel's Everyman, a clever footnote that reveals, after all, that peasant wisdom can be as profound as that of the ancients."

Students are first inclined to see Auden's poem as an indictment of indifference; our own view is that Auden gives the daily world its due, especially in such phrases as "doggy life" and "innocent behind"; that is, he helps us see that all of creation cannot and need not suffer along with heroes. Auden's poem evoked a pleasant reply by Randall Jarrell, "The Old and the New Masters," *Collected Poems* (1959) 332-33. It begins, "About suffering, about adoration, the old masters / Disagree...."

An audiocassette of W. H. Auden reading is available from HarperCollins.

TOPICS FOR CRITICAL THINKING AND WRITING

1. Reread the poem (preferably over the course of several days) a number of times, jotting down your chief responses after each reading. Then, in connection with a final reading, study your notes, and write an essay of 500 words setting forth the history of your final response to the poem. For example, you may want to report that certain difficulties soon were clarified, and that your enjoyment increased. Or, conversely, you may want to report that the poem became less interesting (for reasons you will set forth) the more you studied it. Probably your history will be somewhat more complicated than these simple examples. Try to find a chief pattern in your experience, and shape it into a thesis.
2. Consider a picture, either in a local museum or reproduced in a book, and write a 500-word reflection on it. If the picture is not well known, include a reproduction (a postcard from the museum, or a photocopy of a page of the book) with your essay.

ANNE SEXTON

The Starry Night (p. 915)

We think that one can reasonably call some of the language of this poem surrealistic—particularly the description of a *black-haired tree* that *slips / up like a drowned woman into the hot sky*. (A tree presented as having hair, and a woman drowning *upward* seem to us to qualify; and so does the passage, in the second stanza, about the moon pushing children from its eye).

Surrealism is characterized by dreamlike, fantastic imagery, often presented in finicky detail and therefore (because the realism seems to be at odds with the subject-matter) the more disconcerting. Surrealism is quite different from

Expressionism. Expressionistic painting—and van Gogh is considered to be the father of Expressionism—does not seek to offer the surreal world of dreams and fantasies, nor does it seek to offer the world as perceived by traditional painters, who aimed at reproducing nature. Rather, Expressionist painting, as is evident in many of van Gogh's pictures, seeks to present the artist's emotions, or emotional response to the ostensible subject matter. (Sexton, as a "confessional poet," quite naturally found van Gogh's work of special interest.) Thus, as van Gogh's letters indicate, his picture of his bed (see the text and this manual) was supposed to convey the artist's sense of rest. In *The Starry Night* van Gogh gives us not the dark sky with a thousand points of light that all of us can and do see, but a blazing heaven that expresses his ecstatic feelings about eternity. (Stars are a traditional symbol of eternity.) Also expressive of his feelings, no doubt, is the writhing cypress. In a letter to his brother, van Gogh says that he sees the sunflower and the cypress as both opposite and equivalent. Bright yellow sunflowers embody the life force, but they go to seed and die; dark cypresses are associated with death, but they energetically rise toward heaven. (See Vojtech Jirst-Wasiutynski on van Gogh's cypresses, in *Art Bulletin* 75 [1993], 647-70, especially 657-60.) Also expressive is the little town, which is so slight when compared to the grandeur of nature.

But if Sexton's imagery is surrealistic, her poem is nevertheless tightly ordered. (There is no contradiction here. Surrealists such as Dali and Magritte often use conspicuously formal compositions.) The first two stanzas closely resemble each other, most obviously in the number of lines and of course in the identity of the last two lines of each of these stanzas, but in other ways too; for instance, the first line of each of these stanzas is conspicuously shorter than the second line. Doubtless Sexton counted on the reader perceiving the formal connection between the first two stanzas because much of the force of the poem depends on the fact that the last stanza is truncated—five lines instead of six, and only two syllables in the final line, instead of four. That is, "I want to die" (the ending of the first and second stanzas) is diminished to "no cry," a silent ending to an unheroic extinction of the flesh ("no flag," "no belly").

Having said that the poet imagines an unheroic extinction, we are uncomfortably aware that in the first two stanzas she seems to want to go off in a blaze of light ("Oh starry starry night! This is how / I want to die." Still, our sense is that the third stanza makes a reader see the first two stanzas in a new light.

Two other points: (1) van Gogh's painting, as the quotation from his letter suggests, is a religious painting, or, rather, an expression of the artist's sense of the divinity of nature, whereas Sexton's poem seems to us to have nothing to do with religion. (2) The poem comes from *All My Pretty Ones* (1962), a book of poems much concerned with death. (The book takes its title from *Macbeth* 4.3.216, where Macduff is speaking of the children whom Macbeth slaughtered. Both of Sexton's parents had died within a few months of each other in 1959, and her father-in-law, of whom she was very fond, had died a few months later.)

A Note on the Assignment in the Text: If you use this assignment, which asks students to discuss in what ways the poem does and does not describe the painting, you may want to follow this procedure: Divide the class into two groups. One group, after conferring for 15-20 minutes, would then report on the ways the poem does not reproduce the picture; the other on the ways it does.

WISLAWA SZYMBORSKA

Brueghel's Two Monkeys (p. 916)

The directness of the first line suggests a matter-of-fact speaker, but of course as soon as one talks about dreams one enters a mysterious world. (Perhaps that is why the sky "flutters" and "the sea is taking its bath.") The speaker gives us no clues about his or her identity, but we may assume that the speaker is a person of some education (perhaps a member of a profession), since dreams about final examinations are said to be fairly common among people with academic credentials. (In such dreams the dreamers are usually baffled and humiliated; the customary analysis suggests that these dreamers believe they are frauds, undeserving of their credentials.)

In the poem, since the examination is History of Mankind, the dreamer can be taken as standing for all of us. We all wonder where we came from (and where we are going), and perhaps most of us are familiar with the experience of talking earnestly about mysterious subjects and then perceiving (or thinking) that our hearer "listens with mocking disdain." In the poem, the second monkey, who "seems to be dreaming away"—i.e. who seems to be a kindred spirit to the dreamer—offers help, but of a terrifying sort: "he prompts me with a gentle / clinking of his chain."

Brueghel's painting shows two chained monkeys, and in the poem the chain is the monkey's, not the dreamer's, but it is easy enough for a reader to think of the dreamer as chained, partly because the dreamer in the poem is unable to escape from the dream, and partly because monkeys resemble human beings. Monkeys or apes have been common symbols of humanity, but different artists have put different emphases on the symbolism. In early Christian art the ape symbolizes the devil (a creature who mimics God's concern for humanity, but who really is wicked); in later art the ape often symbolizes (usually satirically) the artist, i.e. the maker of imitations. But the ape can also symbolize lechery, pride, folly, and—as perhaps in Brueghel's painting and in Szymborska's poem—baffled humanity. In *Art Bulletin* 63 (1981): 114-26, Margaret A. Sullivan takes issue with earlier political interpretations of Brueghel's painting, and argues that the monkey at the left symbolizes avarice and the monkey at the right (seated among scattered empty nutshells) symbolizes prodigality. Not relevant to the poem, but we thought you might like to know, even if the interpretation is unconvincing.

To return to the poem: what is the significance of the monkey prompting the poet "with a gentle / clinking of his chain"? If there is one thing we can say with some certainty, it is that there is no one right answer to this question. Still, we take the passage to mean (perhaps among other things) something along these lines: the monkey, clinking his chain, "prompts" or reminds the speaker that all of us are fettered, that is, severely restricted in what we can do (and know). This isn't much of an answer, but it is something, and the rhyme at the end of the poem (it is the only rhyme in the poem) provides a note of closure, as if to say, "Well, we know only that we are fettered, but at least we know *something*."

DANNIE ABSE

Brueghel in Naples (p. 917)

First, a confession: We don't understand the relevance of the title to the rest of the poem. At first we thought that perhaps Abse visited Naples and saw an exhibition of paintings by Brueghel, but we find no record of such an exhibition. Possibly Abse simply thought of Brueghel's picture of the drowning of Icarus while he visited Naples—there's lots of water near Naples. We just don't know.

We quote, in the text, Abse's remark that he wants to deceive and puzzle the reader. Perhaps this aim can be related to Ezra Pound's exhortation, "Make it new." For readers of English and American literature, probably the Icarus story is not Ovid's but Auden's. Abse begins with Auden—in the epigraph—and then goes on to do something of his own, thereby dislocating the story in our minds.

Abse rejects Ovid as well as Auden, and, for that matter, he also rejects Daedalus (lines 1-3). That is, he rejects Ovid's assertion that the sun melted the wax, and he blames Daedalus's shoddy workmanship for the disaster. (Much of the effect of the poem is gained by recounting an ancient story in a modern voice, as in this complaint about the workmanship of "these days.") As Icarus falls, we join him in his topsy-turvy view ("the sea is rearing up" [131], and we are at least for an instant puzzled by such a line a "There's a mountain down there on fire / and I'm falling, falling away from it." (Actually, the writers of this manual continue to be puzzled. Possibly the mountain on fire, from which Icarus falls away, is the sun, but the sun is mentioned a bit later in the poem, and why would Icarus conceive of the sun as a mountain? More likely the mountain on fire is Vesuvius, near Naples, but Icarus fell into the Aegean—at least in the legend before Abse remade it—and Vesuvius therefore would seem irrelevant.)

In the next-to-last stanza Icarus laments that the ploughman and the rest do not see him, and it is his bad luck to be seen only by a jackass of an artist

> interested in composition, in the green
> tinge of the sea, in aesthetics
> of disaster—not in me.

And of course he is right; in the long run an artist, "intent on becoming an Old Master," may be more interested in aesthetics, in the medium of art, than in life. One thinks of various remarks along these lines, such as Shaw's, that he threw his mother into the struggle for life (i.e. he let her support him while he wrote), or Faulkner's coarse and considerably less amusing remark that "If a writer has to rob his mother, he will not hesitate; the 'Ode on a Grecian Urn' is worth any number of old ladies." Remarks of this sort could be supplemented with anecdotes about absent-minded professors and with Browning's grammarian ("This man decided not to Live but Know"). Doubtless there are many comparable anecdotes about scientists dedicated to their subject. (As a physician, Abse must have met other physicians who care more about the disease than about the patient.) From our schooldays we recall (imperfectly) an anecdote about a Greek geometrician who, during a battle, in the seclusion of his tent was contemplating a problem with the aid of circles drawn in the sand. A barbarian soldier burst into the tent, asked what he was doing, and received for an answer only a mumbled "Do not disturb my circles," whereupon the soldier killed the philosopher-mathematician.

Stories of this sort do seem to us to get at what may be the deepest interests of problem-solvers, including artists and writers: They may or may not be passionate about life, but they certainly are passionate about their work. We hope we are saying something relevant to the poem. If we are, and if you want to introduce into the classroom this idea of the artist's obsessive concern with the work, you may find useful the following entry from one of Emerson's journals (March 22, 1839):

> Each work of art excludes the world, concentrates attention on itself. For the time it is the only thing worth doing—to do just that; be it a sonnet, a statue, a landscape, an outline head of Caesar, or an oration. Presently we return to the sight of another that globes itself into a Whole as did the first, for example, a beautiful garden; and nothing seems worth doing in life but laying out a garden.

A friend, William Cain, who called our attention to the passage in Emerson, suggests that the poem can be seen in part as an exercise in point of view—Abse's versus Auden's, and Abse's versus Brueghel's, and above all Brueghel's versus Icarus. On this last relationship Cain observes that we commonly say, of a work of art, "What an interesting treatment of X," but here Abse is prompting us to consider what X (the subject) might have to say about the artist. The idea is serious, Cain suggests, but Abse nicely gives the speaker amusing touches of voice that make the idea interesting but not overly weighty, e.g., when the doomed Icarus says, "My luck. I'm seen / only by a jackass of an artist / interested in composition...."

The second question in the text mentions Abse's superficially strange comment that he wants "to look upon the world with the eyes of a perpetual convalescent." Of course as a physician Abse must know a good deal about the ways in which convalescents experience the world, but it takes only a moment of thought to realize that the convalescent is, so to speak, living in two worlds, the strange world of the past (illness), where everything was dislocated, and the no less strange and now eagerly welcomed world of renewed health. In a way it's the old idea that the healthy don't know of their health; you have to be sick to appreciate—*to see, to feel, to value intensely*—the ordinary life of daily health. And it is the job of artists to make us intensely aware of experience, to make us see. That's exactly the way Conrad put it, in the famous Preface to *The Nigger of The "Narcissus"*: "My task which I am trying to achieve is, by the power of the written word, to make you hear, to make you feel—it is, before all, to make you *see*."

This creed may seem to be the opposite of Abse's Brueghel, who apparently is intent only on art, not on the suffering life around him. Let students think about trying to reconcile them.

GWENDOLYN BROOKS

The Chicago Picasso (p. 918)

As the title and the two epigraphs indicate, "a big steel sculpture" by Picasso was dedicated in Chicago in 1967. A few details about the sculpture, illustrated in the text, may be useful. Strictly speaking, one may quibble, or even seriously argue, that the work is not a "Picasso." The facts are these: Picasso made some drawings, from which a 42-inch metal statue was fabricated. (He did not himself have a hand in making the statue.) From this maquette (preliminary model) a 50-foot statue of Cor-Ten Steel was fabricated in Gary, Indiana, and installed in front of the Civic Center Building in Chicago, a 647-foot structure of 31 storeys. In short: Picasso never worked on the Chicago sculpture, and he seems not to have touched even the maquette. Still, the work *is* based on a design by Picasso, so if we are generous we can call the sculpture a work by Picasso. Speaking of generosity, Picasso refused any fee, though it must also be mentioned that few people knowledgeable about Picasso's work would say that this sculpture adds anything to his reputation.

Why is it in Chicago? Largely because Mayor Richard Daley wanted something by Picasso in Chicago. Why did he want a Picasso? "Picasso is the best artist in the world," he said, "and that is what we care about." When you think about it, this is a most unusual reason for commissioning a civic sculpture. The Picasso has no relevance whatsoever to the site—other than what is implied in Daley's words: Chicago is a place with Big Name Art. What *is* the subject? Roland Penrose, one of Picasso's biographers, sees in it "the head of a woman with ample flowing hair," but Penrose is tolerant of other interpretations: "The two wing-like shapes that are her hair suggest with equal truth the fragile wings of a butterfly or the powerful flight of the eagle, while at the same time the rods that connect them with the profile seem to contain the music of a guitar" (quoted in Ira J. Bach and Mary Lackritz Gray, *A Guide to Chicago's Public Sculpture* [1983], 75). Most viewers are unsure of what they see in the sculpture, but William B. Chapell has shown (*Art International*, October / November 1997: 61-63) that the image is a conflation of Picasso's wife Jacqueline Roque (he had married her in 1961) and his pet Afghan hound, though even when one knows this, it is hard to see the woman or the dog or the combination from some angles. (For additional background on the commissioning of the work, see Harriet F. Senie, *Contemporary Public Sculpture* (1992), 95-100.

As Brooks explains in her *Report from Part One* (1972), Mayor Daley asked her to write a poem celebrating the gift. She had seen only some pictures of the work, not the work itself, and she thought it looked "very foolish" (147), but she explains that she does not consider herself highly knowledgeable about modern art. In this, she realized, she is like most other people:

> I decided that most of us do not feel cozy with art, that it's not a thing you easily and chummily throw your arms around, that it's not a huggable thing. "Does man love Art? Man visits Art...." And we visit it, we pay special, nice, precise little calls on it. But those of us who have not grown up with or to it perhaps squirm a little in its presence. We feel that something is required of us that perhaps we aren't altogether able to give. And it's just a way of saying "Art hurts." Art is not an old shoe; it's something that you have to work in the presence of. It urges voyages. You have to extend yourself. And it's easier to stay home and drink beer." (147-48)

She goes on to insist that she is not satirizing those who stay home and drink beer; on the contrary, she found that when she saw the work she admired it and she urged people to look at it, and to "consider it as they might consider flowers" (148).

If we take all of these comments, along with the poem itself, we find that Brooks raises important issues about art. For instance, the comment that we do not feel comfortable about art can be connected with a remark that we quote by Kafka, to the effect that a book should hammer at our head, and should be like an ice ax, breaking the frozen sea around our heart, radically changing our consciousness. That is, to return to Brooks's poem, a work of art *should* make us "squirm," *should* "hurt" us (lines 1-2).

On the other hand, we should observe the work as we might observe a "flower" (19). Here the implication seems to be that the work should be contemplated merely as an aesthetic object, and that beauty is its own excuse for being. But even here Brooks may be complicating matters. The flower, she says, is as "innocent" and also as "guilty," and as "meaningful" and as "meaningless," as any "other flower in the western field." From this statement we can easily get into a discussion of art as meaningful and meaningless, e.g., *The Tempest* is, on the one hand, a complicated statement about authority, gender relations, love, and a good many other things, and, on the other hand, only a fanciful entertainment, an "insubstantial pageant," a "dream" (4.1.155-57).

We want to make one other point about the poem: Brooks's writing is of quite a different order from the journalistic epitaph that she quotes at the start, in which Mayor Daley appears as a patron of the arts, tugging a ribbon to the "hearty cheer" of the crowd. Writing of *that* sort certainly makes people "squirm."

WILLIAM SHAKESPEARE

Sonnet 55 (Not marble nor the gilded monuments) (p. 921)

The promise of immortality puts this sonnet in the genre of eternizing poetry; it thus has affiliations with the following poem by Landor. The Renaissance promises of monuments that will outlive devouring time is rooted in Roman poetry, for instance in Ovid's *Metamorphoses* 15:871 ("devouring time") and in Horace, *Odes* 30.1-5 ("monuments of brass"). In Shakespeare's *Sonnets* (published in 1609, but probably written in the 1590s) the young man is promised immortality through the poems—and he is instructed in some of the sonnets, though not in this one, to make himself immortal also by marrying and having children.

Sonnet 55 begins with "marble," "monuments," and "princes," but these are said to be less enduring than "you"; the speaker's beloved is less bright than these important things, which are subject to time, and time itself is radically diminished to a negligent houseman ("unswept stone... sluttish time").

In the second quatrain we encounter not mere neglect but energetic evils ("war," "broils," "fire"). Line 7 is especially interesting for several reasons. First, most students are interested to learn that the possessive form of "Mars his sword" (cf. bookplates that are inscribed, "John his book") probably arose from a confusion with the Old English genitive, which was made by adding -*es* to the noun. (The apostrophe in the modern possessive indicates the loss of the *e*.) Second, "Mars his sword" does not really govern any verb in the sentence; "fire" governs "burn," but (one might almost say) in the chaos that the poem is describing, the sword is subsumed by the fire and turned into an instrument that burns. Third, the line is enjambed, perhaps conveying the relentless forward movement or the overthrowing of bounds associated with war.

The third quatrain, however, begins with four consecutive stresses ("Shall you pace forth"), emphasizing the hearer, and suggesting that he need fear nothing. That is, we take the stresses to indicate his steadiness; one might almost say that he walks at a steady pace no matter what accidents surround him. The "you" eternized by the poem is now a prince superior to the princes of line 2, who are subject to mortality.

What of the couplet? The three quatrains have been concerned with the future of "you," and the couple too looks toward the future, with its reference to Judgment Day. But the couplet also emphasizes the present, with "You *live* in this, and *dwell* in lovers' eyes."

For some information about the sonnets, see p. 158 in this manual.

WALTER SAVAGE LANDOR

Past Ruin'd Ilion (p. 922)

We include this poem in this section because although the poem praises the writer and the woman whom he addresses, chiefly it praises poetry. That is, "Past Ruin'd Ilion" is an eternizing poem, as is Shakespeare's Sonnet 55, print-ed earlier in this section. Landor claims, doubtless correctly, that it is the poets who have made Helen of Troy immortal, as they have made Alcestis immortal. Alcestis is an interesting case, since she was rescued from the underworld ("the shades," in line 2) by Hercules, i.e. she gained new life (according to mythol-ogy) even in her own time. But of course she died some years later, and it is the poets (particularly the dramatist Euripides) who have given her the endur-ing life that she possesses.

Our second question in the text asks about the lapidary quality (though we don't use this word) in Landor's poem. The brevity of the poem, the fact that each line rhymes, and especially the fact that each stanza consists of a sin-gle sentence surely are among the factors that remind a reader of concise, authoritative statements that supposedly were inscribed on tombstones. If we look more closely we see several things that suggest a tight structure: in the first stanza the first line is devoted to one heroine, the second line to a second hero-ine; the stanza contains four clauses, each with one verb. The second stanza seems more expansive (it begins with a run-on line), but the sense is complet-ed in the second line, though the last two lines amplify the sense. The popu-lation of the world is shrunk from "all the peopled hills" (line 6) to "the gay, the proud" (very much in the tradition of the elegy), and the poem ends, rather like an epitaph, with a glorification of the beloved—and, in this case, of the lover-author too.

What of the third (later deleted) stanza? We think Landor did well to drop it. On the other hand, although we like the arrogant ending of the revised version, where the speaker imagines himself hailed by future lovers, one can make a case that the third stanza courteously diminished the arrogance by attributing immortality alone to Ianthe. Still (to return to our view that the revision is superior), one can say that the third stanza, which asserts Ianthe's immortality, does not really add anything to what has already been said in the first two stanzas.

If you assign this poem, you may also want to assign Shakespeare's Sonnet 55, "Not marble nor the gilded monuments...," another eternizing poem.

WILLIAM WORDSWORTH

The Solitary Reaper (p. 923)

"The Solitary Reaper" is discussed in Carl Woodring, *Wordsworth*; John Danby, *The Simple Wordsworth*, 122-27; and by G. Ingli James, *Essays in Criticism*, (January 1965) 65-76. What follows is derived from these sources.

The situation in "The Solitary Reaper" is notably Wordsworthian: a single humble figure is in a landscape that is both dreary and richly mysterious. The poem opens with an exclamation of wonder, and a hint of biblical or at least archaic language ("Behold her"); in line 4, with the consecutive stresses on "Stop here," we get one of the poem's very few metrical variations.

In the second stanza the vision widens to include an oasis in Arabia and the Hebrides off western Scotland; her voice is like a nightingale's telling the desert travelers that they approach life and a refreshing coolness, and like the cuckoo's heralding the warm spring in the cold north. In line 15 the trochee in "Breaking" perhaps helps to communicate a suggestion of strength or vitality.

In the third stanza the poet says he cannot understand the words of her song—possibly because she sang in Gaelic, possibly because she is distant. In any case, her song resembles the nightingale's and the cuckoo's in that it is a song and a sign of life, but it differs from theirs in that it is melancholy, and here Wordsworth again extends the vision now to the distant past and the present and the high and the low.

Note, too, that the melancholy is presented in a work of art, and it should be noted that although the song is melancholy there is no evidence that the *girl* is melancholy. Presumably—if the singer is like people in the real world—there is indeed a sort of joy to be gained from singing a melancholy song. We included the poem in this section partly in order to let students discuss this point.

The feminine rhymes ("ending" and "bending," in lines 26 and 28) perhaps suggest the continuity of the song which, so far as the speaker was concerned, did *not* end. The redundancy in "motionless and still" (line 29) perhaps serves to communicate the poet's entranced state, though perhaps it is merely a redundancy.

JOHN KEATS

Ode on a Grecian Urn (p. 924)

Let's begin at the end, with the issue of the punctuation of the last two lines. Does the urn speak the two lines, or does it speak only "Beauty is truth, truth beauty"? The matter has been thoroughly discussed by Jack Stillinger, in an appendix to his book called *The Hoodwinking of Madeline* (1971). The problem is this: when the poem was first published, in *Annals of the Fine Arts* (1819), the lines were printed thus:

> Beauty is Truth,—Truth Beauty—That is all
> Ye know on Earth, and all ye need to know.

When Keats published the ode in his book *Lamia and Other Poems* (1820), the lines were punctuated thus:

> "Beauty is truth, truth beauty,"—that is all
> Ye know on earth, and all ye need to know.

The two printed versions thus set off "Beauty is truth, truth beauty" as a unit separate from the remaining words. But Keats probably did not supervise the publication in *The Annals*, and because he was ill when *Lamia* was in production he may not have read the proofs, or may not have read them attentively. Many scholars therefore do not feel obliged to accept the punctuation of the two printed texts. They point to the four extant manuscript transcripts of the poem (none by Keats, but all by persons close to Keats). Because none of these transcriptions uses quotation marks or a period after "beauty," these scholars argue that the punctuation suggests that the urn speaks all of the last two lines:

> Beauty is Truth,—Truth Beauty,—that is all
> Ye know on earth, and all ye need to know.

Stillinger points out that none of the six readings (the four transcripts and the two published versions) offers conclusive proof of Keats's intention. He goes on to summarize the interpretations, and we now summarize Stillinger:

   1) **Poet to Reader.** The urn speaks the first five words of line 49 ("Beauty is truth, truth beauty"), and the poet, addressing the reader, speaks the rest of the last two lines ("that is all / Ye know on earth, and all ye need to know"). The objection to this view is that earlier in the last stanza the poet and the

reader are "us," and the poet says that later woes will belong to a generation other than "ours." Why, then, does the poet shift the address to "ye," where we would expect "we"? Second, the statement is obviously false; we need to know much more than that "Beauty is truth, truth beauty."

2) **Poet to Urn.** The poet speaks the end of line 49, and all of the last line, to the urn. The poet tells the urn that *it* need know no more—but that we need to know a great deal more. The objection, Stillinger points out, is that "ye" is normally a plural pronoun—though in fact Keats did sometimes use it as a singular. A second objection: What can Keats possibly mean by saying to the urn, "that is all / Ye know *on earth*..."?

3) **Poet to Figures on Urn.** The poet speaks the end of 49 and all of the last line to the figures on the urn. This fits with "ye" as a plural. The objection is that the figures are not "on earth," and, further, that the poet is no longer thinking of them as alive and capable of hearing. Further, *why* should the figures on the urn know this and only this?

4) **Urn to Reader.** The urn speaks all of the two last lines. The objection is that the statement seems to defy common sense, and more important, it is *not* the way the *Lamia* volume punctuated the line. Some critics have suggested that the quotation marks were meant to set off these five words as a sort of motto within a two-line statement by the urn.

It is our impression that most editors today disregard the *Lamia* punctuation, put the whole of the two lines within quotation marks, and take the lines as spoken by the urn to the reader. In any case, a reader is still left to wonder whether the passage is profound wisdom or is nonsense.

Now to begin at the beginning. In the first line "still" probably has several meanings (motionless; as yet; silent); the urn is the "foster-child of silence and slow time" because its real parent is the craftsman who made it, but it has been adopted, so to speak, by silence and the centuries. Although the poet begins by saying that the urn can tell a tale "more sweetly" than a poet can, in fact by the end of the stanza it is clear that the urn cannot tell a tale; it can only (of course) show some isolated moment, and let the viewer try to guess what actions came before and will come after. It is worth mentioning, too, that this stanza praises the urns staying-power ("slow time") but is rich in words that imply transience: "Sylvan," "flowery," "leaf-fringed," "haunts" (suggesting the insubstantial or ethereal). The stanza ends with urgent questions conveying agitation and implying that the urn cannot tell a tale satisfactorily.

The second stanza begins on a note of composure; in the space between the stanzas, so to speak, the poet has stilled his questioning spirit, and has progressed to a state where he can offer something for meditation ("Heard melodies are sweet, but those unheard / Are sweeter"). As the stanza continues, a slightly painful note is introduced: the pastoral landscape will never die—but the lover will never kiss the woman. The poet urges the lover not to grieve, which means that he in fact introduces into this Arcadian world the idea of potential grief. Although the stanza ends by asserting the youth's eternal love, and the woman's eternal beauty, there is something almost painful in the last words of the next-to-last line of the stanza, "though thou hast not thy bliss."

The third stanza begins with a renewed note of joy, again apparently gained in the blank space that precedes the stanza, though perhaps we may also detect a note of hysteria in the repetition of "Ah, happy, happy boughs." This stanza too, despite its early expressions of joy, moves toward distress. We are told that the figures on the urn are "far above" human passion, but the last lines dwell on the pains of human passions: "a heart high-sorrowful and cloyed, / A burning forehead, and a parching tongue."

We cannot quite say that the fourth stanza begins with the by-now expected note of composure, because in fact it begins with a question, but it is true to say that in fact this stanza too begins in a quieter mood. The poet is contemplating with interest a new scene on the urn, a scene showing a "mysterious priest" and a "heifer lowing at the skies, / … her silken flanks with garlands drest." As the poet describes this highly picturesque scene, again we hear a note foreign to the beginning of the stanza. The poet begins by conveying his interest in what he sees—"the mysterious priest," the "heifer," and the "folk, this pious morn"—but then his mind turns to the "little town" that is "emptied of this folk" and whose "streets for evermore / Will silent be." The last two lines of the stanza are deeply melancholy: not a soul to tell / Why thou art desolate, can e'er return." Jack Stillinger, in an essay on the odes (reprinted from his *Twentieth Century Views*) in *The Hoodwinking of Madeline* suggests that "'Desolate' in line 40 is the counterpart of 'forlorn' in *Ode to a Nightingale*. It brings the speaker back to his sole self" (106).

The fifth stanza begins with the expected renewed joy, but it is worth noticing that the urn, which in the first stanza was a "Sylvan historian" capable of telling a "flowery tale" now is a "shape" and a "silent form" and a "Cold Pastoral." The poet by now has clearly seen that what he at first took for a world of idealized love is "cold," and its figures are "marble men and maidens." That is, if it is perfect and permanent it is also cold, bloodless, without the passion that (however painful) is what we want from life. Stillinger puts it this way:

> Like the nightingale, [the urn] has offered a tentative idea—momentarily "teas[ing]" the speaker "out of thought"—but has also led the speaker to understand the shortcomings of the ideal. (108)

Stillinger's comment on the last two lines is also worth quoting:

> The final lines present a special problem in interpretation, but it is clear that, while the urn is not entirely rejected at the end, its value lies in its character as a

work of art, not in its being a possible substitute for life in the actual world. However punctuated, the urn's "message" amounts to what the speaker has come to realize in his speculations—that the only beauty accessible to mortal man exists "on earth." The urn is "a friend to man" for helping him to arrive at this conclusion through just such ponderings as we have witnessed in the course of the poem. (108-09)

Bibliographic Note: For detailed analyses of the poem, see Earl Wasserman, *The Finer Tone* (1953) and Helen Vendler, *The Odes of John Keats* (1983); for briefer discussions, see the books on Keats by Walter Jackson Bate and by Douglas Bush. Also useful is a collection edited by Jack Stillinger, *Twentieth Century Interpretations of Keats's Odes* (1968). Ian Jack, in *Keats and the Mirror of Art* (1967), has an interesting well-illustrated chapter on urns—and pictures of urns—that Keats is likely to have seen, but, unfortunately, no one urn is the model; in fact, "that heifer lowing at the skies" probably came not from an urn but from the Elgin Marbles. Jack's concern is only with identifying motifs; he does not offer an intepretation of the poem.

HERMAN MELVILLE

Art; Greek Architecture (p. 926)

"Art" begins in the realm of fancy, with a reference to the easiness of dreaming or day-dreaming ("in placid hours well-pleased we dream"), in which our schemes are "unbodied." But to convert fantasies into real things—"to give to airy nothings a local habitation and a name" (to quote from the last act of *A Midsummer Night's Dream*)—that is, to actually produce a work of art, a "form," is, according to Melville, an immensely strenuous activity. It requires paradoxical qualities: heat and cold, patience and energy, humility and pride, instinct or native ability and training, boldness or pride and reverence. The idea of course is old; traditionally the creation of art needs both the heat of passion and the coldness of reason, passion to invent, and reason to act as a check or critic. Alexander Pope, for instance, in *An Essay on Criticism*, insists that the writer must be familiar with the works of the past (Melville's "study"), but he must also be able to "snatch a grace beyond the reach of art" (Melville's "instinct" and "audacity"). Here, for instance, are a few lines from Pope:

> Some Beauties yet, no precepts can declare,
> For there's a *happiness* as well as *care*.
> Music resembles poetry, in each
> Are nameless Graces which no Methods teach.

This idea that the creation of art requires opposed qualities is evident in several of the poems we reprint in this section, but perhaps most obviously in Wilbur's "Museum Piece," where we are told that in a painting by Degas we see "grace" and "strain," and "Beauty joined to energy."

In "Art," the first Melville poem that we print in this section, the emphasis is on the need for apparently opposed qualities if the artist is to produce a work of art, a "form" (line 2). In "Greek Architecture" Melville's emphasis is on the form, rather than on the creative process. And this form is, well, classic—that is, not "wilful," not "lavish," not simply vast (cf. "magnitude" in line 1). Greek architecture—notable for its repose—has these qualities, in contrast, for instance, to Gothic architecture, with its exuberance or its elaboration, or in contrast to baroque architecture, with its sense of energy or unresolved tension. The qualities that Melville praises in this poem are pretty much what one means when one speaks of "classic" work (whether architecture or sculpture or painting).

A. E. HOUSMAN

Loitering with a vacant eye (p. 927)

In the world of contemporary art criticism, the equivalent of an extreme version of reader-response theory claims that works of art have no inherent meaning. Works of art "mean" what the viewer makes them mean; the viewer (not the artist) creates the meaning.

What happens, then, when a gay man looks at a work of art? (No one today doubts that Housman was sexually interested in men, and was in love with a fellow-student at Oxford, though the love was unrequited.) Do gay people create distinctive meanings? Until fairly recently, gays argued that they were just like other men except for their sexual preference. Recently, however, a different view is heard: there is a distinctive gay experience, a gay sensibility that informs almost all aspects of behavior. A formulation of the extreme version, offered to straight people, goes this way: "Except for what we do in bed, we are unlike you in every way." In this emphasis on difference, the gay movement more or less parallels the women's movement, which at first argued for equality ("We can hold down the same jobs that men hold down," and "We want to be treated in the same way that men are treated") but more recently has argued for distinctiveness ("Women are more nurturing than men"). One sees something of this emphasis on difference among other groups, too. For instance, some African Americans wear a T-shirt bearing the legend, "It's a black thing; you wouldn't understand."

Although it used to be said that a viewer's response to a nude statue ought to be purely esthetic, today probably most people would grant that there is also an erotic element. This is old ground, discussed in the first chapter of Kenneth Clark's *The Nude* (1956):

> "If the nude," says Professor [Samuel] Alexander, "is so treated that it raises in the spectator ideas or desires appropriate to the material subject, it is false art, and bad morals." This high-minded theory is contrary to experience. {8}

Housman does not, of course, explicitly announce his sexual preference (the poem was published in 1896, a year after Oscar Wilde had been sentenced to two years at hard labor for engaging in homosexual acts), and apparently the homosexual content of Housman's poems was not readily perceived in their day, though it now seems evident enough.

The very first word, "Loitering," suggests that the speaker is up to no good. He is, in effect, cruising the Grecian gallery (the gallery, in the British Museum, where Greek sculpture is displayed). He doesn't specify that the statue is nude, but the fact is that Greek statues of males (though not of females) were nude. Looking at the statue, Housman imagines that it is a kindred soul: "'Well met,' I thought the look would say." Not surprisingly, and completely in accord with what we can call viewer-response theory, the statue says what Housman has in mind. That is, the statue speaks of their mutual alienation from the common lot ("We both were fashioned far away"). Most explicitly: "I, too, survey that endless line / Of men whose thoughts are not as mine." The statue's alienation is evident enough: he is a Greek youth from 2,500 years ago, dwelling among visitors to a London museum. What is the source of Housman's alienation? Of course we can't prove what his "thoughts" were. One might even argue (preposterously) that Housman, who soon was to become renowned as an editor of difficult classical texts, is thinking about his differences with scholars concerning some obscure passage in Manilius. But surely common sense suggests that Housman's deep sense of alienation was rooted in an awareness that in his sexuality he was fundamentally different from most of the men around him, or at least from the man he most admired.

In any case, the speaker puts ideas into the work of art—as we all inevitably do, for instance when we say that a self-portrait by van Gogh shows "a tormented genius," or "a man of deep feeling," or "a man who loved color," or whatever. And then, hearing his ideas formulated ("So I thought his look would say"), he finds himself refreshed, better able to face the world. The poem ends with a paradox: The flesh and bone man is made more "manful"— i.e. is made more able to endure his lot—by the "the man of stone," the work of art.

Housman is touching on an ancient and an important question: what do works of art (of course including literature) *do* to us? Some people would argue that art does nothing—except afford momentary pleasure. Perhaps Archibald MacLeish's "Ars Poetica" (text, 931) makes some such assertion—though if it does, it contradicts its own statement that "a poem should not mean / But be."

In any case, from ancient times to the present, people have assumed that art does (or can do) something to us. Probably most people somehow assume that works of art can improve their lives, and certainly many people (from Plato to Senator Helms) assume that art can do damage. Pornography, for instance, is alleged to corrupt the young, and to stimulate men to do violence against women.

We have moved rather far from Housman's poem, which we enjoy especially for its witty presentation of a human being who feels a kinship with a work of art, and who by the end of the poem feels he can better face an alien world. The stoic philosophy ("Stand, quit you like stone, be strong"), too, is engaging, even if one doesn't quite feel up to its demands. But we think that the poem is especially useful because it gives students the opportunity to discuss ideas about responding to works of art.

A Note on the Text: Some of the changes Housman made in the poem are of interest. (They are given in Tom Burns Haber, *The Making of A Shropshire Lad* [1966].) In line 1, *Loitering* originally was *Moving;* in 3, *brooding* was *thinking;* in 13, *drooping* was *fainting;* in 18, *collar* was *burden.*

WILLA CATHER

The Swedish Mother (Nebraska) (p. 928)

Our first question in the text concerns a child's delight in hearing a story repeated verbatim. Doubtless there is more than one reason why a child likes to hear the same story over and over again. Presumably a familiar story provides the child with reassurance, making the world secure. (Children can get rather nasty when an adult narrator alters the ending of a familiar story. One may hear cries of "No fair," mingled with alarm.) Perhaps, too, the fact that the child knows how the story will turn out allows the child to treasure each part of the story, line by line, without distracting thoughts of where the story is going.

Why do adults sometimes want to hear the same story, i.e. see *King Lear* for a second or third time, or reread a favorite novel? Perhaps for the very same reasons, though we are likely to add that we respond differently on each experience. That is, our response to *King Lear* in college is one thing, and our response to it twenty years later (perhaps when we have lost our parents, or perhaps when we have experienced filial ingratitude) may be quite another thing.

Our second question concerns the mother's sadness as she tells what seems to be a happy story. Why does she smile sadly? Probably chiefly because she is remembering her childhood in the Old Country. That is, she is remembering a time which, whatever the hardships, was a time of relative innocence for her, a time when, for instance, her loving father—"He so young then, big and strong"—would hold her tightly (line 37). The poem ends with the girl looking where the mother gazes, but the girl "Only sees the drifting herd," whereas presumably the mother sees the lost world of her own childhood.

ROBERT FROST

The Aim Was Song (p. 930)

The poem offers a playful, witty fable, in effect telling how man improved upon nature by inventing art. Frost talks about only one art, "song," the art dearest to him, but (as we will see in a moment) the fable implies the other arts too.

Nature is the rough wind, blowing loudly. Art is (to use Alexander Pope's words in *An Essay on Criticism*) "nature methodized." In Frost's playful terms in this poem, nature has to be "converted" (line 11, literally *turned around, transformed*) and changed into something governed "by measure." Poetry of course uses *measure*, i.e. meter (from the Greek *metron*, "measure"), but so the other arts, such as music (where the metronome has its place), architecture (where symmetry is common), and even prose fiction (where one can chart recurring motifs, paired or contrasting characters, foreshadowing, and so forth).

Having said this, we must admit that Frost is talking chiefly about poetry, and in fact about lyric poetry (*song*) where, one might almost say, the sound is more important than the sense. After all, we *do* value some lyrics that barely go beyond *hey nonny nonny.* There is a staying-power in nonsense rhymes, counting-out rhymes, and so forth, and while no one would say that these are the highest kind of poetry, they do serve as reminders that music (measure) is at the heart of poetry.

ARCHIBALD MACLEISH

Ars Poetica (p. 931)

See Donald Stauffer, *The Nature of Poetry*, 121-25, and W. P. Standt in *College English* 19 (October 1957) 28-29. Standt points out that in the first and second sections there are similes, but in the third section we move from similarity to identity; i.e., metaphors replace similes. Moreover, identity is stressed in the quasi-mathematical formula at the beginning of the third section.

This poem, like Moore's "Poetry," easily gets the class into a discussion of the nature of art. (Moore's poem is not concerned explicitly with "modern" poetry, but with new poetry of any period.) And a discussion of MacLeish's poem inevitably gets into whether MacLeish practices his precepts; the abundant detail gives us a sense of felt reality ("be"), but doesn't MacLeish also "mean"? Certainly "a poem should not mean but be" has meaning; and note, too, that MacLeish is not content to give us "An empty doorway and a maple leaf," for he prefaces this with an explanation, telling us that it stands "for all the history of grief."

It is useful to ask students to comment in detail on the figures. The figure of an empty doorway and an autumn leaf standing for grief is clear enough, but how is "a poem... motionless in time / As the moon climbs"? Perhaps the idea is that a poem, because it stirs the emotions, seems to move, yet it is itself unchanging.

An audiocassette of Archibald MacLeish reading is available from HarperCollins.

ELIZABETH BISHOP

Poem (p. 932)

First, the title. We tell students in our composition classes that a piece of writing—whether by a student or by a professional—begins with the title; this poem provides a sort of test case. Bishop's titles are usually less laconic than this one, so we assume that this title too is significant. The poem is partly about a painting, and therefore about the effects of works of art; this title, then, reminds us at the start that we are confronting a work of art, or, to put it a little differently, Bishop's poem is itself, as an artifact, analogous to Uncle George's picture, a work of art, a concrete embodiment of a perception, and an object that will stimulate the mind of the perceivers.

We find touches of wry humor in "that awful shade of brown" ("awful" is also deeply disturbing), in the reference to "the artist's specialty," and in the bird that looks like a flyspeck—or the flyspeck that looks like a bird (12, 25, 26-27); there is a sort of humor, too, in the remembered monologue of the giver of the picture, presumably the speaker's mother or father (39-44). But any wryness that occurs after this last passage lacks humor; the remaining lines are not quite bitter, but they convey a strong sense of diminution or loss, as in "Which is which? / Life and the memory of it cramped, / dim, on a piece of Bristol board...," and especially in "the little of our earthly trust. Not much / About the size of our abidance / along with theirs; the munching cows...."

"Earthly trust" and "abidance" in the lines just quoted have a puritanical ring—though there is probably also a pun in "earthly trust," given the earlier financial references ("dollar bill," "never earned any money in its life," and "handed along collaterally"—another pun here). At the start the diminutive is engaging (the "tiny" cows, the "wisp" of the steeple), but soon the references to the small and the transient or the brief become disquieting. The picture is "done in an hour, 'in one breath'"; Uncle George abandoned Canada; "Life and the memory of it cramped, /dim, on a piece of Bristol board"; the speaker of the remembered conversation, who will "probably never / have room to hang these things again," is quite likely moving to smaller quarters. (Such a move is usually provoked by the loss of part of one's family.) We get "little... for free" (58), and though what we get on earth we treasure in memory, it cannot last. Right now, at least in memory, there are "spring freshets," but autumn and winter will come: the elms will be "dismantled" (64); that is, their covering or mantle of leaves will fall, or perhaps the branches will be lopped and the trees themselves will be chopped down. Although the reference to dismantling is powerful, it is not the last word; the poem ends with "the geese," and, after all, the little picture itself continues to survive. Art—including Bishop's poem (again we emphasize the importance of the title)—is one of the things we "get for free." (One might, in class, compare this poem with Keats's "Ode on a Grecian Urn," another poem about transience and art.) Helen Vendler, in *Part of Nature, Part of Us,* at the end of her discussion of Bishop's poem, offers a somewhat different interpretation:

> As lightly as possible, the word "dismantled"... refutes the whole illusion of entire absorption in the memorial scene; the world of the poet who was once the child now seems the scenery arranged for a drama with only too brief a tenure on the stage—the play once over, the set is dismantled, the illusion gone. The poem, having taken the reader through the process that we name domestication and by which a strange terrain becomes first recognizable, then familiar, and then beloved, releases the reader at last from the intimacy it has induced. Domestication is followed, almost inevitably, by that dismantling which is, in its acute form, disaster....

Earlier in the essay Vendler points out that "the place" depicted in the painting is described three times: first, visually; then, after "Heavens, I recognize this place," as a remembered landscape (but the painting remains a painting, consisting of "titanium whited etc.); and finally as something not merely seen by the eye or contemplated by the mind but perceived (Vendler says) "by the heart, touched into participation." See, in addition to Vendler, Bonnie Costello, *Elizabeth Bishop.*

LAWRENCE FERLINGHETTI

Constantly risking absurdity (p. 934)

Ferlinghetti has insisted that poetry be read aloud, and as a consequence, he writes poetry that is easily intelligible to auditors. (Not surprisingly, the one allusion in Ferlinghetti's poem is not to mythology or literature, but to the liveliest and most popular art, film.) Easy intelligibility, however, means that the poet is "constantly risking absurdity." Of course the point is not to be absurd; absurdity is a risk one runs in trying to "perceive / taut truth" as one approaches "Beauty" and hopes to catch her.

The shape of the poem on the page more or less imitates the progress and the pauses of a performer on a tightrope, and perhaps it also imitates his balancing pole extending far out on each side. The poem is obviously related to many of William Carlos Williams's poems, especially to "The Artist." And it is worthwhile to remind students of Frost's comment that a poem is a "performance in words." In addition to Ferlinghetti's typographical performance on paper, the word-play is part of the act ("climbs on rime," of "balancing on eyebeams," "sleight-of-foot tricks," "with gravity").

RICHARD WILBUR

Museum Piece (p. 935)

The poem begins by glancing at what might seem to be an inartistic aspect of the museum world, the "good gray guardians of art," that is, the bland, colorless guards. It will end on what might seem to be another inartistic or unartistic note, Degas's trousers hanging by the artist's bedside—something we will discuss in a moment.

After the apparently inartistic beginning—but set forth, of course, in an elegant and witty quatrain—the poem in its second stanza introduces a painting by Degas, but still in a jokey way, since the dancer seems to be balanced on the part in the hair of a dozing guard. But this gets us to the heart of the poem: "The grace is there, / But strain as well is plain to see." Perhaps this is the time to mention, in class, Hemingway's famous definition of "guts" (*New Yorker* 30 November 1929): "Grace under pressure." Hemingway was a writer who was determined to stick to his principles, so of course he had to say *guts* where some other writer would have said *beauty*, but beauty is what Hemingway is talking about.

The idea that the most interesting sort of beauty involves strain is ancient, and often was set forth in images of the lyre (the string must be taut if it is to give a musical sound) or the bow (again, the string must be taut if the arrow is to make a graceful flight). Ideas of a work of art as possessing unity *and* complexity also usually involve strain, as is evident in the emphasis on paradox in New Criticism. Or consider this passage from Pope's "Windsor Forest":

> Here hills and vales, the woodland and the plain,
> Here earth and water seem to strive again,
> Not Chaos-like together crushed and bruised,
> But as the world, harmoniously confused:
> Where order in variety we see,
> And where, though all things differ, all agree.
> Here waving groves a checkered scene display,
> And part admit and part exclude the day....

It is easy enough to see tension in Degas dancers, and, for that matter, in most of his paintings—certainly, for instance, in his paintings of his other favorite subject, race horses, those elegant, high-strung creatures.

Wilbur's poem ends with a joke, but a serious one: Degas loved art—he was a great collector—but he also saw art as useful, even as useful in the most pedestrian way, as when he used an El Greco as a support for his trousers.

TOPIC FOR WRITING

Wilbur says that in Degas's picture of a dancer we see not only "Grace" but also "strain." In an essay of about 750 words, explain what Wilbur meant, using his example. Then go on to show how a work of art that interests you shows those qualities too. Don't limit yourself to painting; music, sculpture, architecture, and so on may provide an example.

NIKKI GIOVANNI

For Saundra (p. 937)

Some of your students may be familiar with poems about writing a poem; the most famous perhaps is Langston Hughes's "Theme for English B." Usually these poems end with an announcement—uttered almost to the poet's surprise—that the poem has been written. Giovanni takes a different tack, ending with the assertion that "perhaps these are not poetic / times / at all" but of course the joke is that she has indeed written a poem in the course of describing these unpoetic times.

The first stanza ("revolution doesn't lend / itself to be-bopping") voices a familiar complaint—that in difficult times the work of a poet may seem trivial. The terms of disparagement are almost comic. The comedy is continued in the second stanza, when we meet a neighbor who likes trees and wants a tree poem. (There *are* some significant "tree poems," such as Frost's "Tree at My Window," but chiefly one thinks of Kilmer's not-so-notable "Trees.")

The comedy continues with the speaker noting, apparently with surprise, that when she looks out of her window she sees only asphalt. An attempt to write "a big blue sky poem" is derailed with a dirty joke about Richard Nixon.

The "revolution" mentioned in the first stanza reappears, indirectly, in the next-to-last stanza, with the references to a gun and kerosene, thus helping to prepare for the closure of the final stanza, which reasserts, but in different words, the point of the first stanza.

CHAPTER 21

The Individual and Society

JOSEPH BRANT

Indian Civilization vs. White Civilization
(p. 938)

Because Brant's remarks, like those of Mary Jemison in the next selection, were recorded by whites, one cannot with confidence say that the reported words are exactly what the speaker said. And certainly in Brant's alleged comments we hear a good deal of what sounds suspiciously like eighteenth-century deistic thought, particularly in the idea (in the first paragraph) that "the great Spirit of the universe" has written a message "on the heart of every rational creature."

That is, this formulation whereby the deity has revealed his message to everyone, and this message is "rational," is very much of the time. It certainly is not in accord with much of the history of Judaism and Christianity, where the message is revealed to an elect few, and where the message is far from rational. That is, in most Jewish and Christian thinking, the message is manifested through special revelation, particularly in the Hebrew Bible and in the New Testament, and these books present messages that could never be arrived at through the workings of mere reason.

Brant presents the Indians (to use the word that appears in his text) as more or less in the tradition of the Noble Savage, devoid of "envy and covetousness." (Speaking a bit broadly, we can say that when Europeans first encountered what was to be called America, they developed two opposed strains of thought: the newfound residents were barbarous creatures, little better than animals, and badly in need of the whip, the sword, and the teachings of Jesus, or, on the other hand, the new-found people were almost pre-lapsarian Adam-like persons, Noble Savages who were inherently good. In eighteenth-century America, the Puritans inclined toward the first view, the Deists toward the second.)

Brant does grant that the Indians sometimes are "furious," display "rage," and use torture—i.e. that they are not perfect noble savages—but the torture lasts for "no longer than a day," and (he says) is mild punishment compared with years of imprisonment. Students might be invited to give their responses to Brant's suggestion (paragraph 5) that a day of torture, ending with death, is preferable to a year in prison.

A Note on the Word "Indian." Of course the word is all a mistake; Columbus thought that the people he encountered were natives of India. In recent years *Native American* has often been substituted for *Indian*, but there are some problems. (1) Many of the people who are being described in fact call themselves Indians; (2) these people did not originate here, but (like the Europeans) migrated here, albeit in ancient times; (3) the term *Native American* avoids *Indian* but it nevertheless includes a Eurocentric element, American (named for a European explorer). It is our impression that although Native American is perhaps used more often than Indian by persons of European descent, the people in question are more likely to use *Indian.*

MARY JEMISON

A Narrative of Her Life (p. 940)

If your library has the full version of *The Life of Mrs. Mary Jemison*, you may want to encourage students to do some further reading in the book, and summarize her comparisons between Indian life and white life. At the time we are writing this note (June 1994) a book on a comparable story is receiving much attention, John Demos, *The Unredeemed Captive: A Family Story from Early America*. This scholarly but highly readable study examines the capture (1704) and subsequent history of Eunice Williams and her father and mother. The mother was killed, the father was ransomed, but Eunice was adopted by Roman Catholic Iroquois, and she refused to return to her family. Students might be invited to compare Eunice's experiences—especially her reasons for staying with the Indians—with Mary Jemison's.

One of the things one learns from Demos's book, and indeed glimpses in some of the paragraphs that we give from Jemison's account, is that America in the second half of the eighteenth century was very much a multi-cultural sphere. There were the French, the English, the Americans, the Indians (of various tribes, and including Roman Catholics and Protestants). These groups apparently mixed with some ease, at least some of the time. Notice, for example, Jemison's comment in paragraph 12 that she conversed almost daily "with English people."

Another thing one learns from Jemison's pages is that, for a woman at least, life among the Indians was easier than life among the Europeans. Jemison certainly does not present a simple, idealized world of noble savages, but she does present a world in which women seem to have a good deal more freedom than their Euro-American counterparts.

JUDY BRADY

I Want a Wife (p. 945)

This article originally appeared in *Ms*, so presumably its intended audience is female and its purpose is (as the saying goes) consciousness raising. But readers—male as well as female—can scarcely fail to understand that the essay seeks to be persuasive: it doesn't merely suggest that this is the way things are; rather, it implies that the situation is outrageous and ought to be changed.

Like much other satire, it expresses its outrage not by saying "This is outrageous," but by using an innocent eye, a persona who merely describes, in a simple, apparently objective way, what is going on. (The reader, not the speaker, says "This is outrageous.") Brady's persona or speaker is simply "a Wife." We then get the terrifying list of things that a Wife finds thrust upon her. These are scarcely described in detail, but the mere enumeration of the chores becomes, by the volume of its unadorned accumulation, comic—and stinging. One is reminded of John Dryden's comment, in *Origin and Progress of Satire*, distinguishing between invective (direct abuse) and verbal irony:

> How easy is it to call "rogue" and "villain," and that wittily. But how hard to make a man appear a fool, a blockhead, or a knave, without using any of these opprobrious terms.

Brady's essay is easy, amusing, and widely popular, but doubtless it is also intended to be a serious vision of an old (and still surviving?) way of life. Brady forces men to look at something they rarely face because they simply take it for granted, like the air they breathe.

It's always risky to say that our social system today is free of the abuses that are so obvious in systems of the past. Between, say, 1920 and 1960 it was commonly said that Ibsen's plays were dated. After all, women could now vote, and so on, and so forth. But the Women's Movement helped everyone see that, at its core, a work such as *A Doll's House* is not dated. Judging from Brady, Torvald Helmer is alive and well (or at least was so in 1971, when the essay was first published).

Whether things have changed since then is a question that might be argued. One might also ask (though of course one doesn't expect a balanced view in satire) if things in 1971 really were the way Brady saw them. Did marriage really offer nothing to a wife? No love, no companionship, no security? Were all husbands childish and selfish, and all wives selfless?

NEIL MILLER

In Search of Gay America: Ogilvie, Minnesota (Population 374) (p. 947)

If you ask students to do any interviewing and then to put the results into writing, you may find this piece of special interest. Students should understand, however, that Miller's essay—indeed, his entire book, *In Search of Gay America*—is not an interview with an expert or a celebrity. Rather, the book recounts Miller's attempt to gain, for himself as well as for his readers, a better sense of gay life in this country. This means that the book is in some degree about Miller, specifically about his growing awareness of the kinds of gay life he encounters.

Thus, the first paragraph is about Miller, not about the gay farmers whom he meets in the chapter, In this paragraph he tells us that he had "never assumed that the beef and poultry barn or the cattle barn of a state fair would be a particularly good place to observe gay and lesbian life." Presumably the reader assents, and the next paragraph thus begins with something of a surprise, set forth in a short, emphatic sentence: "I was wrong"—and so, too, is the reader. (It's only "*something* of a surprise" because the mere assertion of the assumption in the first paragraph causes the reader to suspect that the assumption will soon be refuted.) In short, the reader shares in Miller's education. The most obvious point, of course, is that there are gay farmers, but Miller (and along with him, the reader) learns a good deal more. One point of interest, for example, is that the parents of these farmers are at least partly reconciled to their children's sexuality because unlike the other sons these men have continued the family tradition of farming. An instructor might ask students what *they* found especially interesting in the essay. What did they learn about human behavior?

Matters of style, too, are of interest. We have already commented on the way that the opening paragraph is undermined by the emphatic first sentence of the second paragraph. The third paragraph is interesting partly because of its concrete details: "urban sophistication" is clarified by "take-out Szechuan restaurants, the punk rockers," and so on. Similarly, "The connection to the land" is supported by names and other details. On the whole Miller's style appears simple, almost invisible, but it serves him well. Paragraph 14, for example, seems to be a rather routine description of a rather nondescript farm, but in "They didn't grow their own feed or even have a vegetable garden" we hear the voice of the slightly puzzled urban writer who is going to get an education both about gay life and about farm life.

TOPICS FOR WRITING

1.   If you know of any openly gay or lesbian couples, interview them and write an essay concentrating on the way they manage to live their lives in a predominantly straight world.
2.   If you know someone who grew up on a farm but left it, briefly describe the person and then give the reasons he or she moved from farming.

ANDREW LAM

Goodbye, Saigon, Finally (p. 954)

This essay on assimilation may come as something of a surprise to students, who today are more likely to read (or to hear) about multiculturalism, the importance of maintaining ethnic identity, the Untied States as a salad bowl or mosaic rather than as melting pot, etc.

Of course ethnic neighborhoods survive, with their restaurants, butcher shops, groceries, and with foreign languages spoken. But the members of the second-generation are largely assimilated, partly in spite of their efforts to preserve their parents' culture. (It will be interesting to see, in class, if members of different ethnic cultures respond differently to the essay.) In their adolescence they may echo their parents and may even outdo their parents in enthusiasm for the old (in paragraph 11, Lam reports that when his brother said he wanted to be a guerrilla fighter, his father "sighed"), but, as Lam indicates (paragraph 15), growing up in this country probably involves (*mutatis mutandis*) "a little betrayal of Little Saigon's parochialism, its sentimentalities and the old man's outdated passions." In his 16th paragraph Lam suggests (correctly, we imagine) that at least for most people this "betrayal" is unconscious: "When did this happen? Who knows?" One knows only that one is beginning to sound—to think—like an American; one's vocabulary "includes terms like career choices, downpayment, escrow, overtime."

We think Lam is highly successful in communicating the young immigrant's slightly puzzled sense of himself, and especially his slightly critical sense of what he has become. We say "slightly," because although the quoted words about "downpayment, escrow," etc. suggest a not entirely attractive materialism, there really is nothing indecent about these words, and, further, it is clear that life in Saigon is not a viable alternative for him—and indeed it is scarcely tolerable even for those who never left Saigon. What the customs officer calls National Liberation Day is, at the end, admitted to be National Defeat Day. The Saigon of Lam's youth is gone with the wind, and so he and his friends see the film, and presumably they feel, as they see it, a sense of hopeless loss and also a sense of relief that they do not live in that sort of world.

The Book of Ruth (p. 956)

None of the arguments for any date is highly convincing, and some of the arguments are highly technical, based, for instance, on matters of vocabulary and style. Some scholars argue that the gist of the story—in which a Moabite woman is welcomed into the Hebrew community—indicates that the book must precede the anti-foreign decrees of the fifth century B.C.E. found in Ezra and Nehemiah, requiring Hebrew men to divorce foreign wives. On the other hand, other scholars argue that the Book of Ruth is a humane response to those decrees. In short, the book has been placed as early as the 10th century and as late as the third century B.C.E., with perhaps a majority of scholars inclining to a date in the late fifth century. Some scholars, but by no means all, regard the genealogy in 4.18-22 (with its assertion that David is descended from Ruth) as a late addition. Even if it is an addition, we as readers take the story as a whole—that is, we take the genealogy as part of the work.

The author is unknown, but almost everyone assumes the author was a male, though one who was remarkable aware of the feelings of women. (Later we will refer to some feminist readings.)

The story begins with three deaths, the death of Naomi's husband and the deaths of her two sons, and with talk of famine. Naomi is a woman in a patriarchal society, a Jew, a widow, living in Moab, a country not her own, and therefore she is in a desperate plight. The Moabites, who inhabited the plain east of the Dead Sea, were enemies of Israel and Judah. In Deuteronomy we read that "an Ammonite or Moabite shall not enter into the congregation of the Lord" (23.3), and, again, Ezra (10.1-5) and Nehemiah (13.23-27) specifically condemn men who take non-Jewish wives. Against this harsh background we find a story so free from anger or rejection that most commentators find themselves calling it an idyll, a sweet tale of rural life.

Not surprisingly, Naomi decides to leave Moab and to return to her native land, especially since she has heard that "the Lord had visited his people in giving them bread" (1.6), i.e. the country is prospering, a sign of God's favor. Her two Gentile daughters-in-law, Orpah and Ruth, volunteer to return with her, but Naomi counsels them that for their own good they should remain among their own people. Orpah is persuaded, but Ruth insists on accompanying Naomi, in one of the most famous speeches of the Hebrew Bible, all the more impressive because it is uttered by a pagan:

> Intreat me not to leave thee, or to return from following after thee: for whither thou goest, I will go; and where thou lodgest, I will lodge: thy people shall be my people, and thy God my God. (1.16)

The tone of the book is such that Orpah is not blamed for remaining in Moab; there are no villains in this story, only minimally correct human beings (the next-of-kin, who will redeem Naomi's land but will not marry Ruth), decent human beings (Orpah and Boaz), and two heroines (Naomi and Ruth). Again, things proceed so smoothly and the setting is so rural that we overlook the heroism that motivates the women who, at the start, are in a highly perilous situation. But from death (and the apparent extinction of the line of Elimelech, Naomi's husband), comes birth and renewal, in the form of a son born to Ruth and to Boaz. This son, sired by a kinsman of Elimelech in what is called a levirate marriage, is regarded not as the son of the biological father but as the son of the deceased husband, and thus he continues the line of Elimelech.

The story moves, then, from famine, death, and sorrow to birth, harvest (with inevitable suggestions of fertility and fulfillment), and joy, the joy being especially great because the grandson of the newborn son will be the great David. (The three deaths as the beginning of the story are matched by the three births at the end—Obed, Jesse, and David.) In line with this ultimately joyful story, Naomi moves from weakness to strength, counseling Ruth how to behave with her kinsman Boaz. And Ruth, who in 2.10 says to Boaz "I am a stranger" (and thereby brings to the mind of readers familiar with the Bible a host of references to strangers, such as "Ye were strangers in the land of Egypt," in Exodus 22.21), is ultimately joined to a family and a nation. If, then, we look for the themes of the Book of Ruth, we can find at least two, one concerning only Ruth (a human story), and a second concerning the history of the Jews (a national story): 1) Israel welcomes those who, even though of foreign birth, "join themselves to the Lord" (to quote from Isaiah 56.6); 2) God is merciful, sustaining the line of descent from Abraham, even including the Moabite woman Ruth, who becomes the great-grandmother of the heroic David.

The story is entirely plausible on a human level; personality and chance seem adequately to explain what happens (*hap* is a Middle English word meaning "chance"), but some readers find, in what seems to be chance, strong hints of Providence working through faithful mortals, particularly in two passages: "Her hap was to light on a part of the field belonging unto Boaz" (2.3), and "Blessed be he of the Lord, who hath not left off his kindness to the living and to the dead" (2.20). (In this second quotation, it is not clear whether Naomi is speaking of the kindness of the Lord or of Boaz. This very ambiguity, however, is in accord with the issue we are discussing.) One might perhaps add 4.1, where the unnamed next-of-kin appears—apparently by chance—at the gate where Boaz is seated. Chance (happenstance)? Or Providence?

In recent years the book has been the subject of some feminist writing. (For a very brief example, see, for instance, Alice L. Laffey, *Introduction to the Old Testament: A Feminist Perspective* [1988]. For a collection of essays by women, see the book edited by Kates and Reimer, mentioned at the very end of our comment.) Such writing emphasizes the courage of all of the women, including Orpah, who is not blamed for leaving Naomi. Feminist readings also emphasize Naomi's resourcefulness (she instructs Ruth how to approach Boaz), and they sometimes concern themselves with calling attention to the limitations of a patriarchal society that regards a woman as nothing if she is not affiliated with a male, whether father, husband, brother, or son. June Jordan, in a very brief essay in *Out of the Garden*, ed. Christina Buchmann and Celina Spiegel (1994), mentions that she was distressed by what seemed to be the subservience of Ruth and Naomi to men, but then, Jordan says, she realized that "Ruth and Naomi had made brave choices in a circumstance that allowed them no freedom. They had chosen to do whatever would allow them to stay together, without undue penury, or censure by the townspeople of Bethlehem" (86).

Phyllis Trible, writing about the Book of Ruth in the fifth volume of *The Anchor Bible Dictionary*, brings together a theological and a feminist perspective. Here is Trible's summary of the part of her essay headed "Theology":

> Among the book's characters, women predominate. They embody a remnant theology in contrast to patriarchal perspectives. Scene 1 presents Naomi and Ruth all alone; they make their own decisions. This portrayal continues in scene 2, even though the appearance of Boas complicates the situation. The power of the scene is not, however, transferred to him. The women prevail in their struggle for physical survival. Similarly, in scene 3 they summon an Israelite man to responsibility and thereby secure their cultural survival. At its beginning, scene 4 reverts to a traditional mode when males decide the future of widows. At the end, the females of Bethlehem reinterpret the occasion. The newborn child symbolizes a new beginning with men. Overall, the book of Ruth shows females working out their own salvation with fear and trembling, for it is God who works in them" (5: 845).

See also Trible's essay in *Literary Interpretations of Biblical Narrative*, II, ed. Kenneth R. R. Gros Louis (1982).

We can summarize what we have been saying:

1) Ruth, a foreigner, is welcomed into the community of Israel

2) The author is not suggesting that all people should acknowledge the God of Israel; Orpah is not condemned for returning to her people and her gods (1.15-18).

3) The story tells of a family that—with God's help—escaped extinction, and indeed produced the illustrious David (Ruth is David's great-grandmother [4.13-22]).

4) The structure: (a) the story begins with three deaths and famine, and (moving through a period of harvest, with its implications of fulfillment) ends with births (fertility, the revival of Elimelech's line, joy, prosperity); (b) Naomi moves from victim to recipient of a blessing.

5) Feminist readings emphasize the courage of the women (Ruth and Orpah are willing to leave their homeland to be with Naomi; Naomi bravely tells them both to return; Ruth remains loyal to Naomi; Naomi resourcefully tells Ruth what to do to attract Boaz's attention). A second point is that in this patriarchal society a woman is regarded as nothing if not attached to a male.

Additional Suggested References: in addition to the cited works by Trible and by Laffey, we strongly recommend an essay by D. F. Rauber, originally published in *Journal of Biblical Literature* 39, Part 1 (March 1970): 27-37, and reprinted with a slightly different title in *Literary Interpretations of Biblical Narratives*, ed. Kenneth R. R. Gros Louis (1974). Rauber emphasizes the literary aspects of the story, e.g. such matters as foreshadowing and literary allusions. Another useful literary analysis can be found in Leland Ryken, *Words of Delight*, 2nd ed. (1992).

After we wrote all of the above, we encountered a newly published work, *Reading Ruth: Contemporary Women Reclaim a Sacred Story*, ed. Judith A. Rates and Gail Twersky Reimer (1994). Thirty writers—essayists, poets, rabbis, psychologists, scholars—offer a range of fascinating commentary. We cannot attempt to discuss each contribution, but we can give something of the flavor of the work by quoting. We arbitrarily choose to quote from the essays by the two editors. First, from Kates's essay:

> Ruth is a story of women struggling to survive in a man's world. The book begins in the male-centered mode we expect from biblical stories, identifying a "man from Bethlehem in Judah" (1:1) as the principal character and the woman as simply "his wife." The already familiar pattern of movement out of the land of Israel to a neighboring pagan territory in time of famine reinforces the sense that we know this story (compare Genesis 12 or 44).... But the text shatters the familiar narrative, both its pattern and its human center. The place of refuge becomes a place of death. And in death Elimelech becomes simply "Naomi's husband" (1:3). Naomi begins to take center stage, so that by verse 5 she preempts our attention, ironically because she has been left alone: "so the woman was left without her two sons and without her husband." The text enters into her experience of loss, referring to the sons as *yiladeha* (her children) from the root meaning "to give birth," to "bear," rather than *baneha* (her sons). The word poignantly reminds us of the sons' essential meaning to her: they are *yiladeha*, the children she bore, in the very moment when death severs her connection to them. (189)

Now for a brief quotation from the essay by Reimer:

> Naomi's view of women's destiny is evident in her first spoken words, addressed to her daughters-in-law. "Go, return each of you to her mother's house" (1:8). It is at once startling and fitting that, at the crossroads, when Naomi attempts to part from her daughters-in-law, she directs them to return to their "mother's house." Startling because the typical formulation in biblical narratives is "the father's house"; this narrative too, began by defining fathers as the heads of households—"and a man of Bethlehem in Judah, with his wife and two sons, went…" (1:1). And fitting because the "mother's house" to which Ruth refuses to return represents the culture of conventional expectations that Ruth rejects. (97).

The entire collection is well worth reading, though if one can devote only an hour or so to reading about the Book of Ruth, and therefore wants a general introduction, probably one should turn to Trible's essay in *The Anchor Bible Dictionary* or to Rauber's essay in K. R. Gros Louis's 1974 collection, *Literary Interpretations of the Bible*.

NATHANIEL HAWTHORNE

The Maypole of Merry Mount (p. 963)

Our first question in the text asks students to explain the allegory. We find that discussion usually begins by generating a list somewhat along these lines:

Merry Mount	↔	Plymouth
"gayety"	↔	"moral gloom"
laughter	↔	sermons
maypole	↔	whipping post
light	↔	dark (Puritans concealed in forest "frowned… darkly")
bright colors	↔	black
light-footed	↔	weighed down with armor
flowers	↔	"men of iron" (armed soldiers)

Because even in the first paragraph Hawthorne explicitly says that "Jollity and gloom were contending for an empire," it is easy—but probably mistaken—to see in all of this a simple conflict of freedom against oppression, or even more simply, of good (Merry Mount) against evil (Plymouth). Although the sympathies of most readers will, on first reading, lead toward such a view, this opposition is too simple, as Frederick Crews points out in *The Sins of the Fathers*. The life of Merry Mount has about it something not merely natural (in the sense of being in harmony with nature) but bestial. Its revelers are costumed as a stag, a wolf, a goat, and a bear, and soon we hear that "a riotous uproar burst from the rout of monstrous figures." Moreover, Hawthorne suggests that the most engaging aspects of the life of Merry Mount are unreal. One notes "dreamlike" in the first paragraph, and the comparison to a rainbow in the second. Edith, the Lady of the May, soon confesses that she has intimations that the masque is "visionary" and "unreal," and immediately after this expression of her doubts, "down came a little shower of withering rose leaves from the Maypole," causing the lovers to become "sensible of something vague and unsubstantial in their former pleasures." A little later we are told, quite directly, that the inhabitants of Merry Mount reject or pervert "Thought" and "Wisdom." In opposition to these images of dreamlike triviality is the Puritan world, a world that Hawthorne characterizes as the world of "waking thoughts."

But if one's initial view of a simple contrast (Merry Mount = good, freedom; Plymouth = evil, oppression) is thus modified, even nearly reversed, it is (Crews argues) modified and reversed by still further thought. The young couple is indisputably attractive, and the Puritans are indisputably off-putting. (One recalls the famous line from *1066 and All That:* "The royalists were wrong but romantic, the Republicans right but repulsive.") Further (again Crews's point) the Puritans do not represent morality versus pleasure, because the Puritans themselves engage in activities that seem to afford a nasty, sadistic sort of pleasure: slaughter of wolves, of Indians, and of the bear; the use of the whipping post; the mutilation of ears. Moreover, the Puritans no less than the revelers live a life of delusion, for Hawthorne explicitly tells us that they have peopled the wilderness with devils and witches. Given the bestial suggestions attributed to the revelers and the sadistic pleasures of the Puritans, the two groups, Crews suggests, "are less different from one another than they seem."

Still, there is a difference between Merry Mount and Plymouth, and the difference is perceptible to all. For one thing, the revelers in whom we are most interested—Edgar and Edith, the Lord and Lady of the May—perceive the shallowness of the revels. Recall Hawthorne's words about the pair in the passage on the fall of withering rose leaves: "No sooner had their hearts glowed with real passion than they were sensible of something vague and unsubstantial in their former pleasures." Put bluntly, this means that the revelers move from illusion to reality, from life as we would like it to be to life as conventional society recognizes it is, and indeed as it is. The author treats the young May couple sympathetically, but given the emphasis on the unreality of the life of the revelers, and given the piety and strength—and as we know, the success—of the Puritans, and given also Endicott's remarkable sympathy for the young couple (Hawthorne tells us that Endicott "almost sighed for the inevitable blight of [the young lovers'] early hopes"), the story can be seen as being about the education of carefree, irresponsible young lovers into mature, social beings who live under law. This is not to say, it must be noted, that Edith and Edgar give up (or are stripped of) love. Even at the end of the story, removed from their Eden, they retain their garland of roses, and "in the tie that united them, were intertwined all the purest and best of their early joys." There is no reason, then, for them to waste "one regretful thought on the vanities of Merry Mount," for their love, still rooted in the pagan rites of fertility, is now also sanctified by a higher moral and spiritual code.

(For a different view, arguing that at the end "the party of gloom has triumphed completely," see Michael Bell, *Hawthorne and the Historical Romance of New England.*)

Crews's *The Sins of the Fathers* seems to us to be the best account of the story, but useful discussions can also be found in Richard Harter Fogle, *Hawthorne's Fiction,* and in Daniel Hoffman, *Form and Fable in American Fiction.*

TILLIE OLSEN

I Stand Here Ironing (p. 971)

The story ends ("she is more than this dress on an ironing board") with an echo of its beginning ("I stand here ironing"). In a sense, there are two stories in between: the story of the mother, whose monologue we hear, and the story of her nineteen-year-old daughter as told by the mother. The two, of course, are connected. The mother was nineteen when she bore the daughter; the mother and daughter have had a difficult life in the "prerelief, pre-WPA world of the depression"; they both resist the conventions of the conformist society as embodied by the guidance counselor or psychiatrist who has told the mother that her daughter "needs help." As the mother tries to understand the forces that have shaped her daughter, she is also trying to understand the mysterious, irresistible forces that surround us all. Life for mother and daughter has been a struggle—for the mother to work and to make a success of her second marriage and her family, for the daughter to survive nurseries, schools, clinics, and a convalescent home.

Both *have* survived, though not in the view of the counselor who seeks a meeting with the mother to discuss the child's "problems." The child, though damaged, is strong, demanding, and entertaining (she "does not smile easily," but she can compel to laughter a "roaring, stamping audience, unwilling to let this rare and precious laughter out of their lives"). "Let her be" is the mother's strong view. True, "all that is in her will not bloom," she thinks, "but in how many does it? There is still enough to live by." And so we come to the end of this story: whatever the counselor may think, the task is not to manipulate the young woman but "only [to] help her to know... that she is more than this dress on the ironing board, helpless before the iron."

Students are often angry with the mother for sending the girl to a sanitarium, or for now not wanting to talk to the counselor. But the mother—who, like the daughter, resists being flattened like an ironed dress—is distressed by her daughter's suffering. Sometimes she seems to engage in self-justification, blaming the depression and the war, but on the whole we see compassion and (perhaps more important) an intelligent belief that Emily will "find her way," or at least an awareness that even a mother does not have all the answers.

Note: students may need help in seeing that despite the "you" (mentioned in the first line and persistently throughout), the piece is a soliloquy, a reflective monologue. For the most part, the "you" is, as we have mentioned, some sort of conscientious, but insensitive counselor. In the paragraph beginning "Afterwards," however, the "you" is the mother being addressed by the remembered counselor, and we are almost surprised to learn that the counselor has a sense of humor after all, as well as an awareness of talent that enables him (or her) to recognize the child's special gift. But the very next paragraph, beginning "She is coming," indicates that the counselor does not call to commend the child, or to talk about successes and happy days, but to report trouble.

TOPICS FOR CRITICAL THINKING AND WRITING

1. Who is the "you" whom the mother speaks of? Do you think the mother will visit the "you"? Why, or why not?
2. What do you make of Emily's telling her mother not to awaken her for the midterm examination on the next morning?
3. In what way(s) did your response toward the mother change as you progressed through the story?
4. What, if anything, has the mother learned about life?

SHIRLEY JACKSON

The Lottery (p. 977)

This story is based on fertility rituals of the sort described in Sir James Frazer's *The Golden Bough:* a community is purged of its evil, and fertility is ensured, by the sacrifice of an individual, that is, by killing a scapegoat. "Lottery in June, corn be heavy soon," Old Man Warner says. In "The Lottery," the method of execution is stoning, which Frazer reports was a method used in ancient Athens.

Until the last six paragraphs we think we are reading a realistic story about decent small-town life. Probably on rereading we notice that, despite all the realism, the time and the place are never specified; we may feel we are reading about a twentieth-century New England town, but we cannot document this feeling. On rereading, too, we pay more attention to the early references to stones, and to the general nervousness, and of course we see the importance of Tessie Hutchinson's outburst. (Consult Helen E. Nebeker, "'The Lottery':

Symbolic Tour de Force," *American Literature* 46 [1974]: 100-107.) With the last six paragraphs the horror comes, and it is described in the same matter-of-fact, objective tone used in the earlier part of the story.

Inevitably a discussion turns to the question, "Does the story have any meaning for a modern society?" Students in the 1990s may have to be reminded that a lottery was used as recently as the Vietnam War to pick the people who would be subject to slaughter.

In *Come Along With Me,* Shirley Jackson discusses the furor "The Lottery" evoked after its original publication in the *New Yorker* in 1948. Lenemaja Friedman, in *Shirley Jackson* (1975) reports that Jackson said of the theme: "Explaining just what I hoped the story to say is very difficult. I suppose I hoped, by setting a particularly brutal ancient rite in the present and in my own village, to shock the story's readers with a graphic demonstration of the pointless violence and general inhumanity in their own lives." On the other hand, Jack O'Shaughnessy in *The New York Times Book Review* (August 18, 1988, 34), said that after reading the story in the *New Yorker* he wrote to Jackson, asking, "What does it mean?" He says that Jackson replied, on a postcard, "I wish I knew. Shirley Jackson."

Perhaps this story should not be pressed for its meaning or theme. Formulations such as "Society engages in ritualized slaughter," or "Society disguises its cruelty, even from itself," or "Even decent people seek scapegoats" do not quite seem to fit. Isn't it possible that the story is an effective shocker, signifying nothing? As many people have pointed out, much of the effect of the story depends on the contrast between the objective narration and the horrifying subject. The story is clever, a carefully wrought thriller, but whether it is an allegory—something about the cruelty of humanity, a cruelty which is invisible to us because it is justified by tradition—is a matter that may be reasonably debated.

The date of the story is significant, June 27, close to the summer solstice, and the season for planting. Some of the names, too, are obviously significant: the ritual is presided over by Mr. Summers, the first man to draw a lot is Mr. Adams, and conservative warnings are uttered by Mr. Warner. Note, too, that the leaders of the attack on Mrs. Hutchinson are Adams (the first sinner) and Graves (the result of sin was death).

One last point about the ritual: Clyde Dunbar, at home with a broken leg, does not participate. Why? Because a sacrificial victim must be unblemished.

TOPICS FOR CRITICAL THINKING AND WRITING

1. Is "The Lottery" more than a shocker?
2. What is the community's attitude toward tradition?
3. Doubtless a good writer could tell this story effectively from the point of view of a participant, but Jackson chose a nonparticipant point of view. What does she gain?

4.   Let's say you were writing this story, and you had decided to write it from Tessie's point of view. What would your first paragraph, or your first 250 words, be?

5.   Suppose someone claimed that the story is an attack on religious orthodoxy. What might be your response? (Whether you agree or disagree, set forth your reasons.)

ALICE MUNRO

Boys and Girls (p. 983)

A good way to begin the discussion of this story is to have a student read the first paragraph aloud, and then ask if the sentences about the calendar have any relevance to the rest of the story. Of course this passage would be justified if it did no more than give a glimpse of the sort of decorations that might be found on a Canadian fox farm, and one doesn't want to press too hard for a deep meaning, but surely the picture of "plumed adventurers" (male, naturally) who use "savages" as pack animals introduces, however faintly a political note that can be connected with the treatment of distinctions between the sexes.

This is not to say that the story suggests that women are comparable to the Indians who bend their backs in service to the whites. The wife works hard, but so does the husband. And the early part of the story indicates that the female narrator, when a child, eagerly engaged in what the mother must have thought was "man's work." Certainly the girl, feeling quite superior to her little brother, had no sense that she was oppressed. She came to learn, however, that she must "become" a girl. If we hear a note of protest in this statement that society expects us to assume certain roles, the story nevertheless seems also to suggest that females are, by nature rather than by nurture, mentally or emotionally different from males. Despite the narrator's early enthusiasm for her father's work, and despite her sense of superiority to her brother (she can handle the wheelbarrow used for watering the foxes, whereas Laird, carrying a "little cream and green gardening can," can only play at watering), she is more shaken by the killing of Mack than she will admit. "My legs were a little shaky," she says, and later she adds that she "felt a little ashamed," but for the most part she deals with her response by talking about another episode, the time when she endangered Laird's life, and afterwards felt "the sadness of unexorcised guilt." Of course we may think that anyone—male or female— might feel shaky and guilty upon first witnessing the death of a harmless animal, but in fact Laird does not seem even mildly disturbed. Rather, after witnessing the shooting of Mack, Laird is "remote, concentrating."

The guilt engendered by watching Mack die prompts the narrator to let Flora escape. (A question: If the first horse killed had been a female, would the narrator have let the second horse, a male, escape? One answer: The story is right as it is. Don't monkey with it. If the horses were reversed, the story would be less coherent.) The narrator is irretrievably female. (Notice too the passage recounted after the episode with Flora, about the narrator's attempt to pretti-fy her part of the bedroom and, in the same paragraph, the discussion of her new fantasies, in which she no longer performs heroic rescues but is now the person rescued, and is wondering about her hairstyle and her dress.) Having let Flora escape, she of course has no desire to join in the chase, but Laird does, and when he returns, daubed in blood (this passage, however realistic, seems almost a parody of Hemingway and Faulkner on rituals of initiation), he is quite casual about what happened: "'We shot old Flora,' he said, 'and cut her up in fifty pieces.'" Laird, no longer his sister's partner but now firmly aligned with the men, soon betrays the narrator, reducing her to tears. Her father means well in absolving her ("She's only a girl"), but, as the narrator says, the words not only absolve but "dismiss" her. On the other hand, the narrator rec-ognizes that the father's words may be "true."

In teaching this story, one might get around to making the point that a work of literature doesn't "prove" anything. *Hamlet* doesn't prove that ghosts exist, or that one should not delay, or that revenge is morally acceptable. Sim-ilarly, Munro's story doesn't prove that girls are by nature more sensitive to the killing of a horse than boys are. We won't attempt here (or anywhere) to say what a work of fiction does do, but the point is worth discussing—probably early in the course and again near the end, after students have read a fair amount of literature.

TOPICS FOR CRITICAL THINKING AND WRITING

1. What does the narrator mean when she says, "The word *girl* had for-merly seemed to me innocent and unburdened, like the word *child;* now it appeared that it was no such thing. A girl was not, as I had supposed, simply what I was; it was what I had to become."
2. The narrator says that she "could not understand" why she disobeyed her father and allowed the horse to escape. Can you explain her action to her? If so, do so.
3. Characterize the mother.

TONI CADE BAMBARA

The Lesson (p. 993)

It would be hard to find a less strident or more delightful story preaching rev-olution. At its heart, "The Lesson" calls attention to the enormous inequity in the distribution of wealth in America, and it suggests that black people ought to start thinking about "what kind of society it is in which some people can spend on a toy what it would cost to feed a family of six or seven" for a year. That the young narrator does not quite get the point of Miss Moore's lesson— and indeed steals Miss Moore's money—is no sure sign that the lesson has failed. (Presumably, Miss Moore doesn't much care about the loss of her money; the money is well lost if it helps the narrator, who plans to spend it, to see the power of money.) In any case, the narrator has been made sufficiently uneasy ("I sure want to punch somebody in the mouth") so that we sense she will later get the point: "I'm goin... to think this day through." The last line of the story seems to refer to her race to a bakery, but it has larger implications: "Ain't nobody gonna beat me at nuthin."

The difference between Sylvia's response and Sugar's response to Miss Moore's lesson is worth discussing in class. As Malcolm Clark, of Solano Community College, puts it, "The obvious question of the story is, 'What is the lesson?'.... It's clear that Miss Moore is trying to teach these children a lesson in economic inequity.... Sugar learns this lesson, as her comments to Miss Moore indicate. However, Sylvia has also learned this lesson, though she does not reveal her understanding to Miss Moore." As Clark goes on to point out, Miss Moore's lesson is not simply that some people are rich and others are not. She wants to bring the children to a state where they will demand their share of the pie. "And it is in learning this part of the lesson that Sylvia and Sugar part company. Despite Sugar's obvious understanding of the lesson and her momentary flash of anger—strong enough to make her push Sylvia away— her condition is only temporary.

"At the end of the story she is unchanged from the little girl she was at the beginning. It is she who wants to go to Hascomb's bakery and spend the money on food, essentially the same thing they intended to do with the money before the lesson began.... Sylvia, however, is greatly changed. She does not intend to spend the money with Sugar; instead, she plans to go over to the river and reflect upon the lesson further."

TOPICS FOR CRITICAL THINKING AND WRITING

1. In a paragraph or two, characterize the narrator.
2. Let's suppose Bambara had decided to tell the story through the eyes of Miss Moore. Write the first 250 words of such a story.
3. What is the point of Miss Moore's lesson? Why does Sylvia resist it?
4. Describe the relationship between Sugar and Sylvia. What is Sugar's function in the story?
5. Miss Moore says, "Imagine for a minute what kind of society it is in which some people can spend on a toy what it would cost to feed a family of six or seven. What do you think?" In an essay of 500 words, tell a reader what you think about this issue.

ANJANA APPACHANA

To Rise Above (p. 999)

Appachana's story has obvious affinities with Judy Brady's "I Want a Wife," also in this chapter. Perhaps this story, like Brady's essay, is overstated or one-sided, but a reader—even a male reader—nevertheless feels the truth of it. That husband, who invites friends to come for tea, and then to stay for dinner, and who doesn't lift a finger to help! That mother-in-law, who offers to help because she knows the offer must be refused! "To Rise Above" offers a comic but thought-provoking view of the status of wives in India, but it includes a number of little comic details about all sorts of human folly, for instance the college boys who, in paragraph 3, delay a bus in order to protest the irregular service.

Obviously students who have immigrated to this country, or whose parents have, may enjoy writing a story inspired by this one, using a fair number of foreign words. Males as well as females can play the game, just as males can imitate Judy Brady and write "I Want a Husband." But even students whose families have long been part of what can be thought of as mainstream America (i.e. the Northern European or Anglo tradition) doubtless can write versions of life in patriarchal America—or matriarchal, if they wish.

DIANA CHANG

The Oriental Contingent (p. 1004)

The title comes from a remark in paragraph 15, when a voice—presumably belonging to Lisa's Caucasian husband—refers to the two Asian-American women as "the Oriental contingent." Is the remark offensive? The man sees two Asian-Americans together, and he (quite naturally?) sees them as a unit. The Asian-Americans, too, regard themselves (quite naturally?) as having something in common, although it turns out that Lisa, born in Buffalo, was not even brought up by Chinese parents.

It's hard to think of Lisa as Chinese in any significant way, other than that her biological parents were Chinese. And yet, of course, to Caucasians she will always be "Oriental," and when two people like Lisa are chatting they will (in Caucasian eyes) be "the Oriental contingent." And in their own eyes, too, they are not a hundred percent American; at one point Lisa thinks of her "American friends," and then remembers that she too is American. But if an American with Asian features, or, for that matter, with Indian features or black African features is in some degree an outsider to a Caucasian, such an individual is also in some degree—indeed, probably to a much greater degree—an outsider to persons with those features who were born in Asia, India, or Africa. Connie feels inferior to Lisa, who she mistakenly thinks is a more "authentic" Chinese than Connie, but it turns out that Lisa is so fearful of being insufficiently Chinese that she avoids visiting Asia.

One way to talk about the story is to talk about the degree to which any American—even someone from an Anglo background—feels an identity with some ethnic subgroup and therefore sees others as the Other. Of course the old idea was that all who came to the United States were turned into Americans, which more or less meant Anglos, or, let's say, Northern Europeans. America was "melting pot," a term invented or at least popularized by Israel Zangwill in a play, *The Melting Pot* (1914): "America is God's crucible, the great Melting-Pot where all the races of Europe are melting and reforming." The idea was dominant in the late nineteenth century, and survived almost unchallenged into the middle of the twentieth century, but today the image of the melting pot has been replaced by other images, including "the salad bowl" and "the mosaic." These newer images emphasize the idea that each part retains its identity and also contributes to the whole. (You might ask students if they are familiar with other metaphors. In recent years we have noticed the occasional use of America as a kaleidoscope.)

Here are two relevant quotations:

Fortunately, the time has long passed when people liked to regard the United States as some kind of melting pot, taking men and women from every part of the world and converting them into standardized, homogenized Americans.... Just as we welcome a world of diversity, so we glory in an America of diversity—an America all the richer for the many different and distinctive strands of which it is woven. (Hubert H. Humphrey, 1967)

And:

The crucial thing about the melting pot was that it did not happen: American politics and American social life are still dominated by the existence of sharply-defined ethnic groups. (Charles E. Silberman, 1964)

It would be easy to find many quotations in which African Americans call attention to their sense of having two identities as Americans, or call attention to the inadequacy of the image of the melting pot. Here is an example of each:

One ever feels his twoness—an American, a Negro, two souls, two thoughts, two unreconciled strivings; two warring ideals in one dark body, whose dogged strength alone keeps it from being torn asunder. (W. E. B. Du Bois, 1903)

And:

I hear that melting-pot stuff a lot, and all I can say is that we haven't melted. (Jesse Jackson, 1969)

Perhaps in class you may want to examine the following hasty generalizations. How much truth is in any of them?

1) It is probably true that, until some thirty years ago, most people who immigrated to this country wanted to enter the melting pot, i.e. wanted to put "the old country" behind them and to become "Americans."

2) Most African Americans, too, probably wanted to get into the pot, but they were excluded by whites.

3) Even immigrants who were or are eager to become 100% American probably retain a good deal of ethnic identity, perhaps unto the third and fourth generations (an idea implicit in Silberman's quotation).

4) Many recent immigrants emphasize their desire to retain their ethnic identity, but they too—or, rather, their children and grandchildren—will retain very little of the older generation's identity; they will, in fact, be like the Chinese Americans in Chang's story.

"The Oriental Contingent" provides an excellent opportunity for students to write—in journals, and then in essays and in their own fiction—about their ethnic backgrounds or about what they have seen in the behavior of second- and third-generation people of other backgrounds. (You may also want to refer students to Pat Mora's poem, "Immigrants" [in Chapter 14, "Arguing an Interpretation"] and to Martin Espada's poem, "Bully," in this chapter.)

RICHARD LOVELACE

To Lucasta, Going to the Wars (p. 1010)

Teachers of composition will doubtless point out the dangling participle in the title (the speaker, not Lucasta, is "going to the wars"), but the poem provides ample evidence that Lovelace *did* know how to use language.

How to reconcile love and honor, Venus and Mars, pleasure and duty? Lovelace argues that there is not a conflict but, as we shall see, an identity. The dramatic situation (Question 1) here is this: A man (presumably young) is addressing his beloved. He has told her he is leaving, and she has chided him with being "unkind." Perhaps, too, she has suggested he is unfaithful to her. In any case, the second stanza introduces this point ("True, a new mistress now I chase"), but perhaps he has invented it.

The woman, called "sweet," is said to have a "chaste breast." Indeed, her breast is a "nunnery," a word that emphasizes her purity and her devotion to holy ideals. Why would a man leave her? He explains, beginning by taking her charge of infidelity and granting (with a pun) that he chases a new mistress, foes of the king. (Thus, he does fly to other "arms.") There is a bit of broad comedy in the line in which he embraces a horse, but the last stanza is quite serious: his love for her is rooted in his love for honor and so she will approve of his apparent "inconstancy." True, he leaves her, but only because his sense of honor compels him to do so, and it is his love of honor that forms the basis of his love of Lucasta. And since Lucasta is a woman of honor, with a "chaste breast" and a "quiet mind," the speaker can assume that she will accept his argument.

TOPIC FOR WRITING

The speaker of this poem, like the speaker of Donne's "Valediction," offers an argument. Which argument is more persuasive, and why?

ALFRED, LORD TENNYSON

Ulysses (p. 1011)

Robert Langbaum, in *The Poetry of Experience*, and Christopher Ricks, in *Tennyson*, offer some good remarks; Paul Baum, in *Tennyson Sixty Years After*, assaults the poem. Henry Kozicki, in *Tennyson and Clio* (a book on Tennyson's philosophy of history), argues that "Ulysses" reveals Tennyson's optimism about historical progress and his despair about the role of a hero. For a review of much that should not have been written, see L. K. Hughes in *Victorian Poetry* 17 (Autumn 1979): 192-203. By the way, it is worth mentioning to students that Homer's hero wanted to get home, Sophocles's (in *Philoctetes*) is a shifty politician (as is Shakespeare's), and Dante's Ulysses (*Inferno* XXVI) is an inspiring but deceitful talker whose ardent search is for *forbidden* things.

The first five lines emphasize, mostly with monosyllables, the dull world Ulysses is leaving. With line 6 ("I cannot rest from travel") we see a rather romantic hero, questing for experience, and indeed "experience" is mentioned in line 19, but it must be added that something is done in the poem to give "experience" a social context: Ulysses has fought for Troy (17), he wishes to be of "use" (23), and he wishes to do "some work of noble note" (52). Lines 22-23 apparently say the same thing four times over, but readers are not likely to wish that Tennyson had deleted the superbly appropriate metaphor of the rusting sword. "Gray spirit" (30) and "sinking star" (31) help (along with the heavy pauses and monosyllables in 55-56) to define the poem as a piece about dying, though students on first reading are likely to see only the affirmations. Even the strong affirmations in 57 ff. are undercut by "sunset" (60), "western" (61), etc. But the last line, with its regular accents on the meaningful words, affords a strong ending; perhaps the line is so strong and regular that it is a bit too easy. In line 45 Ulysses directly addresses the mariners, yet we hardly sense an audience as we do in Browning's dramatic monologues. If he is addressing the mariners, who are aboard, where is he when he refers to "this still hearth" (2) and when he says, "This is my son" (33)? (Some critics claim that lines 1-32 are a soliloquy: Ulysses supposedly would not speak publicly of Ithaca as stagnant and savage, or of his wife as "aged." Lines 33-43 are his farewell to the Ithacans, and the remainder is an address to his mariners.)

Probably the reader ought to see the poem not as a muddled attempt at a Browningesque dramatic monologue, but as a somewhat different type of poem—a poem in which the poet uses a fairly transparent mask in order to express his state of mind and to persuade his readers to share that state of mind. The poem thus is closer to, say, "Prufrock," than it is to "My Last Duchess."

TOPICS FOR CRITICAL THINKING AND WRITING

1. Ulysses's voice.
2. Ulysses: hero or suicidal egotist?
3. Ulysses as he sees himself, compared with Ulysses as we see him.

ARTHUR HUGH CLOUGH

The Latest Decalogue (p. 1013)

The speaker is, of course, bitterly ironic; it is preposterous to say (but it has been said) that the speaker unwittingly gives himself away as a crass materialist.

Note that the last four lines, with the comment on loving one's neighbor, derive not from the Ten Commandments (the Decalogue, which stands behind the title of the poem) but from the New Testament. When Clough's widow published the poem she deleted these four lines, probably because she felt it was unseemly to satirize or distort a commandment from the New Testament.

A. E. HOUSMAN

The laws of God, the laws of man (p. 1014)

We have known this poem for many years, so it is impossible for us to recall our initial response to the first line, but we imagine that many readers find it sonorous, and expect some sort of solemn praise of the laws of God which manifest themselves in the laws of human societies. If in the first line Housman does indeed set up some such expectation, in the second and third lines he pulls the rug from under the reader's feet: "He may keep that will and can; / Not I." (The two stresses at the beginning of the third line of course emphasize his strong stand.)

Much of the interest in the poem seems to us to reside in the contrast between the rather grand view (or serious topic) that the first line suggests, and the rather chirpy or insolent tone that appears here and there, for instance in "Let them mind their own affairs" (6), "Please yourselves, say I, and they / Need only look the other way" (9-10), "But no, they will not" (11). There is wit, too, of an outrageous sort, in the reference to "man's bedevilment and God's" (16), where God is blended with the devil, and both are blended with "man," i.e. with the laws of society.

But some of the interest is, of course, also in what we can call the plot of the poem, the emotional and intellectual shifts that the speaker goes through: The poem begins by asserting (1-3) that the speaker will *not* keep the laws of God, and concludes with the assertion, in the last two lines, that "we must" keep them, if possible, though to the very end he insists that these laws are "foreign."

In one of our questions we ask the students if they believe the poem is a gay poem. Our own sense is that Housman's awareness that his sexual orientation was illegal—Oscar Wilde had been sentenced to hard labor only a few years before Housman wrote this poem—was in large measure a source for this poem and for many of his other poems, but obviously it does not have to be read only as a poem about homosexuality, and indeed until recently it could not have been read that way except perhaps by the very few persons who knew of his sexual preference. Possibly, then, this poem provides an especially good opportunity to talk about multiple or changing meanings of works of literature. It even allows us the opportunity to talk about whether we can conceivably read the poem in the way it was read in 1936, when it must have seemed to be chiefly a poem by an atheist who pretends to believe that there is a God and that this God has issued oppressive laws.

ROBERT FROST

Mending Wall (p. 1015)

Some critics applaud the neighbor in Frost's "Mending Wall," valuing his respect for barriers. For an extreme version, see Robert Hunting, "Who Needs Mending?" *Western Humanities Review* 17 (Winter 1963): 88-89. The gist of this faction is that the neighbor wisely realizes—as the speaker does not—that individual identity depends on respect for boundaries. Such a view sees the poem as a Browningesque dramatic monologue like "My Last Duchess," in which the self-satisfied speaker unknowingly gives himself away.

Richard Poirier, in *Robert Frost*, makes the interesting point that it is not the neighbor (who believes that "good fences make good neighbors") who initiates the ritual of mending the wall; rather, it is the speaker: "I let my neighbor know beyond the hill." Poirier suggests that "if fences do not 'make good neighbors,' the *making* of fences can," for it makes for talk—even though the neighbor is hopelessly taciturn. For a long, judicious discussion of the poem, see John C. Kemp, *Robert Frost: The Poet as Regionalist* (1979).

TOPICS FOR CRITICAL THINKING AND WRITING

1. Compare and contrast the speaker and the neighbor.
2. Notice that the speaker, not the neighbor, initiates the business of repairing the wall (12). Why do you think he does this?
3. Write an essay of 500 words telling of an experience in which you came to conclude that "good fences make good neighbors." Or tell of an experience that led you to conclude that fences (they can be figurative fences, of course) are detrimental.

ROBERT FROST

The Road Not Taken (p. 1017)

The diverging roads are pretty similar; the speaker chose the one less worn, as "having perhaps the better claim," but three times we are told that the difference was negligible: "just as fair"; "Though as for that, the passing there / Had worn them really about the same"; "equally." It is important to notice that although a reason is given for the choice ("it was grassy and wanted wear"), we are led to doubt that there really was a clear basis for choosing. Certainly there is no moral basis. Moreover, we may feel that had the speaker chosen the other path, the ending of the poem would have been the same; that is, he would remember the alternative path and would fantasize that he might someday return to take it, and would at the same time know that he would not relearn. And so he would find that it too "has made all the difference." The sigh imagined in the last stanza is not to be taken as an expression of regret for a life wasted, but as a semicomic picture of the speaker envisioning himself as an old man, wondering how things would have turned out if he had made a different choice—which is not at all to imply a rejection of the choice he did make.

Students are likely to take the poem too seriously, and to press it too hard for a moral, for example, that Frost says we should choose the "less traveled," the unconventional, path. We have tried to suggest that the first two lines of the last stanza are playful, a reading that is supported by a letter in which Frost spoke of the poem as "my rather private jest." (See *American Literature* 50 [November 1978]: 478-79.) As Lawrance Thompson says in his introduction to *Selected Letters of Robert Frost* (1964), p. xiv, Frost wrote the poem after returning to the United States from England. In England, his friend and fellow poet Edward Thomas liked to take Frost on woodland walks, and then fretted that perhaps he should have chosen a different path, which would have revealed different flora. Of course, this bit of biography does not prove that the poem cannot refer to moral choice, but it may help students to ease up on the highly moral interpretations that many are prone to make.

TOPICS FOR CRITICAL THINKING AND WRITING

1.   Frost called the poem "The Road Not Taken." Why didn't he call it "The Road Taken"? Which is the better title, and why?

2.   Consider a choice that you made, perhaps almost unthinkingly, and offer your reflections on how your life might have been different if you had chosen otherwise. Are you now regretful, pleased, puzzled, indifferent, or what? (For instance, what seemed to be a big choice may, in retrospect, have been a decision of no consequence.)

3.   Suppose that someone said to you that the poem is simply about walking in the woods and choosing one road rather than another. In an essay of 250 words, set forth your response. (You may, of course, agree with the view, in which case you will offer supporting evidence.)

4.   In a paragraph discuss whether it would make any difference if instead of "yellow" in the first line the poet had written "bright green" (or "dark green").

5.   Why do you think that Frost says he (or, more strictly, the speaker of the poem) will later be telling this story "with a sigh"? Set forth your response in a paragraph.

PAUL LAURENCE DUNBAR

We Wear the Mask (p. 1018)

Dunbar is represented elsewhere in this book by "An Ante-Bellum Sermon," a poem in which an African-American preacher preaches revolution through the guise of talking about Moses leading the Israelites out of Egypt, but he assures his audience that "I ain't talkin' bout to-day." In short, he wears the mask. And Dunbar wears it too.

Dunbar wrote poems in dialect that passed as cute, but that we can now easily see had an explosive content. He also wrote some poems, such as "We Wear the Mask," that use what we might call White English to state very directly the African-American's oppressed condition. (Some of your students may be familiar with Dunbar's "I know why the caged bird sings," or at least with the line if not with the poem.)

Students might be invited to discuss not only the "masks" that African-Americans are conventionally associated with but also the masks associated with other minorities in a white patriarchal society, or, for that matter, in any other society that they are familiar with. (Sandra M. Gilbert and Susan Gubar, in the third volume of *No Man's Land, Letters from the Front* [1994], discuss at length "female female impersonation," that is, women's adoption of feminine roles in order to gain at least a degree of power. The idea is interesting; students might be invited to think also of male male impersonation, a topic touched on in Gilbert and Gubar's discussion of Vonnegut's *Welcome to the Monkey House*.)

COUNTEE CULLEN

Incident (p. 1019)

The poem seems to be of the utmost simplicity: twelve lines without any figures of speech and without any obscure words. But it has its complexities, beginning with the title.

Our first question in the text asks students to think about the word "incident." It's our impression that an "incident" is usually a minor affair—something detached from what comes before and after, and of little consequence. For instance: "During the banquet a waiter dropped a tray full of dishes, but apart from this incident the affair was a great success." There are of course plenty of exceptions, such as the famous "Incident at Harpers Ferry," but we think that on the whole an incident is (1) minor and (2) a distinct occurrence.

Cullen's title therefore is ironic; the episode might seem to be a minor, but in fact it has left an indelible mark on the speaker's mind (and on the minds of countless readers). And since it continues to have its effect, it is not something separate and done with. The apparent simplicity, then, of the title and of the entire poem, is deceptive, since this seemingly trivial and unconnected episode stands for, or embodies, an enormous force in American life.

It's a good idea to ask a student to read the poem aloud in class (true for all poems, of course), so that students can hear the rhythms. On the whole, "Incident" sounds like a happy jingle, but of course that is part of the irony. Two details that strike us as especially effective are the enjambments in lines 7 and 11.

T. S. ELIOT

The Love Song of J. Alfred Prufrock (p. 1020)

Among the useful introductory books are Elizabeth Drew, *T. S. Eliot;* Northrop Frye, *T. S. Eliot;* and Grover Smith, *T. S. Eliot's Poetry and Plays.* On "Prufrock," see also Rosenthal and Smith, *Exploring Poetry;* Hugh Kenner, *The Invisible Poet: T. S. Eliot,* 3-12; and Lyndall Gordon, *Eliot's Early Years.* It is well to alert students to the fact that "Prufrock" is not a Browningesque dramatic monologue with a speaker and a listener, but rather an internal monologue in which "I" (the timid self) addresses his own amorous self as "you." (Not every "you" in this poem, however, refers to Prufrock's amorous self. Sometimes "you" is equivalent to "one.") Possibly, too, the "you" is the reader, or even other people who, like Prufrock, are afraid of action.

Among the chief points usually made are these: The title proves to be ironic, for we scarcely get a love song: "J. Alfred Prufrock" is a name that, like the speaker, seems to be hiding something ("J.") and also seems to he some-what old-maidish ("Prufrock" suggests "prude" and "frock"); the initial description (especially the "patient etherised") is really less a description of the evening than of Prufrock's state of mind; mock heroic devices abound (people at a cocktail party talking of Michelangelo, Prufrock gaining strength from his collar and stickpin); the sensuous imagery of women's arms leads to the men in shirt-sleeves and to Prufrock's wish to be a pair of ragged claws.

We print the original (1915) version, from *Poetry* magazine, but in line 19 we give *soot* instead of *spot* (an obvious typo in *Poetry*). When the poem later appeared in book form it differed only in punctuation (e.g., square brackets instead of parentheses) and one verbal change—*no doubt* instead of *withal* in line 114.

An audiocassette of T. S. Eliot reading "The Love Song of J. Alfred Prufrock" is available from HarperCollins. A "Voices and Visions" videocassette of T. S. Eliot is also available from HarperCollins.

TOPICS FOR CRITICAL THINKING AND WRITING

1.   How does the speaker's name help to characterize him? What suggestions—of class, race, personality—do you find in the name? Does the poem's title strike you as ironic? If so how or why?

2.   What qualities of big-city life are suggested in the poem? How are these qualities linked to the speaker's mood? What other details of the setting— the weather, the time of day—express or reflect his mood? What images do you find especially striking?

3.   The speaker's thoughts are represented in a stream-of-consciousness

monologue, that is, in what appears to be an unedited flow of thought. Nevertheless, they reveal a story. What is the story?

W. H. AUDEN

The Unknown Citizen (p. 1024)

In "The Unknown Citizen" the speaker's voice is obviously not the poet's. The speaker—appropriately unidentified in a poem about a society without individuals—is apparently a bureaucrat. For such a person, a "saint" is not one who is committed to spiritual values, but one who causes no trouble.

An audiocassette of W. H. Auden reading is available from HarperCollins.

TOPICS FOR CRITICAL THINKING AND WRITING

1. What is Auden satirizing in "The Unknown Citizen"? (Students might be cautioned to spend some time thinking about whether Auden is satirizing the speaker, the citizen, conformism, totalitarianism, technology, or what.)
2. Write a prose eulogy of 250 words satirizing contemporary conformity, or, if you prefer, contemporary individualism.
3. Was he free? Was he happy? Explain.
4. In a paragraph or two, sketch the values of the speaker of the poem, and then sum them up in a sentence or two. Finally, in as much space as you feel you need, judge these values.

STEVIE SMITH

Not Waving but Drowning (p. 1025)

All his life the dead man in Stevie Smith's "Not Waving but Drowning" sent messages that were misunderstood. His efforts to mask his loneliness and depression were more successful than he intended. His friends mistook him for a "chap" who "always loved larking," as they now mistake the cause of his death. But true friends would have seen through the clowning, the dead man seems to protest, in lines 3 and 4 (when of course it is too late to protest or to explain). The second stanza confirms his view of the spectators. They are imperceptive and condescending; their understanding of the cause of his death is as superficial as their attention to him was while he was alive. But they didn't know him "all [his] life" (11). The dead man thus acknowledges, by leaving them out of the last stanza, that, never having risked honest behavior, he is at least as responsible as others for his failure to be loved and to love.

MITSUYE YAMADA

To the Lady (p. 1026)

First, some background. In 1942 the entire Japanese and Japanese-American population on America's Pacific coast—about 112,000 people—was incarcerated and relocated. More than two-thirds of the people moved were native-born citizens of the United States. (The 158,000 Japanese residents of the Territory of Hawaii were not affected.)

Immediately after the Japanese attack on Pearl Harbor, many journalists, the general public, Secretary of the Army Henry Stimson, and congressional delegations from California, Oregon, and Washington called for the internment. Although Attorney General Francis Biddle opposed it, on February 19, 1942, President Franklin D. Roosevelt signed Executive Order 9066, allowing military authorities "to prescribe military areas... from which any or all persons may be excluded." In practice, no persons of German or Italian heritage were disturbed, but Japanese and Japanese-Americans on the Pacific coast were rounded up (they were allowed to take with them "only that which can be carried") and relocated in camps. Congress, without a dissenting vote, passed legislation supporting the evacuation. A few Japanese-Americans challenged the constitutionality of the proceeding, but with no immediate success.

Many students today may find it difficult to comprehend the intensity of anti-Japanese sentiment that pervaded the 1940s. Here are two samples, provided by David Mura, whose poem about the internment camps appears on page 509 of the text. Lt. General John DeWitt, the man in charge of the relocation plan, said:

> The Japanese race is an enemy race and while many second and third generation Japanese born on United States soil, possessed of United States citizenship, have become "Americanized," the racial strains are undiluted. To conclude otherwise is to expect that children born of white parents on Japanese soil sever all racial affinity and become loyal Japanese subjects.... Along the vital Pacific Coast over 112,000 enemies, of Japanese extraction, are at large today. There are indications that these are organized and ready for concerted action at a favorable opportunity. The very fact that no sabotage has taken place to date is a disturbing and confirming indication that such action will be taken.

One rubs one's eyes in disbelief at the crazy logic that holds that *because* "no sabotage has taken place," such action "will be taken." The second quotation Mura has called to our attention is a remark made in 1942 by Senator Tom Steward, of Tennessee:

They [the Japanese] are cowardly and immoral. They are different from Americans in every conceivable way, and no Japanese... should have the right to claim American citizenship... A Jap is a Jap anywhere you find him. They do not believe in God and have no respect for an oath of allegiance.

By the way, not a single Japanese-American was found guilty of subversive activity. For two good short accounts, with suggestions for further readings, see the articles entitled "Japanese Americans, wartime relocation of," in *Kodansha Encyclopedia of Japan,* 4:17-18, and "War Relocation Authority," in 8:228.

It may be interesting to read Yamada's poem aloud in class, *without* having assigned it for prior reading, and to ask students for their responses at various stages—after line 4, line 21, and line 36. Line 14 poses a question that perhaps many of us (young and old, and whether of Japanese descent or not) have asked, at least to ourselves. The question, implying a criticism of the victims, shows an insufficient awareness of Japanese or Japanese-American culture of the period. It also shows an insufficient awareness of American racism; by implying that protest by the victims *could* have been effective, it reveals ignorance of the terrific hostility of whites toward persons of Japanese descent.

The first part of the response shows one aspect of the absurdity of the lady's question. Japanese and Japanese-Americans were brought up not to stand out in any way (certainly not to make a fuss), and to place the harmony of the group (whether the family, or society as a whole) above individual expression. Further, there was nothing that these people could effectively do, even if they had shouted as loudly as Kitty Genovese did. For the most part they were poor, they had no political clout, and they were hated and despised as Asians. The absurdity of the view that they could have resisted effectively is comically stated in "should've pulled myself up from my / bra straps" (echoing the red-blooded American ideal of pulling oneself up by one's bootstraps), but of course the comedy is bitter.

Then the speaker turns to "YOU," nominally the "lady" of the title but in effect also the reader, and by ironically saying what we would have done points out what in fact we did not do. (The references to a march on Washington and letters to Congress are clear enough, but most students will not be aware of the tradition that the King of Denmark said that he would wear a Star of David [line 27] if Danish Jews were compelled by Nazis to wear the star.)

Thus far the speaker has put the blame entirely on the white community, especially since lines 5-21 strongly suggest that the Japanese-Americans *couldn't* do anything but submit. Yet the poem ends with a confession that because Japanese-Americans docilely subscribed to "law and order"—especially the outrageous Executive Order 9066—they were in fact partly responsible for the outrage committed against them. The last line of the poem, "All are punished," is exactly what Prince Escalus says at the end of *Romeo and Juliet.* Possibly the echo is accidental, though possibly the reader is meant to be reminded of a play, widely regarded as "a tragedy of fate," in which the innocent are victims of prejudice.

ADRIENNE RICH

Aunt Jennifer's Tigers (p. 1027)

We reprint here an effective essay written by a student, Maria Fuentes.

Aunt Jennifer's Screen and Adrienne Rich's Poem

What especially pleases me in Adrienne Rich's "Aunt Jennifer's Tigers" is the combination of neat, tight, highly disciplined stanzas of four rhyming lines (like marching squadrons) with the explosive rebellious content of the poem. Somehow the message seems especially powerful *because* it is so tightly packed, because the form is so restrained.

The poem is, on the surface at least, about what the title says it is about, "Aunt Jennifer's Tigers." Aunt Jennifer has made a screen, in embroidery or needlepoint, showing tigers that "prance." Presumably Aunt Jennifer was a sweet old lady, but she has created a picture of enormous energy, expressing, through her work of art, her own repressed energy.

We learn in the second stanza that she was repressed by the man she was married to:

> The massive weight of Uncle's wedding band
> Sits heavily upon Aunt Jennifer's hand.

The wedding band for her, as for many women in the present as well as in the past, is like a heavy chain. Rich tells us that Aunt Jennifer was "terrified" and was "mastered," obviously by Uncle. Rich makes a pun on the word "ringed," but the joke is very bitter:

> When Aunt is dead, her terrified hands will lie
> Still ringed with ordeals she was mastered by.

And yet, Rich points out, this "terrified" woman created something beautiful, a picture of tigers who "go on prancing, proud and unafraid." Apparently Aunt Jennifer was able, despite being oppressed by Uncle, to make something that gives pleasure to a later generation— just as the poet, however unhappy she may be, produces a work of art that gives pleasure to those who later read it.

Aunt Jennifer's work of art shows, in the prancing tigers, an energy that she apparently felt and understood, but because of her husband and perhaps because of the period in which she lived, she could express herself only in a "ladylike" activity such as embroidering. Aunt Jennifer was "mastered" (line 10), but she has nevertheless "made" (line 11) something depicting creatures who are "proud and unafraid." She was "terrified" (line 9), as many women were terrified by the patriarchal society in which they lived (and still live), but in her art she created an image of energy. Adrienne Rich, too, makes a work of art—a highly patterned poem consisting of three rhymed quatrains—that is as elegantly crafted as a work of embroidery. Rich speaks matter-of-factly and in a disciplined way in her quatrains about Aunt Jennifer and her tigers, but in this elegant poem she conveys energy and outrage on behalf of her terrified aunt who could not openly protest against the role that society had assigned to her.

ADRIENNE RICH

Rape (p. 1028)

We can think of a number of earlier poems about rape—one of them, Yeats's "Leda and the Swan," is in our text—and it occurs to us that in virtually all of them the suffering of the woman is transformed by a mythic vision. (So far as we know, all poems on Philomela turn the violated woman not only into a bird, as Ovid did, but also into a symbol that presumably should be contemplated with sweet melancholy.)

Rich's poem is different. The violated woman is not metamorphosed and mythologized. She is, at the end of the poem as at its beginning, an ordinary woman, a "you" who lives in a violent male world, a world in which everyone else is rapist, cop, father, stallion, unsympathetic confessor. The victim of the rape is victimized a second time when, "the maniac's sperm still greasing your thighs, / ... You have to confess / to him, you are guilty of the crime / of having been forced." In Ovid, the authorities (the gods) take pity on the victim and metamorphose her, but in Rich's poem the police officer takes pleasure in the victim's distress: "the hysteria in your voice pleases him best." The first rapist is a "maniac," but the second, the police officer-confessor, is empowered by society, and so at the end the victim is diminished rather than elevated into the world of myth.

MARGE PIERCY

What's That Smell in the Kitchen? (p. 1029)

Putting aside the title (in which, at least in retrospect, perhaps we hear the voice of the oafish husband comfortably seated in the TV room), the first words of the first line ("All over America women are") might lead us to expect some sort of feminist/Whitmanesque assertion of glorious unity, or of flourishing individuality, and in a sense we get something like this, but in a comic domestic vein. The burnt dinners are fully explained in the final line, but the reason becomes evident fairly soon in the poem—certainly by line 9, with its punning glance at kitchen utensils in "Anger sputters in her brainpan."

MARGE PIERCY

A Work of Artifice (p. 1030)

Bonsai is the art of dwarfing trees by pruning the branches and roots and by controlling the fertilization. The grower shapes the tree by wiring the trunk and the branches. The important point, so far as Piercy's poem goes, is that a bonsai (the word can be used of a specimen itself, as well as of the art) is *not* a special hybrid dwarf, but is a tree distorted by the grower. (The somewhat freakish shape of the poem perhaps imitates the miniaturized tree.) Lines 1-8 give students the gist of what they need to know about bonsai. Students will readily see that Piercy's bonsai is a metaphor; the real "work of artifice" that the poet is concerned with is the female shaped by a dominant male society. The metaphor extends through line 16, when it yields to the closely related image of "the bound feet" (footbinding was practiced in China until well into the twentieth century) and then by easy association to "the crippled brain," which in turn yields to "the hair in curlers." Students might be invited to comment on the connection between these last two images: in what way is "hair in curlers" a kind of crippling (not only of the hair, of course, but of the woman's mind, which is persuaded or bullied into distorting itself in order to be acceptable to men)? The last two lines remind us of an advertisement, perhaps for a soap or skin lotion, but we can't identify it. In any case, in "the hair you love to touch" the reader gets the modern American male's version of the gardener who soothingly "croons" (11) to his tree while he maims it.

JAMES WRIGHT

Lying in a Hammock at William Duffy's Farm in Pine Island, Minnesota (p. 1031)

It seems to us that the title is somewhat paradoxical, in its implication of utter relaxation and apartness—lying *in* a hammock, *at* someone's farm, *in* an island—and (on the other hand) the almost pedantic or fussy specification of the locale. And we find the rest of the poem paradoxical too.

The speaker's eye ranges. He takes in the view above (a natural starting-place for someone lying in a hammock), then looks "Down the ravine," then "to my right," and then, at the end, up again ("I lean back"), when he observes the chicken hawk. In a sense he ends where he began, but meanwhile he has explored (or at least surveyed) a good deal. He has, from his sleep-like condition in the hammock, begun by seeing a bronze-colored butterfly

"Asleep," then has heard the distant cowbells, and has seen "The droppings of last year's horses" (so we get some extension into time as well as into space), and then glances again at the skies. This exploration—all from the hammock—is marked by keen yet imaginative observations.

Let's go back a moment, to the first perception, the "bronze butterfly / Asleep." The poet is describing the color, but the effect is paradoxical, giving the reader a fragile insect made of an enduring material. From perceptions of colors ("bronze," "black," "green") we go to aural perceptions ("the cowbells follow one another") and then back to visual perceptions (the horse droppings, now "golden stones"). In all of this beauty there is a keen sense of isolation—the cows and horses are not present, and even the chicken hawk is looking for home. Now, "as the evening darkens," the speaker has an epiphany, uttered in the final line.

The final line probably comes to the reader as a shock, and perhaps the reader is uncertain about how to take it. Is he kidding? Or is he saying, in dead seriousness, all creatures except me seem to have their place in a marvelously beautiful, peaceful nature, whereas I am not even in my own home? Our own impression is that, whatever he says, *we* feel that he has not wasted his life, since he has so interestingly recorded his perceptions.

AURORA LEVINS MORALES

Child of the Americas (p. 1032)

The author, born in Puerto Rico of a Puerto Rican mother and of a father whose origins went back to the ghetto in New York and beyond that to Europe, came to the United States when she was thirteen, and has lived in Chicago, New Hampshire, and now in the San Francisco Bay Area. Her heritage and her experience thus are considerably different from those of most Puerto Ricans who are now in the United States.

Wheras other Latinas in this book emphasize the difficulties of their divided heritage (see Pat Mora's "Immigrants" and Lorna Dee Cervantes's "Refugee Ship"), Morales celebrates her diversity and apparently is at ease as a Latina in the United States: She is "a light-skinned mestiza of the Caribbean, / a child of many diaspora," she was born "at a crossroads," she is "a U.S. Puerto Rican Jew, / a product of the ghettos of New York," "Spanish is in [her] flesh," but in the next-to-last stanza she insists that she is "not african," "not tafna," "not european." Most significantly, she insists that she is not fragmented but is, on the contrary, "whole."

In short, Morales holds to the old idea of the United States as a melting pot, an idea not heard so often today. The conception of the melting pot has largely given way to the conception of America as a "gorgeous mosaic," a "salad bowl," a kaleidoscope, i.e., a place where there is great variety but where each ingredient maintains its identity.

MARTIN ESPADA

Bully (p. 1033)

The editors of *Literature for Composition* belong to a generation that was taught, in grade school and in high school, that Teddy Roosevelt was a hero. Some of his words entered the classroom, just as half a century later some of the words of John Kennedy—notably the Inaugural Address—entered the classroom. In school we heard such Rooseveltisms as "I wish to preach, not the doctrine of ignoble ease, but the doctrine of the strenuous life" (1899), "In life, as in a football game, the principle to follow is: Hit the line hard" (1901), and "There is no room in this country for hyphenated Americanism.... The one absolutely certain way of bringing this nation to ruin, of preventing all possibility of its continuing to be a nation at all, would be to permit it to become a tangle of squabbling nationalities" (1915). In the text, in our fifth question, we quote yet another (in)famous remark, expressing the opinion that all immigrants should be required to learn English within five years. Persons who doubt that Roosevelt was regarded as one of America's greatest heroes need only call to mind Mount Rushmore National Memorial, in South Dakota, where an enormous bust of Roosevelt, along with busts of Washington, Jefferson, and Lincoln, is carved. Although the sculptures (visible for some sixty miles) were not finished until the 1950s, the monument was dedicated in 1927, and in effect it represents the values of the 1920s.

In our third question in the text we ask about the word "bully," as an adjective and as a noun. Roosevelt used the adjective, meaning "excellent," in a famous comment, to the effect that the presidency is a "bully pulpit." But given Roosevelt's enthusiasm for military action, in particular for the Spanish-American War (a war whose name somehow omits the efforts of the Cuban patriots who fought for independence), it is hard not to think of the other and more common meaning of the word. Certainly in this poem entitled "Bully," where it is said of Roosevelt that "each fist [is] lonely for a sabre," the image that comes across is of someone who pushes other people around. A century ago Roosevelt stormed San Juan with his Rough Riders, but today Puerto Rican children invade Roosevelt High (line 11). The end of the poem, with its reference to Roosevelt's "Victorian mustache / and monocle," present a hopelessly outdated and somewhat comic figure who contrasts with the vitality of the "Spanish-singing children."

PAT MORA

Sonrisas (p. 1034)

Most students will quickly see that the two stanzas stand for the "two rooms" (worlds, we might ordinarily say) in which the Chicano speaker lives. (Interestingly, the word "stanza" comes from an Italian word meaning "room," "stopping place"; a stanza is a room in a poem.) The first room in "Sonrisas" is a room of Anglo culture, "careful," usually unsmiling, and when there are smiles the smiles are "beige" (cautious, neutral, certainly not enthusiastic). This is a world of "budgets, tenure, curriculum," that is the orderly world of the establishment. The second room is a room of Chicano culture, a world of coffee-breaks, "laughter," "noise," scolding (presumably affectionate) and "dark, Mexican eyes" that contrast with the beige smiles and eyes of specified color in the first stanza. If the first stanza hints at the world of power and therefore of money (in "budgets, tenure, curriculum"), this stanza hints very gently at a world of relative poverty in "faded dresses," but it seems evident that for the speaker this world is more attractive, more (we might say) human.

CAROLYN FORCHÉ

The Colonel (p. 1035)

"The Colonel" comes from a book of poems. You may want to talk about the rather undefined genre of the prose-poem. A prose-poem looks like prose but is marked by a strong rhythm (often gained by repetition of grammatical constructions) and sometimes by abundant imagery. (The idea is that the chief characteristics of poetry are rhythm and imagery, and so a short piece of prose with these features can be called a prose-poem.) Having said this, we must add that we don't think there is much point in worrying much about whether "The Colonel" is poetry or prose.

Much of "The Colonel" probably is literally true. During one of her stays in El Salvador, Forché may indeed have visited a colonel, and he may have said and done exactly what this colonel says and does. Until we are told that the ear "came alive" when dropped into the glass of water, there is nothing unbelievable in "The Colonel," partly, of course, because television has informed us that atrocities are committed daily.

Forché's first sentence ("What you have heard is true") suggests that the speaker is addressing someone who has just said, "I heard that you visited Colonel————. Did you really? What was it like?" We get details about what seems to be a comfortable bourgeois existence ("Daily papers, pet dogs") and also some menacing details ("a pistol on the cushion beside him," "broken bottles were embedded in the walls"), all told in the same flat, matter-of-fact voice. The sixth sentence uses a metaphor ("The moon swung bare on its black cord over the house"), but even journalists are allowed to use an occasional metaphor, and a reader probably does not think twice about Forché's metaphor here, except perhaps to notice that it uses the same structure ("The moon swung bare...") as the previous, factual sentences ("I was," "His wife carried," "His daughter filed," "There were"). Again, for the most part the language is flat; when the speaker next uses a metaphor (the ears are "like dried peach halves") she (or he) flatly apologizes for this flight of fancy: "There is no other way to say this." But the next to last sentence takes us into a metaphorical (or mysterious) world: "Some of the ears on the floor caught this scrap of his voice."

Much of the power of "The Colonel" comes from the contrast between the picture of the colonel's bourgeois private life (pets, television, lamb, wine, etc.) and his brutal public life, a contrast that Forché emphasizes by not commenting on it (i.e., by allowing the reader to make the comment). The piece is masterful in what it doesn't say. The colonel asks how the visitor "enjoyed the country," but we don't hear the response. We can, however, guess it by what follows: "There was some talk then of how difficult it had become to govern." Presumably the colonel becomes annoyed with the visitor's comments, though at first we aren't told this in so many words. Instead we are told what the colonel did (he got a sack of ears, dumped them on table, shook one in the faces of his guests, dropped it in a glass of water). Then we hear him: "I am tired of fooling around.... As for the rights of anyone, tell your people they can go fuck themselves." Irked but (as we see it) enormously confident, he says of the severed ears, "Something for your poetry, no?" Students might be invited to comment on the tone the colonel uses here. Is he complacent, wry, naive, or what?

Students might also be invited to comment on the last two sentences of "The Colonel." Does the next-to-last sentence indicate (let's say symbolically) that the oppressed people of the country know what is going on, and will ultimately triumph? Does the last sentence ("Some of the ears on the floor were pressed to the ground") mean that (1) some of the ears were pressed, presumably by being stood on, and (2) the dead were listening (and presumably waiting to be avenged)?

YUSEF KOMUNYAKAA

Facing It (p. 1036)

The title is both literal (he is facing the wall) and figurative (he is confronting the terrible memories of past experiences).

Soldiers in other wars, of course, underwent traumatic experiences, and the experience of a combatant is almost bound to include episodes that seem unreal or surreal. But the fact that the Vietnam War had so little popular support—was not convincingly bolstered by the idea that it was being fought for a good cause—was particularly disconcerting and demoralizing. Much of Komunyakaa's poem catches a sense of unreality, and a sense of the loss of self. Thus, a black man looking at his reflection in the black wall finds his reflection literally disappearing; at the same time, if the wall has caused his reflection to disappear, it has nevertheless caught the man himself, drawn him back into the horrible experiences that the wall in effect memorializes. (Strictly speaking, the wall memorializes those who died, not the war itself. That is, the Memorial does not say that the war was either good or bad, only that certain people died in the war.)

From the title on, the speaker is "facing it"—facing the painful memories aroused by standing in front of the wall and confronting or reliving the war experiences. He sees a vision of the booby trap that killed a comrade, Andrew Johnson, and, as reflected in the wall, the loss of the arm of a veteran, who therefore is standing near the poet. At the end of the poem the violence is transformed by the return to the world outside of the wall. In the wall the poet sees a woman "trying to erase names," that is, apparently engaged in a futile action, though one hopes that the memories of the war can be diminished if not erased. But then he corrects himself, and realizes that the wall is in fact mirroring an act of affection: "No, she's brushing a boy's hair".

Some of your students may have visited the wall. If so, you may want to ask them to report their experience.

HENRIK IBSEN

A Doll's House (p. 1038)

First, it should be mentioned that the title of the play does *not* mean that Nora is the only doll, for the toy house is not merely Nora's; Torvald, as well as Nora, inhabits this unreal world, for Torvald—so concerned with appearing proper in the eyes of the world—can hardly be said to have achieved a mature personality.

A Doll's House (1879) today seems more "relevant" than it has seemed in decades, and yet one can put too much emphasis on its importance as a critique of male chauvinism. Although the old view that Ibsen's best-known plays are "problem plays" about remediable social problems rather than about more universal matters is still occasionally heard, Ibsen himself spoke against it. In 1898, for example, he said, "I must disclaim the honor of having consciously worked for women's rights. I am not even quite sure what women's rights really are. To me it has been a question of human rights" (quoted in Michael Meyer, *Ibsen*, 2:297). By now it seems pretty clear that *A Doll's House*, in Robert Martin Adams's words (in *Modern Drama*, ed. A. Caputi), "represents a woman imbued with the idea of becoming a person, but it proposes nothing categorical about women becoming people; in fact, its real theme has nothing to do with the sexes. It is the irrepressible conflict of two different personalities which have founded themselves on two radically different estimates of realty." Or, as Eric Bentley puts it in *In Search of Theater* (350 in the Vintage edition), "Ibsen pushes his investigation toward a further and even deeper subject [than that of a woman's place in a man's world], the tyranny of one human being over another, in this respect the play would be just as valid were Torvald the wife and Nora the husband."

Michael Meyer's biography, *Ibsen*, is good on the background (Ibsen knew a woman who forged a note to get money to aid her husband, who denounced and abandoned her when he learned of the deed), but surprisingly little has been written on the dramaturgy of the play. Notable exceptions are John Northam, "Ibsen's Dramatic Method," an essay by Northam printed in *Ibsen*, ed. Rolf Fjelde (in the Twentieth Century Views series), and Elizabeth Hardwick's chapter on the play in her *Seduction and Betrayal*. Northam calls attention to the symbolic use of properties (e.g., the Christmas tree in Act I, a symbol of a secure, happy family, is in the center of the room, but in Act II, when Nora's world has begun to crumble, it is in a corner, bedraggled, and with burnt-out candles), costume (e.g., Nora's Italian costume is suggestive of pretense and is removed near the end of the play; the black shawl, symbolic of death, becomes—when worn at the end with ordinary clothes—an indication of her melancholy, lonely life), and gestures (e.g., blowing out the candles, suggesting defeat; the wild dance; the final slamming of the door).

For a collection of recent essays on the play, see *Approaches to Teaching Ibsen's "A Doll's House,"* ed. Yvonne Shafer. Also of interest is Austin E. Quigley's discussion in *Modern Drama* 27 (1984): 584-60:5, reprinted with small changes in his *The Modern Stage and Other Worlds*. Dorothea Krook, in *Elements of Tragedy*, treats the play as a tragedy. She sets forth what she takes to be the four universal elements of the genre (the act of shame or horror, consequent intense suffering, then an increase in knowledge, and finally a reaffirmation of the value of life) and suggests that these appear in *A Doll's House*—the shameful condition being "the marriage relationship which creates Nora's doll's house's situation." Krook calls attention, too, to the "tragic irony" of Torvald's comments on Krogstad's immorality (he claims it poisons a household) and to Nora's terror, which, Krook says, "evokes the authentic Aristolelian pity."

One can even go a little further than Krook goes and make some connection between *A Doll's House* and *Oedipus the King*. Nora, during her years as a housewife, like Oedipus during his kingship, *thought* that she was happy, but finds out that she really wasn't, and at the end of the play she goes out (self-banished), leaving her children, to face an uncertain but surely difficult future. Still, although the play can be discussed as a tragedy, and cannot be reduced to a "problem play," like many of Ibsen's other plays it stimulates a discussion of the questions, What ought to be done? and What happened next? Hermann J. Weigand, in *The Modern Ibsen* (1925), offered conjectures about Nora's future actions, saying,

> But personally I am convinced that after putting Torvald through a sufficiently protracted ordeal of suspense, Nora will yield to his entreaties and return home— on her own terms. She will not bear the separation from her children very long, and her love for Torvald, which is not as dead as she thinks, will reassert itself. For a time the tables will be reversed: a meek and chastened husband will eat out of the hand of his squirrel; and Nora, hoping to make up by a sudden spurt of zeal for twenty-eight years of lost time, will be trying desperately hard to grow up. I doubt, however, whether her volatile enthusiasm will even carry her beyond the stage of resolutions. The charm of novelty worn off, she will tire of the new game very rapidly and revert, imperceptibly, to her role of songbird and charmer, as affording an unlimited range to the exercise of her inborn talents of coquetry and playacting.

Students may be invited to offer their own conjectures on the unwritten fourth act.

Another topic for class discussion or for an essay, especially relevant to question 4: Elizabeth Hardwick suggests (*Seduction and Betrayal*, 46) that Ibsen failed to place enough emphasis on Nora's abandonment of the children. In putting "the leaving of her children on the same moral and emotional level as the leaving of her husband Ibsen has been too much a man in the end. He has taken the man's practice, if not his stated belief, that where self-realization is concerned children shall not be an impediment." But in a feminist reading of the play, Elaine Hoffman Baruch, in *Yale Review* 69 (Spring 1980), takes issue with Hardwick, arguing that "it is less a desire for freedom than a great sense of inferiority and the desire to find out more about the male world outside the home that drives Nora away from her children" (37).

Finally, one can discuss with students the comic aspects of the play—the ending (which, in a way, is happy, though of course Nora's future is left in doubt), and especially Torvald's fatuousness. The fatuousness perhaps reaches its comic height early in Act III, when, after lecturing Mrs. Linde on the importance of an impressive exit (he is telling her how, for effect, he made his "capricious little Capri girl" leave the room after her dance), he demonstrates the elegance of the motion of the hands while embroidering and the ugliness of the motions when knitting. Also comic are his ensuing fantasies, when he tells the exhausted Nora that he fantasizes that she is his "secret" love, though the comedy turns ugly when after she rejects his amorous advances ("I have desired you all evening"), he turns into a bully: "I'm your husband, aren't I?" The knock on the front door (Rank) reintroduces comedy, for it reduces the importunate husband to conventional affability ("Well! How good of you not to pass by the door"), but of course it also saves Nora from what might have been an ugly assault.

TOPICS FOR CRITICAL THINKING AND WRITING

1. To what extent is Nora a victim, and to what extent is she herself at fault for her way of life?
2. Is the play valuable only as an image of an aspect of life in the later nineteenth century, or is it still an image of an aspect of life?
3. In the earlier part of the play Nora tells Helmer, Mrs. Linde, and herself that she is happy. Is she? Explain. Why might she be happy? Why not? Can a case be made that Mrs. Linde, who must work to support herself, is happier than Nora?
4. Write a dialogue—approximately two double-spaced pages—setting forth a chance encounter when Torvald and Nora meet five years after the end of Ibsen's play.
5. Write a persuasive essay, arguing that Nora was right—or wrong—to leave her husband and children. In your essay recognize the strengths of the opposing view and try to respond to them.

AUGUST WILSON

Fences (p. 1090)

Some background (taken from our *Types of Drama*) on the history of blacks in the American theatre may be of use. In the 1940s and 1950s black playwrights faced the difficult problem of deciding what audience they were writing for—an audience of blacks or of whites? The difficulty was compounded by the fact that although there were a number of black theatre groups—for example, the American Negro Theatre (founded by blacks in 1940)—there was not a large enough black theatre-going public to make such groups commercially successful. In fact, although the original ideal of the American Negro Theatre was "to portray Negro life... honestly," within a few years it was doing plays by white writers, such as Thornton Wilder's *Our Town* (not only by a white but about whites) and Philip Yordan's *Anna Lucasta* (by a white, and originally about a Polish working-class family, but transformed into a play about a black family). Further, the aim of such groups usually was in large measure to employ black actors and theater technicians; some of the most talented of these, including Harry Belafonte, Sidney Poitier, and Ruby Dee, then went on to enter the mainstream of white theatre, on Broadway, or—a short step—in Hollywood. Meanwhile, such writers as James Baldwin and Lorraine Hansberry, though writing about black life, wrote plays that were directed at least as much at whites as at blacks. That is, their plays were in large measure attempts to force whites to look at what they had done to blacks.

In the mid-1960s, however, the most talented black dramatists, including LeRoi Jones (Imamu Amiri Baraka) and Ed Bullins, largely turned their backs on white audiences and in effect wrote plays aimed at showing blacks that *they*—not their white oppressors—must change, must cease to accept the myths that whites had created. Today, however, strongly revolutionary plays by and about blacks have difficulty getting a hearing. Instead, the newest black writers seem to be concerned less with raising the consciousness of blacks than with depicting black life and with letting both blacks and whites respond aesthetically rather than politically. Baraka has attributed the change to a desire by many blacks to become assimilated in today's society, and surely there is much to his view. One might also say, however, that black dramatists may for other reasons have come to assume that the business of drama is not to preach but to show, and that a profound, honest depiction—in a traditional, realistic dramatic form—of things as they are, or in Wilson's play, things as they were in the 1950s—will touch audiences whatever their color. "Part of the reason I wrote *Fences*," Wilson has said, "was to illuminate that generation, which shielded its children from all of the indignities they went through."

This is not to say, of course, that *Fences* is a play about people who just happen to be black. The Polish family of *Anna Lucasta* could easily be converted to a black family (though perhaps blacks may feel that there is something unconvincing about this family), but Troy Maxson's family cannot be whitewashed. The play is very much about persons who are what they are because they are blacks living in an unjust society run by whites. We are not allowed to forget this. Troy is a baseball player who was too old to join a white team when the major leagues began to hire blacks. (The first black player to play in the major leagues was Jackie Robinson, whom the Brooklyn Dodgers hired in 1947. Robinson retired in 1956, a year before the time in which *Fences* is chiefly set.) For Troy's friend, Bono, "Troy just came along too early;" but Troy pungently replies, "There ought not never have been no time called too early." Blacks of Troy's day were expected to subscribe to American ideals—for instance, to serve in the army in time of war—but they were also expected to sit in the back of the bus and to accept the fact that they were barred from decent jobs. Wilson shows us the scars that such treatment left. Troy is no paragon. Although he has a deep sense of responsibility to his family, his behavior toward them is deeply flawed; he oppresses his son Cory, he is unfaithful to his wife, Rose, and he exploits his brother Gabriel.

Wilson, as we have seen, calls attention to racism in baseball, and he indicates that Troy turned to crime because he could not earn money. But Wilson does not allow *Fences* to become a prolonged protest against white oppression—though one can never quite forget that Troy insists on a high personal ideal in a world that has cheated him. The interest in the play is in Troy as a human being, or, rather, in all of the characters as human beings rather than as representatives of white victimization. As Troy sees it, by preventing Cory from engaging in athletics—the career that frustrated Troy—he is helping rather than oppressing Cory: "I don't want him to be like me. I want him to move as far from me as he can." But Wilson also makes it clear that Troy has other (very human) motives, of which Troy perhaps is unaware.

A Note on the Word *Black:* The play is set in 1957 and (the last scene) 1965, before *black* and *African-American* were the words commonly applied to persons of African descent. The blacks in the play speak of "coloreds" and of "niggers." *Black* did not become the preferred word until she late 1960s. For instance the question was still open in November 1967, when *Ebony* magazine asked its readers whether the *Negro* should be replaced by *black* or *Afro-American.* The results of polls at that time chiefly suggested that *Afro-American* was the preferred choice, but *black* nevertheless became the established term until about 1988, when *African-American* began to displace *black.*

A 30-minute videocassette of Bill Moyers' interview with August Wilson is available from HarperCollins.

CHAPTER 22

Men, Women, God, and Gods

JILL TWEEDIE

God the Mother Rules—OK? (p. 1139)

Some students—especially those who are church-goers—may be familiar with recent translations that seek to reduce the patriarchal aspects of the Bible and *The Book of Common Prayer.* The Rev. Bruce Metzger, chief translator of the New Revised Standard Version of the Bible, said that his staff sought to circumvent the "inherent bias of the English language toward the masculine gender" by avoiding "he" and "him" in passages where "they" and "them" could reasonably be used, and (in some passages) by using "mortal" or "humanity" instead of "man." But Metzger's version remains fairly conservative; other translators have gone further, refraining from calling God a king or a father, and Jesus the Son of Man. If students have any knowledge of such changes, the discussion can be very lively.

As Tweedie points out in her first paragraph, changes in diction of this sort are sometimes regarded as mere eccentricities. In fact, of course, they reflect the influence of the Women's Movement on theology. From her lively beginning Tweedie moves to the large issue of the patriarchal God versus the goddess, reflecting an important current in feminist thought, one that is represented by many essays in *WomenSpirit Rising.* ed. Carol P. Christ and Judith Plaskow (1979), and in Carol P. Christ's *Laughter of Aphrodite: Reflections on a*

Journey to the Goddess (1987). Students who are interested in the topic can be urged to look at these books. At the risk of oversimplifying, perhaps we can say that Ms. Christ summarized the gist of much of this writing when she says (in "Why Women Need the Goddess," in *Laughter*), "The simplest meaning of the Goddess symbol is an affirmation of the legitimacy and beneficence of female power."

Tweedie is perhaps the liveliest writer in this tradition; she is so lively that some students may object not only to her argument but to her tone. Fine; a good chance to discuss matters of decorum and the degree to which style serves as a form of argument.

W. E. B. DU BOIS

Of the Sorrow Songs (p. 1144)

It is perhaps hard for us to realize that not much more than a century ago African-American spirituals, or sorrow songs, were virtually unknown outside of the southern African American community, and they were probably nowhere thought of as literature. During the Civil War, some Northerners who served in the South heard the songs and were impressed; Thomas Wentworth Higginson, the commander of the first freed slave regiment to fight against the Confederacy, was one, but he is known to literary history chiefly because of his interest in Emily Dickinson. Still, as Du Bois explains in his essay, it was not until 1871, when Fisk University sent a group of singers to Ohio and later to New York in a fundraising effort, that the songs were introduced to large numbers of whites .

Although Du Bois can scarcely be said to be a pioneer in calling the public's attention to the songs—he was writing some thirty years after the successful concerts—his essay nevertheless was important in establishing among the white middle class the importance of the songs. Alain Locke, for instance, in *the Negro and His Music*, says,

> It was one of the great services of Dr. Du Bois, in his unforgettable chapter on "The Sorrow Songs," to give them a serious and proper interpretation as the peasant's instinctive distillation of sorrow and his spiritual triumph over it in a religious ecstasy and hope.

Locke's use of the word "peasant" may give us pause, especially since later in his essay he says that "genuine spirituals are composed in primitive Negro communities even today." Du Bois too uses the word "primitive" in paragraph 3, when he speaks of "a black folk of primitive type," in paragraph 9, when he speaks of "primitive African music," and in several later paragraphs. This word has rightly come in for a good deal of criticism. For instance, today we realize the colonialist implications in characterizing the art of Africa as "primitive art." Behind the word is the now-discredited idea that certain peoples—especially those in agrarian societies—represent an earlier or first (Latin *primus* = *first*) stage of human development, a "natural" condition. "Like all primitive folk," Du Bois writes, "the slave stood near to Nature's heart."

This idea was of course common at the time; if so-called primitive people, uncorrupted by civilization, did not enjoy the benefits of "civilization," they thereby escaped the corruptions of civilization. They were, so to speak, our own natural selves—ignorant, but somehow splendid. In any case, the dominant idea of the time held that at least some of the so-called primitive people might develop into the splendid developed beings represented by white middle class Europeans and Americans. Or—some people felt, they might not; they might not have the brain power that whites had.

Du Bois accepts—as everyone at the time accepted—the use of the word "primitive" to characterize the uneducated (in terms of European civilization) black people of his time. Similarly, he can speak of "the backward races of today," but the context clearly indicates that he means only the people who at this moment in their history are not organized into a certain kind of society. He certainly does *not* accept the view that Africans, or African Americans, are inherently intellectually inferior to white. In fact, thinking of the current Anglo-Saxon ("Teuton") assumptions of racial superiority, he wittily says that any such assumptions would have surprised the ancient world, a world in which the people of the Mediterranean represented high civilization, and the German people were the barbarian hordes. That is, he says, the then current assumption that certain races are "not worth the saving" is

> the arrogance of peoples irreverent toward Time and ignorant of the deeds of men. A thousand years ago such an assumption, easily possible, would have made it difficult for the Teuton to prove his right to life. Two thousand years ago such dogmatism, readily welcome, would have scouted the idea of blond races ever leading civilization.

We want to make one other point about this essay: Du Bois does not assume that the promise of the songs ("the prisoned shall be free") will come about, but in his penultimate paragraph he does at least conceive of a time when the "sunshine" may be available to all. He began his essay with a song of sorrow and of death ("When I lay this body down"), but he ends his essay with "fresh young voices" singing a song of pronounced hope ("Let us cheer the weary traveller / Along the heavenly way"). Presumably, in the past the songs served to sustain the weary, and now, he implies, they may also help to bring to reality the freedom they so often speak of.

We include some spirituals later in this chapter. Also especially relevant in the chapter is Dunbar's "An Ante-Bellum Sermon."

FLANNERY O'CONNOR

A Letter to Alfred Corn (p. 1148)

We think that all of the questions printed in the text lend themselves to writing assignments. But there are plenty of other things in the letter that are also worth discussing, for instance O'Connor's observation that as a college freshman Corn's intellectual life "is already running ahead of [his] lived experience" (paragraph 3), or her statement that "Faith is what you have in the absence of knowledge" (5), or "If you want your faith, you have to work for it" (6).

NATHANIEL HAWTHORNE

Young Goodman Brown (p. 1151)

Lea B. V. Newman's *A Reader's Guide to the Short Stories of Nathaniel Hawthorne* (1979) provides a valuable survey of the immense body of criticism that "Young Goodman Brown" has engendered. (By 1979 it had been discussed in print at least five hundred times.) We can begin by quoting Newman's remark that the three chief questions are these: "Why does Brown go into the forest? What happens to him there? Why does he emerge a permanently embittered man?"

Newman grants that there is a good deal of "ambivalence" in the story, but she finds most convincing the view that Brown is a victim, a man who "is deluded into accepting spectral evidence as conclusive proof of his neighbors' depravity." Newman also finds convincing another version of the "victim" theory, this one offered by psychologists who hold that "Brown is a sick man with a diseased mind who cannot help what he sees in the forest or his reaction to it." But her survey, of course, also includes references to critics who see Brown "as an evil man who is solely responsible for all that happens to him" (342-44).

Various critics—it almost goes without saying—press various details very hard. For instance, one critic says that Faith's pink ribbons symbolize Brown's "insubstantial, pastel-like faith." (Instructors expect to encounter this sort of reductive reading in essays by first-year students, but it is disappointing to find it in print.) How detailed, one might ask, is the allegory? Probably most readers will agree on some aspects: the village—a world of daylight and community—stands (or seems to stand) for good, whereas the forest—a dark, threatening place—stands (or seems to stand) for evil. The old man—" he of the serpent"—is the devil. But, again, as Newman's survey of criticism shows, even these interpretations have been debated.

The journey into the forest at night (away from the town and away from the daylight) suggests, of course, a journey into the dark regions of the self. The many ambiguities have engendered much comment in learned journals, some of which has been reprinted in a casebook of the story, *Nathaniel Hawthorne: Young Goodman Brogan* ed. Thomas E. Connolly. Is the story—as David Levin argues in *American Literature* 34 (1962):344-52—one about a man who is tricked by the devil, who conjures up specters who look like Brown's neighbors in order to win him a damnable melancholy? Does Faith resist the tempter? Does Goodman (i.e., Mister) Brown make a journey or only dream that he makes a journey? Is the story about awareness of evil, or is it about the crushing weight of needlessly assumed guilt? That is, is the story about a loss of faith (Austin Warren, in *Nathaniel Hawthorne*, says it is about "the devastating effect of moral skepticism"), or is it about a religious faith that kills one's joy in life? And, of course, the story may be about loss of faith not in Christ but in human beings; young Goodman Brown perceives his own corruption and loses faith in mankind.

With a little warning the student can be helped to see that the characters and experiences cannot be neatly pigeonholed. For example, it is not certain whether or not Faith yields to "the wicked one"; indeed, it is not certain that Brown actually journeyed into the woods. Richard H. Fogle points out in *Hawthorne's Fiction* that "ambiguity is the very essence of Hawthorne's tale." Among other interesting critical pieces on the story are Marius Bewley, *The Complex Fate;* Thomas Connolly, "Hawthorne's 'Young Goodman Brown': An Attack on Puritanic Calvinism," *American Literature* 28 (November *1956): 370-75;* and Frederick C. Crews, *The Sins of the Fathers: Hawthorne's Psychological Themes.* Connolly argues that Brown does not lose his faith, but rather that his faith is purified by his loss of belief that he is of the elect. Before the journey into the woods, he believes that man is depraved, but that he himself is of the elect and will be saved. In the forest he sees "a black mass of cloud" hide "the brightening stars," and (according to Connolly) his faith is purified, for he comes to see that he is not different from the rest of the congregation.

On the other hand, one can point out (as J. L. Capps does, in *Explicator,* Spring 1982) that only once in the story does Hawthorne use the word "hope" ("'But where is Faith' thought Goodman Brown; and as hope came into his heart, he trembled"), and the word "charity" never appears, indicating that Brown lacks the quality that would have enabled him to survive despair.

Speaking a bit broadly, we can say that critics fall into two camps: those who believe that Goodman Brown falls into delusion (i.e., misled by the devil, he destroys himself morally by falling into misanthropy), and those who believe that he is initiated into reality. Thus, for readers who hold the first view, Brown's guide into the forest is the devil, who calls up "figures" or "forms" of Brown's acquaintances, and it is Brown (not the narrator) who mistakenly takes the figures for real people. Even what Brown takes to be Faith's pink ribbon is for the narrator merely "*something* [that] fluttered lightly down through the air, and caught on the branch of a tree." In this view, (1) the fact that Faith wears the ribbon is proof that Brown has yielded to a delusion, and (2) are to judge Brown by recalling the narrator's objective perceptions. For instance, Brown's guide says that "evil is the nature of mankind," and Brown believes him, but the narrator (who is to be trusted) speaks of "the good old minister" and of "that excellent Christian," Goody Cloyse. There is much to be said for this view (indeed much has been said in journals), but against it one can recall some words by Frederick Crews: "The richness of Hawthorne's irony is such that, when Brown turns to a Gulliver-like misanthropy and spends the rest of his days shrinking from wife and neighbors, we cannot quite dismiss his attitude as unfounded" (*The Sins of the Fathers*, 106).

TOPICS FOR CRITICAL THINKING AND WRITING

1. Ambiguity in "Young Goodman Brown."
2. What are the strengths and weaknesses of the view that Brown is tricked by the devil, who stages a show of specters impersonating Brown's neighbors, in order to destroy Brown's religious faith?
3. Brown's guide says, "Evil is the nature of mankind," but does the *story* say it?
4. Is the story sexist, showing Brown more horrified by his wife's sexuality than his own?
5. Retell the story using a modern setting. Make whatever changes you wish, but retain the motif of the temptation of a man and a woman by evil.
6. What do you think Hawthorne gains (or loses) by the last sentence?

I. L. PERETZ

If Not Higher (p. 1160)

The story is a modern version of the genre of the Hasidic tale, a genre used by Hasidim (members of a Hebrew mystical sect) to teach piety. Behind this story is a traditional folktale of a rabbi who disguised himself to do works of great charity. But Peretz has added a narrative voice (an unquestioning admirer of the rabbi, annoyed by the Litvak's suspicions), and he has greatly enriched the meaning (doing good works on earth may be an activity even more exalted than doing God's will in heaven). The message is close to St. Paul's message in 1 Corinthians 13 that charity (to use the King James word for a word that most later versions translate as *love*, but not so much in the sense of benevolence as of *overflowing love* or *grace*) is what chiefly characterizes a godly person.

The somewhat comic groaning of the rabbi for the sins of his people is a manifestation of his love for them. We take it that the speaker in the third paragraph assumes it is perfectly natural for the missing rabbi to be in heaven;

after all, a rabbi's job is to protect his people, and to put in a good word for them with God, especially during the Days of Awe, which is the period when God is scrutinizing our behavior (including misbehavior) of the previous year.

There is much primitive or folkloric belief here (the marvelous account of Moses fantastically "suspended two and a half feet below heaven"), but there is also realism in the narrative voice ("Go argue with a Litvak!"). There is also, at the end, the delightful touch of the Litvak, still combative; he is thoroughly converted to belief in the rabbi, but he must continue seeing things a bit differently from the rest.

It is worth spending some time in class discussing the narrator, especially the narrator's relation to the reader. He begins by asserting the mysterious in a matter-of-fact way: "Early every Friday morning, at the time of the Penitential Prayers, the Rabbi of Memirov would vanish." Perhaps a modern American reader at first takes this to mean merely that the rabbi kept out of sight, but the next two paragraphs, emphasizing that the rabbi was not in any of the expected places, insist on the mystery.

The narrator assumes an audience who shares his beliefs, or, to put it a little differently, who shares the beliefs of all of the townsfolk: "Who can help us if not the rabbi!" (He goes on to say, "That's what the people thought," but pretty clearly he is one of the people, and he assumes that his audience resembles "the people.") A remark such as "They want to be pious and good, but our sins are so great," shows his identification, and it is easy to assume that "our" includes his audience.

But of course we are not members of the narrator's community, and we presumably are somewhat skeptical of his comments. In this, we are like the Litvak. (The Litvaks were Jews from Lithuania. They were considered to be inclined toward rationalism, and therefore to be hostile to Hasidic mysticism.) In the course of the tale, the Litvak—not the narrator—makes a discovery. The reader, therefore, (who more or less has been trying to keep the somewhat too-intimate narrator at arm's length) is forced (at least briefly) to accept the truth of the narrator's account, though the whimsical final line brings us back from the miraculous rabbi to the assertive Litvak.

We began by saying that the story belongs to the genre of the Hasidic tale, but in a way it is almost opposed to Hasidism, since the thrust of the moral is that the rabbi's efforts to make life on earth a bit easier are equal in value to— "if not higher" than—what he might do in heaven.

KATHERINE ANNE PORTER

The Jilting of Granny Weatherall (p. 1163)

Students do not always understand that there are two narratives here: one of a woman's dying hour and another of the past that floods her mind. The old lady, a tough Southerner or Southwesterner with an intense love of life, has "weathered all," even a jilting; she had expected a groom, George, and was publicly disappointed when he failed to show up. Now, at her death, again a priest is in the house, and again she is disappointed or "jilted": the Bridegroom (Christ) fails to appear. (It surely is worthwhile to call attention to the parable of the wise and foolish virgins, in Matthew 25:1-13, where the bridegroom does appear, but the foolish virgins miss him.) The first jilting could in some measure be overcome, but the second is unendurable.

Porter gives us the stream of Granny's consciousness, and if we are not always perfectly clear about details (did Hapsy die in childbirth?) we are nevertheless grateful for the revelation of an unfamiliar state of consciousness.

Exactly who is Hapsy? We are inclined to think that Hapsy was her last child, "the one she really wanted," and that is why Hapsy plays such an important role in Granny's consciousness. Presumably she had at last come to love her husband. (On this point, it is relevant to mention, too, that one of her sons is named George—presumably for the man who jilted her—and the other son is not named John, for his father, but Jimmy.) But other readers interpret Hapsy differently. Among the interpretations that we find farfetched are (1) Hapsy was a black friend and midwife who secretly delivered Ellen of an illegitimate child, but George learned of this and therefore jilted Ellen, and (2) Hapsy was Ellen's illegitimate child, fathered by George, and George then jilted her.

Also, who is the "he" who, at the first jilting, "cursed like a sailor's parrot and said, I'll kill him for you"? Among the answers usually given are: her father, a brother, the man she later married. Probably the question can't be answered authoritatively. And who is the driver of the cart, whom she recognizes by "his hands"?

These details probably do not affect the overall interpretation of the story. To return to a large matter, what interpretation of the story makes the most sense? What happens if we consider the story chiefly in the light of the Parable of the Ten Virgins? "The Jilting of Granny Weatherall" has engendered considerable comment in books on Porter, in journals, and especially in the instructors' manuals that accompany textbooks, but it is probably fair to say that the story is usually interpreted as setting forth the picture of an admirable—even heroic—woman who finds, at the end of her life, that there is no God, or, more specifically, that Christ the Bridegroom does not come to her. That is, putting aside the matter of the author's own beliefs (and putting the whole matter rather crudely) the story shows us an energetic woman who at the end of her life learns that she lives in a godless world.

This is the way we have long seen the story, and we still have a strong attachment to that view, but a rereading of the parable (Matthew 25:1-13) may raise some doubt:

1   Then shall the kingdom of heaven be likened unto ten virgins, which took their lamps, and went forth to meet the bridegroom.

2 And five of them were wise, and five were foolish.

3 They that were foolish took their lamps, and took no oil with them.

4 But the wise took oil in their vessels with their lamps.

5 While the bridegroom tarried, they all slumbered and slept.

6 And at midnight there was a cry made, Behold, the bridegroom cometh; go ye out to meet him.

7 Then all those virgins arose, and trimmed their lamps.

8 And the foolish said unto the wise, Give us of your oil; for our lamps are gone out.

9 But the wise answered, saying, Not so; lest there be not enough for us and you: but go ye rather to them that sell, and buy for yourselves.

10 And while they went to buy, the bridegroom came; and they that were ready went in with him to the marriage: and the door was shut.

11 Afterward came also the other virgins, saying, Lord, Lord, open to us.

12 But he answered and said, Verily I say unto you, I know you not.

13 Watch therefore, for ye know neither the day nor the hour wherein the son of man cometh.

Before we learned (chiefly from Wimsatt and Beardsley) of "the Intentional Fallacy," we might have studied Porter's letters, prefaces, and other stories in an effort to ascertain her view of the parable—we still might try to do so, but if we do we will be frustrated since Porter apparently did not comment on the parable, except in this story. Nor does the fact that she had a Catholic education tell us much about what she made of the parable. It appears that to understand the story we can do nothing more than read the story, and perhaps read the parable.

Matthew's final line, "Watch [i.e. remain awake] therefore, for ye know neither the day nor the hour wherein the son of man cometh," somewhat confuses the point of the parable, since the wise virgins as well as the foolish virgins slept, but the point nevertheless is very clear: the foolish virgins—foolish because they were short-sighted—overlooked the possibility of the Bridegroom's delay. The Bridegroom came unexpectedly.

Can one (or should one) interpret the story in the light of the evident meaning of the parable? If one interprets it thus, the point or theme might be roughly stated along these lines: Granny, despite all her apparently commendable worldly activity—ministering to the sick, keeping the farm in good repair, and so on—is (in a spiritual sense) improvident. The second Bridegroom does not appear at the moment that she expects him, and she therefore despairs and abandons her belief:

> For the second time there was no sign. Again no bridegroom and the priest in the house. She could not remember any other sorrow because the grief wiped them all away. Oh, no, there's nothing more cruel than this—I'll never forgive it. She stretched herself with a deep breath and blew out the light.

One might also say Granny Weatherall is guilty of the sort of hubris shown by some of Flannery O'Connor's characters, who think (for example) that because they wear clean clothing (the grandmother in "A Good Man Is Hard to Find") or hose down their pigs (Mrs. Turpin in "Revelation") they will be saved. Some support for this reading can be found in this passage:

> Granny felt easy about her soul.... She had her secret comfortable understanding with a few favored saints.

However, another way of looking at the story is to emphasize the point that, although at the end she is deeply disappointed, she remains active; she blows out the light. Against this, David C. Estes argues (Studies *in Short Fiction* 22 [1953]), "Her final act... reveals the ironic futility of all that has kept her so busy."

The interpretation that she is hubristic is offered very tentatively, and certainly not as one that gives *the* meaning of the story. But a reading of the parable is bound to call into question the usual view that "The Jilting of Granny Weatherall" is a story about a strong woman's perception that her faith is delusive.

A video cassette of Katherine Anne Porter's "The Jilting of Granny Weatherall" is available from HarperCollins.

TOPICS FOR CRITICAL THINKING AND WRITING

1. The meaning of the title, "The Jilting of Granny Weatherall."
2. The reader's developing response to Ellen Weatherall.
3. Religious imagery in "The Jilting of Granny Weatherall."
4. The meaning of "duty" in "The Jilting of Granny Weatherall."
5. The two narratives of "The Jilting of Granny Weatherall."
6. The imagery of darkness and light in "The Jilting of Granny Weatherall."

ERNEST HEMINGWAY

A Clean, Well-Lighted Place (p. 1169)

When we teach this story, we think of Cardinal Newman's famous remark on style: "Thought and meaning are inseparable from each other. Matter and expression are parts of one: style is a thinking out into language."

Hemingway's style is spare because the world he sees (so different from Faulkner's rich, fertile, vibrant world) is a world of nada, nothing, meaninglessness. The best that this world can offer is the sympathetic understanding that one person (the older waiter) has for another who with despair perceives nada; that's why the older waiter tries to maintain "a clean, well-lighted place." (God once said, "Let there be light," but for Hemingway human beings have to make what light—order—there is.) This waiter, in contrast to the young waiter (whose unthinking confidence prevents him from understanding the old man's despair), realizes that there are people who "need" a clean, well-lighted cafe, hence he is reluctant to close up for the night. (Notice, too, that he specifies that "this old man is clean." The motif of cleanliness versus messiness is introduced fairly early in the story when Hemingway tells us that when the young waiter poured the brandy "it slopped over.") And there is of course a second, related reason for his reluctance; he himself needs such a place, as is evident when he goes to the coffee bar, thus more or less repeating the old man's visit to the cafe.

Though we call Hemingway's style "spare," and it is often thought of as simple and realistic, it is of course artful, and sometimes it is patently unnatural: "I am of those who like to stay late at the cafe." Obviously Hemingway is trying to give us something of a sense of people speaking Spanish—but we might also say he sets his story in Spain because he wants to be able to give some dialogue an air of formality.

A few words about the point of view in the story: The third-person narrator is omniscient at the beginning (he knows how the old man feels, and what the waiters know about him). Much of what follows is objective, with only a bit of editorializing, as when he observes that the younger waiter uses the syntax of "stupid people." When the waiters separate, the narrator limits himself to the mind of the old waiter, who, of course, is the protagonist.

One other point: many readers have been unsure about which waiter speaks which lines. In fact, the lineation in Hemingway's original text, and followed in all reprints until 1967, contained an indisputable inconsistency. In order to avoid the inconsistency, a line had to be moved, and attached to a previous line. The solution that Scribner's, the publisher, adopted, was to make an alteration in the following passage:

"His niece looks after him."
"I know. You said she cut him down."

Scribner's emended the passage to read:

"His niece looks after him. You said she cut him down."
"I know."

For a detailed discussion of scholarly arguments concerning the assignment of speeches, see David Lodge's *The Novelist at the Crossroads* (1971), 35-56. But the emendation, near the middle of the story, does not affect the opening dialogue, which also puzzles some readers. We lean to the view that the first line of dialogue is spoken by the older waiter, and (of course) the subsequent lines alternate. This means that the last line of this passage, "He has plenty of money," is spoken by the older waiter, although one might at first think that such a remark is out of character—as we come to perceive the character later. But surely the point is that when the younger waiter doesn't grasp the older waiter's special meaning of "nothing" (emptiness), the older waiter then offers a simple explanation that the insensitive younger waiter can comprehend.

For an intelligent discussion of the story, see Steven K. Hoffman, "*Nada* and the Clean, Well-Lighted Place," in *Ernest Hemingway*, ed. Harold Bloom (1985) 173-92.

FLANNERY O'CONNOR

A Good Man Is Hard to Find (p. 1174)

In the early part of this story the grandmother is quite as hateful as the rest of the family—though students do not always see at first that her vapid comments, her moral clichés, and her desire to be thought "a lady" are offensive in their own way. Her comment, "People are certainly not nice like they used to be," can be used to convince students of her mindlessness and lack of charity.

The Misfit, like Jesus, was "buried alive"; he believes that "Jesus thrown everything off balance," and he finds no satisfaction in life (i.e., his life without grace). Life is either a meaningless thing in which all pleasure is lawful (and, ironically, all pleasure turns to ashes), or it derives its only meaning from following Jesus. The Misfit, though he does not follow Jesus, at least sees that the materialistic view of life is deficient. Confronted by the suffering of The Misfit, the nagging and shallow grandmother suddenly achieves a breakthrough and is moved by love. She had earlier recognized The Misfit ("'You're The Misfit!' she said. 'I recognized you at once'"), and now she has a further recognition of him as "one of her own children," that is, a suffering fellow human. Faced with death, she suddenly becomes aware of her responsibility: her head clears for an instant and she says, "You're one of my own children." This statement is not merely an attempt to dissuade The Misfit from killing her; contrast it with her earlier attempts, when, for example, she says, "I know you come from nice people! Pray! Jesus, you ought not to shoot a lady. I'll give you all the money I've got." Rather, at last her head is "cleared." This moment of grace transfigures her and causes her death. The Misfit is right when he says, "She would of been a good woman if it had been somebody there to shoot her every minute of her life."

On the "moment of grace" in O'Connor's fiction, see *College English* (27, December 1965): 235-39, and R. M. Vande Kiefte in *Sewanee Review* 70 (1968): 337-56. Vande Kiefte notes that the description of the dead grandmother ("her legs crossed under her like a child's and her face smiling up at the cloudless sky") suggests that death has jolted the grandmother out of her mere secular decency into the truth of eternal reality. See also Martha Stephens, *The Question of Flannery O'Connor.*

For Flannery O'Connor's comments on this story, see our text, In her collected letters, entitled *The Habit of Being,* O'Connor says (letter to John Gawkes, Dec. 26,1959) that she is interested in "the moment when you know that Grace has been offered and accepted—such as the moment when the Grandmother realizes The Misfit is one of her own children" (367).

TOPICS FOR CRITICAL THINKING AND WRITING

1. Explain the significance of the title.
2. Interpret and evaluate The Misfit's comment on the grandmother: "She would of been a good woman if it had been somebody there to shoot her every minute of her life."
3. O'Connor reported that once, when she read aloud "A Good Man Is Hard to Find," one of her hearers said that "it was a shame someone with so much talent should look on life as a horror story." Two questions: What evidence of O'Connor's "talent" do you see in the story, and does the story suggest that O'Connor looked on life as a horror story?
4. What are the values of the members of the family?
5. Flannery O'Connor, a Roman Catholic, wrote, "I see from the standpoint of Christian orthodoxy. This means that for me the meaning of life is centered in our Redemption by Christ and what I see in the world I see in relation to that." In the light of this statement, and drawing on "A Good Man Is Hard to Find," explain what O'Connor saw in the world.

FLANNERY O'CONNOR

Revelation (p. 1185)

This story, like "A Good Man Is Hard to Find," is concerned with a moment of grace, which most obviously begins when Mary Grace hurls a hook at Mrs. Turpin—an action somewhat parallel to The Misfit's assault on the grandmother. The doctor's office contains a collection of wretched human beings whose physical illnesses mirror their spiritual condition. There is abundant comedy ("The nurse ran in, then out, then in again"), but these people are treated sympathetically too. Mrs. Turpin's pitiful snobbery—especially her desperate effort to rank people in the eyes of God—is comic and horrible, but it at least reveals an uneasiness beneath her complacency, an uneasiness that finally compares well with the monumental hatred that characterizes Mary Grace. Yet Mary Grace, a pimply girl, is a messenger of grace. And so when the blow comes (from a book nicely called *Human Development*), it is not in vain.

The girl's accusation ("Go back to hell where you came from, you old wart hog") strikes home, and later, among the pigs that Mrs. Turpin so solicitously cleans, the message produces a revelation, a revelation that forces upon her an awareness of the inadequacy of "virtue" (her horrible concept of respectability) as she has known it. Virtue is of as little value to fallen humanity as a hosing-down is to a pig; in her vision she sees that even virtue or respectability is burned away in the movement toward heaven.

On the one hand, some students have difficulty seeing that Mrs. Turpin is not simply a stuffy hypocrite; on the other, some students have difficulty seeing that her respectability is woefully inadequate and must be replaced by a deeper sympathy. But perhaps students have the greatest difficulty in reconciling the comic aspects of the story with its spiritual depth, and here the instructor can probably not do much more than read some passages and hope for the best.

In O'Connor's writings the sun is a common symbol for God. Here, the light of the sun transforms the hogs, so that they appear to "pant with a secret life," a parallel to the infusion of grace into Mrs. Turpin, which causes her to see the worthlessness of her earlier "respectable" values.

The story is deeply indebted to the Book of Revelation, traditionally attributed to St. John the Evangelist and probably written at the end of the first century A.D. (A revelation is, etymologically, an "unveiling," just as an apocalypse is, in Greek, an unveiling. What is unveiled in the Book of Revelation is the future.) Numerous details in O'Connor's story pick up details in the biblical account: O'Connor's "red glows in the sky echoes the fiery heaven of Revelation; the "watery snake" that briefly appears in the air echoes the water-spewing "serpent" of Revelation (12:15), and even the "seven long-snouted bristling shoats" echo the numerous references to seven (angels, churches, seals, stars) in Revelation. But the details should not be pressed too hard; what matters most is the apocalyptic vision of the oppressed rejoicing and shouting hallelujah at the throne of God.

The story is not difficult, and no published discussions of it are essential reading, though it is of course discussed in books on O'Connor and in general comments on her work, such as A. R. Coulthard, "From Sermon to Parable: Four Conversion Stories by Flannery O'Connor" *American Literature* 55 (1983): 55-71. Two essays devoted entirely to "Revelation" are "'Revelation' and the Book of Job" by Diane Rolmedo, *Renascence* 30 (1978): 78-90, and Lame Love Slone's "The Rhetoric of the Seer: Eye Imagery in Flannery O'Connor's 'Revelation,'" *Studies in Short Fiction* 25 (1988): 135-145.

TOPICS FOR CRITICAL THINKING AND WRITING

1.   Why does Mary Grace attack Mrs. Turpin?
2.   Characterize Mrs. Turpin before her revelation. Did your attitude toward her change at the end of the story?

3. The two chief settings are a doctor's waiting room and a "pig parlor." Can these settings reasonably be called "symbolic"? If so, symbolic of what?

4. When Mrs. Turpin goes toward the pig parlor, she has "the look of a woman going single-handed, weaponless, into battle." Once there, she dismisses Claud, uses the hose as a weapon against the pigs, and talks to herself "in a low fierce voice." What is she battling, besides the pigs?

LESLIE MARMON SILKO

The Man to Send Rain Clouds (p. 1200)

The church—especially perhaps the Roman Catholic Church—has often adapted itself to the old ways and beliefs of new converts, sometimes by retaining the old holidays and holy places but adapting them and dedicating them to the new religion. For instance, although the date of birth of Jesus is not known, from the fourth century it was celebrated late in December, displacing pagan festivals of new birth (e.g., the Roman *Saturnalia*, which celebrated the sowing of the crops on December 15-17, and the feast of the *Natalis Solis Invicti*, celebrating the renewal of the sun a week later).

Practices of this sort have facilitated conversion, but from the church's point of view the danger may be that the new believers retain too much faith in the old beliefs. In Silko's story the priest has every reason to doubt that his parishioners have fully accepted Christianity. The unnamed priest—he's just "the priest" or "the young priest," not anyone with a personal identity, so far as the other characters in the story are concerned—is kind and well-meaning, and he is even willing to bend the rules a bit, but he knows that he does not have the confidence of the people. He is disturbed that they didn't think the Last Rites and a funeral Mass were necessary, and he is not at all certain that they have given up their pagan ways: "He looked at the red blanket, not sure that Teofilo was so small, wondering if it wasn't some perverse Indian trick—something they did in March to ensure a good harvest...." He is wrong in suspecting that Teofilo (the name means "beloved of God," from the Greek *theos* = God, and *philos* = loving) is not in front of him, but he is right in suspecting that a " trick" is being played, since the reader knows that the holy water is wanted not to assist Teofilo to get to the Christian heaven but to bring rain for the crops. In Part One we hear Leon say, "Send us rain clouds, Grandfather"; in Part Three we hear Louise express the hope that the priest will sprinkle water so Teofilo "won't be thirsty"; and at the very end of the story we hear that Leon "felt good because it was finished, and he was happy about the sprinkling of the holy water; now the old man could send them big thunderclouds for sure."

We aren't quite sure about what to make of the passage in which the water, disappearing as soon as it is sprinkled on the grave, "reminded" the priest of something, but the passage is given some emphasis and surely it is important. Our sense is that the priest vaguely intuits an archetypal mystery, something older and more inclusive than the Roman Catholic ritual he engages in.

During most of the story the narrator neither editorializes nor enters the minds of the characters; we are not told that the characters are reverential, and (for the most part) we are not allowed to hear their thoughts. Rather, we see them perform ceremonies with dignity, and, because the point of view is chiefly objective, we draw our own conclusions. Possibly, too, by keeping outside of the minds of the characters the narrator helps to convey the traditional paleface idea that Native Americans are inscrutable people, people of few words. Certainly Leon hoards words when, responding to the priest's admonition not to let Teofilo stay at the sheep camp alone, he says, "No, he won't do that any more now." But we do get into the priest's mind, notably in the passage in which he suspects trickery, and we get into Leon's mind at the end of the story when, in what almost seems like a thunderstorm of information, we are told his thoughts about the water.

Because the narrator, like the characters, is taciturn, some readers may think that Leon and his companions are callous. "After all," one student said, "don't they first round up the sheep before attending to the burial rites? And why don't they weep?" Class discussion can usually bring out the dignity of the proceedings here, and some students may be able to provide specific details about burial customs unfamiliar to other members of the class.

We do not know if the different colors of paint—white, blue, yellow, and green—have specific meanings, but perhaps blue suggests the sky and the water, yellow suggests corn meal, and green suggests vegetation. White is a fairly widespread sign of purity, but we have not been able to find out how Pueblo people regard it. (If you know about these things, we'll be most appreciative if you write to us, in care of the publisher.)

TOPICS FOR CRITICAL THINKING AND WRITING

1. How would you describe the response of Leon, Ken, Louise, and Teresa to Teofilo's death? To what degree does it resemble or differ from responses to death that you are familiar with?
2. How do the funeral rites resemble or differ from those of your community?
3. How well does Leon understand the priest? How well does the priest understand Leon?
4. At the end of the story we are told that Leon "felt good." Do you assume that the priest also felt good? Why, or why not?
5. From what point of view is the story told? Mark the passages where the narrator enters a character's mind, and then explain what, in your opinion, Silko gains (or loses?) by doing so.

Psalms 1, 19, 23, 121 (pp. 1204-07)

Modern Bibles with fairly brief but highly useful apparatus (e.g. an introduction to the Psalms, and helpful annotations) include *The HarperCollins Study Bible, The Oxford Study Bible,* and *The Jerusalem Bible.* The multivolume *Interpreter's Bible* (the Psalms are in volume 4) has fuller apparatus, but it is somewhat dated; still, it is worth consulting if time is available. The entry on Psalms in *The Anchor Bible Dictionary* (vol. 5), running to about 14 double-column pages, also provides an excellent survey, though it does not have commentary on each psalm.

Psalm 1. This psalm, one of the group known as "Wisdom Psalms," is part of a larger body of wisdom works such as Proverbs, Job, and Ecclesiastes. It was probably put in the first position in the Psalter (another name for The Book of Proverbs) because it summarizes the moral teachings found in the book.

In verse 3, the image of a tree planted by the water is a striking image of life, especially since large trees were not common in Palestine.

Psalm 19 C. S. Lewis, in his *Reflections on the Psalms* (1958), says that Psalm 19 is "The greatest poem in the Psalter and one of the greatest lyrics in the world" (63). Lewis, like many other commentators, calls attention to the structure, which he sees as "six verses about Nature, five about the law, and four of personal prayer." The usual academic view is that the psalm probably consists of two poems that at some point were joined, one (1-6) a poem celebrating the revelation of God in nature, and the other (7-14, probably later) a poem praising the revelation of God's will in the Mosaic law. Lewis takes the psalm as a unified poem with transitions that only seem abrupt. He says of the author:

> First he thinks of the sky; how, day after day, the pageantry we see there shows us the splendor of its Creator. Then he thinks of the sun, the bridal joyousness of its rising, the unimaginable speed of its daily voyage from east to west. Finally, of its heat... The key phrase on which the whole poem depends is "there is nothing hid from the heat thereof." It pierces everywhere with its strong, clean ardor. Then at once, in verse 7 he is talking of something else, which hardly seems to him something else because it is so like the all-piercing, all-detecting sunshine. The Law is "undefiled," the Law gives light, it is clean and everlasting, it is "sweet." No one can improve on this and nothing can more fully admit us to the old Jewish feeling about the Law; luminous, severe, disinfectant, exultant. One hardly needs to add that this poet is wholly free from self-righteousness and the last section is concerned with his "secret faults." As he has felt the sun, perhaps in the desert, searching him out in every nook of shade where he attempted to hide from it, so he feels the Law searching out all the hiding-places of his soul. (63-64)

Two additional points:

(1) the device called *synonymous parallelism* is nicely evident twice in the first verse, where *the heavens* is paralleled by *the firmament,* and *the glory of God*

is paralleled by *his handiwork*. The second verse, too, contains synonymous parallelism, in *uttereth speech* and *showeth knowledge*, but it also illustrates *antithetic parallelism*, since *day unto day* contrasts with *night unto night*.

(2) In the King James Version, verse 3 runs thus: "There is no speech nor language, where their voice is not heard." Virtually all modern scholars agree that the addition of *where* is a mistake. The KJV version loses the synonymous parallel of the original, which says that the glories of the heavens have "no speech nor language," and that "their voice is not heard." That is, the KJV gives us something consistent (the heavens speak, and they are heard wherever people speak), but it loses the parallelism of the original and it also loses the implied paradox of the original, which in effect says that the heavens are silent—but they nevertheless speak to us.

Psalm 23. A profession of faith. The extended discussion by Leland Ryken, in *Words of Delight*, 2nd ed., is helpful. The following discussion draws heavily on Ryken.

Ryken says that the psalm implies a journey: Human beings, guided by the Lord, are like sheep, who are led from the sheepfold to places of grazing, and then safely home. (In fact one might argue that the pastoral imagery disappears after the third verse, except for a possible recurrence in the "rod and... staff" of the fourth verse.) God is the good shepherd, who finds sustenance for the sheep, and who guards them from predators. "I shall not want" sounds rather general, but it turns out that the provision is physical (food and water) and spiritual (comfort, goodness, mercy). In "He maketh me to lie down in green pastures... still water," we get an image of restfulness (i.e. the sheep are not eating and drinking, but are lying down). In the words "He restoreth my soul," *soul* probably meant something like *life* or *personality*, rather than any special religious entity. In verse 3, "paths of righteousness" is better translated as "right paths," "safe paths [as opposed to paths that might be dangerous for the sheep]," i.e. the original does not have the strong moral quality evident in the translation.

Notice the shift from speaking of the Lord as *he* (2, 3) to *thou* (4). Presumably the speaker feels a greater degree of intimacy as he utters his words.

Psalm 23 is also discussed, in a rather informal, personal way, by John Hollander in an essay on the Psalms, in *Congregation*, ed. David Rosenberg (1987). In part Hollander says:

> The rough pentameters, frequently dactylic, of "Yea, though I walk through the valley of the shadow of death" (with the assonantal pattern of the last phrases pointing up the stresses), of "thou anointest my head with oil; my cup runneth over," and the final couplet made of lilting fourteeners and pentameter: "Surely good and mercy shall follow me all the days of my life: / And I will dwell in the house of the Lord forever"—these cadences were always alive in the language for me. (297-98)

Psalm 121. Psalms 120-34 are designated *psalms of ascent.* A student who is interested in the psalms may want to write a research paper on this category. Good places to begin are the annotated Bibles mentioned above, at the beginning of this discussion of the psalms.

SPIRITUALS

Deep River; Go Down, Moses; Didn't My Lord Deliver Daniel (pp. 1208-09)

The introductory note in the text mentions that one of the chief themes is the desire for release, and that this theme is often set forth with imagery from the Hebrew Bible, but some additional points should be mentioned. Most of what follows here is derived from Albert J. Raboteau, *Slave Religion* (1978).

Although the passages about release undoubtedly refer to the release from slavery, the songs should not be taken only as disguised statements about secular life. Many slaves—like at least some of their masters—believed that the Bible was the book of the acts of God, which is to say that they "believed that the supernatural continually impinged on the natural, that divine action constantly took place within the lives of men, in the past, present, and future" (Raboteau 250).

Raboteau makes a second very important point:

> Identification with the children of Israel was, of course, a significant theme for white Americans, too. From the beginnings of colonization, white Christians had identified the journey across the Atlantic to the New World as the exodus of a new Israel from the bondage of Europe into the promised land of milk and honey. For the black Christian, as Vincent Harding has observed [in *The Religious Situation*, ed. Donald R. Cutter], the imagery was reversed: the Middle Passage had brought his people to Egypt land, where they suffered bondage under Pharaoh. White Christians saw themselves as a new Israel; slaves identified themselves as the old. (250-51)

Instructors who have time for some additional reading may wish to consult—for a survey of scholarship on the topic—John White, "Veiled Testimony: Negro Spirituals and the Slave Experience," in *Journal of American Studies* 17 (1983): 251-63. White is especially concerned with adjudicating between those who see spirituals (of the type that we reprint) as highly revolutionary and, on the other hand, those who see the songs as in effect serving the cause of the masters, since the songs seem to suggest that suffering in this world is transient, and that God will later reward the sufferers. (As an example of this second view, White quotes

E. Franklin Frazier, an African-American scholar who in *The Negro Church in America* [1964] rejected "the efforts of Negro intellectuals... encouraged by white radicals, to invest the spirituals with a revolutionary meaning.")

Other recommended works (in addition to Raboteau and White): John Lovell, *Black Song: The Forge and the Flame* (1972); James H. Cone, *The Spirituals and the Blues* (1972); and Lawrence Levine, *Black Culture and Black* (1977).

Obviously these songs (like all oral literature) really ought to be heard, not simply read. Many excellent recordings are available, but if you are lucky you may find a student who will give a live performance in class.

If you teach any of the spirituals we include, you will probably find it effective also to teach Du Bois's essay (still regarded as seminal) and also Dunbar's "An Ante-Bellum Sermon."

WILLIAM SHAKESPEARE

Sonnet 146 (Poor soul, the center of my sinful earth) (p. 1211)

Shakespeare's Sonnet 146 is well discussed in Edward Hubler, *The Sense of Shakespeare's Sonnets*, and more learnedly and elaborately discussed by Michael West in *Shakespeare Quarterly* 25 (Winter 1974): 109-122. Also useful is *A Casework on Shakespeare's Sonnets*, Gerald Willed and Victor B. Reed, eds. See also an article by Charles A. Hatter, "The Christian Basis of Shakespeare's Sonnet 146," *Shakespeare Quarterly* 19 (Autumn 1968): 355-65, which rejects a reading that the poem ironically argues that spiritual health is achieved by bodily subjugation. The rejected reading holds that the advice that the soul exploit the body must be ironic, since if it were not ironic, the soul would be guilty of simony, the sin of buying (or attempting to buy) salvation. According to this ironic reading, the poet really is pleading for the life of the body against a rigorous asceticism which glorifies the spirit at the expense of the body. But Huttar argues (by citing Biblical sources and Christian commentaries) that the poem argues in behalf of the traditional Christian doctrine that the soul should be the master of the body; the body (which must in any case die) should not be allowed to cause the soul to "pine." The poem, Huttar says, is close to Jesus's words in Matthew 6:20: "Lay up for yourself treasures in heaven, where neither moth nor rust doth corrupt, and where thieves do not break through and steal."

TOPICS FOR CRITICAL THINKING AND WRITING

1.   In line 2, "My sinful earth" is doubtless a printer's error, an unintentional repetition of the last words of the first line. Among suggested emenda-

tions are "Thrall to," "Fooled by," "Rebuke these," "Leagued with," "Feeding." Which do you prefer? Why?

2. How would you characterize the tone of the first two lines? Where in the poem does the thought take its chief turn? What do you think is the tone of the couplet?

3. What does "array" (line 2) mean?

4. Explain the paradox in lines 13-14.

5. In a poem on the relation between body and soul, do you find battle imagery surprising? Commercial imagery (lines 5-12)? What other imagery is in the poem? Do you think the sonnet is a dull sermon?

JOHN DONNE

Holy Sonnet IV ("At the round earth's imagined corners") (p. 1211)

The octave commands the angels (almost in God's voice) to introduce Judgment Day; the sestet humbly petitions God to postpone the event and to teach the speaker "how to repent." Or we might say that the octave forcefully imagines a future event, and the sestet (recoiling from the imagined sight) reflects upon the present in the light of the future. The octave is expansive ("round earth's imagined corners") and filled with "numberless infinities" (line 3) and events (the catalog in lines 6-7); the sestet shifts from "there" (before God, on Judgment Day) to "here on this lowly ground" (line 12), with Donne as the only human being, talking with some intimacy to God. For a discussion of the poem, calling attention especially to the sound effects, see Reuben Brower, *The Fields of Light.*

JOHN DONNE

Holy Sonnet XIV ("Batter my heart, three-personed God") (p. 1212)

"Batter my heart" has been discussed several times in *Explicator* (March 1953, Item 31: December 1953, Item 18; April 1954, Item 36; October 1956, Item 2). In *College English* 24 January 1963): 299-302, John Parrish summarized these discussions, rejecting the idea that in the first quatrain, especially in lines 2 and 4, God is compared to a tinker mending a damaged pewter vessel, and offering his own reading. All these are conveniently reprinted in the Norton critical edition of *John Donne's Poetry*, ed. A. L. Clements.

Our own winnowings from these essays follow. Although the first line introduces the "three-personed God," it is impossible to associate each quatrain with only one of the three persons. Still, the idea of the trinity is carried out in several ways: "knock, breathe, shine" becomes "break, blow, burn." And there are three chief conceits: God as a tinker repairing the speaker, damaged by sin; the speaker as a town usurped by satanic forces; God as a forceful lover who must ravish the sinful speaker; or (lest one get uneasy at the thought that Donne presents himself as a woman) God as a lover who must fully possess the speaker's soul (the soul is customarily regarded as female). "O'erthrow" in the first quatrain, in line 3, leads to the image of the besieged town in the second quatrain; "untrue" at the end of the second quatrain leads (because it can refer to marital infidelity) to the conceit of the lover in the third quatrain; and "ravish" in the final line can take us back to "heart" in the first line of the poem.

A useful, relatively long explication by M. T. Wanninger appeared in *Explicator* (December 1969), Item 37. M. H. Abrams, *Natural Supernaturalism*, 50-51, points out that in "Batter my heart" Donne draws on Revelation 21:5 ("Behold, I make all things new"), and that "the ultimate marriage with the Bridegroom, represented as the rape of the longingly reluctant soul" draws on "commonplaces of Christian devotion."

TOPIC FOR CRITICAL THINKING AND WRITING

How do you feel about an observation made in *Explicator* (Spring 1980), to the effect that "no end" (1.6) is an anagram for "Donne"? What is the point? According to the author of the note, "This anagram is, I think, another of the many ingenious samples of Donne's playing upon his name for poetic effect." Is this reading helpful? Why? Why not?

GEORGE HERBERT

Easter Wings (p. 1213)

The following discussion summarizes a few of the points made by Helen Vendler in *The Poetry of George Herbert* (1975). The first two lines are a rather unexciting, even platitudinous account of the Fall of Man, or, rather, the Fall of Adam, though Herbert says that through Jesus he (Herbert) can "rise" to heaven. In the second stanza Herbert sees the fall in more personal terms ("My tender age"); and although in the first stanza he asked to be allowed to "sing" of the victories of the Resurrection, in the second stanza he asks to "feel" the victory of Jesus. "The poem... admits personal suffering and grief as apparent impediments to personal resurrection, but then explains them therapeutically as an imposition by God in just punishment for sin and as an imitation of Christ as well" (146).

GEORGE HERBERT

The Altar (p. 1214)

Students probably will enjoy working out the allegory: The altar is made of the pieces of a broken (i.e. contrite) heart; the cement is the tears of contrition; God is the stonemason. Remember, of course, that in the Christian church the altar is derived from the altars mentioned in the Hebrew Bible, upon which sacrifices were made to atone for human sin.

Helen Vendler, in *The Poetry of George Herbert* (1975) expresses unhappiness with the allegory. For instance, she says that there is some uncertainty about whether the heart is or is not contrite. The heart is said in line 10 to be "hard," and she asks, therefore, why this "hard" heart should praise God. Perhaps the answer is that the speaker's heart has in fact been humbled ("cut"), but—precisely because the speaker is humble—he thinks his heart is still hard. In any case, no allegory can be pressed hard; what counts is the gist, or certain details and not other details.

For a rather elaborate reading of the poem, see Stanley Fish, *Self-Consuming Artifacts*.

GEORGE HERBERT

Discipline (p. 1214)

Herbert's "Discipline" is discussed by Helen Vendler in *The Poetry of George Herbert.* Among the points she makes are these: the poem's appeal stems "not only from the child-like plea asking God to 'throw away' his wrath as though it were an object external to himself, but also from the exceptional lilt of the metrics"; "the anomalous third line calls attention to itself by slowing down the pace, and the effect of this slowness is one of taking thought." Between the first stanza and the last (which is a variant on the first) so long as Herbert "describes his own efforts at virtue" the poem is "static," but when midway "he abandons his useless attempt to compel God by demonstrating his own virtue," the poem gains "momentum." The whole of Vendler's discussion is strongly recommended.

JOHN MILTON

"When I consider how my light is spent" (p. 1216)

Milton's sonnets have been carefully edited by Ernst Honigmann (1966). Argument about the date Milton became blind need not concern us (Miltonists wonder how literally to take "Ere half my days"), but it should be noticed that one critic argues that the sonnet is not about blindness, (The common title "On His Blindness" has no authority; it was first used by a printer in 1752.) Lysander Kemp held *(Hopkins Review,* 6 [1952], pp. 80-83) that the sonnet deals with the loss not of vision but of poetic inspiration, but Kemp's view has not been widely accepted. The most sensible view (to draw on Honigmann) is that the octave assumes that God requires ceaseless labor, and the sestet enlarges the concept of service to include those who though inactive are eagerly prepared for action. Additional notes: in line 2, "this dark world and wide" suggests not only the dark world of the blind man but is also a religious stock expression for the sinful world; in line 7, "day-labor" suggests not only labor for daily wages but also labor that requires daylight, i.e., the power of vision; in line 14, "wait" perhaps means not only "stay in expectation" but also "attend as a servant, to receive orders."

WILLIAM BLAKE

The Lamb (p. 1216); The Tyger (p. 1217)

E. D. Hirsch, Jr., in *Innocence and Experience,* Harold Bloom, in *The Visionary Company,* and Hazard Adams, in *William Blake,* discuss these poems. "The Tyger" has engendered much comment. Of special interest are Martin K. Nurmi, "Blake's Revisions of 'The Tyger,'" *PMLA* 71 (September 1956): 669-85; Harold Bloom, *Blake's Apocalypse;* and two pieces by John Grant and Hazard Adams reprinted in *Discussions of Blake,* ed. John Grant. See also, for a collection of essays and extracts from books, *William Blake: The Tyger,* ed. Winston Weathers.

In the course of arguing on behalf of reader-response criticism, Stanley Fish, in *Is There a Text in This Class?,* has some fun calling attention to the diversity of opinions. He points out that in *Encounter* (June 1954), Kathleen Raine published an essay entitled "Who Made the Tyger?" She argued that because for Blake the tiger is "the beast that sustains its own life at the expense of its fellow-creatures," the answer to the big question (" Did he who made the

Lamb make thee?") is, in Raine's words, "beyond all possible doubt, No." Fish points out that Raine, as part of her argument, insists that Blake always uses the word "forest" with reference "to the natural, 'fallen' world." Fish then calls attention to E. D. Hirsch's reading, in *Innocence and Experience* (1964), in which Hirsch argues that "forest" suggests "tall straight forms, a world that for all its terror has the orderliness of the tiger's stripes or Blake's perfectly balanced verses." In short, for Hirsch "The Tyger" is "a poem that celebrates the holiness of tigerness." Hirsch also argues that Blake satirizes the single-mindedness of the Lamb.

We find all of this very baffling. We are not specialists in Blake, but it seems to us that both poems celebrate rather than satirize or in any way condemn their subjects. In "The Lamb" (such is our critical innocence), innocence is celebrated; in "The Tyger," energy is celebrated.

In "The Lamb" the speaker is a child, or is an adult impersonating a child. He asks the lamb a question and then gives the answer according to traditional Christian thinking. (In the Gospel of John [1.29, 35] John the Baptist twice greets Jesus as the Lamb of God, presumably drawing on the idea of the lamb as a sacrificial offering. And behind this idea is the Suffering Servant of Isaiah 53, who is compared to "a lamb that is led to slaughter.") The speaker uses a simple vocabulary (words of one and two syllables), and he uses end-stopped lines (one thought to a line). Lamb, God, speaker, and child are all united at the end of the poem.

In "The Tyger" the animal is "burning bright" because of its fiery eyes (6) and presumably because of its orange stripes, also flame-like. (Since the tiger is imagined as being created in a smithy, the poem also includes other images of fire in such words as "forge" and "furnace.")

Blake's question in effect is this: Was the tiger created in hell ("distant deeps") or in heaven ("skies")—and by Satan or by God? Blake hammers these questions into our minds, but it seems to us that Blake clearly implies an answer: The creator is "immortal," daring, "dread," and—most important—creative. In traditional Christian thinking, then, the answer is that God created the tiger.

Lines 17-18 ("When the stars threw down their spears / And watered heaven with their tears") have engendered much commentary. Possibly the lines allude to the war in heaven in Milton's *Paradise Lost*, and Blake's gist might be paraphrased thus: "When the rebel angels cast down their spears in defeat, did the triumphant God smile as his success, i.e. What were God's feelings when he had to be tiger-like to an aspect of his own creation?" This makes sense to us, but we admit that, strictly speaking, in *Paradise Lost* the rebellious angels never do "cast down their spears," i.e. never surrender.

One last comment. Harold Bloom probably understands Blake as well as anyone else alive. In *The Oxford Anthology of English Literature* he gives this footnote, which we can't quite bring ourselves to believe. You may want to think about it, and to try it out on your students.

However the poem is interpreted, the reader should be wary of identifying the poem's chanter with Blake, who did not react with awe or fear to any natural phenomenon whatsoever.

Blake probably had considerable satirical intention in this lyric, as a juxtaposition of his verbal description of the Tyger with his illustration seems to suggest. [The illustration shows an unimpressive beast.] The poem's speaker, though a man of considerable imagination (quite possibly a poet like William Cowper), is at work terrifying himself with a monster of his own creation. Though Blake may mean us to regard the poem's questions as unanswerable, he himself would have answered by saying that the "immortal hand or eye" belonged only to Man, who makes both Tyger and Lamb. In "the forests of the night," or mental darkness, Man makes the Tyger, but in the open vision of day Man makes the Lamb.

TOPICS FOR CRITICAL THINKING AND WRITING

1.   What do the lamb and the tiger symbolize?
2.   In "The Tyger" Blake asks a great question, "Did he who made the lamb make thee?" What is the answer?

EMILY DICKINSON

Those—dying, then (p. 1218)

The faith of her ancestors is, Dickinson apparently feels, no longer possible, but it serves to enrich behavior. An *ignis fatuus* (a phosphorescent light—caused by gases emitted by rotting organic matter—that hovers over a swamp) presumably resembles, however weakly, the beautiful flames of heaven and the demonic flames of hell. It is only a will-o'-the-wisp, but at least it is *some*thing. The image of amputation is shocking, but it can be paralleled in the Bible, for example by "And if thy right eye offend thee, pluck it out, and cast it from thee.... and if thy right hand offend thee, cut it off, and cast it from thee" (Matthew 5:29-30).

TOPICS FOR CRITICAL THINKING AND WRITING

1.   In a sentence or two, state the point of the poem.
2.   Is the image in line 4 in poor taste? Explain.
3.   What is an *ignis fatuus?* In what ways does it connect visually with traditional images of hell and heaven?

EMILY DICKINSON

There's a certain Slant of light (p. 1219)

The poem seems difficult to us, and any questions about it therefore lead to difficulties, but perhaps our fifth question, below, on the rhyme scheme, is fairly straightforward. Some students may recognize that metrically the poem is close to the "common meter" or "common measure" (abbreviated C. M. in hymnals) of a hymn. (C. M. can be defined thus: stanzas of four lines, the first and third in iambic tetrameter, the second and fourth in iambic trimeter, rhyming *abcb* or *abab*.) In fact no two stanzas in the poem are metrically identical (if we count the syllables of the first line of each stanza, we find seven, six or seven, six, and eight), but despite such variations, the meter and especially the rhyme scheme (*abab*) seem regular. The second and fourth lines of each stanza have five syllables, and these lines end with exact rhymes, though the first and third lines of each stanza rely less on rhyme than on consonance. The regularity of the rhyme scheme, especially in such short lines, is something of a tour de force, and (because it suggests a highly ordered world) it might seem more suited to a neat little poem with a comforting theme than to the poem Dickinson has given us. Further, since the meter and some of the rhymes might occur in a hymn ("Despair," "Air"; "breath," "Death"), there is an iron-ic contrast between the form (a hymn, that is, a poem celebrating God's good-ness) and the content of the poem.

But what, in fact, is the content? And what is the "certain Slant of light" that, perceived on "Winter Afternoons," makes "Shadows—hold their breath"? No two readers seem to agree on the details, but perhaps we can offer a few inoffensive comments. Like Hopkins (cf. "God's Grandeur" [1223]), Dickinson sees a divinity behind phenomena, but her nature-suffused-with-divinity differed greatly from his. "There's a certain Slant of light" begins with "light," which might suggest life and eternal happiness (think of Newman's "Lead, kindly light"), but soon becomes darker, and ends with "the look of Death." The ending is not really a surprise, however, since the "certain Slant of light" is seen on "Winter Afternoons," that is, a season when the year may be said to be dying and when light is relatively scarce, and a time of day when light will soon disappear.

This "Slant of light," we are told, "Oppresses, like the Heft / Of Cathedral Tunes." Surely "Oppresses" comes as a surprise. Probably most of us think that cathedral tunes (even funeral music) exalt the spirit rather than oppress it, and so most of 115 might have written something like, "That elevates, like the Lift / Of Cathedral Tunes." But of course most of us couldn't have written even this, since we would not have had the imagination to think of light in aural terms ("Tunes") and in terms of weight ("Heft").

In any case, a certain appearance in nature induces in the poet a sensation that requires such words as "Oppresses," "Hurt," "Despair," "affliction," "Shadows," and "Death." These words might of course appear in a traditional hymn, but, if so, the hymn would move toward the idea that God helps us to triumph over these adversities. Dickinson, however, apparently is saying that on these wintry afternoons the slant of light shining in the air gives us a "Heavenly Hurt," that is, it moves us to a painful consciousness of God and nature, and to a sense of isolation. In the final stanza presumably we are back to the "Winter Afternoons" of the first. Projecting herself into the surrounding world, the speaker personifies nature: "the Landscape listens"—but hears nothing further. (By the way, "listens" to or for what? A "Slant of light"? Again, as in the earlier comparison of light to "Cathedral Tunes," Dickinson uses synesthesia.) If during the moment when one perceives the light or "listens" there is no further insight, and certainly no amelioration of the "Heavenly Hurt," when "it goes" there is an intensification of despair, since one is left with "the look of Death." Is Dickinson evoking an image of the remote stare of a corpse? And is she suggesting that this stare corresponds to the paralyzed mental condition of those who have perceived the "Slant of light"?

Earlier in this brief discussion we contrasted Hopkins with Dickinson. But, as Charles R. Anderson points out in *Emily Dickinson's Poetry*, there is a connection between the two. The perception in this poem resembles Margaret's perception in "Spring and Fall" (622), where the child senses "the blight man was born for."

TOPICS FOR CRITICAL THINKING AND WRITING

1.   In the first stanza, what kind or kinds of music does "Cathedral Tunes" suggest? In what ways might they (and the light to which they are compared) be oppressive?

2.   In the second stanza, the effect on us of the light is further described. Try to paraphrase Dickinson's lines, or interpret them. Compare your paraphrase or interpretation with that of a classmate or someone else who has read the poem. Are your interpretations similar? If not, can you account for some of the differences?

3.   In the third stanza, how would you interpret "None may teach it"? Is the idea "No one can instruct (or tame) the light to be different"? Or "No one can teach us what we learn from the light"? Or do you have a different reading of this line?

4.   "Death" is the last word of the poem. Rereading the poem, how early (and in what words or images) is a "death" suggested or foreshadowed?

5.   Describe the rhyme scheme. Then, a more difficult business, try to describe the effect of the rhyme scheme. Does it work with or against the theme, or meaning, of the poem?

6.   What is the relationship in the poem between the light as one might experience it in New England on a winter afternoon and the experience of despair? To put it crudely, does the light itself cause despair, or does Dickinson see the light as an image or metaphor for human despair? And how is despair related to death?

7.   Overall, how would you describe the tone of the poem? Anguished? Serene? Resigned?

EMILY DICKINSON

This World is not Conclusion (p. 1220)

First, a brief comment about Dickinson and religion. She clearly was not fond of the patriarchal deity of the Hebrew Bible. "Burglar! Banker—Father," she wrote of this deity, and in a note to Thomas Wentworth Higginson she says that the members of her family, except for herself, "address an Eclipse every morning—whom they call their Father." She seems to have been amused by preachers. She said, of one, that "the subject of perdition seemed to please him somehow." Still, in the words of Charles R. Anderson, in *Emily Dickinson's Poetry* (1960), no reader can doubt that she "faced creation with a primal sense of awe" (17). And, as Anderson and everyone else points out, the Bible was "one of her chief sources of imagery" (18).

Now for "This World is not Conclusion." The first two lines sound like the beginning of a hymn ("Conclusion" presumably means "ending," not "inference drawn"). The poem is not divided into stanzas by white spaces, but clearly it moves in units of four lines. The first four lines assert that although a world beyond our own is (like music) invisible, we strongly sense it. "Positive" in line 4 perhaps refers both to our conviction that it exists and also to its goodness.

Line 5 introduces a complication: "It beckons, and it baffles." Although the rest of the stanza (i.e., lines 6-8) seems to affirm the initial confident (positive) assertion, it also raises doubts in the reader, since it dismisses "Philosophy" and "Sagacity," and it characterizes life (or is it death?) as a "Riddle."

Lines 9-12 seem more positive. They remind us that although human experience "puzzles Scholars," martyrs have given their lives to affirm religious faith, to affirm (in the words of the first line) that "This World is not Conclusion."

Lines 13-16, however, present "Faith" in a somewhat less heroic light: "Faith slips—and laughs, and rallies—Blushes, if any see." Surely this is in a much lower key than "Men have borne / Contempt of Generations," a couple of lines earlier. The enduring power of faith is still affirmed (Faith "rallies"), but in "slips" and "Blushes, if any see" we seem to be presented with a rather adolescent world. Further, the last two lines of the stanza (15-16) similarly diminish Faith, showing it clutching after "a twig of Evidence," and inquiring of a "Vane" (a weathervane, a most unstable thing). Perhaps, too, "Vane" hints at emptiness, insubstantiality (Latin, *vanitas*).

The final four lines at first seem more affirmative. They begin with a strong assertion that calls up a picture of a vigorously gesticulating preacher, and they reintroduce imagery of music (now "Strong Hallelujahs roll"), but these lines at the same time are unconvincing, or, rather, almost comic. A reader may find in the preacher's abundant gestures a lack of genuine conviction. (One thinks of the marginal note in the politician's speech: "Argument weak; shout here.") The "Strong Hallelujahs" may strike a reader as less potent than the "Music" that was "positive" in lines 3-4. Are the gestures and the hallelujahs "Narcotics" that don't quite work, that is that don't quite convince us of the pious forthright assertion that "This World is not Conclusion"? Yet the poem ends with the word "soul"; if "Much Gesture, from the Pulpit" reveals a preacher who is not wholly convincing, we nevertheless cannot therefore lapse into the belief that this world is conclusion. Something "nibbles at the soul."

TOPICS FOR CRITICAL THINKING AND WRITING

1. Given the context of the first two lines, what do you think "Conclusion" means in the first line?
2. Although white spaces here are not used to divide the poem into stanzas, the poem seems to be constructed in units of four lines each. Summarize each four-line unit in a sentence or two.
3. Compare your summaries with those of a classmate. If you substantially disagree, reread the poem to see if, on reflection, one or the other of you seems in closer touch with the poem. Or does the poem (or some part of it) allow for two very different interpretations?
4. In the first four lines the speaker seems (to use a word from line 4) quite "positive." Do some or all of the following stanzas seem less positive? If so, which—and what makes you say so?
5. How do you understand "Much Gesture, from the Pulpit" (line 17)? Would you agree with a reader who said that the line suggests a *lack* of deep conviction? Explain.

CHRISTINA ROSSETTI

Amor Mundi (p. 1221), Uphill (p. 1222)

The two poems were written and originally published several years apart ("*Amor Mundi*" was written in 1865 and published in 1875, "Uphill" in 1858 and published in 1862), but later, in her *Poems* (1876), Rossetti printed them next to each other—with the earlier poem placed second, as we give it—inviting the reader to read them as a pair, with "Uphill" as a response to *"Amor Mundi."*

Doubtless Rossetti meant to suggest that although "the downhill path is easy" *("Amor Mundi"* line 3), the uphill road is the one to take. The idea of life as an arduous journey along a road is ancient, and one especially common in Christian writing. One thinks, for instance, of Biblical passages (the "strait gate" versus the "broad way" in Matthew 7:13), and of Bunyan's *Pilgrim's Progress* (where "progress" itself means a journey or stepping forward). In *Hamlet,* to draw on a work in this book, Ophelia reminds Laertes (I.iii.49-54) of the difference between "the steep and thorny way to heaven" and "the primrose path of dalliance." In these lines from Shakespeare, one notices that the references to a path and a way *must* be metaphorical; but suppose Shakespeare had written only of "the steep and thorny way" versus "the primrose path"—how can one be sure the passage is metaphorical? This is part of what we are getting at in our first question on "Uphill," in which we ask the student to respond to a reader who assumes the speaker is making inquiries preparatory to a bit of touring. The question is not meant to be frivolous. Instructors know that this is a poem about larger matters. but that's because instructors are used to reading poems and to figurative language. Most students are unfamiliar with the ways poems work—which is why they sometimes read too literally and why, on other occasions, they read too freely, imposing irrelevant, highly personal and eccentric readings on the text.

The two poems lend themselves to comparison, most obviously because of the contrast between "the downhill path" and the winding "uphill" road, but there are other connections. To begin with, both poems make use of questions and answers. Few if any students will be aware that the questions in *"Amor Mundi,"* with their repeated structure ("Oh what is that...?"), derive from popular ballads, but they can nevertheless try to distinguish the speakers in each poem. In "Amor *Mundi"* it's our impression (based on "dear she was to dote on" in line 7) that a man is seduced by a *femme fatale,* or let's say, the devil (through a woman, or in the guise of a woman) seduces a man. If so, a man asks the question given in the first two lines, and a woman replies in the next two. Though it is a convention in love poetry to say that the woman seems to walk not on the ground but on air, here the association of her feet with pigeons faintly introduces Venus (whose chariot is drawn by a pair of doves); given the title, the allusion indicates that this love is misdirected, and really is lust. Possibly we are making a fuss over nothing. but most students assume that a male is seducing a female, whereas in our reading of the poem a female seduces a male from the path of virtue.

The use of quotation marks in *"Amor Mundi"* emphasizes the distinction between the two speakers of the one poem, or to put it the other way around, the lack of quotation marks in "Uphill" suggests the possibility that the speaker is answering his (or her) own question. By the way, we don't know exactly what to make out of the suggestion of a student that the answerer in "Uphill" is a ghost, that is, someone who has made the journey and therefore answers authoritatively. We do find the answers (with their dry understatement, as in "You cannot miss that inn," i.e., "Don't worry, you will certainly die") chilling as well as comforting, but we are unconvinced that a reader is supposed to imagine a dialogue between the poet and a revenant. Rather, we believe (guided by Jerome J. McCann's essay on Christina Rossetti in his The *Beauty of Inflections*) that the poet is speaking with what McCann calls "her divine interlocutor', (p. 242). McCann points out that the ending of "Uphill" is easily misinterpreted. Rossetti is not saying that the pilgrimage of the Christian soul ends with an eternal sleep. Rather, she is alluding to the Anabaptist doctrine known as "Soul Sleep" (technically, psychopannychism), which holds that at death the soul is put into a condition of sleep until the millennium. On the Last Day the soul awakens and goes to its final reward. McCann fully discusses the point in his essay.

By placing "Uphill" after *"Amor Mundi,"* Rossetti was rejecting the last line of the latter, which says "there's no turning back": That is, once one starts on a life of sin, there is no hope for salvation, an idea that the reader surely is meant to reject. Still, the sense of finality in *"Amor Mundi"* is emphasized by the fact that the last words of the last stanza ("no turning back") pick up the last words of the first stanza ("never turning back"). The final stress, too, makes for emphasis, especially given the jingling quality produced partly by the anapests, feminine rhymes, and internal rhymes (a sort of equivalent to frolicking downhill?).

In "Uphill" the physical arrangement of lines on the page perhaps helps to suggest the plodding, wearisome journey, with lots of pauses. Suppose one compares the physical appearance of the poem with that of *"Amor Mundi."* If instead of using internal rhymes in *"Amor Mundi"* Rossetti had chosen to end each line wherever she uses a rhyming word, we would get stanzas of eight short lines, rhyming *aaabcccb*. This arrangement, compared with that of "Uphill," might indeed have seemed appropriately skipping, but perhaps Rossetti believed that the form she in fact used in *"Amor Mundi,"* with its lines of relatively uniform length, suggested easy and steady progress (downhill).

Finally, something should be said about the diction of the two poems, Some words, of course, are found in both: "you," "I," "uphill," "and"; but *"Amor Mundi"* includes some "poetic" or, let's say, romantic words, words of a sort that cannot be paralleled in "Uphill": "love-locks," "glowing." "an it please ye," "honey-breathing," "soft twin pigeons," etc. In "Uphill" we do get "morn" (instead of "morning") and "wayfarers," but these two are about the only words with romantic associations. For the most part we get commonplace monosyllabic words, such as "road," "night," "roof," "dark," and "beds," though of course—given the fact that the entire poem is metaphorical—these words have rich meanings.

GERARD MANLEY HOPKINS

God's Grandeur (p. 1223)

The world (including the human world) has divinely created beauty in its charge (care), but "charged" in line 1 is also a scientific term (referring to electricity), leading to "flame out" in the next line; "foil" in line 2, Hopkins explained in a letter, refers to "foil in its sense of leaf or tinsel." Most of the first quatrain asserts the grandeur of God, whose divine energy may be manifested either suddenly ("flame out") or slowly ("ooze of oil / Crushed"). "Crushed," at the beginning of line 4, is part of this celebration (probably alluding to olives or seeds), but this word itself of course also suggests destruction, and the rest of the octave is about human corruption of the self and of nature. "Man's smudge" in line 7 probably alludes to original sin as well as to the destruction wreaked on the countryside by factories. The octave thus moves from an excited or urgent proclamation of God's grandeur to a melancholy reflection on our insensitivity to this grandeur. The sestet reintroduces a joyous affirmation of God's grandeur. Lines 13 and 14 allude to the traditional representation of the Holy Ghost as a dove, but of course Christ is here seen also as the dawning sun, giving warmth and light, and thus we go back to the reference to light in line 2; "bent world" probably evokes the curvature of the horizon, the world distorted by sin, and perhaps backbreaking labor.

Paul L. Mariani, in his excellent *Commentary on the Complete Poems of Gerard Manley Hopkins*, suggests that the last lines are connected with the first quatrain: "If we can picture the dawning sun before it breaks over the horizon, we may recall how the rich light seems precisely to 'gather to a greatness' in density and brightness... until the orb of the sun itself seems to spring forth, and then the sun flames out in strong rays like wings from its center." W. H. Gardner, in *Gerard Manley Hopkins*. II, 230, suggests that the obvious meaning of the poem is that the world is a reservoir of divine power, love, and beauty, and that the deeper meaning is that life must be jarred before the presence of God can be felt. On "verbal resonance" and other sound effects in the poem, see Brooks and Warren, *Understanding Poetry*, 4th ed., pp. 538-40. See also Terry Eagleton in *Essays in Criticism*, 23 (1973), 68-75. Students might be invited to compare the poem with this entry (8 Dec. 1881) from one of Hopkins's notebooks, reprinted in *The Sermons of Gerard Manley Hopkins*, ed. Christopher Devlin, 95: "All things therefore are charged with love; are charged with God and if we know how to touch them give off sparks and take fire, yield drops and flow, ring and tell of him."

GERARD MANLEY HOPKINS

Pied Beauty (p. 1224)

Of the five poems by Hopkins in this book, "Pied Beauty" seems to be for most students the most accessible and the most enjoyable, But in fact (not surprising, of course) it has much in common with Hopkins's other poems, and students can be invited to see the connections, especially the connections with "God's Grandeur," which also celebrates nature and sees in nature the creative power of God. But where "God's Grandeur" speaks of "man's smudge" and sees human beings chiefly as fallen creatures, "Pied Beauty" celebrates—along with skies, trout, chestnuts, and landscapes—"all trades, their year and tackle and trim." (The human world—which Question 1 asks about—is first implied in the "plotted" landscape of line 5, with its folds [pens] and its fields, both those that are left fallow and those that are ploughed. In the next lines, of course, the human world is more evident.)

There is something of a Whitmanesque delight in the sheer variety of existence, including human existence, Behind the poem, however, is the venerable idea that underlying all of this beautiful variety is the Creator, "whose beauty is past change." We say "venerable" because Hopkins is probably drawing on the medieval doctrine of plenitude (things that may seem imperfect to the human eye play a part in God's scheme) and also on the Bible's emphasis on God as the unchanging creator of change. For instance, James 1:17 says: "Every good gift and every perfect gift is from the Father of lights, with whom is no variableness, neither shadow of turning."

In Hopkin's "Curtal-Sonnet" (i.e. curtailed sonnet, consisting of a sestet and a quatrain, plus a line of only two syllables—which adds up to a sort of compressed version of an octave and a sestet), we move from the specificity of the sestet, with its trout and so forth, to abstractions ("Whatever is fickle, freckled," etc.), and finally to the source of all of these. "Finally," however, is not the right word, since the poem begins with "Glory be to God." The last words, then, "Praise Him," bring us back to the beginning, for the poem is, from first to last, a sort of *Laudate Dominum*.

But isn't there a difference between "Glory be to God" and "Praise Him"? To our ear, the first sounds like an ejaculation, an emotional outcry, whereas "Praise Him" sounds like a more controlled utterance, as though the speaker is saying, in effect, "Now that I have shown you why, praise the Lord."

GERARD MANLEY HOPKINS

The Windhover (p. 1225)

This is a difficult poem for instructors as well as students, but we have found that even students with little interest in literature can enjoy it.

The dedication, "To Christ Our Lord," can be used as a way into the poem. In itself, the dedication suggests no more than that the poet is offering what he hopes is an acceptable gift to Christ, but it helps the reader to perceive the bird, with its wings outstretched, as an image of Christ on the cross. The octave describes the flight of a kestrel (a close relative of the American sparrow-hawk), commonly called the windhover because it hovers for as long as a minute in the wind. The first two lines, calling the bird the beloved or favorite ("minion") of daylight and the heir to the throne ("dauphin"), suggest that the bird is of great importance to the speaker. The bird is the dauphin, not the king ("Our Lord," of the title), but as the dawn of the morning leads to sunrise, so the bird leads to Christ. In addition, the rest of the octave effectively conveys the bird's "mastery" of flight, which stirs the speaker's "heart in hiding" (the priest's heart usually hides or withdraws from earthly things, but is ere drawn to the bird by its achievement).

The second stanza (the first tercet of the sestet) begins by asserting the bird's qualities ("Brute beauty and valour and act"); then, in line 10, comes the endlessly discussed "Buckle," which can mean "join" (i.e., "combine") or "collapse" (i.e., "give way"). There seems to be no way to decide between these meanings, though "join" is preferable if the idea is that, at this point, the bird joins its wings as it dives down to its prey. "Thee" in line 10 and "chevalier" (mounted nobleman) in line 11 can be the bird, or Christ, or both.

The final three lines begin quietly, reflectively, rather than with the excitement of the earlier lines: "No wonder of it." Even slow brute energy ("sheer plod") makes a horse-drawn plough "shine" as it turns clods to create a furrow. (Perhaps the blade strikes stones, or perhaps the idea is that the new surfaces of the clods catch the light and seem to shine.) By the way, students may need to remember that in Hopkins's day, ploughs were pulled by horses, not by tractors. The horse, then, not mentioned but of course present in the mind of Hopkins's reader, is a weighty, earthy version of the airy creature that "rung upon the rein of a wimpling wing" in line 4, and of the "chevalier" in line 11, prepared for by "riding" in line 2. From the implied clods of the "sillion"—or ridge—in line 12, come the "blue-bleak embers" of line 13. These are just what Hopkins says they are: blue-bleak (grayish) embers that, when they are poked or when they fall of their own weight, reveal their glowing inner nature. And of course the words "Fall, gall themselves, and gash gold vermilion," in the context of a poem dedicated "To Christ Our Lord," evoke thoughts of the crucified Christ whose ascent onto the cross and descent into death—his arms stretched upward by the weight of his body—suggest the bird in his descent. Christ performed an act even more daring and more masterful than the windhover's soaring and plummeting. In connection with the "blue-bleak embers" that turn to "gold-vermilion," it should be mentioned that the windhover or kestrel, though bluish gray on the head (which looks like a medieval helmet) and on the back, is rosy or buff and dappled on its underside.

GERARD MANLEY HOPKINS

Thou Art Indeed Just (p. 1225)

"Thou Art Indeed Just" has been well discussed, with emphasis on the speaking voice, by Reuben Brower, in *The Fields of Light*. Yvor Winter complains (*On Modern Poets*) about the "banks and brakes" of line 9: the poet, Winter says, "goes into a trivial passage about the banks and braes [sic]; the birds and blossoms which he describes here are outside of the moral order and are irrelevant to the problem which he has posed."

PAUL LAURENCE DUNBAR

An Ante-Bellum Sermon (p. 1226)

Instructors may find it useful to put Dunbar's poem in a context established by Booker T. Washington. Washington, born into slavery, in *Up from Slavery* (1901) comments on the time just before emancipation:

> As the great day [of emancipation] grew nearer, there was more singing in the slave quarters than usual. It was bolder, had more ring, and lasted later into the night. Most of the verses of the plantations songs had some reference to freedom. True, they had sung those same verses before, but they had been careful to explain that the "freedom" in these songs referred to the next world, and had no connection with life in this world. Now they gradually threw off the mask; and were not afraid to let it be known that the "freedom" in their songs meant freedom of the body in this world. (In *Three Negro Classics* [965], 39.)

Dunbar's poem has been discussed at great length in the context of the African-American sermon by David T. Shannon, in "'An Ante-bellum Sermon': A Resource for an African American Hermeneutic," in *Stony the Road We Trod*, ed. Cain Hope Felder (1991): 98-123. Shannon cites many interesting secondary works, for instance Bruce A. Rosenberg, *The Art of the American Folk Preacher* (1970), Philip S. Foner, *The Voice of Black America* (1975), and Henry Mitchell, *Black Preaching* (1979). Toward the end of his article, in a section entitled "Hermeneutical Reflections," Shannon says that the early African American sermons, like Dunbar's imitation, "address the issues of (1) *contextuality*, (2) *correlation*, (3) *confrontation*, and (4) *consolation*. He goes on to explain (we quote a few passages):

> "*Contextuality:* The early African American sermons demonstrate a clear awareness of the role of the context of oppression in the human predicament and in the spiritual condition of the hearers."

"*Correlation:* The sermons harmoniously correlate the ancient biblical stories and changing historical situations."

"*Confrontation:* In their presentation of the biblical message the preachers used double entendre and humor as methods of confrontation."

"*Consolation:* The sermons present the basic biblical theme of divine presence in the midst of oppression and suffering a basic for hope."

ROBERT FROST

Design (p. 1229)

On Frost's "Design," see Randall Jarrell, *Poetry and the Age;* Richard Poirier, *Robert Frost;* Reuben A. Brower, *The Poetry of Robert Frost;* Richard Ohmann, *College English* 28 (February 1967): 359-67; *Frost: Centennial Essays;* and Reginald Cook, *Robert Frost: A Living Voice,* especially 263-67. Brower is especially good on the shifting tones of voice, for example from what he calls "the cheerfully observant walker on back country roads" who reports "I found a dimpled..."—but then comes the surprising "spider, fat and white"—to the "self-questioning and increasingly serious" sestet. Here, for Brower, "the first question ('What had the flower to do...') sounds like ordinary annoyance at a fact that doesn't fit in." The next question brings in a new note, and irony in "kindred." For Brower, with the last question ironic puzzlement turns into vision: "What but design of darkness to appall?" And then Brower says that in the final line "The natural theologian pauses—he is only asking, not asserting—and takes a backward step."

The title echoes the "Argument from Design," the argument that the universe is designed (each creature fits perfectly into its environment: the whale is equipped for the sea; the camel for the desert), so there must be a designer, God. Notice that the word—"design"—has two meanings: (1) pattern and (2) intention, plan. Frost certainly means us to have both meanings in mind: there seems to be a pattern and also an intention behind it, but this intention is quite different from the intention discerned by those who in the eighteenth and nineteenth centuries argued for the existence of a benevolent God from the "Argument from Design."

"Design" was published in 1922; below is an early 1912 version of the poem, entitled "In White":

A dented spider like a snow drop white
On a white Heal-all, holding up a moth
Like a white piece of lifeless satin cloth—
Saw ever curious eye so strange a sight?—

Portent in little, assorted death and blight
Like the ingredients of a witches' broth?—
The beady spider, the flower like a froth,
And the moth carried like a paper kite.

What had that flower to do with being white?
The blue prunella every child's delight.
What brought the kindred spider to that height?
(Make we no thesis of the miller's plight.)
What but design of darkness and of night?
Design, design! Do I use the word aright?

The changes, obvious enough, are discussed by George Monteiro, in *Frost: Centennial Essays,* published by the Committee on the Frost Centennial of the University of Southern Mississippi, 35-38.

By the way, an ingenious student mentioned that the first stanza has eight lines, corresponding to the eight legs of a spider. And the second stanza has six, corresponding to the six legs of a moth. What to do? We tried to talk about the traditional structure of the sonnet, and about relevant and irrelevant conjectures, and about the broad overlapping area. About as good a criterion as any is, does the conjecture make the poem better?

TOPICS FOR CRITICAL THINKING AND WRITING

1.   Do you find the spider, as described in line 1, cute or disgusting? Why?
2.   What is the effect of "If" in the last line?
3.   The word "design" can mean "pattern" (as in "a pretty design"), or it can mean "intention," especially an evil intention (as in "He had designs on her"). Does Frost use the word in one sense or in both? Explain.

ROBERT FROST

The Most of It (p. 1229)

The "he" of the poem is not the speaker; of course; we are totally dependent on the speaker for our impression of this person and we don't get even a single phrase of reported speech. Judging from what the speaker tells us, the "he" is a rather unimaginative person, someone who (at least in the first half of the poem) finds nothing of significance outside of himself. The world around him offers "but the mocking echo" of his own voice. As Richard Poirier suggests, in his shrewd analysis in *Robert Frost* (1977), 165, this is someone who cannot "*make* the most of it," someone, we might say, who is not a poet. But the reader, as distinct from the "he," perceives the grandeur of the surroundings—and this grandeur is so presented that as we read it we more or less project ourselves into the mind of the spectator, who stands in this landscape "bathed in a mythological heroism" (Poirier 165), and we feel we are experiencing his experience. What we and the spectator get is not what the spectator wanted at the start, but is (again in Poirier's words) "a vision of some fabulousness beyond domestication" (165).

T. S. ELIOT

Journey of the Magi (p. 1231)

The first twenty lines of "Journey of the Magi," in which "and" occurs fourteen times, seem to be a matter-of-fact account, almost an entry in a journal. Except for "we regretted" in line 8, the speaker reveals almost nothing of his feelings. That is, we get nothing of the exuberance of the Magi as we know them in Christmas carols, or as the Bible describes them ("They rejoiced with exceeding great joy"). The second part (lines 21-31) resembles the first, but the lines on the whole are longer, the rhythm easier, and the references to the New Testament (three trees—suggesting the three crosses on Golgotha—white horse, vine, wineskins, dicing for silver) all help to mark a change in tone, though there is still great restraint, notably in "(you may say)" in line 31. The speaker does not report anything that looks much like a picture of the infant Christ surrounded by adoring shepherds and angels. In the third (final) section the speaker gives his reactions and reveals the impact of the experience: he does not know its meaning, but he senses its importance, and, no longer at ease in his world, he longs for a death that will liberate him. The conversion, as the Magus moves from his old life toward a new one, is not sudden and satisfying, but slow and disturbing. He yearns for "another death"—his own—to release him from his spiritual struggle. The poem doubtless has autobiographical elements. Eliot published it in 1927, the year that he was confirmed in the Anglican Church. On "Journey of the Magi" see Kenner, *The Invisible Poet*, 243-50; and see D. A. Harris, language, History, and Text in Eliot's 'Journey of the Magi,'" *PMLA* 95 (October 1980), 838-56. Eliot reads "Prufrock" on *T. S. Eliot Reading His Poetry* (Caedmon Recording, TC 1045).

TOPICS FOR CRITICAL THINKING AND WRITING

1. The role of landscape in "Journey."
2. Unifying devices in "Prufrock."
3. The role of allusion in "Prufrock."
4. In a paragraph characterize Prufrock as he might be characterized by one of the women in the poem. Then, in a paragraph or two, offer your own detached characterization of him.

KRISTINE BATEY

Lot's Wife (p. 1232)

If one had to state the theme of this poem, perhaps one could do no better than to quote the title of a poem by Richard Wilbur: "Love calls us to the things of this world." Lot's wife loves her children, of course, but also worldly possessions (line 22), the animals (lines 23-26), and her friends. The poem suggests that Lot, "the conscience of the nation" (line 1), sees the "City of Sin" (line 4) but—so enamored is he of God—not the world of human feelings to which his wife is attached. Thus, "On the breast of the hill, she chooses to be human" (line 35), where "breast" emphasizes the human and specifically maternal power of the world Lot rejects. It seems obvious to us that Batey approves of Lot's wife's choice, in contrast, for instance, to Milton's disapproval of Adam's weakness in the moving passage where Adam announces his decision to sin with Eve rather than to follow God's command:

> "And me with thee hath ruined, for with thee
> Certain my resolution is to die.
> How can I live without thee, how forgo
> Thy sweet converse and love so dearly joined,
> To live again in these wild woods forlorn?
> Should God create another Eve, and I
> Another rib afford, yet loss of thee
> Would never from my heart; no, no! I feel
> The link of nature draw me: flesh of flesh,
> Bone of my bone thou art, and from thy state
> Mine never shall be parted, bliss or woe."
>
> (*Paradise Lost*, 906-16)

Students may have to be reminded that Jesus did not put familial bonds above the bond between the individual and God:

> Think not that I come to send peace on earth: I come not to send peace, but a sword. For I am come to set a man at variance against his father, and the daughter against her mother, and the daughters-in-law against her mother-in-law. And a man's foes shall be they of his own household. (Matthew 10:34-6)

JUDITH ORTIZ COFER

Latin Women Pray (p. 1233)

The first two lines are innocent enough, and so perhaps is the first half of the third, but by the end of the third line, when the contrast is established between the women praying in Spanish and the "Anglo God," one senses that one is in for satire, or at least humor. Cofer goes on to say that this Anglo God has "a Jewish heritage," and although the statement is historically correct enough, it furthers the comic contrast.

In the fifth line, when the Anglo God with the Jewish heritage is called a "Great White Father," probably most readers hear an echo of what the Native Americans are reported (by Anglos) to have called the president of the United States, and so again we hear a wry note—which is emphasized a moment later when the white father is contrasted with his "brown daughters."

The second stanza begins, like the first, with language that might well appear in a religious poem, but the last two lines make a bitter joke. The women are and are not laughed at; the speaker is amused by the spectacle of the pious and persistent women, but she also suggests that the women are aware that their prayers have not been answered, and that their fervent hopes are not without limit.

When we first encountered the poem, we were a trifle surprised by the subjunctive "be" ("hoping / That if not omnipotent / At least he be bilingual") in the last line. Surely almost no speakers and only the most fastidious writers would use "be" instead of "is" in the sentence. Apparently Cofer is one of the few surviving people who think that precision in language really matters. But the more we think about the line, the more we see that "be" is exactly right; the sentence concerns linguistic ability, and the writer shows that she has it.

SOPHOCLES

Oedipus the King (p. 1236)

Though interpretations are innumerable, most fall into the following categories:

1. The gods are just; Oedipus is at fault. The gods are innocent because foreknowledge is not foreordaining. (Jesus predicted that Peter would thrice deny him, but this prediction does not mean that Jesus destined Peter to deny him.) The prophecy told what Oedipus would do, but Oedipus did it because of what he was, not because the gods ordained him to do it. As we watch the play, we see a man acting freely—pursuing a course that leads to the revelation of who he is. (See especially Bernard Knox, *Oedipus at Thebes* 33-41.) Though Oedipus is often praised for relentlessly pursuing a truth that ultimately destroys him, the fact is that—until very late in the play—he believes he is searching for someone other than himself, and moreover, in this search he too easily assumes that other people are subversive. Oedipus is rash and even cruel

in his dealings with Teiresias, Creon, and the shepherd. His rashness is his *hamartia*, and the gods punish him for it. Given the prophecy that was given to Oedipus, a man less rash would have made it his business never to have killed anyone, and never to have married. (But he thought Polybos and Merope were his parents, and he knew that the old man [Laios] was not Polybos and that the queen in Thebes [Iocaste] was not Merope.)

2. The gods are at fault; Oedipus is innocent. When Oedipus asked the oracle who his parents were, the god answered in such a way as to cause Oedipus to leave a place of safety and to go to a tragic destination. Oedipus is a puppet of the gods; his *hamartia* is not rashness (a moral fault) but simply a mistake: He *un*intentionally killed his father and married his mother. The oracle was not conditional (it did not say, "If you do such and such, then such and such will happen"). The play is a tragedy of destiny; notice that at the end of the play no one justifies the gods; that is, no one exonerates them from forcing evil on Oedipus.

3. Oedipus is on the whole admirable (he pities his suffering kingdom; he has a keen desire to know the truth), but he is not perfect. The matter of his *intention* is irrelevant because the deeds of patricide and incest (irrespective of motive) contain pollution. The gods are mysterious, and though they sometimes shape men's lives terribly, they are not evil because they cannot be judged by human standards of justice or morality.

4. Sophocles is not concerned with justice; the play is an exciting story about a man finding out something about the greatness of humanity and about human limitations.

Walter Kaufmann, *Tragedy and Philosophy*, has a long discussion of *Oedipus the King*, in the course of which he finds five themes:

1. The play is about man's radical insecurity (epitomized in Oedipus's fall); Oedipus was the first of men, but he fell.

2. The play is about human blindness. Oedipus did not know who he was (i.e., he was ignorant of his parentage); moreover, he was blind to the honesty of Creon and Teiresias.

3. The play is about the curse of honesty. Oedipus's relentless desire to know the truth brings him to suffering. (If one wants to hunt for a tragic "flaw," one can see this trait as a flaw or vice, but a more reasonable way of looking at it is to see it as a virtue. Would we regard a less solicitous ruler as more virtuous?)

4. The play is about a tragic situation. If Oedipus abandons his quest, he fails his people; if he pursues his quest, he ruins himself.

5. The play is about justice or, more precisely, about *in*justice, that is, undeserved suffering. (Here we come back to Kaufmann's third point: The re-

ward of Oedipus's quest for truth is suffering. It is not even clear that he is being justly punished for killing Laios, for Oedipus belongs to the old heroic world, where killing an enemy is celebrated.) Another point about the play as a play about justice: Sophocles talks of *human* justice too. When Oedipus curses the unknown killer of Laios, he does not think that the killer may have acted in self-defense. And Oedipus's desire to punish Creon and Teiresias similarly shows how wide of the mark efforts at human justice may be.

The Norton critical edition of *Oedipus Tyrannus*, ed. L. Berkowitz and T. F. Brunner, includes a translation, some relevant passages from Homer, Thucydides, and Euripides, and numerous religious, psychological and critical studies, including Freud's, whose key suggestion, in *The Interpretation of Dreams*, is that the play "moves a modern audience no less than it did the contemporary Greek one" because there is a "voice within us ready to recognize the compelling force of destiny [in the play] .... His destiny moves us only because it might have been ours—because the oracle laid the same curse upon us before our birth as upon him. It is the fate of all of us, perhaps, to direct our first sexual impulse towards our mother and our first hatred and our first murderous wish against our father."

An instructor who uses this quotation in class may wish to call attention to the male chauvinism: Freud's "all of us" really means "all males," although he did make various efforts to account for the Oedipus complex in women. It may also be relevant to mention that if the Oedipus of the play did have an Oedipus complex, he would have wanted to go to bed with Merope (the "mother" who brought him up) rather than Iocaste. Note, too, that when he kills Laios, Laios is to him a stranger, not his father. Indeed, his flight from Corinth is a sign that he does not wish to sleep with his mother or to kill his father. But Perhaps such a view is too literal. Perhaps this is a convenient place to mention that Oedipus's solution of the riddle of the Sphinx (a human being is the creature who walks on four feet in the morning, two at noon, and three in the evening) is especially applicable to Oedipus himself (the weakest of infants, the strongest of men in his maturity, and desperately in need of a staff in his blind old age), but of course it applies to all the spectators as well.

In addition to the Norton edition, the following discussions are especially interesting: Stanley Edgar Hyman, *Poetry and Criticism*; H. D. F. Kitto, *Greek Tragedy* and his *Poeisis*; Richmond Lattimore, *The Poetry of Greek Tragedy*; Cedric Whitman, *Sophocles*; Bernard Knox, *Oedipus at Thebes*; Charles Rowan Beye, *Ancient Greek Literature and Society*, especially 306-12; Brian Vickers, *Toward Greek Tragedy*, Vol. I; R. P. Winnington-Ingram, *Sophocles*.

A videocassette of Sophocles's *Oedipus the King* is available from HarperCollins.

TOPIC FOR WRITING

By today's standards, is Oedipus in any sense guilty, and if so, of what?

SOPHOCLES

Antigone (p. 1271)

On *Antigone,* consult two books by H. D. F. Kitto, *Greek Tragedy,* and especially *Form and Meaning in Drama.* See also D. W. Lucas, *The Greek Tragic Poets;* Cedric H. Whitman, *Sophocles;* and R. P. Winnington-Ingram, *Sophocles.* Hegel's view, most often known through Bradley's essay on Hegel in Bradley's *Oxford Lectures* (and reprinted in *Hegel on Tragedy,* ed. Anne and Henry Paolucci), claims that both sides are right and that both are also wrong because they assert they are exclusively right. (For a long anti-Hegelian reading, see Brian Vickers, *Toward Greek Tragedy,* which insists that Creon is brutal and Antigone is thoroughly admirable.) Bradley says, "In this catastrophe neither the right of the family nor that of the state is denied; what is denied is the absoluteness of the claim of each."

Most subsequent commentators take sides and either see Creon as a tragic hero (a headstrong girl forces him to act, and action proves ruinous, not only to her but to him), or see Antigone as a tragic heroine (a young woman does what she must and is destroyed for doing it). The critical conflict shows no sign of terminating. Mostly we get assertions, such as D. W. Lucas's "There is no doubt that in the eyes of Sophocles Creon is wrong and Antigone right," and Cedric Whitman's "Antigone's famous stubbornness,... the fault for which she has been so roundly reproved, is really moral fortitude." One of the most perceptive remarks on *Antigone* is by William Arrowsmith, in *Tulane Drama Review* 3 (March 1959): 135, where he says that Antigone, "trying to uphold a principle beyond her own, or human, power to uphold, gradually empties that principle in action, and then, cut off from her humanity by her dreadful heroism, rediscovers herself and love in the loneliness of her death." He suggests, too, that the play insists on "not the opposition between Antigone and Creon, but [on] the family resemblance which joins them in a common doom."

John Ferguson, in *A Companion to Greek Tragedy,* offers a fairly brief, commonsensical, scene-by-scene commentary on the play. Toward the end he argues that Hegel was utterly wrong in his view that both Creon and Antigone are right. Ferguson points out that Creon "behaves as a tyrant: and that Creon's law "is disastrous for the state." And Antigone is "wrong," Ferguson says, because although her "view of the situation is the true one," as a woman it was her duty to obey Creon. The play is about Antigone's *hubris,* and therefore it is properly titled.

TOPICS FOR CRITICAL THINKING AND WRITING

1. What stage business would you invent for Creon or Antigone at three points in the play?
2. In an essay of 500 words, compare and contrast Antigone and Ismene. In your discussion consider whether Ismene is overly cautious and whether Antigone is overly cold in her rejection of Ismene.
3. Characterize Haimon, considering not only his polite and even loving plea when he urged Creon to change his mind, but also his later despair and suicide. In what way is he like his father and also (in other ways) like Antigone?

Index of
Authors
and Titles

313